Ancient Human Migrations

Foundations of Archaeological Inquiry

James M. Skibo, series editor

ANCIENT HUMAN MIGRATIONS

A Multidisciplinary Approach

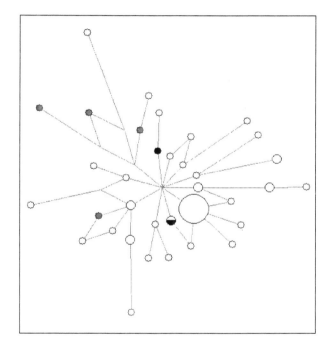

Edited by
**Peter N. Peregrine, Ilia Peiros,
and Marcus Feldman**

THE UNIVERSITY OF UTAH PRESS
Salt Lake City

FOUNDATIONS OF ARCHAEOLOGICAL INQUIRY
James M. Skibo, series editor

The Defiance House Man colophon is a registered trademark
of the University of Utah Press. It is based upon a four-foot-tall,
Ancient Puebloan pictograph (late PIII) near Glen Canyon, Utah.

12 11 10 09 08   1 2 3 4 5

LIBRARY OF CONGRESS CATALOGING-IN-PUBLICATION DATA

Ancient human migrations : a multidisciplinary approach / edited by Peter N. Peregrine, Ilia Peiros,
and Marcus Feldman.
        p. cm.
    Includes bibliographical references and index.
    ISBN 978-0-87480-942-8 (pbk. : alk. paper) 1. Human beings—Migrations. 2. Civilization,
Ancient. I. Peregrine, Peter N. (Peter Neal), 1963- II. Peiros, Ilia. III. Feldman, Marcus W.
    GN370.A525 2009
    304.8—dc22   2008047507

Contents

Contents

Figures

Tables

Preface

Murray Gell-Mann

This volume presents the ideas of some of the world's foremost scholars of language, genes, and culture, but there is one name that is, sadly, missing—Sergei Starostin. Sergei died unexpectedly in late September of 2005, shortly after the workshop from which this volume stems had been finalized. Much of the work presented here is a direct product of Sergei's lifelong quest for understanding the origins and spread of human language, and all of it is influenced by him.

There are currently about six thousand languages on our planet, some of them spoken by millions and some by only a few dozen people. Sergei Starostin and I established the Evolution of Human Languages project at the Santa Fe Institute with the basic goal of providing a detailed classification of these languages and organizing them into a genealogical tree. Considerable progress has been made toward this goal. But since all representatives of the species *Homo sapiens* presumably share a common origin, it would be natural to presume that all human languages also go back to some common source. Before his death, Sergei proposed Borean as a candidate for the common source for most languages of Eurasia, North Africa, and Oceania. The hypothetical Amerindian superfamily may also belong to Borean. Borean is not without problems as a potential source, the most vexing of which is its apparent shallow time depth—only about 17,000 years.

Whether or not Borean will stand as an early, perhaps original, human language, Sergei and other scholars working on the Evolution of Human Language project have aided in clearly establishing a number of protolanguages; that is, early forms of large language families today. The presence of these protolanguages raises several interesting questions, one of which is directly addressed in this volume: how did these languages spread from their place of origin? Did these languages move independently of individuals, transferred from speaker to nonspeaker on the edge of a "wave of advance"? Or, perhaps more likely, did these languages spread along with their speakers, through a process of migration?

Migrations are, and always have been, essential features of human lifestyle. Through migrations, prehistoric humans populated the world. Many ancient civilizations were created and modified through migrations. Numerous migrations of later periods gave rise to the modern ethnic map of the world. Multiple migrations during the last century have drastically changed the ideology, economy, and politics of the modern world.

This volume seeks to address a number of important questions about migrations: How can one detect a migration without historical records? How can one distinguish a migration from contact-determined similarities? How can one identify and stratify multiple prehistoric migrations? Sometimes, languages or physical characteristics of population can be used as "markers" of prehistoric migrations. Are there any other markers? Can one use the spread of certain cultivated plants or agriculture in general as markers of migration? What about material culture, belief systems, or folklore?

Beyond these rather basic research questions, this volume also seeks to address the processes through which migrants decide to move. A traditional community is tightly linked to the environment it inhabits, which affects all aspects of the community's life. What factors cause a community to abandon its original habitat? How do people learn to survive in a new climatic or ecological zone? Were there any ecological restrictions to prehistoric migrations?

Migrations can be conducted by a monolingual group or by a conglomerate of groups who speak different languages, and this has a direct influence on how languages may spread through migration. Are the outcomes of monolingual and multilingual migrations different? In many cases we find that a language has spread from a very restricted area to a large region, replacing all or nearly all the other languages spoken in the region. What kind of migration caused such spread? If Borean does represent an early human language, what led to the spread of this language? Why, with a few exceptions, have only members of the Borean language family survived in Eurasia?

I hope it is clear that the chapters in this volume address fascinating questions that are fundamental to our understanding of human language, culture, and genetics. Indeed, these questions are fundamental to our understanding of human history and our understanding of ourselves. The questions addressed by the chapters in this volume were central to the life work of Sergei Starostin, and it is to his memory and the continuation of his work that we dedicate them.

1

Ancient Human Migrations

A Multidisciplinary Approach

Peter N. Peregrine, Ilia Peiros, and Marcus Feldman

This book is about human migration, a topic that has engendered a vast literature, surely attesting to its importance in understanding human history and culture. But why another book on human migration? And if another book is necessary, why make it an edited collection? Our answer is that we are at a turning point in the study of human migration, or at least of ancient human migration. This book both identifies the turning point and charts a course for the future. Generations of scholars in history, archaeology, and linguistics have charted the movement of peoples and their languages across space and time. Thirty years ago geneticists joined them, first employing mitochondrial DNA, then Y-chromosome, and now nuclear DNA to trace human movements (1, 2). A small group of scholars, primarily at Stanford and Cambridge, began to combine information from genetics, linguistics, history, and archaeology to produce more comprehensive views of ancient human migrations, work that is now appearing in summary volumes and even the popular press (3–5).

There is today a general consensus about where and when humans evolved, and how we populated the earth (6, 7). There is a less complete but growing consensus about the spread of human language families (8, 9). Coherence has been recognized between the spread of people and the spread of language in some parts of the world, and interesting archaeological and historical evidence to approach the question of why those people moved (10–12). In short, we are at

a point where many of the "big" questions about ancient human migrations have been answered, at least initially. The important question at this point is where we need to focus our efforts. The study of ancient human migrations today is in danger of fragmenting, with scholars pursuing divergent questions and potentially contradictory goals. This volume attempts to chart a course into the future by establishing key questions and productive goals for the study of ancient human migrations.

A fundamental fact of any research on ancient human migrations, either today or in the future, is that it must be multidisciplinary. No single discipline can provide adequate data and methods for its study. Thus our approach here, in charting a course for future research, is explicitly multidisciplinary. We use the term *multidisciplinary* rather than *interdisciplinary* because we think that a truly interdisciplinary study of ancient human migrations is impossible, given the vast differences in knowledge and methods required to be a productive scholar in the disciplines represented here. Linguistics, archaeology, history, genetics—each demands that its practitioners acquire a vast knowledge base before they can be conversive. A handful of extraordinary scholars have become conversant in several of these disciplines, but these are rare intellects. We feel it is unreasonable to expect all scholars to achieve such an extensive interdisciplinary knowledge base. Rather, we propose that scholars should pursue multidisciplinary research as a group, working together on a common problem, with each individual contributing his or her own expertise.

This book attempts such a multidisciplinary approach to ancient human migrations. We begin with four chapters that introduce important concepts underlying the study of human migration. Eight case studies follow, each employing one or more primary research tools (e.g., comparative linguistics, comparative genetics) to describe a particular ancient human migration. Each case study stands alone as a compelling piece of research, but together we think they capture the current state of the field. In our concluding chapter we use the picture provided by the case studies to propose an agenda for future research.

The Introductory Chapters

Dean Snow begins the volume with a masterful overview of migration research, providing background on the various disciplines that contribute data and definitions of many key concepts. Snow highlights Robert Sokal's comparative research on migration and the terms he used to describe various forms (13). We will use these terms elsewhere in the volume as a means of comparison and contrast. Snow also provides a set of variables concerning migrations, and these too will be used elsewhere in the volume. Finally, Snow provides several case studies which allow him to illustrate the basic concepts set forth in his chapter, as well as to make six strong conclusions. We will revisit his conclusions in our final chapter.

Sohini Ramachandran and Marcus Feldman follow Snow in providing an overview of migration research, but their chapter focuses on population genetics and potential links between genetics and language. The link between language spread and migration is a central one to research on ancient human migrations, and has been at the core of the Santa Fe Institute workshops from which the case studies in this volume were taken. Ramachandran and Feldman simplify difficult concepts in population genetics to help us clearly understand the models that geneticists use to explore migrations, and how those models might also allow us to explore language movement.

Peter Peregrine, Carol Ember, and Melvin Ember discuss the potential contribution of cross-cultural research to identifying the homelands of protolanguage groups and to the study of language spread. They argue that material correlates of cultural features such as postmarital residence can be identified through cross-cultural research. Once these material culture correlates are identified, the archaeological record can be examined to identify ancient cultures with unique features. If these features can be tied to protolanguage terms, this may provide important evidence for the homeland and spread of the language. Peregrine, Ember, and Ember further their argument by demonstrating that material culture can be used to predict language families among ethnographically described populations. Their chapter provides an important link between the archaeological record and language.

The final introductory chapter, by Ilia Peiros, provides an overview of historical linguistics. Peiros begins with a discussion of the general features of language, and how those general features provide opportunities for languages to change over time. Peiros goes on to explain how linguists study these changes and, in particular, how they go about reconstructing ancestral languages and their spread. To illustrate his points, Peiros examines the Austronesian language family, his area of expertise. He discusses the "mainstream" reconstruction of proto-Austronesian and its homeland, but goes on to demonstrate problems with that reconstruction and significant questions concerning assumptions and potential biases that underlie it. Peiros's discussion provides both an education in historical linguistics and a cautionary tale about the nature of protolanguage reconstructions.

The Case Studies

The volume's eight case studies are organized into two groups. The first concerns territorial expansions; the second, peopling of new lands. We separated the case studies because we see the processes of migration differing in important ways. Most fundamentally, there are existing populations in cases of territorial expansion, and the interactions between migrating and existing populations play a central role in the migration process. The case studies themselves were chosen from among the papers presented at three workshops held at the Santa Fe Institute between 2003 and 2005 (14). These eight were selected because they represent a broad sample of those presented and discussed at these workshops, and because they provide useful cases for comparison and contrast.

Henry Wright's chapter on Holocene population movements in the Old World is the first case study. Wright focuses on material culture as an important source of data for the study of ancient human migrations, and he does an excellent job of showing how material indicators can be used to trace population movements. The scale of migration Wright considers is enormous: the entire Old World for the period from roughly 18,000 to 23,000 years ago. Ironically, the population numbers involved are relatively small, with perhaps only a few dozen people participating in any one migration event. Indeed, the migration processes Wright discusses seem deceptively simple. They appear to describe a unidirectional flow of people, language, and culture out of Africa. But was the situation this simple? Modern humans did not move out into a blank landscape: there were people in Eurasia before. By what processes did humans displace premoderns? Recent Neandertal DNA evidence suggests little or no interbreeding (*15*), and although humans apparently came into close enough contact with *Homo erectus* populations to exchange head lice (*16*), it seems unlikely that modern humans mixed with these ancient populations. We also have to ask why Borean, the language of the most ancient super-super-family proposed by Starostin, is only 17,000 to 18,000 years old. Archaeologists see evidence of modern language capabilities by at least 26,000 years ago, and perhaps more like 50,000 years ago (*17*). What happened to those earlier languages? And what of the people who spoke them?

The next chapter, by Yuri Berezkin, is one of the most important in the volume, offering a remarkable new method for exploring ancient human migrations. Over the past decade Berezkin has worked to assemble a worldwide database of myths that he has coded according to major themes, not unlike Thompson's great catalogue of European folklore (*18*). Berezkin's coding, however, is explicitly designed to allow for large-scale cross-cultural analyses of myths. Focusing on death motifs, Berezkin identifies, much like Wright, what appears to be a fairly simple migration of people out of Africa and across the Old

World. But again, we must ask, what of the people already there? It seems reasonable to think that Neandertals and even *Homo erectus* had myths of their own. Were these incorporated or lost? Can we know? Were there perhaps earlier myths than those Berezkin identifies, ones perhaps linked to pre-Borean languages? Berezkin offers an important new tool and uses it not only to provide an interesting case study of migration, but also to introduce a variety of new and fascinating questions.

Roy King's chapter presents a more traditional approach to the study of ancient human migrations. The geographic and temporal scales are large, and the focus is on not one, but a series of migrations that together form a general pattern of population movement out of the Levant and into the Aegean and Mesopotamia. King also employs a more traditional mix of genetic, linguistic, and material culture evidence to make his case, which is an important one. King argues that the spread of people out of the Levant and Anatolia, much discussed in terms of the spread of agriculture and Indo-European languages into Europe, occurred in the context of significant admixture and reverse migration; in other words, there was a blending of populations, not a replacement. In Mesopotamia, King finds that there was no clear dominant population, and although Hurrian and other Semitic languages came to dominate the region, the genetic evidence points to assimilation between migrant and local populations, probably in the context of agropastoralism. In the Aegean, migration seems more strongly associated with agriculture, and locals appear to have adopted language and (through intermarriage) genetic traits from migrant agriculturalists. But even here the genetic pattern is one of blending, not replacement.

Vladimir Petrukhin's chapter requires a bit more of an introduction than the other case studies. It focuses on a fascinating period of eastern European history, the late ninth and early tenth centuries, a time of what appears to be dramatic population movements that set the stage for the emergence of the historically known peoples of the region. In particular, Petrukhin examines historical records of the period to identify the homelands and migration routes of the Magyars. The Magyars were apparently Finno-Ugric speakers who originally came from the Urals, migrating south and west across the steppe over the course of several hundred years. They arrived in the area of present-day Hungary in the mid-ninth century and, as Petrukhin makes clear, rapidly gained control from local Slav populations and settled down (*19, 20*).

Petrukhin's chapter provides us with an important lesson: migrations are messy. One unified population does not simply move into another and displace it, nor is it a unified population that always moves. Migrations are not unidirectional phenomena in the picture Petrukhin paints; rather, assimilation and blending seem to be key processes. Petrukhin's chapter thus offers cadence at the end of the first group of case studies, for all of them suggest that beneath what may appear to be a fairly simple process of migration is a rather messy process of admixture. The relationship between these two pictures—the clear one on the top and the messy one underneath—is what we focus on in our concluding chapter.

The case studies in the second group focus on migration to new, previously unpopulated lands. Merritt Ruhlen's chapter summarizes his long-time interest in the history of New World languages. Both the geographic scale and time involved are long: migrants to the New World crossed from Asia over the course of several millennia and, according to Ruhlen, in at least three major waves. Ruhlen outlines the three major families of New World languages proposed by Joseph Greenberg (*21*) and gives new evidence supporting the existence of Greenberg's hypothetical Amerind language family. He then explains that the presence of these three families, in addition to archaeological and physical traits found in ancient and modern Native Americans, supports the idea that there were three migrations to the New World, one roughly 13,000 years ago of Amerind-speaking peoples, a second roughly 8,000 years ago of Na-Dene–speaking people, and a third of Eskimo-Aleut–speaking peoples about 4,000 years ago.

Interestingly, Steven Zegura, coauthor of the next chapter with Tatiana Karafet and Michael Hammer, was an early proponent of the three-migration model for the populating of the New World, but in this chapter he and his coauthors argue that the picture is not that clear. Focusing on evidence from the Y chromosome, Zegura, Karafet, and Hammer suggest that there may have been only one migration, roughly 16,000 years ago. If this is the case, then we face a key question: what accounts for the stark linguistic diversity discussed by Ruhlen? A key issue raised in the chapter is that as we obtain more data, patterns that once seemed clear become more confused. Migration (or migrations) to the Americas was not a simple affair, but involved complex processes, some of which we may not yet understand.

Karafet, Zegura, and Hammer continue this line of argument in their chapter on the peopling of Japan. It has long been assumed, based on both linguistic and archaeological data, that Japan is one of the clearest cases of migration available. The Japanese language belongs to the Altaic linguistic family, possibly related to Korean, but the Japanese people have long seen themselves as genetic isolates: direct descendants of Yayoi agriculturalists who replaced Jomon hunter-gatherers around 2,300 years ago. What Karafet, Zegura, and Hammer demonstrate through the analysis of Y-chromosome DNA is that, again, the picture is not at all clear. Like the migrations to the New World, what appears on the surface may not be what actually happened. The Y-chromosome data suggest that migrations to Japan were a messy process that involved several waves and considerable admixture.

The final case study, by Alexander Adelaar, presents a complex linguistic argument about the peopling of Madagascar. Like Petruhkin's chapter, this one requires a bit of background. Madagascar lies only some 250 miles off the coast of Mozambique, yet this huge landmass was not populated by humans until about 1,400 years ago. It seems obvious that Africans would have peopled this nearby island, and yet the island's indigenous language (Malagasy) is Austroneasian. How did Austroneasians arrive in Madagascar, and, perhaps more interesting, where did they come from? Adelaar attempts to answer these questions using comparative linguistic data. His data and arguments are detailed and compelling. What Adelaar demonstrates is that the migration of Indonesians to Madagascar was a complicated process that included both direct ocean crossings and interaction with peoples in India and Africa. Like the other case studies of peopling new lands, Adelaar's study demonstrates that migrations which may look fairly direct and simple on the surface appear much more complicated as one acquires more data.

The Concluding Chapter

In our concluding chapter we attempt to summarize what we have learned from the case studies, and to suggest a new direction for research on ancient human migrations. What we argue is that the study of ancient human migrations is at a turning point. We have established new methods for studying ancient human migrations (including Berezkin's comparative mythology, which

we believe will be a crucial new tool) over the past decade and have acquired vast new data sets. What once appeared to be fairly clear processes of demic expansion and replacement are clearly more complicated. The case studies presented here suggest that admixture is an important process, and that migration affects the migrants as much as (and in some cases more than) the established populations they move into. How is research to move forward in this new, more complicated world? Our answer is that it requires a multidisciplinary, rather than interdisciplinary, approach.

Notes

1. L. Cavalli-Sforza, M. Feldman, *Nature Genet.* 33, 266–275 (2003).

2. R. Cann, *Science* 291, 1742–1748 (2001).

3. C. Renfrew, K. Boyle, eds., *Archaeogenetics* (McDonald Institute for Archaeological Research, Cambridge, 2000).

4. P. Bellwood, C. Renfrew, eds., *Examining the Language/Farming Dispersal Hypothesis* (McDonald Institute for Archaeological Research, Cambridge, 2003).

5. S. Wells, *The Journey of Man* (Random House, New York, 2002).

6. P. Underhill et al., *Ann. Rev. Hum. Gen.* 65, 43–46 (2001).

7. M. Hammer et al., *Mol. Biol. and Evol.* 18, 1189–1203 (2001).

8. M. Ruhlen, *The Origin of Language* (Wiley, New York, 1996).

9. J. McWhorter, *The Power of Babel* (Harper Collins, New York, 2003).

10. L. Cavalli-Sforza, *Genes, Peoples, and Languages* (Univ. of California Press, Berkeley, 2001).

11. J. Chen, R. Sokal, M. Ruhlen, *Hum. Biol.* 67, 595–612 (1995).

12. J. Diamond, P. Bellwood, *Science* 300, 597–603 (2003).

13. R. Sokal, N. L. Oden, C. Wilson, *Nature* 351, 143–145 (1991).

14. Acknowledgments to SFI, MacArthur Foundation, and papers not included here.

15. J. P. Noonan et al., *Science* 314, 1113–1118 (2006).

16. D. L. Reed et al., *PLoS Biology* 2(11), e340 (2004). DOI: 10.1371/journal.pbio.0020340

17. R. Klein, *The Human Career*, 2nd ed. (Univ. of Chicago Press, Chicago, 1999).

18. S. Thompson, *Motif-Index of Folk Literature* (Indiana Univ. Press, Bloomington, 1955–1958).

19. M. Molnár, *A Concise History of Hungary* (Cambridge Univ. Press, Cambridge, 2001).

20. R. Milner-Gulland, *The Russians* (Blackwell, Oxford, 1997).

21. J. Greenberg, *Language in the Americas* (Stanford Univ. Press, Stanford, 1987).

2

The Multidisciplinary Study of Human Migration

Problems and Principles

Dean R. Snow

The problems of greatest interest to me and to many other people interested in human origins are inherently interdisciplinary. The difficulty with this perspective on the world is that many scientists restrict themselves to their particular disciplines and draw conclusions from selective sets of evidence. Consider an encounter between a geneticist, an archaeologist, and a historical linguist, all of them interested in the origins of some particular seventeenth-century culture. It would not be surprising to find that each of them has sorted through several alternative hypotheses designed to explain data derived from their separate domains. Each of them has selected the most parsimonious hypothesis, and each has proposed that it is the most likely of all those tested. Regrettably, the three favored hypotheses are all mutually exclusive. The available genetic, archaeological, and linguistic data lead to three explanations that cannot all be simultaneously valid. Yet all three of the scientists have conducted the research correctly by the lights of their respective disciplines.

The larger problem is that none of the scientists in this scenario has considered all of the available evidence. To do so, they must all adopt a broader perspective, yet they are all reluctant to move outside their own areas of expertise. This problem is much more common than many practicing scientists are willing to admit, and it seriously handicaps modern archaeology in particular. Thus when a colleague tells me that the available evidence from his disciplinary domain does not necessarily require human migration to explain some phenomenon, he may be quite right. But that is only because he has defined the problem very narrowly, silently assuming that all other variables are constant or irrelevant. However, in archaeology and other historical sciences it is rarely if ever the case that all other things are equal. Examples discussed below show how disciplinary specialization can impede scientific progress. The situation is made even worse when there is a bias against a particular line of explanation for some reason that is extraneous to science. That is why I favor evolution and ecology as a theoretical approach and an empirical approach that includes the full range of phenomena that can inform the student of human migration, not just data from narrower domains such as archaeology, linguistics, or biology.

Accommodating Different Disciplinary Principles

The case studies in this volume, like many other publications in recent decades, attempt to draw together the separate findings of genetics, osteology, archaeology, and historical linguistics. This is not easy to accomplish because each of these fields has not just a distinctly different data field but also its own internal logic, which is too often left implicit (cf. Chapter 14, this volume). Moreover, the ways in which one can assess adaptive evolutionary change varies considerably from one disciplinary domain to another. Table 2.1 presents a very simplified summary of factors

TABLE 2.1. Factors Affecting the Accommodation of Different Disciplinary Principles

	Retrospective	Continuity	Precision	Codification
Genetics	Convergent	High	High	High
Osteology	Generalizing	High	Low	High
Archaeology	Generalizing	Low	Low	Low
Language	Convergent	High	High	High
Speech Community	Generalizing	Low	Low	Low

affecting the accommodation of different disciplinary principles. While genetics and osteology must be understood in terms of biological evolution, archaeology must be understood in terms of cultural evolution, which operates under different principles. Historical linguistics must contend with both because languages evolve in ways analogous to biological evolution, while the communities that speak them are subject to the forces of cultural evolution. Consequently, it is useful to review the operating assumptions of each discipline briefly but explicitly before examining how they can be used together in a multidisciplinary effort to understand general patterns of human migration.

Genetics

Two branches of biology, genetics and osteology, have been at the forefront of discussion of migration in recent years. The internal logics of even these two closely related areas of study differ in important ways. Genetic data are ideally gathered from large samples of individuals and on large numbers of genetic markers. Genes, haplotypes, or other markers are then often used to identify lineages. A basic assumption is that genetic lineages diverge as random mutations create new lines. The number of such mutations appears to have been manageably small, and the rate at which they have occurred has been both slow and steady. Studies have tended to focus on female lineages detected in mitochondrial DNA (mtDNA) and male lineages found on the Y chromosome.

Much was made some years ago of a mitochondrial "Eve," a female who probably lived perhaps 200,000 years ago and from whom all living mitochondrial lineages later diverged (1). Of course there never was a time when there was only one female human because all species necessarily live in breeding populations of at least hundreds of individuals unless they are on the verge of extinction.

Genetic data indicate that even in a period of severe selection that occurred about 74,000 years ago there were around 25,000 humans making up our ancestral breeding population (2). Some say that the number of survivors of that demographic bottleneck was less than a tenth of that, but that still comes to 2,500 individuals. It would not be surprising if one individual in such a population had the good fortune to carry a highly adaptive mutation, such that other lines died out as the descendants of that one individual reproduced more effectively over the long term. For the human population generally, the near-fatal episode around 74 millennia ago led to the rapid evolutionary selection for language and related skills, and positioned humans for a new adaptive expansion (3).

The main point is that the lines of evidence used by geneticists tend to converge on single individuals as researchers work upstream against the flow of time. Consequently, haplotypes tend to be specific hallmarks that stand for ancient breeding populations rather than being traits that all individuals in those breeding populations necessarily shared.

Osteology

Osteology generally and paleoanthropology more specifically rely on the lucky discovery of skeletal remains. There are only a few of these relative to the sizes of the past breeding populations they represent, and osteologists are compelled to assume that some amount of sampling error is an unavoidable problem. To the extent that larger samples are available to characterize some past human population, the individuals in that sample are assumed to be representative of the whole population. There is no equivalent of the genetically reconstructed mitochondrial Eve in such a sample because the logic used by osteologists is statistical, not deterministic.

In a few cases intact DNA has been extracted from ancient human bone, but these successes do not change the basic difference between the logics of osteological and genetic approaches to our biological history. Any particular fossil find might be that of an individual who has millions of living descendants, or (perhaps more likely) it might be that of an individual who has no living descendants at all. It is but one representative of a long gone breeding population. On the other hand, projections into the past that are based on genetic data are necessarily founded on samples of living individuals in modern populations. Those of us alive today are the descendants of the better adapted (or merely luckier) minorities in ancient populations. Thus while biological evolution shaped the outcomes observed by both geneticists and osteologists, the epistemologies of the two disciplines are different and must be kept in mind as their results are compared and analyzed.

Archaeology

Archaeologists work with artifact assemblages, settlement patterns, and the spatial and temporal distributions of these and a variety of other data drawn from allied disciplines. Reconstructed archaeological cultures tend to be based on statistical generalizations derived from archaeological data, and in this sense the logic of archaeology is similar to that of osteology. Both lack the precision we might prefer, and both are forced to rely on samples that are unknown fractions of larger phenomena of unknown size as a means to make generalizations about those larger phenomena. Archaeologists do not often work backwards from living populations in a systematic way, a neglected approach that probably holds some promise for future research. In other words, retrospective experimental archaeology might yield more benefits than have been realized thus far.

Archaeology enjoys poorer continuity over time than osteology because while archaeology deals mainly with cultural evolution, osteology is grounded in biological evolution. The individual is the unit of selection in both biological and cultural evolution, but in the latter case individual transformation is relatively easy. Individuals can switch language and culture rather easily, but not their genes. This is the most important difference between the basic principles of biological evolution and those of cultural evolution (4).

Because samples are often small and the phenomena being sampled uncertain, archaeology shares poor precision with osteology. Archaeologists do their best to overcome this shortcoming, but the fact remains that human culture in general is not codified in the ways that languages and genetics are. Moreover, although individuals cannot change their genetic codes, or make wholesale changes in language codes, they often can modify other parts of their cultures piecemeal. Some parts of human culture may be highly codified and durable, at least in some cultures, but other parts are not. Archaeology has to contend with the imprecision and lack of continuity that this freedom entails.

Historical Linguistics

Historical linguists work backwards from data derived from modern, living speech communities. While those communities are analogous to breeding populations, linguists often work with one or just a few informants. This usually succeeds because languages are highly codified, and speech is remarkably consistent within speech communities. Idiolects vary a bit, of course, but the need for precise communication and the importance of subtle consistencies for group identities keeps that variability largely in check.

Historical linguists reconstruct the vocabularies of protolanguages from those of their surviving descendant languages. It is a laborious process that depends on a thorough knowledge of sound shifts and considerable technical skill. For my purposes here, it is sufficient to point out that the analytical process of historical linguists is analogous to genetic projections into the past because it tends to converge as analysis moves backwards in time. It may well be that at the time the protolanguage was spoken, it was part of a widespread language complex spoken by a very thin population of hunter-gatherers, something similar to the Cree-Montagnais-Naskapi language complex found across the vast boreal forest of eastern Canada. But the protolanguage is not representative of the whole language complex that once existed. Instead, the working assumption is that the protolanguage was but one tiny variant within the larger language complex, the other dialectical variants having left no descendants.

Of course linguists recognize that there must have been other forces at work. Internal migration, intermarriage, and language switching muddy the internal consistency and history of any language complex. But the default assumption is that a reconstructed protolanguage was once a single dialect, not an abstract representative of all the related dialects spoken at that time.

Speech Community

Although linguistic and genetic approaches are both retrospectively convergent in the sense of converge used above, and as one works upstream in time, there is an important difference that has hindered attempts to map one on to the other. The continuity of a language over time is much better than the linguistic continuity of a human speech community. Thus while the evolutionary continuity of English is one thing, the continuity of speech in Ireland (where English largely replaced Gaelic) is something else. It is important for our purposes to be careful about this distinction because when we use historical linguistics together with archaeology or genetics, the sometimes poor continuity of language within an evolving community can be a serious confounding factor. Although historical linguistics must necessarily deal with both, confusing a language with the community that speaks it can frustrate attempts to relate findings to archaeological, genetic, and osteological phenomena.

An individual cannot abandon one set of genes for another, but an individual *can* abandon one language for another. Breeding populations keep their genetic characteristics even while switching from one language to another, a process that can be completed easily in only two generations. Many examples of this process can be found among immigrant populations, but there are also examples of stationary populations in which one generation spoke language A, the next generation was bilingual in languages A and B, and

the following generation spoke only B (5). Indo-European languages apparently spread across Europe in much this way, with dozens or even hundreds of local speech communities switching to the language(s) of a relatively small population of new elites (6). It happened again in the first millennium CE when the residents of France, Italy, Spain, Portugal, and Romania opted for local dialects of Latin over their probably more numerous traditional languages. It happened again when Anglo-Saxon speech spread to England, and nearly happened there a second time after the Norman conquest (see cases below). Language switching of these kinds can confound efforts to map linguistic ontology onto genetic ontology (7). This means that while continuity over time is good for genetic analysis and reasonably good for the study of languages, it is relatively poor in historical linguistic analyses that attempt to reconstruct the descent of speech communities.

Some Definitions and Axioms

Quite apart from the different logics and operating principles of the disciplines we use to reconstruct general patterns of migration are the assumptions we have about how human beings behave over time and space, and the terms we use to describe those behaviors. I offer here an ontology of definitions and operating assumptions, along with some explication of synonyms or alternatives that are designed to improve communication. Many terms are already generally accepted, while some here are new. I have provided references for novel usages I have adopted from others.

Human migration is defined here as the intentional long-term or permanent movement of human beings across space and over time.

1. Many anthropologists prefer the term *demic diffusion* to *migration* because of the many special and often confusing definitions that have been associated with the latter term (8).
2. Seasonal movements (including transhumance), commuting, and other short-term movements, whether regular or irregular, are excluded from this definition. "Transhumance is a system of semi-nomadic livestock farming with migration or transport of the stock normally between two,

occasionally between more, only seasonally usable pasture grounds, which differ in their location as regards altitude, climatic conditions and vegetation" (*9*). I am mindful that if adopted by ornithologists, this definition would mean that migratory birds do not migrate.

3. Migration may involve any number of people, from a single individual to the entire national society.
4. Low-density, low-intensity foragers tend to marry distantly, whereas later high-density, highly invested cultivators tended to marry locally, meaning that among foragers migration can be the cumulative effect of moves prompted by marriage (*10*).
5. At a larger scale, migrations of long duration by large societies may result from the cumulative effects of migrations by relatively small subsets over relatively short distances.
6. Migrations may be either voluntary or coerced.
7. Internal migration is migration that takes place within the territory of a national society. External migration is migration that takes place across the borders of distinct national societies.
8. Local migration is a special case of internal migration (*11*), or what Lee would refer to as a change in residence (*12*).
9. The absolute distance of any migration is variable, contingent upon the prevailing means of transportation.
10. Much of the confusion observed among studies of migration results from a failure to explicate intentionality. To qualify as human migration, the movement must be intentional. This is not a factor in nonhuman cases of migration. No ruby-throated hummingbird will decide this year to cancel its migration across the Gulf of Mexico on the basis of its thoughtful consideration of compelling circumstances. This level of intentionality is unique to human behavior. Intentionality is a confounding factor in any discussion of human migration when it is left implicit. It makes sense to define human migration as necessarily intentional in order to get past this conceptual obstacle.

I assume that all voluntary movements are adaptive at some level, even though some may eventually prove to be maladaptive due to changing or misperceived circumstances. In other words, whatever individual human beings do is rational to them at the time, even when hindsight reveals mistakes in judgment. Specifically, a decision to stay put or to move is rational by definition, even if it strikes an objective observer distant in space or time as irrational. It is sometimes necessary for an investigator to acquire a fuller understanding of the knowledge available to the actor(s) when their decisions appear to have been irrational. That said, evolutionary forces select in favor of the more adaptive decisions, rewarding some decisions and reproving others despite each having been a good idea at the time. The point of this for human migration is that it is important to determine (or at least hypothesize) agency. Given that migration is intentional, where did the decision reside? Was it the collective result of many individual decisions or a centralized leadership decision? Was it voluntary or coerced? If these questions cannot be immediately answered, then assumptions about them should be made explicit and alternative hypotheses may be in order.

Sokal's Terminology
Robert Sokal has compiled 3,460 documented instances of population movement in Europe. The terms he uses to describe types of population movement were chosen for their practical utility (*13*). He defines migration in terms equivalent to those used here, and the additional definitions and modifiers he uses are helpful supplementary terms. Sokal's terms are shown here in italics They are presented in no particular order and are subject to further refinement and reorganization.

1. *Peopling* is defined as the initial occupation of a region by humans. Expansion of a population into previously unoccupied marginal environments is excluded from this definition inasmuch as even marginal environments would have been traversed and occasionally used by earlier people. In most cases it is intentional only locally.
2. *Partial migrations* involve movement of only a fraction of the whole.

3. *Territorial expansions* usually characterize dominant populations growing and expanding at the expense of subordinate ones. Intentionality varies, and specification of it allows for finer distinctions.
4. *Territorial contractions* usually occur as reactions of subordinate populations to the expansions of dominant ones. Contractions may be preceded by or associated with numerical declines. Numerical declines can involve either emigration or a reduction of total size as a consequence of mortality being greater than fertility. Intentionality is local for the contracting population.
5. *Conquest* involves the expansion of a dominant society over one or more subordinate ones. It is always intentional. Conquered societies do not necessarily move, and dominant societies can be very small relative to the conquered ones if their relative technological or organizational advantages are sufficiently great.
a. *Coerced migration* often occurs when dominant conquest societies resettle conquered societies within imperial boundaries.
b. *Colonial settlements* or *military garrisons* may be established as enclaves in the territories of subordinate societies. These are special forms of displacement that often presage conquest.
c. *Military attacks* are often the first stage of conquest or settlement by territorial empires. Naval attacks are special cases often associated with the expansion of overseas empires. Unless they are followed by other forms of population movement, attacks of both kinds often have only relatively minor long-term consequences for the attacked populations.

Scaling of Variables

Migration variables can be scaled along a small number of well-defined parameters. This sometimes allows researchers to quantify meaningful variation in addition to merely classifying types of migration.

1. Distance of the migration (may be measured as a function of time as a means to adjust for variation in transportation technology)
2. Size of the migrating group (may be measured as absolute size or as a fraction of the parent group)
3. Duration of the relocation (a measure of permanence)
4. Degree of coercion (carrot and stick factors)
5. Relative sizes of competing populations (not a factor in peopling)
6. Relative cultural dominance of competing populations (either technological or organizational dominance, or both)
7. Cultural persistence (the degree to which the migrating group abandons old cultural norms and adopts new ones)
8. The number and sizes of obstacles that inhibit movement

Consequences and Alternatives

Large-scale migrations (adaptive expansions) can involve the expansion of dominant populations at the expense of subordinate ones. The dominant population can be numerically smaller. The possible consequences for the subordinate populations are:

1. Displacement
   a. Expulsion
   b. Marginalization
2. Absorption (assimilation)
3. Extirpation (annihilation)

Each of these cases produces its own typical pattern of trait transfer. Absorption of large numbers of subordinates can dilute the genetic distinctiveness of the dominant population, as in the Northern Iroquoian case in northeastern North America, but research has shown that even in that case identifiable genetic differences remain detectable (*14*).

Small-scale migrations can involve the movement of subordinate populations into or within the territorial limits of dominant populations. The possible consequences for the subordinate populations over the long term are:

1. Absorption (assimilation)
2. Isolation (insulation, marginalization)
3. Extirpation (annihilation)
4. Expulsion
5. Return migration

Each of these cases produces its own typical pattern of trait transfer.

Diffusion is the transfer of traits across societal boundaries in the absence of migration. It is often useful as a first step to find ways to exclude diffusion because in some cases it has been misinterpreted as migration.

1. *Transculturation (15)* is trait exchange without the loss of identity, a special form of trait diffusion. Genetic, osteological, or language continuity can be used to show that population movement has been minor or has not taken place at all.
2. *Acculturation (15)* is another special form of diffusion in which a society gradually loses its unique identity through the replacement of endogenous traits by exogenous traits. As in the case of transculturation, genetic and osteological lines of evidence will show continuity, but archaeological and language typically show discontinuity.

A basic assumption is that individuals are the units of transformation (4). Another is that societies (broadly defined) can propagate or dissolve rapidly as individuals join or abandon them. Several forms of migration require individuals to abandon previous social memberships and acquire new ones. This is a simpler and clearer way of stating the factors listed by Lee (12). It is also a way of defining the factors such that they can be used for further analysis.

Some Instructive Cases

A few case studies illustrate the general principles outlined above. Many others are possible, and multidisciplinary research into the study of human migration would be advanced by detailed examination of such cases.

The Cheyenne

The earliest references we have that might refer to the Cheyenne place them in a series of small villages near the uppermost Mississippi in northern Minnesota before 1680 CE. According to Hennepin, by 1680 they were living among the Dakota in the area between the Mississippi and Mille Lacs, where they practiced some horticulture but were still dependent on hunting and harvesting of wild rice. Their dwellings were wigwams or possibly bark tipis. Expeditions to hunt buffalo required them to trek south or southwest to reach the prairie of southern Minnesota.

Jonathan Carver found the Cheyennes in two villages on the Minnesota River in 1766, 200 km south of their previous location. The valley was forested, but the Minnesota River cut across open prairie, affording anyone living there direct access to herds of buffalo. By moving to these locations the Cheyennes gained better access to buffalos and had better conditions for growing corn, but at the cost of moving out of the range of wild rice. Carver noticed that some Cheyennes were by this time living in skin tipis, good evidence that buffalo hunting was increasing in importance. Others, however, were living in earth lodges, permanent dwellings that could only have been possible if their reliance on corn had also increased.

Another Cheyenne village was founded by 1724 at the Biesterfeldt site on the Sheyenne River of North Dakota (16). Here too they lived in earth lodges up to 10 m in diameter. Most houses held around 15 people, and the total population of the village was probably around 900. This would have been no more than a third of the total Cheyenne population at the time.

Some Cheyennes moved later to the Missouri River valley where it crosses the modern boundary between North and South Dakota. The Cheyennes from the Biesterfeldt site took refuge there after the Chippewas attacked and burned their village around 1780. From there, Cheyenne villagers still later moved to new locations west of the Missouri on the Grand River tributary. The Cheyennes were still farmers and still lived in earth lodges, but their movement to west of the Missouri put them just northwest of the Black Hills and on the edge of the high plains. From there they needed only horses to prompt them to abandon farming and settled life for nomadism and full-time buffalo hunting (17–19) (see Figure 2.1).

So long as they maintained earth lodge villages, the Cheyennes had to defend them from raids by other groups looking to capture food stores. Even after acquiring horses, they were compelled to leave some men at home to defend

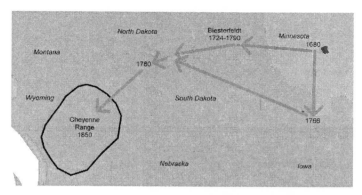

FIGURE 2.1. Movements that took the Cheyenne people from the Minnesota woodlands in 1680 to nomadic lives on the Great Plains in less than two centuries.

the villages while others hunted. The Chippewas had driven them onto the plains with such raids. Once there they had to put up with raiding by the Arikaras. A shift to nomadism enabled them to concentrate all their men on hunting, to keep women and children close, and to deny the Arikaras and other enemies the temptation to attack poorly defended permanent villages. Mobility allowed them to pursue the buffalo herds wherever they went rather than waiting for them to wander within range of settlements. Mobility also opened up vast new opportunities for trade. In terms of evolution and ecology it was all very sensible.

Horses were available from the south, guns from the north and east. The skin tipis could be dragged from place to place on horse-drawn travois. The prophet Mutsiev (Sweet Medicine) made a trip to the Black Hills and came back with a bundle of sacred arrows and word that a new set of ceremonies would make the abandonment of their villages ideologically possible. However, the Cheyennes also needed to have enough horses to make the change. As farmers they had only enough grass to pasture a relatively small number of horses around their villages. For a few years they solved the problem by planting crops and then temporarily abandoning the villages and growing crops in order to pasture their growing herds. Finally, when the number of horses equaled or exceeded the number of people, the Cheyennes changed from village farmers to quintessential Plains nomads.

The challenge for an archaeologist is to find a way to track a rapidly evolving culture like this one across time and space. It is unlikely that we could do so easily without historical documentation, linguistic analysis, and genetic evidence. There is a rough hierarchy of archaeological evidence that is usually accepted as indicating migration and intrusion. These classes of evidence are what one would expect to find preserved from the donor culture in the destination area, probably more so in situations involving stratified societies than in cases like the Cheyenne. In order of significance they are:

1. Burials
2. Architecture
3. Ceramics
4. Economy

Other technological items (especially those associated with metallurgy) are not good indicators because they move so easily through transculturation. Mode of burial tends to be very conservative, architecture generally a little less so, and so on. But we see from the Cheyenne case that architecture and economy both changed dramatically more than once over a couple centuries. Their mode of burial might have persisted with less change over time, and their ceramics might be a good indicator of continuity. If we had access to enough well-selected samples of mtDNA we might be able to track the Cheyenne migration, but any such effort would require much more information than we currently have. Historical linguistics is more useful, and this is the thread of continuity that informs the Cheyenne case.

Moore's ethnohistory of the Cheyenne nation emphasizes the dispersal of bands after they left northern Minnesota and their eventual reunion in the nineteenth century (19). Thus the ethnogenesis of the nomadic Cheyenne bison hunters was a rhizomic process rather than a simple dendritic one in the sense that they dispersed and reassembled themselves over time rather than simply branching (18). This is an important point, and one that applies to many small migrating American Indian communities during the contact period. Population decline, mainly from epidemic diseases, led many small remnant groups to amalgamate as they relocated. This is something that biological species, once separated, cannot do. A multiethnic community in which five or ten different languages were spoken typically evolved into a cohesive society in which everyone spoke the same language. That language was either the dominant one among the various Indian languages or one of the colonial languages. The southeastern Creek nation formed this way, as did the Seminole nation that derived from the Creeks. There are many more such examples.

The Cheyenne case shows that culture change can take place very rapidly while constituent communities are also relocating across multiple ecological boundaries. Were it not for documentary records, there would be virtually no solid evidence to lead researchers to conclude that the Cheyenne nomads of the nineteenth-century Great Plains descended from wild rice gatherers in the northern Minnesota forests a mere two centuries earlier.

New England Pilgrims

The migration of English religious dissidents to Massachusetts in the early seventeenth century is a very well-known case. David Anthony points out that migrating groups typically replicate the culture of the parent society in simplified form. However, he does not fully explore the underlying processes. One might expect migrants to express a simplified version of the parent culture if only because they represent a small subset of the original culture that is adapting to a new environment, but there is more. It is important to realize that migrants are often (perhaps usually) self-selected; consequently, they are going to be a coherent subculture, not just a random subset, of the parent culture. Thus the Puritans of eastern England migrated in order to get away from the diversity of the larger regional English society. They found many features of the larger society repugnant, and their explicit goal was to shed those features and establish a new colonial society that would endure without the traits they were deliberately leaving behind. We should hardly be surprised that Plymouth, Massachusetts, displays less diversity than did Anglia in the 1630s.

The case of the New England Pilgrims illustrates the cultural simplification that often attends concerted human migration. There is a deliberately imposed founder effect in this process, which is analogous to allopatric speciation in biological populations. Archaeologists and historical linguists must be mindful of this process when studying migrant populations.

Northern Iroquoians

In 1995 I shook up the world of Iroquoian archaeology by publishing a new hypothesis that the Iroquoians had expanded into New York and Ontario from the south about a millennium ago, after they acquired maize horticulture (20, 21). Undisciplined migration scenarios had led Northeastern archaeologists to shun migration as a demographic option five decades earlier. The "in situ" hypothesis of Northern Iroquoian origins subsequently became the controlling model for interpreting their development. Eventually, however, contrary evidence accumulated to the point that the in situ hypothesis of Northern Iroquoian origins could no longer withstand close scrutiny and testing. The practical problem for me was that the in situ hypothesis had solidified into dogma, and several distinguished reputations had been built on its framework. The bearers of those reputations did not receive the new hypothesis well. Nevertheless, by 1995 it was clear that the in situ hypothesis—which required that all archaeological explanations in the region had to assume as a first principle that no migration occurred in the past—had to be abandoned.

The immediate archaeological ancestor of the Northern Iroquoians appears to have been the Clemsons Island (archaeological) culture of central Pennsylvania, which flourished after 775 CE. I have been able to demonstrate the subsequent expansion of Northern Iroquoians out of that area into New York, Ontario, and Quebec on empirical archaeological grounds (22). No one has yet defined the source population for Clemsons Island culture other than to presume that it was one shared by the Cherokee, the sole survivors of the Southern Iroquoian branch of Iroquoian who lived in the southern Appalachian Mountains. While the Iroquoian migration hypothesis remains controversial among archaeologists, it is supported by recent genetic research (14). No alternative hypothesis explains discontinuities in the archaeological record, the genetic evidence, or the presence of Iroquoian languages in Northeast North America as economically.

The migration hypothesis of Northern Iroquoian origins has been disputed more recently by some scholars. For example, John Hart argues that matrilocality and maize horticulture can be explained in terms of each other, and that other variables need not be considered (Hart 2001). Unfortunately, Hart's effort to simplify the problem leads to an unrealistic selective use of the evidence. The Northern Iroquoian case demonstrates the need to use all lines of relevant evidence that are available. Only a multidisciplinary approach can succeed in such cases because disciplinary constraints often produce artificially narrow perspectives.

Indo-European

Ammerman and Cavalli-Sforza have pulled together a variety of archaeological, historical, linguistic, and genetic evidence to show that the spread of agriculture from various developmental hearths around the world was typically carried by expanding populations of cultivators. Their demographic expansions involved both rapid growth in numbers and spreading out beyond their regions of origin. This was typically at the expense of demographically stationary and less dense populations of nonagriculturalists who were displaced or absorbed. The result of this process is a widespread modern population of agricultural populations that show less internal genetic diversity than those that have been in place longer (23, 24). Recent research has shown that a demic model for the spread of agriculture

to India matches up with both linguistic and genetic evidence, another instructive example (25).

Colin Renfrew made the same observation, and it led to his controversial book on the expansion of Indo-European languages across Europe (26). The problem with this case is that the expansion of agriculture out of Anatolia cannot be matched convincingly with either the evolution and spread of Indo-European languages or the genetic evidence (27, 13). It is likely that Renfrew is right, and that language(s) did spread with the expansion of agricultural communities across Europe—they just were not Indo-European languages. But even this expansion appears not to have involved wholesale population replacement; at least some geneticists argue that Europe has been genetically stable since the Upper Paleolithic (28, 29).

Indo-European speech almost certainly arrived much later and then spread by a very different mechanism. The most economical hypothesis currently available is that the process by which Indo-European became established across Europe was basically the same as the process by which Latin later became established across most of what is now France and Spain, as mentioned earlier. A dominant elite established a series of polities that each dominated several preexisting languages and a multitude of dialects. Adoption of the elite language became adaptive because local folks needed both a common language and access to political power in the new, larger polity. The elite language provided them with both.

There are many examples of the spread of language without migration, or at least only minor migration. English is an excellent example. The process by which Latin became established in France and Spain was replicated by English in India. Both English and French spread widely through colonial empires in the nineteenth and twentieth centuries. Spanish spread similarly across Latin America in the sixteenth and seventeenth centuries. The spread of English largely (but not entirely) with the migration of Euroamericans across North America is probably an exception to the more common pattern for that language.

While the expansion of relatively dense agricultural populations often carries waves of new speech, the Indo-European cases show that languages can also spread across existing farming populations with little or no population movement. Celtic is a particularly informative specific case within Indo-European.

Celts

Techniques, particularly new and innovative ones such as iron swords, diffuse rapidly across cultural boundaries. However, sword styles can vary without functional consequences, so we should expect them to be more diagnostic than other tools for purposes of detecting migration. Arguing against this, however, is the example of La Tene, an artifact complex that is often associated with, and argued to be evidence of, the spread of Celtic-speaking populations across Europe and into the British Isles. The problem is that La Tene artifacts were probably the blue jeans, CDs, and Coke bottles of their time—highly valued items that spread rapidly through and between populations. One did not have to be a Celtic speaker to covet them, and I doubt that La Tene artifacts can be safely associated with any particular population or language.

Archaeologically there is no evidence to indicate that Celtic speech arrived in the British Isles as the result of large-scale migration (27). Like the spread of Indo-European generally, Celtic was probably established there as a lingua franca by a dominant elite that offered a common language to what had become a linguistic mosaic of older languages across the islands. This is how French, initially a creole version of Latin, became established across Roman Gaul. Interestingly, Latin subsequently failed to become established in the same way in Celtic Great Britain, probably because the Romans did not stay long enough, and local populations remained outside the political and economic power structure. An interesting aside is that when the Romans pulled out of Great Britain they left behind a unit of 5,500 Sarmatians in the vicinity of Hadrian's Wall. These migrants, who probably arrived speaking their own language, disappeared into the Celtic and later English populations of the island.

Variants of Old English later became established in Great Britain and replaced earlier Celtic languages in what is now England. Old English survived to become standardized as modern English even after 1066, when the ruling class brought French to the island. Had chaotic internal migration not prompted English language standardization during the reign of hapless King Stephen, this book might be written in some form of French. If nothing else, the case illustrates that we cannot map language classifications onto human biological classifications except perhaps in very general ways. The observation calls into question at least some of the conclusions published by Cavalli-Sforza (Cavalli-Sforza and Cavalli-Sforza 1995).

Basques

The Basques are famous for being the only non–Indo-Europeans in Europe, and for having been in place for a very long time. Their relevance to a discussion of migration is that they probably reflect the situation in many parts of the world prior to the time when small, dominant, migrating groups established themselves and their speech over large domains. There are eight dialects of Basque spread over only 10,000 km2 of Spain and France. That degree of diversity in a much larger area would ripen over a millennium into numerous mutually unintelligible languages and an even larger number of dialects in the absence of efficient transportation and long-distance communication. This would have set the scene for the kind of process that led to the establishment of Indo-European in Europe, French in Gaul, English in Ireland, and Pidgin-English in New Guinea. In each of these cases a territorially large political system was imposed on a mosaic of languages, and the language of the new political leadership came to dominate over the course of a few generations.

The alternatives for modern Basque are to (1) switch to French or Spanish, (2) maintain their current diversity and risk extinction, or (3) opt for the choice made by English speakers during the reign of King Stephen. The English might have adopted the French speech of the dominant elite, but instead they generalized the various dialects of Germanic Old English by simplifying grammar and standardizing vocabulary, a move that was facilitated (if not forced) by widespread population dislocations. Thus there must be a tipping point on one side of which subject peoples resist the language of the dominant elite, and on the other side of which they adopt it and abandon traditional languages. The critical difference might be the degree to which the elites allow subjects access to ideological or political power, and/or the degree to which broader economic opportunities replace traditional local economies.

The Basque case is a rare example of stubborn linguistic persistence. Many American Indian languages persist in the same way, their speakers proudly conscious of the impracticality of their perseverance. Fortunately, examples of such doggedness also help research of the kind found in this volume.

Huns

"Hun society by its very nature was such that we can never expect to discover many traces of it in the archaeological record" (*30, p. 7*). The Huns were a Turkic society that arose in central Asia like so many other nomadic peoples. Their great military advantage was that they used a new and very efficient compound bow, one that was larger and stronger than the earlier Scythian bow. Their arrows were longer and tipped with steel, such that they immediately rendered obsolete the armor of the heavy Sarmatian cavalry. After sweeping aside the Massagetae and Sacians by around 16 BCE, they turned their attention westward.

The eastern Roman Empire went to war against Persia in 420, moving legions there and stripping the northeastern border of much of its military protection. Perceiving the weakness, the Huns began attacking Thrace in 422. In 433 the Huns began their ferocious expansion to the west and north, galvanized by a single leader. Attila was for them what the ideology of organized religion later was for Muslim and Christian armies.

Beyond the new bow, the principal reason for the military success of the Huns was their cavalry. Because they virtually lived on horseback, the Huns were a ready-made army that could be instantly mobilized. Every able-bodied adult male could be transformed in minutes into a cavalryman, and an entire tribe could launch a sudden mobile attack on even a distant enemy with unprecedented alacrity.

The empire of the Huns was perhaps more parasitic than any the world had known up to that time. By 450 the empire stretched from the Caspian Sea to France, from the Balkans to the Baltic. The organizational structure, which depended on an overextended network of personal relationships and loyalty founded on charisma and a constant flow of loot, was stretched, fragile, and dependent on subject populations. Eventually the Romans recovered enough to defeat the Huns in battle at least some of the time, to refuse extortion demands, and to even deny the Huns access to key market towns. As Hunnish bonds of personal loyalty fragmented, and their leaders grew older, local leaders looked to their own interests, and the empire dissolved in place.

The Huns, by that time dispersed all over Europe, had few means of production of their own. They had long since abandoned pastoralism and had become dependent on subject populations for food and clothing. Many individual Huns must have been annihilated by their former subjects, while others fled eastward. Some held out in Hungary for a while, then followed those that had already retreated back to the steppes. Still others were recruited into the local populations. Thus thousands of Huns disappeared into the populations they had briefly dominated (*30*). According to newspaper accounts, in April 2005 some Hungarians who claimed Hunnish descent failed to gain recognition as a minority population from the Hungarian government.

The case of the Huns shows how small, temporarily dominant populations can disappear into larger, more permanently established ones. Readers of historical atlases might often wonder what happened to ethnic groups like the Avars, the Langobards, the Ostrogoths, the Vandals, the Picts, and many others who seem to have disappeared, leaving no descendants. In fact they all have many descendants, but names and languages change over time.

Some General Conclusions

Many other cogent cases exist, but the cases discussed above are sufficient to support some tentative conclusions. Moreover, readers with Type A personalities have already skipped ahead to this section. As an archaeologist, I am most interested in a few general observations that will allow me to make sense of the archaeological record in terms of major demographic processes, especially migration. Put in terms of research questions, what are the archaeological signatures of the processes discussed above, and how can we infer different forms of migration (or the lack of it) from those signatures? Some specific, but still tentative, conclusions are possible, and these can be used as working principles in the effort to understand the range of phenomena that we have pulled together under the umbrella of migration.

1. *The gross archaeological signatures of population expansions often mimic those of the spread of highly adaptive traits and innovations in the absence of substantial population movement.* This circumstance is what misled Colin Renfrew to infer that the spread of Indo-European speech was coincident with the spread of agriculture across Europe. However, not all archaeologically observable phenomena will display this kind of equifinality. Researchers should consider the potential test implications of the following principles:

    a. Distributions resulting from population expansions (often horticulturally driven)
        i. will show relatively little internal genetic diversity, and
        ii. will show uniformity in conservative traits that differ from those of the previous residents of the region.

    b. The spread of artifact types or language without substantial demic expansion
        i. will result in the persistence of genetic diversity in the population so defined, and
        ii. will not result in the replacement of typically conservative traits.

2. *Migrating populations often carry simplified forms of the cultural inventories of their source populations. Dissident factions such as Massachusetts Pilgrims or more recent Amish immigrants to Pennsylvania are good examples.* In these cases one should look for genetic continuity with the presumed source population, although one must be mindful of the founder effect and the probable genetic bottleneck created by a small founding population. One should also expect to encounter persistence of conservative traits in the simplified inventory. Genetic traits will vary in their persistence depending on whether the migrating population recruits

from the outside, as in the case of the Pilgrims, or bars outsiders, as in the Amish case.

3. *Migration is not convincingly disconfirmed by studies that artificially limit the scope of analysis.* For example, Hart asserted that researchers need not necessarily infer demic diffusion in the Northern Iroquoian case because both matrilineality and maize horticulture can be explained more simply by their mutual adaptability, and without any necessary reference to migration (31, 32). However, Hart omits consideration of genetic evidence and the archaeological evidence of ceramics, lithics, and architecture from his discussion—three conservative classes that all show discontinuity with earlier evidence in the region occupied by Northern Iroquoians over the last millennium. When all the evidence is considered, only a hypothesis that includes provision for migration covers all the known facts.

4. *Migration was a common demographic phenomenon in the past, made to seem less so in recent decades by scholarly bias.* American archaeology came to be biased against discussion of migration in the second half of the twentieth century because of earlier, undisciplined use of migration scenarios. Rouse argued long ago that the burden of proof rested on migration, the default hypothesis being one that assumed no movement at all. Rouse's criteria for demonstrating migration were very stringent and, accordingly, rarely met (33):

1. Identify the migrating people as an intrusive unit in the region it has penetrated.
2. Trace this unit back to its homeland.
3. Determine that all occurrences of the unit are contemporaneous.
4. Establish the existence of favorable conditions for migration.
5. Demonstrate that some other hypothesis, such as independent invention or diffusion of traits, does not better fit the facts of the situation.

To these David Sanger added a sixth requirement, namely that one had to establish the presence of all cultural subsystems in any hypothesized migratory group, as opposed to an isolated one such as burial practices (*34*). The bias against migration as a common feature of human evolutionary ecology persisted in American archaeology until the 1990s. An article by David Anthony marked a turning of the tide (*11*). A better stance is to assume that migration is one of several commonly seen demographic processes, and that it is better to find ways to force choices between them than to preempt research by assuming at the outset that migration is the least likely of them to occur.

5. *If cultural simplification is the consequence of deliberate self-selection, then most migrations are bound up in the process of ethnogenesis.* This is a feature of migration that has not yet been fully explored for the Iroquoian case or many others of its kind. The way it would have worked in the Iroquoian case is that a subset of Iroquoians who saw the advantages of adopting full-time horticulture, multifamily houses, and compact villages would have migrated away from a parent society having a more diverse set of subsistence and settlement characteristics. More generally speaking, migrants who guess wrong die out or come home with their tails between their legs. Those that guess right live and prosper, and the parent societies either come along belatedly in chain migration, dwindle in place, or continue with a different (and perhaps still more diverse) adaptation. We see this over and over again in the record. This is what the Cheyenne did twice in a matter of decades. This process describes the Puritans in New England, the Mormons in Utah, the Spanish in Cuba, the Pipil in El Salvador, the Mongols in China, and many others. People usually migrate in part to reinvent themselves by keeping what they value and leaving behind what they detest. There is often a strong religious or other ideological component. Thus it should not surprising that migrant groups look like simplified versions of their parent societies.

6. *Major demic expansions of dominant cultures can result in their absorption by subordinate societies if they spread themselves too thinly over conquered territories.* The Huns are the best example. The colonial Spanish might have experienced the same fate in Latin America had smallpox and other epidemic diseases not reduced the native populations as dramatically as they did. When absorption happens, the only surviving evidence is often genetic or archaeological.

My hope is that scientists from the range of disciplines brought together for this volume will continue to learn how to use their complementary disciplinary strengths along with the definitions, axioms, and working principles I have outlined to unravel general patterns of human migration and the ways they have played out over time around the world. This complex of interrelated problems can be solved only by multidisciplinary teamwork, and the workshops at the Santa Fe Institute that led to this volume have demonstrated that the will and the means to make progress in this fascinating area of research are at hand. The chapters that follow summarize our best efforts and point to avenues for new research.

Notes

1. R. Cann, M. Stoneking, A. Wilson, *Nature* 325, 31 (1987).

2. H. Harpending, S. Sherry, A. Rogers, M. Stoneking, *Curr. Anthropol.* 34, 483 (1993).

3. S. Elena, V. Cooper, R. Lenski, *Science* 272, 1802 (1996).

4. D. Snow, in *Darwin and Archaeology*, J. Hart, J. Terrell, eds. (Bergin and Garvey, Westport, 2002), 161–181.

5. E. Burch, E. Jones, H. Loon, L. Kaplan, *Ethnohistory* 46, 291 (1999).

6. J. Mallory, *In Search of the Indo-Europeans* (Thames and Hudson, New York, 1989).

7. L. Cavalli-Sforza, F. Cavalli-Sforza, *The Great Human Diasporas* (Addison-Wesley, New York, 1995).

8. P. Bogucki, ed., *Case Studies in European Prehistory* (CRC, Boca Raton, 1993).

9. B. Hofmeister, in *Erdkunde* (Univ. of Bonn, Bonn, 1961), 121–135.

10. A. Fix, *Migration and Colonization in Human Microevolution* (Cambridge Univ. Press, New York, 1999).

11. D. Anthony, *Am. Anthropol.* 92, 895 (1990).

12. E. Lee, in J. A. Jackson, ed., *Migration* (Cambridge Univ. Press, Cambridge, 1969), 282–297.

13. R. Sokal, N. Oden, C. Wilson, *Nature* 351, 143 (1991).

14. R. Malhi, B. Schultz, D. Smith, *Hum. Biol.* 73, 17 (2001).

15. I. Rouse, *Migrations in Prehistory* (Yale Univ. Press, New Haven, 1986).

16. W. Wood, *Biesterfeldt,* (Smithsonian Institution, Washington, D.C., 1971).

17. J. Moore, *The Cheyenne Nation* (Univ. of Nebraska Press, Lincoln, 1987).

18. J. Moore, *Am. Anthropol.* 96, 925 (1994).

19. J. Moore, *The Cheyenne* (Blackwell, Cambridge, MA, 1996).

20. D. Snow, *Am. Antiq.* 60, 59 (1995).

21. D. Snow, *Am. Antiq.* 61, 791 (1996).

22. D. Snow, in *Methods in the Mountains: Proceedings of Congrès International des Sciences Prèhistoriques et Protohistoriques Commission IV Meeting* (1994), Mount Victoria, Australia, August 1993.

23. A. Ammerman and L. Cavalli-Sforza, *The Neolithic Transition and the Genetics of Populations in Europe* (Princeton Univ. Press, Princeton, 1984).

24. J. Diamond, P. Bellwood, *Science* 300, 597 (2003).

25. R. Cordaux, E. Deepa, H. Vishwanathan, M. Stoneking, *Science* 304, 1125 (2004).

26. C. Renfrew, *Archaeology and Language* (Cambridge Univ. Press, New York, 1987).

27. J. Mallory, T. McNeill, *The Archaeology of Ulster* (Institute of Irish Studies, The Queen's Univ. of Belfast, Belfast, 1991).

28. C. Faurie, M. Raymond, *Biol. Lett.* 271, S43 (2004).

29. W. Haak et al., *Science* 310, 1016 (2005).

30. E. Thompson, *The Huns* (Blackwell, Oxford, 1996).

31. J. Hart, *J. Archaeol. Method and Theory* 6, 137 (1999).

32. J. Hart, *J. Archaeol. Method and Theory* 8, 151 (2001).

33. I. Rouse, in Thompson, ed., *Migrations in New World Culture History*, (Univ. of Arizona, Tucson, 1958), 63–68.

34. D. Sanger, *Arctic Anthropol.* 12, 60 (1975).

3

Theory of Migration

Implications for Linguistic Evolution

Sohini Ramachandran and Marcus W. Feldman

In studies of human evolution, the population is often the unit of interest. The population genetics framework, which formalizes the effects of evolutionary forces on genes in populations of organisms, is applied to understand more about evolutionary relationships between modern human populations. Such studies use statistical techniques (1), some of which are general, while others have been developed specifically for genetic studies. It follows that we might apply this statistical framework to study the history of other important characteristics, such as languages, between which there might be genealogical connections.

Evolution is defined as the process of descent with modification, a definition that has two important consequences. First, traits in a descendant are often determined by corresponding traits in ancestors; this reasoning applies to genetic traits and to other (for example, cultural) traits such as chosen profession in humans (2). If these ancestors differ markedly in the traits of interest, then their descendants observed today will reflect a history of admixture that can be revealed using statistical methods. In this chapter, we consider admixture at two levels: first, in an individual with ancestry from different places; and second, in a population with a history of migrants. Note that in genetics, admixture is a property of the individual, while in linguistics admixture only makes sense as a cultural property of the language spoken by a group of individuals. The

second consequence of this definition of evolution is that it requires the existence of variation. Without variation, and therefore the forces that produce variation, evolution cannot take place.

Thus, when interpreting evolutionary relationships between languages, we need to identify the possible sources of variation in a language. In genetics, mutation and recombination generate new nucleotide combinations, but an important generator of variation in genetics, which also drives change in languages, is migration (3, 4). Vertical transmission, from parent to child, preserves the status quo with respect to variation (2). On the other hand, languages are likely to change a great deal due to horizontal transmission (e.g., borrowing of new words, pronunciations, or expressions, when groups speaking different languages come into contact) (2); with migration, linguistic admixture is generated. The existence of horizontal transmission—in biology (e.g., in prokaryotes [5]) or in linguistics via migration and/or borrowing—greatly complicates the reconstruction of phylogenetic relationships (Figure 3.1). This is why migration, both of linguistic features and their human carriers, is an important process to consider in linguistics and phylolinguistics. The term *migration* thus encompasses physical movement of the speakers of a language or a dialect of a language, as well as cultural diffusion, which entails the spread of a feature or features of a language by contact between individuals but without actual movement of the carriers of the features.

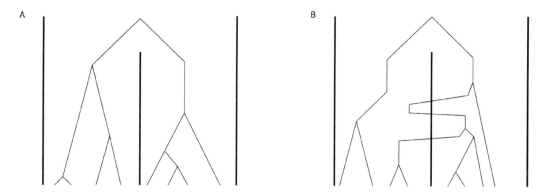

FIGURE 3.1. Diagrams of coalescence: *A,* a model with no migration after divergence; *B,* a model with considerable migration post-divergence. The center line separates the two descendant populations, and the phylogeny is drawn for samples of eight lineages taken in the present, four from each descendant population.

In order to distinguish between these alternatives, additional information, especially genetic or archeological evidence, may be useful (3).

Before proceeding, we should describe the generators and measures of variation in both the genetic and linguistic contexts.

Generators of variation: In genetics, the origin of all variation is mutation, which generates de novo changes that become heritable. Mutation can be thought of as a change at the level of the nucleotide sequence due to mistakes in DNA replication, or the rearrangement of a chromosome through an inversion or translocation event. Although mutation provides the raw material for evolutionary change, in the absence of other forces it is relatively weak in changing allele frequencies. Another source of genetic variation is recombination, which brings different combinations of genes together on the same chromosome.

At the population level, migration is an important source of genetic variation, allowing variant forms to spread to groups outside their population of origin. With respect to languages, it is clear that migration, either in the demic sense or through cultural diffusion, can generate variation. However, we must not overlook de novo changes analogous to mutation in language; indeed, such newly arising changes may be important in the formation of new dialects. Changes in a language may have a physiological explanation, such as the changing of voiceless consonants to voiced consonants when occurring between vowels in some languages (6), while other changes

such as a newly arising word may be harder to explain. For example, a new technology or concept requires a verbal description (i.e., a name) for its communication. The intentionality inherent in this kind of change to language differentiates it from the randomness of genetic mutation. Although we know little about the mechanism of change in a single language, there should be no doubt that similarities between two languages in words, orthography, or grammatical structure likely indicate some historical relationship between the pair.

Measures of variation: The rate of mutation for a gene gives us an initial idea of how often variation is being newly generated in a population; these genic rates can be quite low, on the order of 10^{-4} to 10^{-6} new mutations per gene per generation (7). Mutation can generate new alleles at a locus in a population; thus counting the number of alleles and their frequency is one natural way of studying genetic variation. One of the most basic measures of genetic variation is heterozygosity, whose expectation under Hardy-Weinberg equilibrium is one minus the sum of allele frequencies squared, averaged over loci and individuals.

The term used to describe the nonuniformity of a population's geographic distribution is *population substructure.* An important consequence of population substructure is a reduction in heterozygosity across subgroups relative to that expected under random mating with no subdivision; that is, there is a dearth of heterozygotes in the total population, even though random mating occurs within each subpopulation. Sewall Wright developed the concept of hierarchical population structure and heterozygosity at different levels (i.e., subpopulations, regions, and total population) and formalized these values in the hierarchical F-statistics, of which F_{ST} is prominently used in population genetics to quantify the reduction in total heterozygosity due to population substructure (*8–10*). F_{ST} theoretically ranges from 0 (indicating no genetic divergence between subpopulations) to 1. Across 52 globally distributed human populations, F_{ST} has been estimated to be between 5 and 7 percent for one class of genetic markers (*11*). Overall, it is reasonable to claim values between 5 and 15 percent for the widest array of genes (*1*). In other words, the fraction of all genetic variation that can be attributed to differences between individuals in different populations is between 5 and 15 percent, with the remaining 85 to 95 percent occurring between individuals in the same population. In addition to F_{ST}, other statistics are widely used in anthropological genetics to measure distances between individuals, populations, or groups of populations. Such statistics can be used to compare genetic distances between different pairs, or groups, of populations with geographic or cultural distances between the same groups in order to distinguish likely historical patterns of migration or cultural diffusion (*12*).

Linguistic studies tend to measure variation in terms of the preservation of basic words (such as "one," "two," "mother," "father") across language families. Other approaches have included examining similarities in word order and grammatical or structural features of language. One important note regarding these different strategies is that linguistic markers may vary in type and strength of evolutionary constraints; for example, consonant systems may change more easily than the ordering of subject, verb, and object. This would be especially important to consider when comparing phylolinguistic conclusions based on different types of linguistic markers (*13, 14*).

In genetics, classification into categories entails finding groupings of observed data, calculated using measures like those discussed earlier, that minimize differences between individuals in the same subpopulation. In contrast, the phylolinguistic approach is to look for similarities between two languages, either for words with conserved sound and meaning or grammatical structures that are preserved (such as word order [*15, 16*]). Thus linguistic classification operates on the premise that similarities between words across languages are not likely to have been the result of chance, and, as in genetics, we can explain these similarities by descent from a common ancestor, with alternative explanations being convergence or horizontal transmission as a result of migration either through physical movement of people or cultural diffusion among sedentary groups (i.e., borrowing).

Genetic Models of Migration

In this section we discuss migration in the population genetic context in more depth and present models of migration whose analysis may be useful in studying linguistic evolution.

Geneticists' initial interest in the spatial structure of populations arose from the idea that dispersal prevents genetic differentiation into subpopulations, and, if too high, dispersal may prevent genetic adaptation to spatially varying environments (thought to be the first step necessary for allopatric speciation). Little evidence exists for the idea that population structure is essential for adaptation (*17*), but the question of how structure affects the process of natural selection remains.

Natural selection acts on variation generated by mutation in ways that can be formally modeled in terms of differential survival rates, fertilities, and abilities to find and keep mates. Population subdivision by local inbreeding or geographic or ethological barriers may, in the absence of migration, produce genetic nonuniformity across the species range. This lack of uniformity is further promoted by small demographic size of the local interbreeding subpopulations.

The presence of population substructure makes accounting for random fluctuations in allele frequencies due to finite population size important, as even a favored genetic variant may be lost through the stochastic sampling procedure that generates the genetic makeup of the next generation (known as random genetic drift). Thus structure can confound the inference of selection, and we need to measure drift at both a local geographic scale and at the level of the total population. We will define F_{ST} here in more detail and discuss its behavior under two different models that may be applicable to the study of linguistic evolution. Under these models genetic variation is considered to be neutral; that is, different alleles do not have different effects on the number or survival of individuals' offspring.

Wright's F_{ST} Under the Infinite Island Model and Isolation by Distance

To quantify random differentiation between subpopulations, Wright considered the behavior of the ratio

$$\frac{Var(p)}{\bar{p}(1-\bar{p})} \quad (18, 19)$$

where $Var(p)$ is the variance of allele frequencies among different subpopulations (assumed to be subject to the same conditions) at a locus and $\bar{p}$ is the mean allele frequency among subpopulations (18); this quantity later became known as F_{ST} (20, 21). We can see from this definition that F_{ST} becomes large when the variance in the frequency of alleles across subpopulations grows. This variance will be greatest when each subgroup is fixed for a different allele at a given locus; that is, when alleles are homogeneous within subpopulations but different across subpopulations.

Suppose we have an infinite number of demes (subpopulations), each consisting of N diploid adults where gametes disperse independently from any deme to any other deme with probability m. This is known as the infinite island model (22), and F_{ST} has a simple expression under these assumptions such that for large N and small m,

$$F_{ST} \approx \frac{1}{1+4Nm}.$$

From this expression, Nm determines the amount of genetic differentiation we expect to see in the presence of population structure; a large value for Nm means less random genetic drift (if N is large) and/or more genetic input from migrants (if m is large), which brings local allele frequencies closer to the average frequencies observed in the total population and, therefore, lowers F_{ST}. Thus the compound quantity Nm, the effective number of migrants from each deme, is informative as to the relative amounts of within- and between-population genetic variance that

exist; the size of Nm may also influence linguistic similarity across groups, although the meaning of m must be considered carefully since, as mentioned above, it may involve migration of people (demic diffusion) or just an aspect of language (cultural diffusion).

Under the infinite island model, $\bar{p}$ and $Var(p)$ are regarded as fixed, not as random variables. It is assumed that mutation is occurring at a high enough rate to keep allele frequencies stable in the total population despite being in flux in the subpopulations. Suppose we incorporate mutation at rate μ into the infinite island model; a quantity of interest in genetics is the probability that two sampled alleles are "identical by descent"; that is, that two sampled alleles descended without any mutation from their most recent common ancestor. This probability at equilibrium under the infinite island model with mutation is approximately

$$\frac{1}{1+4N(\mu+m)} \quad (23).$$

Often μ is thought to be much smaller than m and is thus discarded from the above expression, leading to an interpretation of F_{ST} as probability of identity by descent (24). One important analogous consideration when studying phylolinguistics is the relative strength of de novo changes versus the frequency of either physical migration or the rate of cultural diffusion, or both.

The infinite island model is a natural first scenario to study the effects of dispersal, but it hinges on the assumption that all immigrants into a deme come with equal probability from any other deme. But, dispersal in most species— including *Homo sapiens* for most of our history—is spatially restricted, and individuals interact more often with neighbors. The expected genetic consequence of more localized dispersal is that genetic similarity between subpopulations will be correlated with geographic distance between subpopulations, a phenomenon known as "isolation by distance" (Figure 3.2).

More generally, we can consider a migration matrix M with entries m_{ij}, where m_{ij} is the probability that an allele sampled in deme i at the present time had its parent in deme j one time unit before the present. A sample matrix for a system of four demes may be

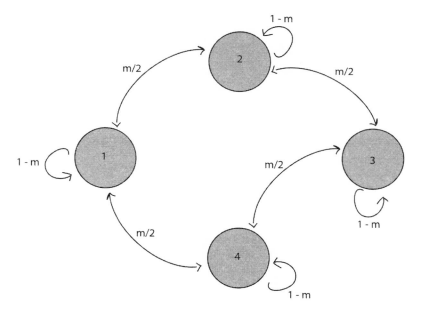

FIGURE 3.2. Schematic of an isolation by distance model with four demes indicated by gray circles. The migration rates between demes correspond to the entries in migration matrix *M*.

$$M = \begin{bmatrix} 1-m & m/2 & 0 & m/2 \\ m/2 & 1-m & m/2 & 0 \\ 0 & m/2 & 1-m & m/2 \\ m/2 & 0 & m/2 & 1-m \end{bmatrix}$$

For human populations, entries in such a matrix can be calculated using parish registers with birthplace information for parents and offspring (25). However, it would be difficult to construct an empirical matrix for prehistoric populations.

The entries of the matrix product M^TM, namely $(M^TM)_{ij}$ where M^T is the transpose of M, would give the probability that two alleles i demes apart from each other after dispersal were j demes apart before dispersal, and the behavior of this matrix applied to a vector of allele frequencies will help us form expectations about genetic differentiation under isolation by distance. Two important predictions result from this model at equilibrium: (i) when total dispersal is low, local differentiation is similar to that predicted by the island model (26); and (ii) in a one-dimensional habitat, differentiation increases linearly with distance, while it increases with the logarithm of distance in a habitat described by a two-dimensional lattice (27, 28).

Empirical studies have shown the logarithmic increase in genetic differentiation with geographic distance for protein variants and blood group polymorphisms within regions (1); however, a linear increase in F_{ST} with geographic distance was observed for genetic data drawn from 53 globally distributed populations (29), and this pattern was found to be related to a decrease in the amount of genetic diversity, the heterozygosity, within a population, with distance from Ethiopia (the putative origin of *Homo sapiens*; see Figure 3.3).

Migration generates both variation and uniformity in genetics and linguistics. In the genetic context, migration prevents the divergence of subgroups by dampening the effect of random genetic drift. In this way, migration is qualitatively like mutation at the subpopulation level, although migration rates between subpopulations are generally much higher than mutation rates of a gene. While migration may bring new alleles into subgroups, it also has a homogenizing effect that prevents divergence across subgroups.

Figure 3A

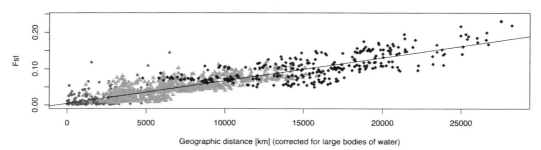

Geographic distance [km] (corrected for large bodies of water)

Figure 3B

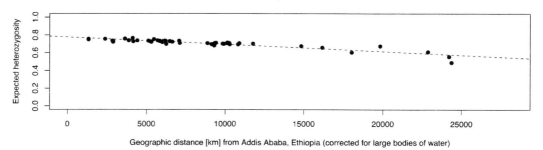

Geographic distance [km] from Addis Ababa, Ethiopia (corrected for large bodies of water)

FIGURE 3.3. The relationship between genetic diversity and geographic distance in human populations (from Ramachandran et al. 2005 [26]): A, the relationship between F_{ST}, genetic distance, and geographic distance for pairs of 53 globally distributed human populations computed using great circle distances and obligatory waypoints. R^2 for the linear regression of genetic distance on geographic distance is 0.7835. The regression line fitted to the data [$F_{ST} = 4.35 \times 10^{-3} + (6.28 \times 10^{-6}) \times$ (geographic distance in kilometers)] is drawn in black. Circles denote within-region comparisons, triangles indicate comparisons between populations in Africa and Eurasia, and diamonds represent comparisons with America and Oceania; B, the decay of heterozygosity plotted against geographic distance between populations and Addis Ababa, Ethiopia (9N, 38E), a possible origin of the human expansion. Distances were corrected for large bodies of water. The equation of the regression line is heterozygosity = 0.7780 − (8.17 × 10^{-6}) × (distance from Addis Ababa); R^2 = 0.8289. This equation corrects typographical errors in Ramachandran et al. 2005 (29).

Limited migration can, however, result in private alleles (alleles confined to one or two subpopulations); if the migration rate is low enough, rare alleles may not occur in migrating individuals and thus will remain in their population of origin until they reach a frequency high enough to be dispersed by migration. For this reason, rare alleles play an important role in the inference of population structure among humans (30); in fact, Slatkin (31) showed that migration rates may be estimated using the average frequency of private alleles.

An important property of a language is the number of people that speak it. Ninety-five percent of the world's languages are spoken by only

6 percent of the world's population (32), and the effect of small population size on linguistic characters can be formally the same as on genes. Biological characters having no apparent selective advantage in a large population might, if that population became fragmented, achieve a high frequency in one or more subpopulations. After a sufficiently long period of isolation for any reason, the subsequent linguistic evolution of the isolated population may be expected to show little relationship to that of its larger progenitor population or other isolates. This is the effect of what might be called "random linguistic drift." Some fraction of linguistic differences between sub-

populations almost surely reflects such purely random and nondirected phenomena.

Under the infinite island model, we see the importance of Nm in the process of differentiation. $Nm > 1$ predicts genetic uniformity and leads to low values of F_{ST}; with respect to language, this means a large enough rate of borrowing contributes to mutual intelligibility. Also, we expect, under a process of limited dispersal, as in isolation by distance, that subpopulations in close proximity will be more genetically and linguistically related than subpopulations that are geographically distant. Note, however, that dispersal as discussed in this section is thought to be a continuous process over time; contrast this with a one-time migration, such as conquest, that may result in a dramatic alteration in language. One-time migration is more analogous to a macro-mutation, bringing about sudden change. Consider the Norman conquest and the resultant influx of French and Latin words into English, or the Lombard invasion's effect on Italian. War may also result in a language being outlawed, as with Catalan during Franco's reign. These effects are important to distinguish from continuously occurring linguistic changes that may be intentional.

We have not presented genetic models with different migration rates for the sexes here, but there is some debate as to whether males and females have migrated at different rates in the past, and whether this may have left a genetic signature in societies that are patrilocal or matrilocal (33–35). Sex-specific migration in either the physical sense or by cultural diffusion may play a role in linguistic evolution as mothers and other female caregivers likely influence the language a child speaks more than male members of a population.

The mathematical models in common population genetic usage do not accommodate linguistically important events such as conquest, coercion, and military attacks, as suggested by Sokal et al. (36). However, other models of migration, such as the one introduced by Fisher (37), have been successfully applied to the study of diffusion of early farming from the Near East (3, 38). This model, which portrays the feature under study as being carried by a wave of advance due to some advantage that it has over a competing feature of the resident population, does allow some parametric

estimation; for example, Ammerman and Cavalli-Sforza (38) estimate that farming spread at about 1 km per year from the Fertile Crescent to western Europe. Genetic analysis of populations across the route of this expansion suggests that this expansion of farming was a case of demic diffusion; that is, people moved and carried the innovation with them. Renfrew (39) incorporated the ideas of Ammerman and Cavalli-Sforza (38) into his analysis of the eastward expansion of Indo-European languages from the Fertile Crescent, which was mediated by the spread of early farming. This "wave of advance" formulation is a useful alternative to the migration matrix approach, especially at the macro level.

Confounds

Just as population geneticists began studying population structure because it confounded the inference of selection, we should consider processes affecting linguistic evolution that may confound the interpretation that linguistic change is due to an influx of migrants. That is, what forces besides migration would lead to changes in some aspects of a language? We have already discussed de novo changes analogous to genetic mutation and potential effects of conquests, but other confounds remain.

Demographic change and social stratification can lead to linguistic divergence, especially at the level of dialects, such as the variations of English spoken by different social classes in England. These can leave a striking signature in politically colonized areas; for example, the sounds characteristic of American, Australian, New Zealand, and South African English may reflect those parts of England (and Holland) from which the original settlers came. In biology, these effects that result from the random choice of initial colonizers are called "founder effects." The evolution subsequent to that colonization has been such that, for example, Americans, Australians, South Africans, and Englishmen all recognize each other's dialect as distinct. In biology, speciation is the analogous phenomenon. The meaning of words can also change with political structures. The movement of Romance language terms, especially French words, into English most often occurred in the upper classes; for example, describing meat using the words "beef" (derived from *boef*) or "mutton" (from *moton*) versus words like "rump" and "tripe" to describe the cuts of meat eaten by the poorer classes.

Isolation by distance can generate a gradient in some biological features of the individuals in a population; such a gradient is known as a cline. In biology, the existence of a cline is generally understood to reflect some more or less continuously varying feature of the environment. Of course, movement of individuals mitigates against genetic divergence, but if local selective differences were large enough, they might outweigh the unifying effect of migration and still result in a discontinuity in the biological trait. For example, a number of phenotypes, such as body size, vary systematically in the north-south dimension of the species range. In a continuously distributed human population, the forces that would result in a geographic linguistic gradient would likely be sociocultural. That is, restricted movement across economic or racial boundaries, or restrictions on the extent of diffusion across linguistic boundaries, could produce the effect.

Similarly, actual ecology may play a role in generating a gradient from, say, a coastal fishing society to an inland agricultural one where word usage may differ. Again, an isolation by distance effect might result, but distance would be measured economically or educationally as well as geographically. Here, rather than large-scale linguistic divergence, something more akin to ecotypes in biology would emerge, where any stratum is recognizably coherent and different from any other, but there is a high degree of mutual interintelligibility. Cultural selection might promote the maintenance of the stratification, but without some geographic isolation, it is hard to imagine this sort of geographic gradient resulting in linguistic isolation (see 12).

Although change in language is likely often due to dispersing individuals, language can change by imitation without new human carriers entering a population. The extent to which cultural evolution is driven by demic or cultural diffusion has been subject to debate (40); contrast the movement of the Spanish language into the Americas via boat and conquest to the movement of English into China via science and technology in recent times.

Tools for Studying Linguistic Evolution

We have focused on what aspects of the population genetics framework might be applicable to studying and understanding linguistic evolution. Here we will discuss more specifically what questions need to be answered to make satisfactory estimates of phylolinguistic parameters and to assess the contribution of migration (in both of the senses used here) to the current distribution of languages and linguistic characters in global populations.

The first question is basic: Can we depict linguistic relationships using a phylogeny? A phylogeny is essentially a pictorial representation of a correlation matrix. If the rate at which borrowing occurs (for example, the parameter Nm in models like the island model) is high, then depicting correlations across languages with a phylogeny might prove very difficult. Estimating Nm would make more clear whether the phylogeny is like a bifurcating tree or if linguistic characters spread in lateral network like an epidemic. In order to assess the importance of Nm, we need to know more about population sizes and the migration rates of human populations, about which we have little information for groups existing more than 5,000 years before the present.

Further information is also needed on the background "mutation" rate of linguistic characters and the mutational mechanism in language; linguists assume that independent convergence of words is very unlikely. However, for genetic markers with high mutation rates like microsatellites, homoplasy—when characters are similar but not derived from a common ancestor—can make the inference of phylogenetic relationships difficult.

One hurdle to estimating the mutation rate of linguistic characters is the possibility that de novo change most likely arises at different rates for different types of characters. Further, different aspects of a language will differ in their potential to be affected by borrowing, dialectical diffusion, or physical migration, mutation, and drift (41); that is, some linguistic characters will have different constraints to change from others, as recently shown by Pagel et al. (42). Just as different levels of divergence (or its opposite, conservation) exist across species for different pieces of DNA—protein-coding versus regulatory (transcription-controlling) versus nontranscribed segments within genes—divergence measured with respect to sounds, words, and rules would be expected to be different.

A method that overcomes some of these problems involves comparing linguistic differentiation with genetic differentiation (43) or other distances estimated between human populations (for example, of the temporal arrival of technologies like agriculture [40]), using a Mantel test. Although genetic admixture might not exist simultaneously with linguistic admixture, the concomitance of these two phenomena does occur in human populations. While there may be instances of the movement of language without a genetic effect (cultural diffusion, such as with English into India during the era of the British Empire), it is likely that contact between peoples was a prerequisite for linguistic borrowing until recently in human history. Thus genetics and archaeology can be used to establish time depth when making inferences in phylolinguistics. However, the time scales at which different linguistic markers change, due to the differing constraints discussed earlier in this section, might make the alignment of these phylogenies based on various data types more difficult.

Some assessment of variation within a language group versus variation between language groupings may also establish ideas of how much change is needed, or what types of linguistic markers need to vary, before two languages are categorized in different families. The study of within- and between-population F_{ST} values in population genetics (11, 44) has shown empirically that there is much more diversity within human populations than between human populations. It would be interesting to see how the amount of variation observed between language groups at linguistic markers compares to the variation observed among different dialects of the same language. This would require careful scaling to ensure that relatively similar properties were measured within and between linguistic groups and dialects of a language.

Conclusion

In genetics and linguistics, migration has the effect of generating variation across populations but also of homogenizing groups. When categorizing relationships between languages, linguists often assume that similarities between languages are unlikely to have been due to chance and instead are due to a historical relationship between the groups speaking these languages. In order to assess the contribution that historical migration has had on the distribution of language and linguistic markers throughout the world, we need more information about the rate of linguistic borrowing between groups that come into contact and also about the mechanism of mutation in language. Population genetic models, along with empirical genetic and archaeological data, can help us in writing a cohesive narrative of history that explains the genealogical connections between different traits in human populations.

Notes

1. L. Cavalli-Sforza, P. Menozzi, A. Piazza, *The History and Geography of Human Genes* (Princeton Univ. Press, Princeton, 1994).

2. L. Cavalli-Sforza, M. Feldman, *Cultural Transmission and Evolution* (Princeton Univ. Press, Princeton, 1981).

3. A. Ammerman, L. Cavalli-Sforza, *Man* 6, 674–688 (1971).

4. L. Cavalli-Sforza, W. Wang, *Language* 62, 38–55 (1986).

5. H. Ochman, J. Lawrence, E. Groisman, *Nature* 405, 299–304 (2000).

6. M. Ruhlen, *The Origin of Language* (Wiley, New York, 1994).

7. D. Hartl, A. Clark, *Principles of Population Genetics* (Sinauer Press, Sunderland, MA, 1997).

8. S. Wright, *Genetics* 6, 111–178 (1921).

9. M. Slatkin, *Genet. Res.* 58, 167–175 (1991).

10. M. Slatkin, *Genetics* 139, 457–462 (1995).

11. N. Rosenberg et al., *Science* 298, 2381–2385 (2002).

12. B. Hewlett, A. De Silvestri, C. Guglielmino, *Curr. Anthropol.* 43, 313–321 (2002).

13. E. Holman, C. Schulze, D. Stauffer, S. Wichmann, *Linguistic Typology* 11, 395–423 (2007).

14. S. Wichmann, A. Saunders, *Diachronica* 24, 373–404.

15. E. Sapir, *Language: An Introduction to the Study of Speech* (Harcourt, Brace, New York, 1921).

16. J. Greenberg, in J. Greenberg, ed., *Universals of Grammar*, 73–113 (Massachusetts Institute of Technology Press, Cambridge, 1963).

17. J. Coyne, N. Barton, M. Turelli, *Evolution* 51, 643–671 (1997).

18. T. Dobzhansky, S. Wright, *Genetics* 26, 23–51 (1941).

19. S. Wright, *Genetics* 28, 114–138 (1943).

20. S. Wright, *Ann. Eugenics* 15, 323–354 (1951).

21. S. Wright, *Evolution and the Genetics of Populations* (Univ. of Chicago Press, Chicago, 1969).

22. S. Wright, *Genetics* 16, 97–159 (1931).

23. G. Malécot, *The Mathematics of Heredity* (Masson, Paris, 1948).

24. M. Slatkin, *Genet. Res.* 58, 167–175 (1991).

25. L. Cavalli-Sforza, W. Bodmer, *The Genetics of Human Populations* (Freeman, San Francisco, 1971).

26. M. Kimura, T. Maruyama, *Genet. Res.* 18, 125–131 (1971).

27. F. Rousset, *Genetics* 145, 1219–1228 (1997).

28. F. Rousset, *Genetics* 151, 397–407 (1999).

29. S. Ramachandran et al., *PNAS* 102, 15942–15947 (2005).

30. N. Rosenberg, L. Li, R. Ward, J. Pritchard, *Am. J. Hum. Genet.* 73, 1402–1422 (2003).

31. M. Slatkin, *Evolution* 39, 53–65 (1985).

32. R. Gordon, ed., *Ethnologue*, 15th ed. (SIL International, Dallas, 2005).

33. M. Seielstad, E. Minch, L. Cavalli-Sforza, *Nature Genet.* 20, 278–280 (1998).

34. H. Oota et al., *Nature Genet.* 29, 20–21 (2001).

35. J. Wilder et al., *Nature Genet.* 36, 1122–1125 (2004).

36. R. Sokal, N. Oden, C. Wilson, *Nature* 351, 143–144 (1991).

37. R. Fisher, *Ann. Eugenics* 7, 355–369 (1937).

38. A. Ammerman, L. Cavalli-Sforza, *The Neolithic Transition and the Genetics of Populations in Europe* (Princeton Univ. Press, Princeton, 1984).

39. C. Renfrew, *Archaeology and Language* (Cambridge Univ. Press, New York, 1987).

40. R. Pinhasi, J. Fort, A. Ammerman, *PLoS Biology* 3, 410 (2005).

41. S. Thomason, T. Kaufman, *Language Contact, Creolization, and Genetic Linguistics* (Univ. of California Press, Berkeley, 1988).

42. M. Pagel, Q. Atkinson, A. Meade, *Nature* 449, 717–720 (2007).

43. L. Cavalli-Sforza, E. Minch, J. Mountain, *PNAS* 89, 5620–5624 (1992).

44. R. Lewontin, *Evol. Biol.* 6, 381–398 (1972).

4

Cross-Cultural Research in the Study of Migration

Cultural Features and Language

Peter N. Peregrine, Carol R. Ember, and Melvin Ember

The most common form of cross-cultural research uses worldwide ethnographic information to test hypotheses about cultural variation and evolution. Now we can also use worldwide archaeological information to study cultural variation and evolution. In combination, these two kinds of cross-cultural research can provide a Rosetta stone for inferences about cultural variation and evolution. In particular, we argue here that these two kinds of cross-cultural research can help us find the original homelands of protolanguage groups and aid us in tracing the migrations of their descendant populations.

The developments and possibilities that make it feasible to study the homelands and migrations of protolanguage speakers include the following:

1. Systematic efforts by historical linguists have reconstructed words, and will be reconstructing others, in the basic and cultural vocabularies of numerous protolanguages.
2. Worldwide cross-cultural studies of the traditional kind (i.e., comparative ethnographic studies) have produced hundreds of statistically tested predictions about patterned relationships between cultural traits, and between cultural traits and environments (physical and social; see Table 4.1).
3. Cross-cultural researchers could use these and future findings to discover archaeologically recoverable indicators of the social customs and environmental features that are

implied by the words reconstructed for the protolanguage.
4. Using those archaeological indicators, we could discover the likely homelands of protolanguage groups, testing hypotheses against the data in the archaeological record, which is now more accessible than ever before through the nine-volume *Encyclopedia of Prehistory* (1) and the annually growing eHRAF Archaeology on the Web.
5. Using morphological and DNA analyses of archaeological bone and other remains (from humans and domestic animals), we can test hypotheses about how the protolanguage groups spread through time and space.

Cultural Features

To make their inferences about homelands, linguists have had to rely primarily on connecting reconstructed words to geographical and environmental features such as flora and fauna. These correspondences have high face validity, but they are not likely to narrow the focus enough to particular archaeological sites or regions. Cultural features may provide more sensitive indicators. For example, historical linguists Alexander Militarev and Christopher Ehret disagree about the homeland of Proto-Afroasiatic (PAA)—the protolanguage that gave rise to Arabic, Hebrew, the Chadic and other languages of Africa. Using reconstructed words primarily describing the environment of PAA, Militarev (2) hypothesizes a

PAA homeland roughly corresponding to that of the Natufians in the Levant, with the Natufians spreading from there after 9000 BCE. Ehret (3), on the other hand, hypothesizes that the PAA homeland was in the southern Ethiopian highlands, and its speakers started to move from there after 15,000 BCE to other areas, including that of the Natufians who, Ehret agrees, could have spoken Afroasiatic.

Employing cultural features adds a critical dimension to this debate. For example, Militarev has reconstructed words in PAA for "iron weapon" and "cast metal." These only appear in a very restricted area at the estimated time depth of PAA (Figure 4.1). Similarly, Militarev has reconstructed a word for "a block of houses." Again, the region where such dwellings existed is fairly limited (Figure 4.2). Based on the overlap between these two indicators, it would appear that the PAA homeland was probably somewhere in the Levant and not in the Ethiopian highlands. The presence of metal and block houses both have high face validity in the archaeological record, and we do not need comparative ethnographic research to establish their presence if there are words for them. But there are other realms for which reconstructed words do not clearly imply archaeological features. Examples are terms for kin terms, social structural features, war-related terms, rank, and status.

How can we discover archaeological indicators of social customs and environmental conditions? The methodology for doing so already exists (4–6). Table 4.1 presents a summary of our current knowledge about material culture correlates of behavior. Future research will undoubtedly uncover more.

Previous cross-cultural research has established a strong correlation between type of residence (patrilocal versus matrilocal) and floor area of dwellings (see Table 4.1). We also know from cross-cultural research that different types of social structures are associated with different types of kin terminology (7). If linguists can reconstruct likely kin terms in PAA, that may suggest whether the people were matrilineal or patrilineal, and the correlated house size would be expected. Additional cross-cultural comparisons would be needed to verify the inferences. Is house size an equally strong predictor of matrilineal

versus patrilineal descent groups? Does the presence of certain cousin terms indicative of matrilineality (patrilateral cross-cousins terminologically merged with father's brother and father's sister) also predict house size? Cross-culturally, does a special term for "mother's brother" predict matrilocal residence?

Archaeologists are beginning to infer warfare on the basis of the probable causes of death in skeletal populations (8). But we do not always have skeletal populations. Hence an archaeological indicator of war may be more useful. Peregrine has suggested that the degree of what he calls "settlement impermeability" is an accurate indicator of war frequency (9). Using graph theory, he counts the number of "steps" it takes to enter the innermost part(s) of the settlement from outside the settlement. This is the index of impermeability. Consider a settlement or habitation site that consists of one-room dwellings. If it takes one step to enter each dwelling (i.e., move from the outside to the inside through one entrance), the impermeability index is 1. If there is an outer fence around the dwelling or community, the index is 2. If there is a trench in addition, the impermeability index is 3. If houses have inner rooms that can be entered only from outer rooms, additional steps are added to the score (10). Peregrine found that societies in the ethnographic record that have an impermeability index of 3 or more almost always have war at least once every two years; those that have an index of 1 or 2 almost always have little or no war (codings of war frequency are from Ember and Ember (11, 12). Judging by the Embers' experience, investigators can maximize the reliability of codings by omitting cases that independent coders disagree about appreciably in their initial ratings. Appreciable disagreement generally reflects ambiguity in the original full-text data, and so near-unanimity or unanimity between independent coders means that the coding is likely to be reliable.

How would inferring the presence or absence of frequent war help us in reconstructing the homeland of PAA? What we need are linguistic correlates of war that might emerge from comparisons of extant vocabularies in societies with known frequencies of war. We would expect societies with more war to have a fairly large vocabulary dealing with specialized weapons,

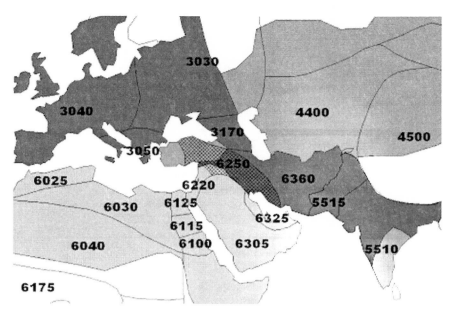

FIGURE 4.1. Languages and metalworking ca. 7000 BP. Numbered areas represent archaeological traditions as defined in the *Encyclopedia of Prehistory* (1). Dark gray represents the Altaic language family, medium gray the Indo-European family, and light gray the Afroasiatic family. Cross-hatching indicates where metalworking is found.

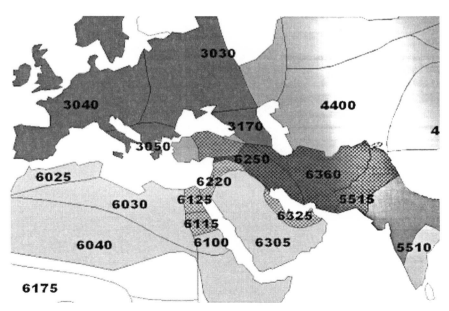

FIGURE 4.2. Languages and brick dwellings ca. 7000 BP. Numbered areas represent archaeological traditions as defined in the *Encyclopedia of Prehistory* (1). Dark gray represents the Altaic language family, medium gray the Indo-European family, and light gray the Afroasiatic family. Cross-hatching indicates where brick dwellings are found.

TABLE 4.1. Archaeological Indicators of Behavior Identified through Comparative Ethnology

Archaeologically Recoverable Indicators	Ethnographic Correlates of Archaeological Indicators Known (in bold) Suspected (not bold)	Ethnographic Correlates of Features in Column 2 Known (in bold) Suspected (not bold)
Residential floor area 14.5–42.7 m^2	**Patrilocal residence** (23–25)	**Internal war (societal population usually > 21,000)** (26–28, 31) **Bride-price, sister exchange, or bride-service** (29) **Tendency toward community exogamy and single kin group communities** (26, 30) **In non-state societies with warfare, patrilineal descent with territorially contiguous groups and lineages** (30)
Residential floor area 79.2–270.8 m^2	**Matrilocal residence** (23–25)	**Purely external war (societal population usually < 21,000)** (26–28) **Insignificant economic transactions at marriage** (29) **Females do as much or more subsistence work** (26, 31) **Tendency toward community agamy or endogamy** (26) **In non-state societies with warfare, matrilineal descent, mixed kin communities, clans, phratries, or moieties (in populations under 9,000)** (30) **Recently migrated; languages unrelated to those of neighboring societies** (27)
Square meters of total residence floor area	**6 m^2/ person** (25, 32)	
Rectangular dwellings only (including an inner court)	**Fully sedentary** (33, 34)	
Elliptical dwellings only	**More likely sedentary** (33)	
Circular dwellings only	**Most are nomadic** (33, 34) Nomadic also among foragers (35) **Most are polygynous** (33) (The converse, that most groups in rectilinear dwellings are monogamous, is not true.)	
Circular as well as rectangular or elliptical dwellings	**Seminomadic** (33)	

TABLE 4.1. Archaeological Indicators of Behavior Identified through Comparative Ethnology

Archaeologically Recoverable Indicators	Ethnographic Correlates of Archaeological Indicators Known (in bold) Suspected (not bold)	Ethnographic Correlates of Features in Column 2 Known (in bold) Suspected (not bold)
Multiroom dwellings	**Extended families or wealth distinctions** (33)	
Surface dwellings	Nomadic among foragers (35)	
Roof and walls made of the same material	Nomadic among foragers (35)	
Elaborate outside house decoration	Long-distance trade (36; only peasant households evaluated)	
Change in settlement location more than once a year	Communal ownership; sharing; no specialized craftsmen; sporadic trade; no taxes; no classes; informal social control; spirits most important; no religious hierarchy; individual religious rites; infrequent group ceremonies; no temples (37, 38)	
Semipermanent settlement	Communal ownership; no specialized craftsmen; no taxes; no classes; spirits most important; no religious hierarchy; individual religious rites; infrequent group ceremonies; no temples (37, 38)	
Community not normally moved	Hoarding; inherited moveable property; no taxes; classes; no religious hierarchy; frequent group ceremonies; no temples (37, 38)	
Center with surrounding satellites	Mostly private ownership; hoarding; inherited moveable property; extensive trade; classes; coercive political leader; formal social control; frequent group ceremonies; temples (37, 38)	
Hierarchy of centers (political state)	Private ownership; hoarding; inherited moveable property; specialized craftsmen; extensive trade; taxes; classes; coercive political leader; formal social control; powerful gods; religious hierarchy; common good religious rites; frequent group ceremonies; temples (37, 38)	

TABLE 4.1. Archaeological Indicators of Behavior Identified through Comparative Ethnology

Archaeologically Recoverable Indicators	Ethnographic Correlates of Archaeological Indicators Known (in bold) Suspected (not bold)	Ethnographic Correlates of Features in Column 2 Known (in bold) Suspected (not bold)
Communities with fewer than 50 people	**Bilocal residence among foragers** (28)	
Severe and rapid depopulation	**Bilocal residence (or alternative residence patterns)** (28, 39) **First-cousin marriage in societies with 1,000 to 25,000 people** (44)	Ambilineal descent when warfare is present in non-state societies; Hawaiian kin terminology
Three or more barriers to enter innermost part of a settlement (e.g., trench, outer fence, door)	**Warfare at least once every two years** (9)	
Unpredictable environment with adverse effect on food supply	**High frequency of war (including internal and external warfare)** (11, 12)	
Burials with ostentatious displays	**Two to four levels of political hierarchy beyond the local community** (40) **Societal norms that allow individuals to accumulate wealth or power** (40)	
Decorations using simple repetitive elements, symmetry, empty space, few enclosed figures	**Egalitarian social structure** (41)	**No games of strategy** (45, 46)
Complex, integrated designs, asymmetry, little empty space, enclosed figures	**Presence of wealth distinctions, social classes, castes** (41, 42)	**Games of strategy** (45, 46) **(particularly with high political complexity)**
Money economy	**Neolocal residence** (43)	Decline of kin groups; Eskimo kin terminology
Two or more distinct levels of settlement size	Chiefdom or state	**Belief in a high god or supreme being** (47–49) **Presence of malevolent practitioners as well as priests** (50)
Three or more distinct levels of settlement size	State	**Games of strategy** (45, 46)

Note: Numbers in parentheses refer to notes citing sources.

fortifications, gates, protective gear, and types of fighting, whereas more peaceful societies should have a more restricted vocabulary. If such relationships could be established, an archaeological indicator of the presence or absence of frequent war combined with reconstructed PAA vocabularies might help point to possible homelands.

Thus, cross-cultural research can provide a kind of Rosetta stone for translating the meaning of reconstructed words into predictions about correlations and sequences that could be tested against the ethnographic and archaeological data. In our experience, just about any variable that is commonly described qualitatively (in words) in the ethnographic and archaeological records can be measured ordinally, which means that all kinds of causal hypotheses, including complex multivariate ones, can be tested statistically (*13*). A worldwide cross-cultural test is the best way to ensure that an explanation or prediction is more or less universally valid; testing theory against the widest possible range of variation is our best protection against being wrong (*14*). Regional comparisons within language families are also possible and often desirable (*15*).

How can we trace the spread of cultures in prehistory, which may help to suggest homelands? Conventionally, archaeologists compare sites to see if and how supposedly related cultures are similar in regard to their cultural repertoires. If similarities are evident, more detailed analyses of material objects (ceramics and metals in particular) can indicate their original source and empirically demonstrate movement. But are there associations between language and material culture?

Language

Welsh, Terrell, and Nadolski tested the association between language and material culture using a sample of 31 village sites on the north coast of New Guinea from which material culture items were collected for the Field Museum between 1900 and 1913 (*16*). They measured propinquity by geographic distance between villages, linguistic similarity by lexicostatistics, assemblage similarity by Driver's G. They found significant (but not strong) correlations between Driver's G and both language similarity (r^2 = .1046, p < .005) and geographic distance (r^2 = .0752, p < .005). Language

explained almost none of the variation in Driver's G when controlling for geographic distance (in multiple regression). They concluded that "there is no necessary correlation between language and other cultural traits."

Moore and Romney suggested that the data used by Welsh, Terrell, and Nadolski were more suited to analyses using multidimensional scaling rather than Driver's G, and also argued that Welsh and colleagues had misinterpreted their own analyses (*17*). They employed correspondence analysis in place of Driver's G to measure assemblage similarity, and scaled both geographic distance and language similarity in two dimensions. Moore and Romney found that language and propinquity account for about the same amount of variance in assemblage similarity (roughly 70 percent) and that that the addition of either language or distance increases the variance accounted for by roughly the same amount (11 percent).

Roberts, Moore, and Romney suggested that hierarchical log-linear modeling could be used to identify whether geographic propinquity or language similarity explained more variation in assemblage similarity (*18*). They found that propinquity and language each account for about 30 percent of the variation and about 40 percent together, a significant improvement in fit. They concluded that "both distance and language contribute to the distribution of artifacts among sites."

So there is some disagreement about the association between language and material culture. The authors of this paper attempted to sort out these disagreements by replicating previous studies using different samples and different variables. The sampling universe we started with consists of the 172 western North American Indian cultures with precoded data published in Joseph Jorgensen's *Western Indians* (*19*). This sampling universe was reduced to the 105 cases representing three language phyla (Aztec-Tanoan, Penutian, and Hokan). Two random samples of 30 cases were chosen from the 105 valid cases for analysis. Multidimensional scaling (ALSCAL procedure in SPSS) was used to create the variables used in the analyses that follow.

Three sets of variables were created for each case: geographic propinquity, linguistic similarity, and assemblage similarity. Multidimensional

TABLE 4.2. Pearson Correlation Coefficients for Two Samples

	Assemblage Similarity (Dimension 1)	Assemblage Similarity (Dimension 2)	Propinquity (Dimension 1)	Propinquity (Dimension 2)	Language Similarity (Dimension 1)
Assemblage Similarity (Dimension 1)					
Assemblage Similarity (Dimension 2)	.183 -.127				
Propinquity (Dimension 1)	.888** .801**	.001 -.027			
Propinquity (Dimension 2)	.199 -.001	.317 .405*	.000 .000		
Language Similarity (Dimension 1)	.090 .124	-.360 .189	.211 .293	-.046 -.118	
Language Similarity (Dimension 2)	.376* .489**	-.361* .01	.379* .495**	.212 -.324	.003 -.002

*p < .05, two tails   **p < .01, two tails

Note: Values for Sample 1 are listed above the values for Sample 2. There were 30 randomly chosen societies in each sample.

TABLE 4.3. Regression Analyses Predicting Assemblage Similarity (Dimension 1)

	Sample 1 Model 1 Std. Beta	Sample 1 Model 2	Sample 1 Model 3	Sample 2 Model 1	Sample 2 Model 2	Sample 2 Model 3	Combined Samples Model 3
Propinquity (Dimension 1)	.888***		.871***	.801***		.740***	.705***
Language Similarity (Dimension 2)		.376*	.047		.489**	.123	.215
N	30	30	30	30	30	30	60
R	.888	.376	.889	.801	.489	.808	.848
R^2	.789	.142	.791	.641	.239	.652	.719
P-value	.000	.040	.000	.000	.006	.000	.000

* p < .05, two tails   ** p < .01, two tails   *** p < .001, two tails

TABLE 4.4. Nominal Regression Analyses with Language Phylum as Dependent Variable

	Independent Variable	X_2	Sig.	Pseudo R_2 (Cox & Snell)
Sample 1	Propinquity (Dimension 1)	13.928	.001	.371
	Assemblage similarity (Dimension 1)	15.788	.000	.409
	Both	15.979	.003	.413
Sample 2	Propinquity (Dimension 1)	14.232	.001	.378
	Assemblage similarity (Dimension 1)	8.725	.013	.252
	Both	15.398	.004	.401

scaling was used to "map" the relationship between each case and the other 29 in the sample in *n*-dimensional space using separate measures of geographic location, language, and material culture. The score of each case on each dimension was retained and used in the analyses below. Geographic propinquity scores were calculated using Euclidean distance measures based on the west longitude and north latitude of each case. Linguistic similarity scores were calculated using chi-squared as the dissimilarity measure (calculated within the ALSCAL procedure in SPSS) based on the language phylum and language family of each case. Assemblage similarity scale scores were calculated using chi-squared as the dissimilarity measure based on 38 archaeologically recoverable material culture traits for each case. Only two statistically valid dimensions were derived for both geographic propinquity and linguistic similarity, and for that reason only the first two dimensions derived for assemblage similarity were retained.

Our results suggest that there are significant correlations between assemblage similarity and both propinquity and linguistic similarity. Table 4.2 shows Pearson correlation coefficients for each sample. Eight of the 30 correlations are significant. The strongest correlations are between propinquity (Dimension 1) and assemblage similarity (Dimension 1)—.888 and .801 in Samples 1 and 2, respectively. Propinquity Dimension 2 and assemblage similarity Dimension 2 are moderately correlated. Linguistic similarity in Dimension 2 is moderately correlated with both assemblage similarity Dimension 1 and propinquity Dimension 1. In our next set of analyses we limit ourselves to assemblage similarity (Dimension 1),

propinquity (Dimension 1), and language similarity (Dimension 2) because these dimensions produced the highest Pearson correlations with the other variables.

To explore the possible independent effects of propinquity and language similarity on assemblage similarity, we performed a number of regression analyses on the two samples separately (Columns 1–6 of Table 4.3) using assemblage similarity as the dependent variable. The columns labeled Model 3 show the standardized beta weights for each of the two independent variables: propinquity and language similarity. The columns labeled Model 1 show the effects of propinquity alone, and the columns labeled Model 2 show the effects of language similarity alone. Language similarity is not significantly related to assemblage similarity when propinquity is in the model, suggesting that propinquity is more important in explaining assemblage similarity than language similarity. However, it is possible that language is not significant because of a small sample size. Accordingly, we retested Model 3 using the combined sample of 60 societies (see last column). Language similarity is more strongly related to assemblage similarity in this larger sample, but is still not significantly related.

Because it is the ability to predict language from material culture that is our real interest, we also performed a multinominal logistic regression analysis (using the NOMREG procedure in SPSS) with language phylum as the dependent variable and assemblage similarity (Dimension 1) and propinquity (Dimension 1) as the independent variables. Table 4.4 shows the results of this analysis. Here it appears that propinquity and assemblage similarity predict linguistic phyla equally well. Thus, we conclude that all of the previous analyses are basically correct. Language, material culture, and propinquity are interrelated. The most important thing to note for our focus here is that material culture can predict language.

Genetics

Chen, Skokal, and Ruhlen have shown that, like material culture, there is also a modest but fairly clear association between genes and language (20). They carried out a worldwide comparison of 11 genetic markers in 130 populations speaking 117 different languages. As we did in our study of material culture, Chen, Skokal, and Ruhlen calculated distance measures between the populations; in their study these were based on propinquity, language, and genes. They conducted pairwise (e.g., language and genes, language and propinquity) and partial (language and genes, controlling for propinquity) correlations of the distance measures and found modest but statistically significant positive correlations between genetics and language, even when propinquity is held constant.

This is an important finding, for it suggests that we may be able to use genetics, like material culture, to predict language. The physical traits of archaeologically derived skeletal populations (both the shape and size of skeletal features, as well as discrete traits such as the presence of shovel-shaped incisors) can provide reliable information on the genetic relationships between ancient populations (21). And recent advances in the recovery, purification, and analysis of ancient DNA may make it possible to conduct direct genetic analyses of ancient populations (22). Thus genetics may soon provide us with yet another source of information about the homelands and spread of protolanguage groups.

Conclusions

It appears that material culture, as described by ethnographers as well as archaeologists, can be very useful in identifying language homelands and studying migration from those homelands. Material culture is related to language, and reconstructed words from protolanguages can be used to identify unique material culture traits. Genetics appears to be related to language and may also be used to identify protolanguage groups and to track their migrations. In combination, comparative ethnography, comparative archaeology, and comparative genetics can provide a Rosetta stone for linking linguistic reconstructions to the material record of prehistory.

In this and other ways, cross-cultural research could reliably establish the homelands of protolanguages. It would start with reconstructed words in the protolanguage and then see if cross-cultural research (comparative ethnography and comparative archaeology) and comparative genetics could confirm the relationships (correlational, genetic) implied by the reconstructed words. This scenario is not just the product of wishful thinking. With modern statistical methods, available computer software, known modeling techniques, and the new technology of computerized databases (particularly the eHRAF collections on the Web), we can make worldwide tests relatively quickly. It is now much easier to model and choose between alternative hypotheses, and to combine them when the test results call for combination. This is precisely the type of multidisciplinary approach called for in this volume, and we look forward to working towards the realization of this approach. We believe it holds great promise.

Acknowledgments

The material presented in Table 4.1 was initially presented by Carol R. Ember to the Language and Prehistory Working Group at the Santa Fe Institute, April 2003. The idea that cross-cultural research could be a Rosetta stone for discovering language homelands was developed by Melvin Ember in his presentation "Integrating Windows onto the Past" at the Santa Fe Institute in April 2003 and several subsequent presentations. Peter Peregrine first presented the analysis of language, propinquity, and material culture in a presentation at the Santa Fe Institute in March 2004, and his identification of homelands with archaeological data was first presented at the Santa Fe Institute in February 2006.

Notes

1. P. Peregrine, M. Ember, eds., *Encyclopedia of Prehistory* (Kluwer/Plenum, New York, 2001–2002).

2. A. Militarev, L. Kogan, A. G. Belova, *Semitic Etymological Dictionary* (Ugarit-Verlag, Münster, 2000–2005).

3. C. Ehret, *An African Classical Age* (Univ. Press of Virginia, Charlottesville, 1998).

4. M. Ember, C. Ember, *J. Archaeol. Res.* 3, 87–111 (1995).

5. P. Peregrine, *Ann. Rev. Anthropol.* 31, 1–18 (2001).

6. P. Peregrine, *J. Archaeological Res.* 12, 281–309 (2004).

7. G. Murdock, *Social Structure* (Macmillan, New York, 1949).

8. D. Frayer, D. Martin, *Troubled Times: Osteological and Archaeological Evidence of Violence* (Gordon and Breach, Langhorne, PA, 1997).

9. P. Peregrine, *North American Archaeologist* 14, 139–151 (1993).

10. R. Blanton, *Houses and Households* (Plenum, New York, 1993).

11. C. Ember, M. Ember, *J. Conflict Resolution* 36, 242–262 (1992).

12. C. Ember, M. Ember, *Behav. Sci. Res.* 26, 169–226 (1992).

13. C. Ember, M. Ember, *Cross-Cultural Research Methods* (AltaMira, Walnut Creek, CA, 2001).

14. M. Ember, C. Ember, *Ethnology* 39, 349–363 (2000).

15. M. Burton, D. White, *Behav. Sci. Res.* 25, 55–78 (1991).

16. R. Welsh, J. Terrell, J. Nadolski, *Am. Anthropol.* 94, 568–600 (1992).

17. C. Moore, A. Romney, *Am. Anthropol.* 96, 370–392 (1994).

18. J. Roberts, C. Moore, A. Romney, *Curr. Anthropol.* 36, 769–788 (1995).

19. J. Jorgenson, *Western Indians* (W. H. Freeman, San Francisco, 1980).

20. J. Chen, R. Sokal, M. Ruhlen, *Hum. Biol.* 67, 595–612 (1995).

21. C. Larsen, *Bioarchaeology* (Cambridge Univ. Press, New York, 1997).

22. D. Reed, *Biomolecular Archaeology* (Southern Illinois Univ. Press, Carbondale, 2005).

23. M. Ember, *Am. Antiq.* 38, 177–182 (1973).

24. W. Divale, *Behav. Sci. Res.* 12, 109–115 (1977).

25. B. Brown, *Behav. Sci. Res.* 21, 1–49 (1987).

26. M. Ember, C. Ember, *Am. Anthropol.* 73, 571–594 (1971).

27. W. Divale, *Behav. Sci. Res.* 9, 75–133 (1974).

28. C. Ember, *Behav. Sci. Res.* 10, 199–227 (1975).

29. M. Ember, in R. Naroll, R. Cohen, eds., *Handbook of Method in Cultural Anthropology* (Natural History Press, Garden City, NY, 1970), pp. 697–706.

30. C. Ember, M. Ember, B. Pasternak, *J. Anthropol. Res.* 30, 69–94 (1974).

31. C. Ember, *Behav. Sci. Res.* 9, 135–149 (1974).

32. R. Naroll, *Am. Antiq.* 27, 587–589 (1962).

33. J. Whiting, B. Ayres, in K. Chang, ed., *Settlement Archaeology* (National Press Books, Palo Alto, CA, 1968), pp. 117–133.

34. M. Robbins, *Minnesota Archaeol.* 28, 2–26 (1966).

35. L. Binford, *J. Anthropol. Res.* 46, 119–152 (1990).

36. R. Blanton, *Houses and Households* (Plenum, New York, 1993)

37. C. McNett, The Inference of Socio-Cultural Traits in Archaeology (Ph.D. diss., Tulane Univ., 1967).

38. C. McNett, in R. Naroll, R. Cohen, eds., *Handbook of Method in Cultural Anthropology* (Natural History Press, Garden City, NY, 1970), pp. 872–886.

39. C. Ember, M. Ember, *Southwestern J. Anthropol.* 28, 382–400 (1972).

40. K. Kamp, *Cross-Cultural Res.* 32, 79–115 (1998).

41. J. Fischer, *Am. Anthropol.* 63, 80–83 (1961).

42. P. Peregrine, *Cross-Cultural Res.* 41(3), 223–235 (2007).

43. M. Ember, *Trans. New York Acad. Sci.* 30, 291–302 (1967).

44. M. Ember, *Behav. Sci. Res.* 10, 249–281 (1975).

45. J. Roberts, M. Arth, R. Bush, *Am. Anthropol.* 61, 597–605 (1959).

46. G. Chick, *Cross-Cultural Res.* 32, 185–206 (1998).

47. G. Swanson, *The Birth of the Gods* (Univ. of Michigan Press, Ann Arbor, 1960).

48. W. Davis, Societal Complexity and the Nature of Primitive Man's Conception of the Supernatural (Ph.D. diss., Univ. of North Carolina, Chapel Hill, 1971).

49. P. Peregrine, *Cross-Cultural Res.* 30, 84–112 (1996).

50. M. Winkelman, *Behav. Sci. Res.* 20, 17–46 (1986).

5

Languages and Migrations

What Can Linguistics Tell Us About Prehistory and Prehistoric Migrations?

Ilia Peiros

The main function of any human language is to maintain reliable communication among its speakers. From this point of view, a language can be seen as a formal device that allows its speakers to represent what they want to say in a text (spoken or written). Applying a similar device to a text, the listener should be able to understand what the speaker intends to convey. This is the Meaning <<==>> Text model put forward by Mel'chuk about 40 years ago (1).

In any text we find only morphemes and the rules governing their combinations. There are two types of morphemes: (1) lexical morphemes, which somehow reflect entities of the real world; and (2) grammatical morphemes, which represent language-specific grammatical relations. Languages have thousands of lexical morphemes. It is highly possible that the number of lexical morphemes is more or less the same in all spoken languages regardless of the cultural achievements of their speakers. Lists of lexical morphemes of Walparli (Australia), Cebuano (Philippines), Yao (Southern China), or Selkup (Western Siberia) consist of about 3,000 to 5,000 entries each. The number of grammatical morphemes depends on the grammatical systems of individual languages, ranging from just a few, as in Classical Chinese, to several hundreds in many morphologically rich languages of North America, the Caucasus, and elsewhere.

A word is a unit that consists of at least one lexical morpheme and one grammatical morpheme.

It is hard to estimate the number of words known by speakers of a given language (tens of thousands?). Any morpheme is a triplet <meaning, form, syntactics> (1). For example, the word "oxen" consists of two morphemes: a lexical morpheme "ox" and a grammatical morpheme "-en" indicating it is plural. The lexical morpheme has its meaning: "certain animal…," the form "ox," and syntactics; i.e., a rule that tells us (among other things) that if we want to make the plural form we must use morpheme "-en."

The link between the three parts of most morphemes is usually arbitrary and has no motivation for the speakers. English speakers simply know which animal should be named "ox" and how to say "two oxen." At the same time, most of them have no idea why they must use the morpheme "ox" and not, for example, "byk." This arbitrary connection between parts of a morpheme has great implications for comparative linguistics. When a significant number of morphemes in different languages are similar, this cannot be just a coincidence. This observation forms the foundation of comparative linguistics.

People who speak the same language belong to the same speech community. However, a speech community can be formed by several different ethnic communities, usually the result of relatively recent events in those communities. Therefore, one can assume that, originally, any given language was associated with only one ethnic community.

Two types of ethnic communities are found: those maintaining a traditional lifestyle, and those in the process of change leading to the loss of identity and language. A traditional community maintains tight control over its members, governing all aspects of their lives, including how the community's language is used. Thus in traditional communities, speakers always follow norms of language usage adopted in their community. In smaller communities, the norms of language usage must be stricter and more uniform.

It is very difficult to estimate how large a traditional community can become. Recorded cases range from fewer than fifty members to several thousand. However, it is unlikely that a traditional community could be found with, say, 50,000 members, since without modern technology there are no means to maintain acceptance of the same norms by so many people. If such a community were found, it means that its language had expanded recently (200 to 300 years), and different centers did not have enough time to develop and to "tear apart" the existing norms.

Each traditional community has at least one language, known to all its members, with grandparents speaking the same language as their grandchildren. This language (L) is either inherited from the ancestors or has been borrowed from neighbors. It is a basic assumption in comparative linguistics that new human languages can never be created. If a community is multilingual (using more than one language), all its languages are either inherited or borrowed. A territory where language L is spoken is usually well known to linguists; that is, its climate, geography, fauna, and flora are well described. In some cases we also have information about how many people speak L, their primary activities, and their neighbors.

So long as people are able to maintain their traditional lifestyle, their language is well adapted to their everyday needs. It has means to name all relevant features of the surrounding world (environment, animals, plants of any importance, etc.), social distinctions of the community, its material culture, and so on. An ability to use a language for these purposes is one of the main conditions of a successful command of any language. Usually, naming is done by words or their combinations ("dog," "guard dog"). One can assume that the

majority of such words include only one lexical morpheme (this assumption, however, has never been fully investigated).

The situation is quite different when a community faces something new. It could be new features of environment, new objects of material culture, or anything else unfamiliar. Often this happens as a result of migration or cultural contacts: the community has migrated, new people established contacts, or traders have brought new objects. The community's language is ill equipped for these new demands and lacks appropriate ready-made names. Therefore it has two main strategies to fix the problem: (1) to borrow a name from another language or (2) to create a new word using its own lexical morphemes ("hornless deer" = "horse").

People normally do not invent new lexical morphemes. A few invented cases (e.g., radar) are known only from the last century. On the other hand, words can be created, but this is always done with the help of existing morphemes.

All human languages have borrowings. In some languages up to 70 percent of lexical morphemes are borrowed, as in Vietnamese, where thousands of morphemes have been borrowed from Chinese, Tai, or Khmer. Borrowings come to a language not only from neighboring languages. If a borrowing is connected to a certain object, it can travel from one language to another until it settles in a language where we finally find it. Borrowings can tell us a lot about the cultural history of a community. However, to use this valuable source of information, we need to know (1) what language was the donor for this borrowing and (2) when the borrowing took place.

A spoken language is in a constant process of change. These changes affect both formal linguistic devices and the norms of their usage. A community's control ensures that changes are accepted by all speakers of the community's language. Over centuries, accumulated changes make a daughter language different from its parent. This is a universal process found in all spoken languages. If several independent centers substitute for the original control center, they begin to support different sets of norms, which leads to the accumulation of different changes. Over time this will cause a split in the original language and the emergence of several new languages, each being a daughter language of the original one.

When three generations of speakers (grandparents, parents, and children) live in the same stable community, they always use the same language. Children have full access to the language, communicating with speakers of at least three generations: grandparents, parents, and other children. In such cases, language transmission from one generation to another is rather smooth. The command of the language remains the same for all generations, regardless of various minor changes that are accumulated in the language of younger generations. The situation is much more complicated when a community adopts another language. Two different scenarios are found in this case: (1) language shift and (2) language formation.

Language shift usually occurs when one community (A) is exposed to the strong influence of another, more powerful, community (B). Under the influence of various political, economic, cultural, or other forces, some members of A begin to use the language of B, first to communicate outside their community, but later also within it. After a certain period of time, a gap occurs between generations: grandparents speak language A but their grandchildren speak only language B. In such cases, a community can shift from one language to another in only 50 years or so. Usually a language shift takes place when a community has no way to protect itself by means of isolation (geographical or cultural).

An exceptionally capable individual can learn to speak a language as well as a native speaker, but there are no examples of groups of adults who learned to speak a new language perfectly. Full command of any language can be achieved only if it is learned by children from many different speakers. It is not known for certain how many speakers are needed to spread a language, but it seems reasonable that more than a handful would be required. A community adopts its new language through intensive contacts with another group, probably via sharing the same settlement.

A language associated with some kind of power might begin to "absorb" other languages. Over time, simply the number of speakers of the language could make it so powerful that it would continue to "suck in" other languages, sometimes despite the political power of the corresponding community. The history of Chinese is a good example. Its spread from several valleys of northern China was a result of the conquest of neighboring groups until the Chinese culture became dominant in East Asia. For centuries, non-Chinese groups joined by learning the Chinese language. Even when China was occupied and ruled by Mongolians and later Manchurians, these rulers and their followers switched to the Chinese language, being unable to resist its overwhelming power.

Language formation takes place when speakers of different languages need a vehicle for communication. Good examples are pidgins and creoles, which form when people are brought by force from different places and are supposed to live and work together. They share no common language, so they have to communicate using the language of their masters. These workers have no direct access to the dominant language, so they begin to use its lexical morphemes, dropping all or most grammatical and phonological rules of the donor language, B. Over time, such variants of B become fully developed languages with their own generations of native speakers.

Even in such unfavorable situations, languages are not invented, but instead adopted for the needs of emerging new communities. A new language may be quite different from its donor in phonology, grammar, or syntax. Nevertheless, a significant number of its lexical morphemes are preserved from the donor language.

Linguistic Migrations

The geographic distribution of modern languages can tell us about migrations. A language map of southern Southeast Asia reveals all possible patterns of distribution (Figure 5.1). Some languages, like Thai or Vietnamese, are spoken over vast territories. From historical sources we know that speakers of both languages are associated with dominant groups and for a long time enjoyed various advantages over other groups. It is recorded, for example, that what is known now as Southern Vietnam was a territory of Khmer speakers, with Saigon being an important Khmer town. Linguistic data confirm these migrations, as we have located the homelands of Proto-Tai and Proto-Vietic, both once spoken much farther north. Various place-names of Khmer ori-

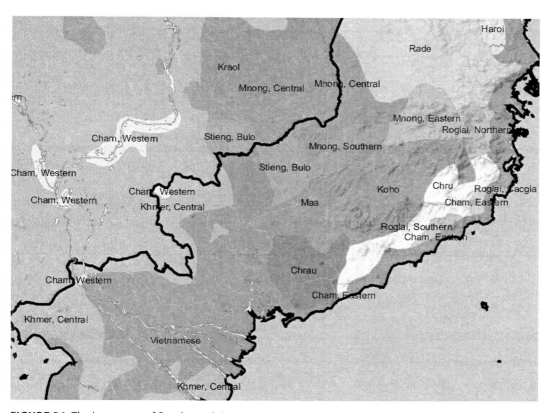

FIGURE 5.1. The languages of Southeast Asia.

gin and Khmer borrowings in these languages are also good indications of their spread. On the other hand, we don't know how this actually happened. Was it caused by movement of population from the north, or by a language shift in local groups? It is highly possible that both processes took place.

A more complex picture is presented by Chamic languages, most of which are spoken in central Vietnam. There are small groups of Chamic-speaking people in Cambodia, which is a result of recent movement. From linguistic reconstructions, we know that Chamic languages are specifically related to Malay, Acehnese, and some other Malayic languages. The homeland of Proto-Malayic must have been somewhere on the islands of Indonesia, from where Proto-Chamic speakers have moved to the north to settle on the coast of modern Vietnam, where its descendants are still found. Some tribal people of the mountains of central Vietnam speak Chamic languages, while their neighbors, who share a very similar lifestyle, speak Bahnaric languages

of Mon-Khmer origin. The Chamic languages of these tribes are full of Bahnaric borrowings, as is Proto-Chamic. So how did these tribal groups get their languages? Are they Chams who moved to the mountains, or local people who adopted the language of the lowlands?

A different story is revealed by the Pearic languages found in isolated places across Cambodia, separated from each other by the Khmer language. This is a typical picture showing a recent spread of Khmer into Pearic lands. The original population has survived only in safe havens that the Khmers have not yet penetrated. Linguistic information about Proto-Pearic is very limited, so one cannot identify the location of their homeland. What is clear, however, is that Proto-Pearic and its daughter languages have many hundreds of Khmer borrowings, indicating its huge impact.

Similar types of distribution are found on the map of northern Southeast Asia (Figure 5.1). Various Miao groups live there surrounded by speakers of other languages. The explanation of this picture, however, is quite different. There are about fifteen Miao languages spoken in southwest China, where, presumably, the Proto-Miao homeland was located. Only one of these languages is found outside their original territory. This patchy settlement pattern can be explained in part by their agricultural methods and cultural tradition. Miao people always build their villages on hilltops, avoiding the wet valleys below. The Miao language distribution may be a good example of the effect of migrations to new settlements where community members at first did not communicate much with other groups in the region.

There are, however, problems related to the languages of the same territory that so far have not been resolved. It is well known that speakers of Mon-Khmer (MK) languages represent two types of communities: agriculturalists (the majority) and hunter-gatherers. At least three main groups of hunter-gatherers are known: Ruc speakers of the Lao-Vietnamese border, Mlabri speakers of the Thai-Lao border, and speakers of Northern Aslian languages of northern Malaysia.

The Ruc language belongs to the Vietic branch of MK. Ruc and its closest relative, Arem of Laos, are very archaic and retain some very important characteristics of Proto-Vietic. As far as we know, Ruc people do not maintain contacts with other groups and do not speak other languages. Most of the Vietic languages are spoken in agricultural communities. The Arem speakers are now also agriculturalists, but the transition to agriculture must have occurred over the last 50 years.

The Mlabri people live in the mountain jungles of the Thai-Lao border. Their language belongs to the Khmuic branch of MK. Mlabri are very secretive people, and until recently, outsiders had no access to their camps. The small Mlabri community is monolingual, although Mlabri men go to work in the fields of their neighbors, who speak languages of other groups. No information is available about the contacts of Mlabri with other Khmuic languages in Laos.

So what is the history of Ruc and Mlabri? Are they the former agriculturalists who lost their skills but retained their language? Are they hunter-gatherers who have adopted the language of their neighbors? Do they maintain their original lifestyle? The last possibility seems to be the least likely. My cultural reconstructions have

suggested that Proto-MK speakers and their descendants—Proto-Vietic, or Proto-Khmuic speakers—knew agriculture.

The situation with Northern Aslian languages is very similar, with one addition: their speakers are physically different from most of the local population, belonging to "Negrito" type as it is called in the old literature. This can be seen as an indication that these groups must have borrowed their language from their neighbors, but how could this happen? One possibility is that those situations are results of migrations, reflected in a mismatch of linguistic and nonlinguistic features of these communities.

The Austronesian Case

To illustrate the principles and problems outlined above, I turn to the case of Austronesian languages. The mainstream view on the homelands of Austronesian languages is stated concisely by Ross (2):

> It is reasonably well established that the Austronesian homeland was on the island of Taiwan…whence Austronesian speakers spread through the Philippines, via Borneo and Sulawesi into Malaysia and western Indonesia, than eastwards through east Nusantra, skirting New Guinea to occupy the Bismarck Archipelago around 3500 BP. From here, speakers of Austronesian languages rapidly occupied the rest of Melanesia, radiating outward from there into Micronesia and Polynesia.

Similar statements can be found in many other publications ranging from encyclopedias like Britannica or Wikipedia to articles in Nature and Science (3, 4).

Austronesian is often seen as one of the best examples of correlation between archaeological and linguistic reconstructions. Let us examine, however, the linguistic evidence, checking it against the theoretical requirements for comparative studies. One of the fundamental notions of comparative linguistics is that of "genetic relations." Strictly speaking, two languages, A and B, are genetically related if and only if linguists know their common ancestor (Δ). This ancestor may be represented in written form or may be reconstructed. French and Italian are related because they both are daughter languages of Latin.

We know that English and German are related because linguists have reconstructed their common ancestor: Proto-Germanic. For each ancestral Δ we must know its phonology, lexicon, and grammar. We also need to know the processes of how languages A and B developed from Δ. If Δ is not well known, any claim about genetic relationship remains hypothetical. Some of these claims are more promising than others, but without reconstructed Δ, they must be seen only as hypotheses.

Languages A and B are specifically related if and only if: (1) there is a language C related to A and B through their common ancestor Δ', and (2) A and B have their own common ancestor Δ, which is not an ancestor of C. English and German are specifically related because they are descendants of Proto-Germanic, but many other Indo-European languages (including French, Russian, and Greek) are not descendants of Proto-Germanic. Both Proto-Germanic and Proto-Indo-European have been reconstructed.

What about Austronesian? The AN family includes 800 to 1,000 languages. Some of these languages are intensively studied, whereas others, spoken in such remote and hostile areas as Borneo or New Guinea, are still not sufficiently known. Published data for about a third of all AN languages is not sufficient even for lexicostatistical analyses (5).

The language families formed by daughter languages transparently related to each other provide a good starting point for our discussion of AN. These may be called "basic" language families. Usually it is not very difficult to reconstruct protolanguages of basic families. To do so, linguists need to compare recorded languages and perform the following tasks:

1. Identify a system of phonological correspondences between most if not all languages of the family. On the bases of these phonological correspondences, a phonological system of the protolanguage must be reconstructed.
2. Compile an etymological dictionary of the family containing the maximum number of protolanguage morphemes. A systematic search for these morphemes in individual languages must be conducted. Thus, if a reflex of a protomorpheme is missing in the

dictionary, it indicates that such reflex does not exist and is not omitted at random.
3. Conduct a full-scale grammatical reconstruction.

Territories occupied by AN languages can be divided into five blocks. The languages and people of each block share common features, which might or might not be due common origin. The blocks are:

1. Taiwan: about 25 languages, with about 15 still spoken, subdivided into 9 to 11 basic families.
2. Mainland Asia, Philippines, western Indonesia, and Madagascar: about 500 languages forming about 25 basic families (Adelaar 2005, Ross 1995c).
3. Eastern Indonesia (Malukus, Timor, Bima, Flores, etc.): about 150 languages, which may be grouped into 16 to 20 basic families.
4. New Guinea and surrounding islands: about 300 languages, which may form 25 to 30 basic families.
5. Pacific islands (Solomon, Vanuatu, New Caledonia, Fiji, Polynesia, Micronesia): about 200 languages belonging to possibly 18 to 20 basic families.

The total number of basic AN families is about 100. So, according to the well-established tradition of modern comparative linguistics, one would expect to see numerous reconstructed protolanguages for these basic families. However, one can hardly find such reconstructions. In a few lucky situations linguists have published comparative phonologies supported by a few hundred lexical comparisons selected to justify reconstructed phonologies. Only a few etymological dictionaries of basic families are available. Among them, there are dictionaries of Chamic (6) and South-Sulawesi (7), representing families from Block 2 and of two families from Block 3: Central Pacific (Fiji, Rotuman, and Polynesian) (8, 9) and Micronesian (10). For other, even relatively well-known basic families, systematic etymological research has never been conducted.

Without reconstructions for most basic families, it is not even possible to make well-supported claims about deeper connections within Austronesian. So what is reasonably supported among linguistic statements about Austronesian linguistic history? In our search for the answers we shall limit the discussion to phonological and lexical issues, which are more conclusive in comparative research.

Comparative Phonology

Dempwollf's (11) work, which established the foundation of AN comparative linguistics, immediately put this family among the few better-known language families of the world. Dempwollf presented an AN "phonological" reconstruction and a detailed comparative dictionary. Formally, however, both the comparative phonology and the etymological dictionary have been presented as the comparison of a few languages: Javanese, Tagalog, Malay, Malagasy, Ngaju Dayak, and Toba Batak (representing six different basic families from Block 2); two closely related dialects, Sa'a and Ulawa; and Fijian and Polynesian (representing only two basic families of Block 4).

One important aspect of this great work, unfortunately forgotten by most modern linguists, is Dempwollf's attempt to find an explanation for everything preserved in the languages used in the study. As a result, each phoneme or phonemic cluster of individual languages was analyzed and explained in the reconstruction. Most etymologies represented in his sources were also identified. In this way, Dempwollf created a very solid foundation for modern Austronesian linguistics.

Dempwollf's reconstruction was subjected to severe scrutiny from several generations of linguists, who changed his phonological reconstruction and etymologies (12). Based on these changes, the system of protophonemes which gave rise to the systems of all languages from Blocks 2–4 is often seen as:

*p	*b	*m	*w		
*t	*d	*n	*l	*r	
	(*ʒ)	*ń			*s
*k	*g	*ŋ			
*q				γ	h

We might also need to add another new phoneme to the list (*Z), but this reconstruction can be challenged.

Current studies of historical phonologies of Austronesian languages demonstrate two competing approaches, which can be called Oceanic and Taiwanese.

The Oceanic Approach

More than 700 Oceanic languages may form a branch of AN (see the discussion below). Their phonological systems differ considerably:

The Tagula (Sudest) language, spoken on an island in the southeast of the Milne Bay Province of Papua New Guinea, has the following phonological system (13):

p	b	ᵐb	m	v		
pʷ	bʷ	ᵐbʷ	mʷ	vʷ	w	
t	dⁿ	d	n	δ	l	r
s	ʒ	ńʒ	ń		γ	
k	g	ᵑg	ŋ	γ		
kʷ	gʷ	ᵑgʷ	ŋʷ	ᵑγʷ		

In contrast, the Northern Marquesan language spoken in the Marquesas Islands, French Polynesia, has the following phonological system (14):

p		m	v
t		n	
k			
ʔ			h

Finally, a suggested Proto-Oceanic consonantal system is as follows (15):

*p	*b	*m			
*pʷ	*bʷ	*mʷ	*w		
*t	*d	*n	*l	*r	*dr
*c	*ʒ	*ń			
*k	*g	*ŋ			
*q				*R	h

It is not so difficult to derive the phonological system of Marquesan and other Polynesian languages from this protosystem and to find supporting etymologies; however, the same cannot be done, with full confidence, for Tagula. The relevant phonological correspondences are given in Ross (*16*), but no lexical support is found anywhere. The same is true for quite a few other Oceanic languages and basic families.

It is believed that the Oceanic system developed from the Proto-Austronesian (PAN) system through "mergers and splits, the introduction of new phonemes, and one deletion" (*15*). How this happened and what the conditions of these mergers or splits were remain unclear. Usually they are explained away as innovations caused by local contacts or by unknown internal factors. The obscure idea of "nasal grades" is used to account for mismatches of the stops in protolanguages. Such explanations, however, would never be accepted in better-known language families, where linguists are expected to identify the factors that caused individual changes.

The Taiwanese Approach

The phonological systems of the AN languages of Taiwan, which all are less complex than those of some Oceanic languages, cannot be simply derived from Dempwolff's system.

For example, the phonological system of Pazeh is as follows (*17*):

p	b	m	w				
t	d	n	l	r	s		z
k	g				x		
ʔ					h		

As comparison, here is the phonological system of Bunun (*18*):

p	ʔb	m	v			
t	ʔd	n	δ	l		s
k		ŋ				
q						
ʔ					h	

The treatment of these systems differs, however, from that of Oceanic. The unique features of these languages are usually seen as archaic and thus are traced back directly to the PAN level. In the cases where slightly different phonological correspondences are found between the Formosan languages, some linguists even postulate several different AN phonemes ($*S_1$, $*S_2$, etc.).

Such special treatment of the Formosan languages was started by Dyen (*19*), but I found no solid justification of this approach in any of his publications. An observation that, say, a distinction of $*t$ and $*C$ is found only in the Formosan languages and not elsewhere does not automatically lead to the conclusion that it must be of PAN origin. A simple fact that a phoneme in language L does not correspond to any particular phoneme in the protolanguage is not sufficient to add a new phoneme to the protolanguage. One must demonstrate that the distinction is not conditioned by other factors (e.g., contact influence).

As one can see, the attitudes towards facts from Taiwan and Oceania are completely different. Is this a result of personalities? Would the fate of AN comparative phonology be different if Dyen had concentrated his attention on the Oceanic languages?

Reading modern AN literature, one gets a feeling that protolanguage phonemes are well known, and what is left is to link individual languages or basic families with this protosystem. This feeling is not, however, supported by proper investigation. To demonstrate such links, linguists have to apply a step by step process of research, first reconstructing phonological systems of basic families, then those of more ancient groups, and eventually the PAN system. Otherwise there is a good chance of losing important information and missing some original distinctions.

I believe that modern AN linguistics studies have accumulated enough data to conduct new phonological reconstructions of the protolanguage. However, this work must be done according to the formal requirements for any reconstruction, and not simply by relying upon the guesswork of other linguists, regardless of their stature in the field. At first, protosystems of the basic family must be reconstructed. Phonological correspondences linking all languages of the family must be established and then supported by a reasonable number of examples. At the next stage the results must be compared to obtain reconstructions of deeper levels. It is not possible at present to say how many intermediate reconstructions would be needed to reach the PAN level. My estimation is that such step by step reconstruction (three to five levels) could be done over the next five to seven years.

Etymological Studies

To restore a morpheme of a protolanguage, we must reconstruct both its form and meaning, and, if possible, its syntactics. To reconstruct a morpheme's form, linguists have to follow phonological correspondences, established beforehand, that tell them what should be reconstructed. Form reconstruction is probably the most strict and sophisticated procedure used in the study of languages. Therefore, any protoform can be verified, and researchers working independently must be able to restore the same forms.

Semantic reconstruction is not yet formalized, and linguists have to use common sense as well as their experience in restoring meanings. In many cases, semantic differences between reconstructed morphemes cannot be identified. Consequently, one might find several morphemes for "nose" or "moon" in the same etymological dictionary. In other cases, compilers use their views and preferences to reconstruct a meaning ("the speakers were animal breeders, so the meaning is 'cattle'"; "the speakers were hunters, so the meaning is 'wild cattle' or even 'wild animal'"). So far there are no generally accepted methods to verify semantic reconstructions, which can lead to rather different cultural interpretations drawn from the same data.

We expect an etymological dictionary to be complete. If a language reflex is missing in a reconstruction, this must indicate that a reflex was searched for but not found. Random selection of reflexes undermines conclusions based on etymologies.

Another treacherous aspect of etymological studies is how to identify the chronological level to which an etymology belongs. If a morpheme is found in two daughter languages, say Germanic and Celtic, should it be attributed to the Proto-Indo-European (PIE) level? How should we treat etymologies found in a couple of branches, but

not in all of them? No general answers can be given.

A very impressive number of AN etymologies have been collected over nearly a century of research. Many of them were included in Dempwolff's study. A compendium of reconstructions, but not full etymologies, is given in Wurm and Wilson (20). An impressive number of new etymologies have been published by Blust (21–25), who is working on a new Austronesian etymological dictionary. Currently, however, it is still a challenge to find etymology and to demonstrate its protolevel attribution.

Genetic Classification

Genetic classification of languages represents the process of development from a single protolanguage toward its descendants of various chronological levels. Therefore, in the process of building a classification, we are facing three different problems: (1) what languages should be included in the classification, (2) which languages are specifically related, and (3) how to establish chronological correlations within a classification. While there are still some languages for which an AN status is not fully supported, let us concentrate on the last two problems.

A language family is a result of long process of splits. At first, its protolanguage splits into a few daughter languages. As time passes, some of these disappear, while others become ancestors of their own daughter language. Such understanding of family development requires a tree-type model of classification. Each family tree consists of a number of nodes connected by arcs. Nodes represent (proto) languages, while arcs represent relationships between the nodes. Thus, we are facing two quite different problems, which can be labeled as problems of grouping and branching.

Grouping deals with the question of how many different groups or daughter families are found in a family (how many nodes are needed in the tree). For example, the Indo-European family (IE, referred to here in the narrow sense, without the Anatolian languages) is formed by a number of daughter families, such as Germanic, Indo-Iranian, Celtic, and so on. In order to reconstruct Proto-IE we have to reconstruct protolanguages of each of these groups (26). In some cases, these daughter languages are also formed by even younger groups for which ancestors also should be reconstructed. Therefore, one can suggest that the number of groups in a family is equal to the number of (proto) languages needed to reconstruct its protolanguage. To study IE, we need to know Proto-Germanic, Proto-Indo-Iranian (with Proto-Iranian and Proto-Indic), Proto-Celtic, and Proto-Balto-Slavic (based on Proto-Baltic and Proto-Slavic) as well as Greek, Latin, Armenian, and some other languages. If such reconstructions are available, it is easy to decide group affiliation of a language: it belongs to the group represented by its protolanguage. No shortcuts, such as a search for innovations, are needed.

Branching deals with the question of relative distances between various groups in a family (e.g., "Are Celtic and Latin closer to each other, than, say, Celtic and Germanic or Slavic?"). Traditional methods of comparative linguistics do not provide us with generally accepted tools to solve such problems. Consequently, we still lack a well-established tree for the IE family. Some linguists (including me) use modified lexicostatistics for these purposes, but most of them reject this method out of hand. Instead, they use innovations, assuming that shared common features always indicate that languages must be classified together.

In a tree representation, arcs link pairs of nodes, representing an ancestral language with each of its direct descendants. A node may have several descending and only one incoming arc. A language always has only one ancestor, but may develop into several daughter languages. The root of a tree does not have an entering arc, even if further connections of the family are known. In well-studied cases, the number of descending arcs is not very big. So, if a genetic tree has a node with five to seven departing arcs, in most cases this indicates problems with the classification.

Another issue related to branching is how to incorporate chronological information in a tree model. Traditional comparative linguistics deals only with relative chronology based on the position of languages in a family tree. Within this framework, there is no way to find out the age of Proto-Germanic or Proto-Iranian. Absolute datings are provided by glottochronology, another method rejected by mainstream linguistics.

More or less generally accepted AN classification is (*17*):

1. Formosan languages forming nine primary branches of AN
2. Malayo-Polynesian
   2a. West-Malayo-Polynesian (not a genetic unit)
   2b. Central-East-Malayo-Polynesian
      Central-Malayo-Polynesian
      East Malayo-Polynesian
      (a) South-Halmahera-West-New-Guinea
      (b) Oceanic

This classification was first suggested 30 years ago by Blust, who later strengthened his views in several papers (*27–29*). The method used by this prominent scholar requires, however, some comments. According to Blust, languages can be classified using innovations of various types (phonological, grammatical, or lexical). Languages that share common innovations are seen to be specifically related (*30*). In regard to this approach in Austronesian studies, several general questions should be asked.

It is obvious from the very notion of innovations that they can be identified only if we know reconstructions of chronological stages. Blust's classification postulates 16 daughter languages (even counting West-Malayo-Polynesian as a single unit). But we have phonological reconstructions and short comparative vocabularies for only a few of the Formosan branches. For the rest of families, no detailed reconstructions are available. In the absence of detailed reconstruction of PAN or any of its ancient daughter languages, how can one be sure that a chosen feature is a real innovation and not a retention, or that it is not caused or even borrowed though contact? I strongly suspect that at the current stage of AN studies these conditions cannot be met.

Blust's classification has two noticeable features. First, languages of two blocks mentioned above (Taiwanese and mainland Asia, Philippines, western Indonesia, and Madagascar) do not represent groups but form two unclassified bunches, one attributed to the PAN level and another to the Malayo-Polynesian one. Second, other nodes of his classification seem to be treated as "real" genetic groups.

In his 1999 paper, Blust listed sets of phonological innovations (= mergers) specific to individual languages of Taiwan, thus justifying that these languages belong to different families (*17*). This, however, does not demonstrate that the languages of Taiwan could not be grouped together in a single Formosan family, as has been proposed by Dyen (*19, 31*).

The nonexistence of West-Malayo-Polynesian unity is also justified by the lack of shared innovations between western languages. Blust wrote that "no phonemic innovations characterize the WMP languages as a group, and a hypothetical PWMP is thus phonologically indistinguishable from PMP" (*17*). This argument creates, however, a catch-22 situation. As already discussed, the PMP phonological reconstruction is based mainly on WMP languages. Not surprisingly, the PWMP phonological system is now identical to that of the PMP, which has never been properly reconstructed. This observation, even proven, does not necessarily demonstrate that WMP unity is a fiction. A language is not just a collection of phonemes. What about its lexicon?

The situation with the nodes in the classification is not simple. Their justification is also found by Blust in innovations. But how can we talk about innovations in CMP if neither the ancestor (CEMP) nor its second branch (EMP) are known? There are no reconstructions for these branches.

The Oceanic node has problems of its own. There are more than 600 languages called Oceanic. According to Lynch, Ross, and Crowley (*15*), the family can be divided into:

1. Admiralties family: Manus, its offshore islands and small islands to the west;
2. Western Oceanic family: the north coast of Irian Jaya, Papua New Guinea (excluding the Admiralties), and the western Solomons; and
3. Central/Eastern Oceanic family: other areas of Oceania.

Many Oceanic languages are still poorly known, and only a few basic families are historically studied. Two full-scale reconstructions are known: Proto-Polynesian (*8, 9*) and Proto-Micronesian (*10*). Ross (*16*) gives a summary of phonological correspondences from most known Oceanic languages of the Admiralties and Western Oceanic families. There is no comprehensive Oceanic etymological dictionary, but a significant number of etymologies are known from literature (*2, 16*).

Some Oceanic languages are found in the same areas where non-AN languages are also spoken. Intensive contacts between Oceanic and Papuan languages have been reported, but without reconstructions and study of these contacts, no well-supported classification of the family can be suggested. For example, what are the arguments to attribute Central Pacific (Fijian, Polynesian, and Rotuman) and Micronesian languages to Central/East Oceanic? (Lynch et al. [*15*] put non-Austronesian Utupua and Vanikoro into the same group, but they are not included in the group in later versions of the same classification [*32*]). Is this supported by innovations? If so, what are they? How they can be identified without a reconstructed protolanguage of the family?

The above discussion demonstrates that we still do not have a trustworthy Austronesian classification. Neither grouping nor branching problems have been firmly solved. Available information does suggest, however, the existence of at least three major groups of AN languages: Formosan, WAN, and Oceanic. None of these groups is supported by a detailed reconstruction, but it seems that none of them can be treated as a daughter of another. So four competing classifications may be suggested:

I.	1. Formosan	II.	1. a. Formosan
	2. WAN		b. WAN
	3. OC		2. OC
III.	1. Formosan	IV.	1. a. Formosan
	2. a.WAN		b. OC
	b. OC		2. WAN

Why has it been assumed that the third one is the best? All are equally plausible, given the current state of knowledge.

The Austronesian Homeland and Ancient Migrations

A reconstructed protolanguage is believed to be another "normal" human language. It must therefore be associated with a particular traditional community and be able to meet all of its communication demands. Therefore, there is a strong belief that information about this protocommunity should be found in its reconstructed protolanguage—namely, in its lexicon. This makes the role of etymological dictionaries even more significant.

Choosing a (lexical) morpheme for lingoarchaeological analysis we need to know:

1. Its attribution (Is the morpheme known in all daughter groups? Is it known only in a few groups which may be in contact?)
2. The reliability of its reconstruction (Is there an alternative reconstruction?)
3. The accuracy of its reconstructed meaning (Is it bias-free? Are we really talking about domesticated fowl?)

An analysis of a reconstructed lexicon can also provide linguists with information about the cultural achievements of protolanguage speakers, such as their knowledge of metals, certain domestic animals, agricultural habits, and so on. The same type of analysis may permit us to identify major features of the homeland (tropics, sea coast, mountains, etc.) and sometimes even the languages spoken by neighbors. However, linguistics alone can never pinpoint any homeland with a place on a map. This can be done only via multidisciplinary studies.

Two different lines of reasoning about the AN homeland are known: one based on the geographic distribution of languages, the other on lexical "pinpointing." Accepting Blust's AN classification, it is quite natural to assume that the homeland was on Taiwan, where 9 of the 10 main branches of the family are still found. If so, all AN

migrations must have originated from this island, with possible routes of these migrations predicted by local geography: first to the Philippines, then southwest to the islands of modern Indonesia and southeast towards New Guinea. As the languages around New Guinea are not very similar, one might suggest that at this stage there was a split, with one group moving along the southern coast of the island towards eastern Indonesia, while the other one followed the northern coast, eventually reaching Oceania (*33*). This picture seems to be quite convincing, but what about linguistic facts?

The AN family belongs to the so-called Austric macrofamily and thus is genetically related to three other families of eastern Asia: Austroasiatic, Tai-Kadai, and Miao-Yao (*34, 35*). This fact suggests that the most archaic variety of PAN must be also spoken on the mainland. A good set of examples of lexical similarities exists between PAN and Chinese. These examples can be explained either as traces of common genetic origin (compare *36, 37*) or as borrowings (*38*). The contacts between Old Chinese and PAN must have taken place after the disintegration of Proto-Sino-Tibetan, which happened approximately 6,000 to 6,500 years ago (*39*).

If all languages of Taiwan can be traced back to Proto-Formosan, then Taiwan was not the center of major diversity of AN languages, and there is no need to look for the homeland there. Instead, one can suggest that Proto-Formosan was the only AN language to be brought to Taiwan. The rest of the family remained on the mainland coast. From there, one or several different migrations might have taken other AN languages to the islands of the south. At this stage it is not possible to identify exactly how this happened. However, I think that the Philippines was populated from the south rather than the north. This would explain the lack of similarities between the local and the Formosan languages (*31*).

Notes

1. I. Mel'chuk, *Dependency Syntax* (State Univ. of New York Press, 1988).

2. M. Ross, in A. Pawley, R. Attenborough, J. Golson, R. Hide, eds., *Papuan Pasts* (Pacific Linguistics, Canberra, 2005), pp. 15–66.

3. J. Diamond, *Science* 287, 2170 (2000).

4. A. Gibbons, *Science* 291, 1735–1736 (2001).

5. My estimate is based on the lexicostatistical study of AN conducted as part of the Evolution of Human Languages program, Santa Fe Institute, Santa

Fe, NM; 100-word lists for the study were collected from all possible published sources.

6. G. Thurgood, *From Ancient Chamic to Modern Dialects* (Univ. of Hawaii Press, Honolulu, 1999).

7. R. Mills, Proto-South-Sulawesi and Proto-Austronesian Phonology (Ph.D. diss., Univ. of Michigan, Ann Arbor, 1975).

8. B. Biggs, *POLLEX (Comparative Polynesian Lexicon)* (computer data base, Univ. of Auckland, 1991).

9. J. Marck, *Topics in Polynesian Language and Cultural History* (Pacific Linguistics, Canberra, 2000).

10. B. Bender et al., *Oceanic Linguistics* 42(1), 2–110; 42(2), 271– 328 (2003).

11. O. Dempwolff, *Vergleichende Lautlehre des Austronesischen Wortschatzes*, 1–3 Zeitschrift für Eingeborenen-Sprachen (Reimer, Berlin, 1934–1938).

12. It's worthwhile to mention, however, that most new etymologies came from languages not used by Dempwolff.

13. M. Anderson, M. Ross, in J. Lynch, M. Ross, T. Crowley, eds., *The Oceanic Languages* (Curzon Press, London, 2002), pp. 322–346.

14. J. Lynch, in J. Lynch, M. Ross, T. Crowley, eds., *The Oceanic Languages* (Curzon Press, London, 2002), pp. 865–876.

15. J. Lynch, M. Ross, T. Crowley, eds., *The Oceanic Languages* (Curzon Press, London, 2002).

16. M. Ross, *Proto-Oceanic and the Austronesian Languages of Western Melanesia* (Pacific Linguistics, Canberra, 1988).

17. R. Blust, in E. Zeitoun, P. Li, eds., *Selected Papers from the Eighth International Conference on Austronesian Linguistics* (Academia Sinica, Taipei, 1999), pp. 31–94.

18. P. Li, *Bull. Inst. of History and Philology* 59(2), 479–508 (1988).

19. I. Dyen, *Asian Perspectives* 7, 261–271 (1963).

20. S. Wurm, B. Wilson, *English Finderlist of Reconstructions in Austronesian Languages (Post-Brandstetter)* (Pacific Linguistics, Canberra, 1975).

21. R. Blust, *Oceanic Linguistics* 9, 104–162 (1970).

22. R. Blust, *Oceanic Linguistics* 19, 1–181 (1980).

23. R. Blust, *Oceanic Linguistics* 22–23, 29–149 (1983–1984).

24. R. Blust, *Oceanic Linguistics* 25, 1–123 (1986).

25. R. Blust, *Oceanic Linguistics* 28, 111–180 (1989).

26. In fact, in the IE studies began as a comparison of old written languages, which in most cases are quite similar to the protolanguages of the daughter families.

27. R. Blust, *Working Papers in Linguistics of the Univ. of Hawai'i*, 9(2), 1–15 (1977).

28. R. Blust, in S. Wurm, L. Carrington, eds., *Second International Conference on Austronesian Linguistics* (Pacific Linguistics, Canberra, 1978), pp. 181–234.

29. R. Blust, in P. Li et al., eds., *Austronesian Studies Relating to Taiwan* (Academia Sinica, Taipei, 1995), pp. 585–650.

30. The validity of innovation-based classification has been discussed in several talks given by S. Starostin and me at various meetings at SFI and other places. Our conclusion was in favor of lexicostatistics: innovations are never free from undetected regional influence.

31. A. Adelaar, in A. Adelaar, N. Himmelmann, eds., *The Austronesian Languages of Asia and Madagascar* (Routledge, London, 2005), pp. 1–42.

32. M. Ross, A. Pawley, M. Osmond, eds., *The Lexicon of Proto-Oceanic* (Pacific Linguistics, Canberra, 2003).

33. Compare branches of Blust's classification: (1) Formosan/the rest = MP; (2) WMP/the rest = CEMP; (3) CEMP divides into CMP and EMP.

34. I. Peiros, *Comparative Linguistics in Southeast Asia* (Pacific Linguistics, Canberra, 1998).

35. I. Peiros, S. Starostin, *Austric Etymologies* (computer database, Santa Fe Institute, Santa Fe, NM, 2005).

36. L. Sagart, *J. Chinese Studies* 8, 195–223 (1995).

37. S. Starostin, *J. Chinese Studies* 8, 225–251 (1995).

38. I. Peiros, S. Starostin, *Computational Analyses of Asian and African Languages* 22, 123–127 (1984).

39. I. Peiros, S. Starostin, Sino-Tibetan Classification (Manuscript, Santa Fe Institute, Santa Fe, NM, 2005).

6

Humanity at the Last Glacial Maximum

A Cultural Crisis

Henry T. Wright

Several years ago, speaking with Sergei Starostin about his argument regarding an early Sino-Caucasian language phylum, I mused, "It must be the mammoth hunters." "Who?" Sergei asked. "The Gravettians," I replied. "The people who expanded across Eurasia exploiting the mammoths, bison, and horses of the steppe-tundra about 25,000 years ago." "Too old," said Sergei. I had no idea what he meant.

The Roots of Language

I subsequently learned how the efforts of Starostin and his colleagues to estimate the dates at which the earliest definable protolanguages began to differentiate have produced an interesting and somewhat puzzling result. On the one hand, the Afri-Eurasiatic "Old World"—Eurasia, Africa, Sahul (New Guinea and Australia together), and major offshore islands—was fully occupied by human ancestors 40,000 or more years ago. On the other hand, new glottochronological studies, many of them not published before Sergei's tragically early death, indicate that the earliest language groupings began diverging only after about 18,000 years ago. Groups in very different parts of the Old World seem to have begun differentiating about the same time. If human groups migrated to the distant corners of the Old World and settled in to local environments long before, why are these dates for language differentiation not earlier?

There seem to me to be two possibilities that need to be considered. The first is that these lexico-statistically estimated dates are not correct. I am not an historical linguist and will not suggest how erroneous estimates—in this case, dates that are too young—might have arisen. Indeed, linguists who have modeled language change suggest that smaller language communities such as foragers will have faster rates of language change (1, 2). Perhaps, however, evidence will show that different interaction patterns in forager societies generate slower language change than that observed in recent tribal and urban societies. I hope that historical linguists will continue to investigate such issues.

The second possibility is that the dates are approximately correct and some conjunction of events worked to reduce the original diversity of languages and to initiate the differentiation of languages after about 18,000 years ago. In fact, something extraordinary did happen on this planet about 21,000 years ago: planetary temperatures reached a minimum, and continental glaciers throughout the northern hemisphere reached their maximum extent, covering most of northwestern Eurasia and northern North America and higher mountain massifs everywhere. These continental accumulations of ice lowered sea level about 130 m, changed the flow of ocean currents, and lowered the humidity of air masses, expanding the arid zones and changing the structure and distribution of grasslands and forests. Could the end of this episode, termed the Last Glacial Maximum, or LGM, by geologists and paleoclimatologists, and the subsequent opening of the "bottle-necks" have influenced the movement and growth of human populations in such a way as to initiate rapid language differentiation? To evaluate this idea, I am going to look at the evidence of human communities in various parts of the Old World from 23,000 to 18,000 years ago. First, however, we need some discussion of archaeological and paleoenvironmental methods and more consideration of the paleoenvironmental and archaeological background.

How Archaeologists Learn About Pleistocene Peoples

Archaeologists are dependent on people's garbage to learn about their actions and thoughts. However, precise estimates of the age of archeological samples and characterization of the environments in which ancient people lived requires collaboration with specialists in physics, chemistry, geology, and biology.

The ages of archaeological materials in the time span of interest is determined almost exclusively with radiocarbon dating. Conventional carbon dates did not account for fluctuations in the cosmic radiation that transforms nitrogen into unstable carbon 14, and are expressed as *bp* or *rcybp*, *bp* being short for "before present," the radiocarbon "present" being conventionally AD 1950. Radiocarbon determinations can now be calibrated to yield estimates of actual age, expressed here as years BC or BCE. For the period considered here, bp determinations are 2,000 to 3,000 years younger than actual dates. Calibration does not eliminate the ever present hazards of sample contamination or error on the part of archaeologists (misinterpreted layers, roots or cigarette butts in the sample, mixed sample labels, etc.). Some of the sites discussed below are more securely dated than others.

The local environments of sites are inferred from geological sediments, associated plant pollen or microfauna, and temperature-sensitive isotope ratios, and they are more secure when based on multiple sources of evidence.

The animals people hunted are indicated by variously selected, cut, and burned bones. The plants people gathered are a more difficult issue. Carbonized nut fragments have long been observed, and the recovery of small carbonized seeds by water flotation is now widespread. However, fungi and partly digested stomach contents so important in the arctic, and the tubers and many fruits particularly important in the tropics have only recently become identifiable through new methods involving the characterization of surviving starches and phytoliths (silica casts of surface cells of leaves, bark, and fruits). We get additional vital information about diet and health from human skeletons, through observation of such varied features as growth and mortality patterns, bone chemistry, and tooth wear. Skeletons datable to the LGM are rare, however, and often all we have are rough estimates of population size based on the sizes and numbers of sites, without useful information on the biological condition of that population.

Methods to infer the use of tools are now widely available. The actions performed and materials worked can be determined, but the procedures are time-consuming and expensive. Stylistic variation in material items has often been taken to mark ethnic or linguistic groups. In particular, ceramics, often richly decorated with structured designs, have been taken to mark such distinctions. While there has been a reaction against enthusiastic abuse of ceramic style—under such aphoristic rubrics as "pots do not speak" or "pots are not people"—careful use of ceramic and linguistic evidence has proved very fruitful (3, 4). During Paleolithic times, alas, ceramic use was very limited, and archaeologists have relied on the presumed stylistic features of stone tools. Recent research on stone tools, however, has shown that much of the variability is a result of the potentials of different raw materials, technological motor habits, and the uses to which tools were put. Very little stone tool variability can be attributed to social patterning. We will have to focus on the social implications of shared technological habits and the distance of social contacts implied by the procurement of exotic raw materials.

A very useful effort to assess some of these variables was made almost 20 years ago in an excellent set of volumes entitled *The World at 18,000 BP* (5, 6), and this work still provides a basic guide to the issue. It is very heartening how much new work has been published since these publications. The inevitable lack of comparability between reports—the lack of plant remains in some areas, the lack of understanding of raw materials in others, and limited publication of the stone tool samples in yet others—should not divert us from attempting to achieve a broader understanding than was possible a few decades ago.

The World of 21,000 Years Ago: The Last Glacial Maximum

Because of reduced solar energy, the LGM was a time of lower temperatures. This began about 23,000 years ago and extended to 18,000 years ago. Because this resulted principally in a reduction of maximum, rather than minimum, temperatures, climatic conditions did not simply displace vegetation zones southward, but created plant communities not seen on the earth today (7). In addition, many animals now extinct still flourished. No less important were the ice masses that changed atmospheric and oceanic movements, which in turn changed total precipitation and its distribution, generally expanding areas of arid and hyperarid deserts and of subarid steppes and diminishing forests. Lowered sea levels opened new migration routes for humans and their prey. The configurations of barriers to migration and communication, areas of limited resources, and areas of rich resources conducive to the growth of human populations are determined by local circumstances and are described by geographic area below. At a general level, however (Figure 6.1), one can see a broad swath of environments very difficult for human communities, extending from the hyperarid Sahara, across very arid Southeast Asia, and up into the polar and high-altitude deserts of Central Asia. Temperate and tropical grasslands, savannas, and forests more conducive to human foraging were compressed into refugia between this broad swath and other arid areas in southern Africa and south and Southeast Asia. The human groups that moved across these landscapes were fully modern representatives of the genus Homo, evidenced by the appearance more than 50,000 years ago of symbolic capacity in the form of stylistic ornamentation, exchange, and mortuary ceremony (8). Though the size of archaeological sites indicates that social groups were usually small, the patterns of hunting and use of technologies that generated blanks or pre-forms—often prismatic blades struck one after the other from special blade cores—adaptable to

different end uses indicate a planning capacity little different from that of recent humans.

Africa

We start our *tour du monde* not in western Eurasia—where Paleolithic archaeology began and where local archaeological sequences are richly documented, a history that might bias our assessment of its importance—but in Africa, simply because it was the long ago first home of the genus *Homo*.

Africa at this time (Figure 6.2) was little affected by sea level change. It was, however, dry, the rain forests having shrunk into small refuge areas in the central Congo Basin and on the west coast. The continent was dominated by two expanded hyperarid zones, the Sahara to the north and the region of the Namib and Kalahari deserts to the south, both much larger than today. Only via the Nile Valley could people have easily moved across the Sahara to and from the better watered Mediterranean coasts. There was also a possible route toward South Asia via Arabia. People could only have moved easily between East Africa and southern Africa along the eastern coast. The far south was much cooler, 5°C along the coasts and 10°C in the interior, as indicated by $^{16}O/^{14}O$ ratios.

In southern Africa human technologies were changing from earlier Late Stone Age industries, with tools both on flakes of Middle Stone Age type and on blades, into classical Late Stone Age industries with even more use of blades, particularly very small microblades as tool blanks. These people lived in large rockshelters near the coast, hunting large herd grazers such as Cape buffalo, zebra, eland, and various kinds of antelope. There is little evidence of plant use, but somewhat later foragers in this region harvested nuts and fruits. As an example, I illustrate the Early Robberg Industry at Boomplaas Cave in the inner Cape region overlooking a valley forested with acacias, dated from about 21,800 BP (18,500 bp) and later (Figure 6.3) (9, 10). The industry uses both large disc cores (Figure 6.3g) and small blade cores (Figure 6.3e, f) of silcrete, chalcedony, chert, and quartz, most available in the area. Various end scrapers (Figure 6.3a, b) and retouched pieces (Figure 6.3c, d) were made on flakes. Small microblades, apparently struck rather than punched

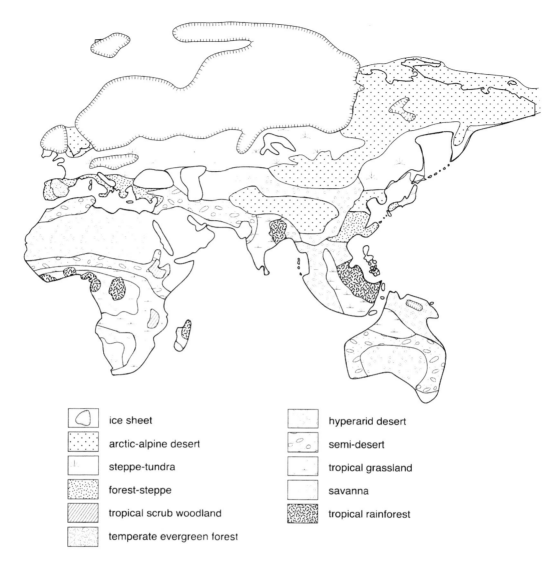

FIGURE 6.1. Afro-Eurasian environments during the Last Glacial Maximum (adapted from Ray and Adams 2001).

(Figure 6.3h–k), sometimes have steep backing (Figure 6.3l–r) and steep retouch or backing (Figure 6.3s, t), perhaps to create projectile elements. Bone tools, tortoise shell bowls, and ostrich eggshell beads also occur.

Contemporary industries are known farther north in eastern Africa, but I take as a second exemplary area for Africa a community of the Nile Valley. Despite the intense aridity of the desert, the Nile flooded regularly. The people in the valley and the animals they hunted were closely tethered to the water and fringe of vegetation near the river. Human groups lived close to the Nile in small seasonal camps of circa .10 ha, hunting gazelles, hartebeest, and wild cattle; taking and drying large catfish and perch; and collecting both aquatic tubers and wild annual seeds.

Well-studied examples are the sites excavated and meticulously reported by Wendorf and colleagues (11) in the Wadi Kubbaniya near Aswan

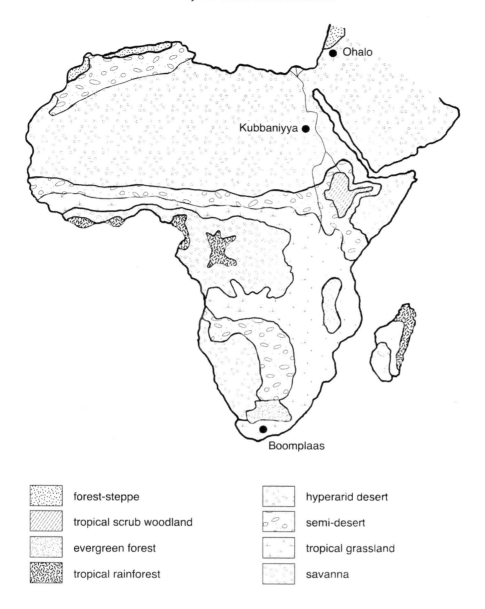

FIGURE 6.2. African environments during the Last Glacial Maximum (adapted from Ray and Adams 2001).

dated to about 20,500 BP (17,600 ± 250 bp). Site E-78-4 exemplifies the chipped stone technology (Figure 6.4). The only cores illustrated are splintered bipolar cores (Figure 6.4i) and microblade cores (Figure 6.4j). The assemblage has small struck blades, some with backing (Figure 6.4k–p), some scrapers (Figure 6.4a–d), denticulates (Figure 6.4g–h), and burins (Figure 6.4e, f), mostly on local stones, but some on flints from

150 km up the Nile. These people also had a varied grinding technology, probably for preparing plant foods.

Western Eurasia

Moving northward across the Mediterranean, a barrier to travel even in this time of lower sea level, we arrive in a Europe severely limited environmentally (Figure 6.5). Ice masses covered the

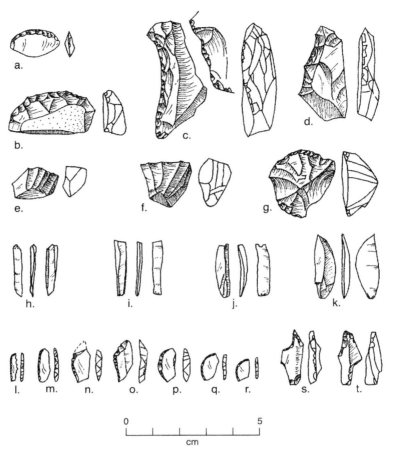

FIGURE 6.3. The Early Robberg stone tool assemblage from Boomplaas Cave, Cape Province, South Africa (adapted from Deacon 1990: Fig. 7.4).

Pyrenees and the Alps, and continental glaciers centered in Scandinavia and northern Britain reached south to cover most of the North German Plain. While areas near the coasts of the Mediterranean were more temperate, a vast belt extending from the now-flooded floor of the Bay of Biscay on the east, across the narrow corridor between the Scandinavian and Alpine ices masses, and across the plains of the Ukraine and southern Russia was polar desert and steppe tundra, bitter in the winter but providing rich herbaceous grazing for large herds of elephants, cervids, and bovids during the summer.

Several regional stone tool industries had developed from the earlier, widespread Gravettian stone tool industries, which used predominantly large blades or flakes as blanks to make a diversity of scrapers, large points, and burins (thought to be whittling and chiseling tools for working wood, horn, and bone).

In the southwest, in southwestern France and the Iberian Peninsula, Solutrean industries typified by bifacially flaked projectile points appeared. Specialists disagree about whether this technology developed locally from the earlier Gravettian or Aurignacian traditions, from a group driven from northern Europe by glacial conditions, or from some other antecedent. However, after 22,000 BP, as settlements disappeared in northwest Europe, the number of settlements in Cantabrian Spain increased threefold, suggesting it was a refuge area for people from the north. Pollen evidence indicates the area was dry and had few trees.

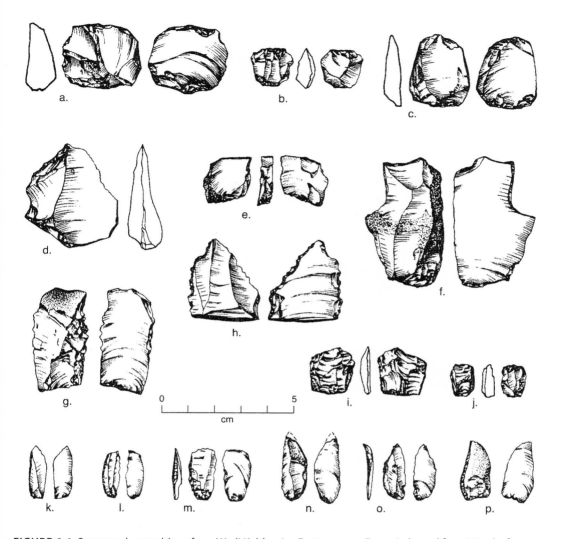

FIGURE 6.4. Stone tool assemblage from Wadi Kubbaniya E-78-4, upper Egypt (adapted from Wendorf, Schild, and Close 1980).

As an example, let us consider the well-studied cave of La Riera in a small valley at the foot of the Cantabrian mountains, 10 km from the seacoast at that time (*12, 13*). Though relatively small, with about 0.011 ha of floor area, the cave was intensively occupied during the glacial maximum and later. The inhabitants of La Riera hunted ibex in the nearby mountains, but later shifted to hunting more red deer in the coastal plain. They intensively processed bone for maximum recovery of fats, and they also collected limpets from rocks in protected bays on the coast and caught a few salmon and trout in the rivers. The intensive

exploitation of mammals and small shellfish is concordant with the idea that the region was a refugium with a relatively high population density exploiting resources to the maximum. There is no evidence of plant foods, but cobbles with evidence of pounding suggest some plant exploitation. The stone tool technology (Figure 6.6) was focused predominantly on flake production, with some manufacture of blades and struck bladelets, from multi-use cores (Figure 6.6c). It had many bifacially flaked, leaf shaped, or shouldered projectile points (Figure 6.6a, b) thought to have been used with spear throwers, many end

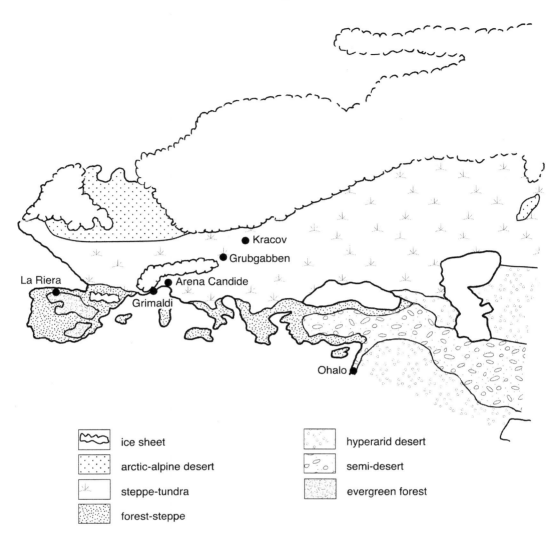

FIGURE 6.5. West Eurasian environments during the Last Glacial Maximum (adapted from Ray and Adams 2001).

scrapers (Figure 6.6d–f), denticulated flakes (Figure 6.6g), retouched flakes (Figure 6.6h), burins on flakes and blades (Figure 6.6i, j), occasional truncated (Figure 6.6k) and notched pieces (Figure 6.6l), and a few bladelets, some backed and some with fine denticulate retouch (Figure 6.6m–p). Study of the stone raw material indicates that more than half are local quartzites and cherts, but exotic stones are common, particularly during the earlier Solutrean occupations, when the site was more specialized for the hunting of ibex in the interior. Points of Catalan stylistic affinity are found in the Basque region, indicating regular social exchange over a distance of more than 200 km. Various kinds of pointed bone tools and bone pendants and perforated teeth, probably used as ornaments, were common. Although the Solutrean communities represented here by La Riera focused on flake production and a distinctive projectile technology, other aspects of their technologies—such as the production of scrapers, burins, and backed microblades—are similar to those elsewhere in Africa and Eurasia.

Elsewhere, in middle and eastern Europe, technologies were later developments from Gravettian traditions. During the crisis of the LGM, these developed into or were replaced by various kinds of "Epi-Gravettian" industries, in which people

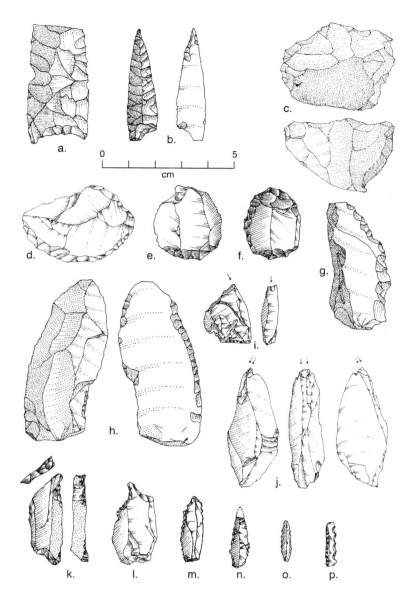

FIGURE 6.6. Stone tool assemblage from La Riera Layers 5–8, Cantabria, Spain (adapted from Straus and Clark 1986: Figs. 8.17 –8.34).

began to use smaller blades, particularly blades with heavy lateral retouch, often called "micro-Gravette" points. The people using this technology lived in a diversity of cave and open air sites, some with huts constructed of wood or bone frames and skin coverings.

The Epi-Gravettian assemblages of the Mediterranean regions is here represented by samples from Grotte delle Arene Candide in Liguria in northern Italy, occupied ca. 20,000 bp (Figure 6.7). This large cave had a number of hearths. The faunal remains indicate much hunting of ibex. There is no information on plant use. The Grimaldi caves, closer to the seashore, have evidence of fishing and the collecting of shellfish. Also found at Grimaldi were people buried with costumes of varying elaboration indicating publicly recognized social differences. Similar coastal

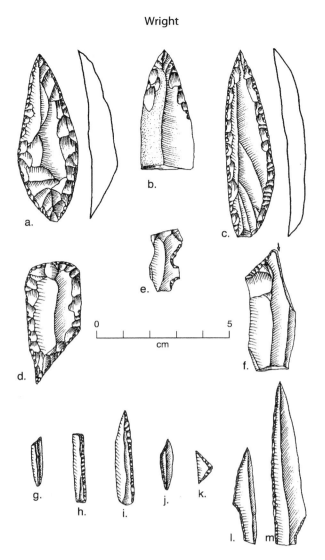

FIGURE 6.7. Stone tool assemblage from Grotte delle Arene Candide 6-4, Liguria, Italy (adapted from Mussi 1990:129, Fig. 7.3).

sites elsewhere must have been covered by rising sea levels during glacial retreat. The stone tool industry (Figure 6.7) is characterized by large blades used to make scrapers (Figure 6.7d), notched tools (Figure 6.7e), burins (Figure 6.7f), and leaf-shaped points flaked only on the upper surface (Figure 6.7a–c), and small blades used to make many kinds of backed tools, including some micro-Gravette points (Figure 6.7g–m). There is no information on stone procurement.

To the north and east, a very different settlement system emerged, with groups having Epi-Gravettian technologies spending the winters in sheltered regions to the south, such as the valleys of lower Austria and Moravia, then moving north 170 km or more into the steppe-tundra during the summers.

One example of a southerly winter site is Grubgraben, in Lower Austria not far north of the Danube (14), occupied about 21,500 BP (ca. 18,500 bp). During its main occupation, Layers AL 2–4, during a brief humid period in the height of the glacial maximum, the site covered at least 0.18 ha of a small promontory overlooking a larger valley and had a number of cobble pavements thought to be hut floors. The inhabitants hunted

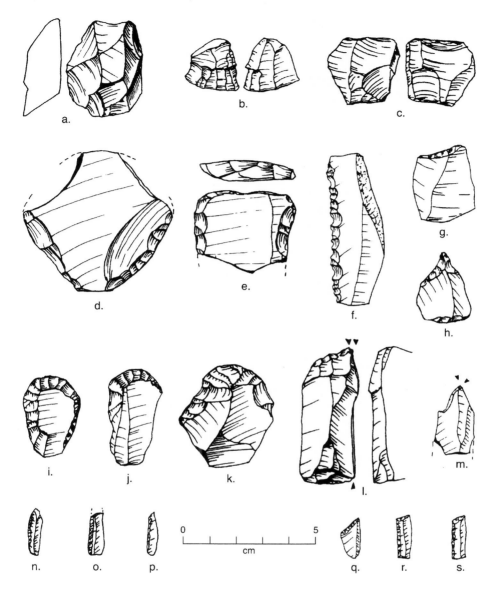

FIGURE 6.8. Stone tools from Krakov-Spadzista C2 II, southern Poland (adapted from Kozlowski 1990c, 129: Figs. 11.6, 11.7).

primarily reindeer and horse, with some taking of ibex and cattle. The tool industry included round and oblong hammer stones used to produce a range of flakes, struck blades and bladelets, from flake (Figure 6.8a), blade (Figure 6.8b), and bipolar (Figure 6.8c) cores. Side scrapers on flakes (Figure 6.8d) and large blades (Figure 6.8e), denticulates on blades (Figure 6.8f), truncated pieces (Figure 6.8g), and borers (Figure 6.8h), end scrapers on blades (Figure 6.8i, j) and flakes (Figure 6.8k), burins on blades (Figure 6.8l, m) and backed (Figure 6.8n-p) and truncated (Figure 6.8q-s) bladelets were produced. Some local quartz was used, but most of the raw material was flints and radiolarites brought from Moravia, 100 km away, and even from the upper Vistula area, 250 km to the northeast. Most of the cores were intensively worked until exhausted, and up to a quarter of all flakes and blades were retouched, indicating the value of these imported materials.

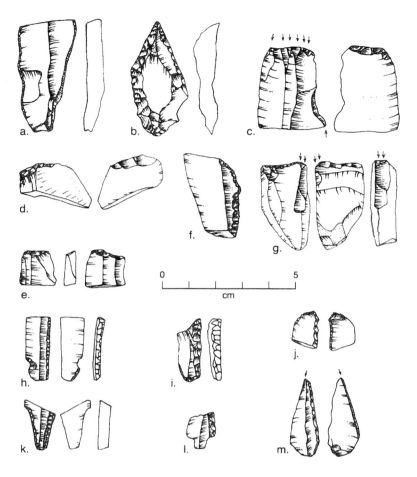

FIGURE 6.9. Stone tool assemblage from Grubgraben AL 2-4, Austria (adapted from Montet-White 1990: Figs. VIII-4, IX-4, 9,12,13).

In addition there were beads made from animal teeth, limestone, and dentalium shell, probably from the Mediterranean.

An example of a northerly summer site is the site of Krakov-Spadzista C2 II in the upper Vistula Valley, occupied about 23,500 BP (ca. 20,000 bp.) The inhabitants hunted reindeer, horse, and mammoth. The stone tool industry (Figure 6.9) includes some tools made on flake blanks (Figure 6.9b), but more common are large blades used to make retouched tools (Figure 6.9a, f), pointed tools (Figure 6.9b), end scrapers (Figure 6.9d–f), and possible hafted tools (Figure 6.9k), and small blades to make various kinds of backed items (Figure 6.9j), some probably fragments of micro-Gravette points (Figure 6.9h, i). Much of the

flint used at Krakov-Spadzista was brought from Moravia and some comes from sources in Slovakia, 270 km to the southwest, probably as a result of exchange.

Communities using similar technologies exploited the steppe tundra, as least in the summer months, from the Atlantic to the Urals, at least into the latest phases of the glacial maximum.

Eastern Eurasia

Eastern Eurasia is larger and even more diverse than western Eurasia (Figure 6.9). To the south, the Middle East, southern Asia, and Southeast Asia were dry and cool but tempered by oceans and widely inhabited. The plateau lands of Anatolia, Iran, and Central Asia were very dry and cold, and lack evidence of inhabitants during the glacial maximum. The high massif of the Himalayas and Tibet is poorly known. To the north, however, the steppe-tundra that extended across Siberia and the now-flooded Beringia all the way into central Alaska was widely exploited. The Pacific coast of Eurasia was transformed by the lower sea level, which exposed vast areas of continental shelf. Though cooler, it was largely park-woodland, and a rich region for food collectors.

In the Middle East, along the well-studied Levant, the large flake and blade industries of the earlier Upper Paleolithic Levantine Aurignacian were replaced by the Early Kebaran blade industries using a variety of small blade tools about 23,000 BP. Many small campsites in caves and in the open air are known, many with evidence of the hunting of gazelle in more open areas and fallow deer in more forested areas. I take as an example, however, an exceptionally preserved and recently meticulously excavated site, Ohalo II in the Jordan Valley (*15*) on the shore of the Sea of Galilee, then lower because of the cool, dry conditions of the glacial maximum. This site dates to around 23,000 years ago (ca. 19,500 bp.) The site covered more than 0.20 ha. The remains of at least four small brush huts (*15*), adjacent large hearths, and a burial were found. In addition to evidence of hunting, predominantly gazelle and water birds, this substantial campsite has evidence of the collecting of wild grain and fruits, and of fishing with nets or traps. The plants exploited, the seasonal preferences of the birds, and the ages of the animals indicate occupation during most seasons of the year. Food processing occurred in working areas in and around the small huts. Ohalo II allows insight into how communities of the LGM could become larger and more sedentary in particularly favorable environments. As one would expect on a site with such diverse activities, the tool industries involve several manufacturing sequences using flake, blade, and bladelet cores made from rolled pebbles, probably locally available. The struck blades and bladelets are notably variable and often curved, a feature that Nadel attributes to the expedient nature of stone industries in less mobile communities. Many functional forms occur, dominated by microblades, many with backing and fine retouch and some truncated, but including a few scrapers,

awls, burins, and denticulates. A comprehensive summary of the chipped stone industry is not yet available, and no illustration is provided here. Grinding or pounding technologies for processing plants have not yet been reported. The presence of beads made of marine shells—a few from the Red Sea (350 km to the south), but most from the Mediterranean (only 55 km to the west)—indicate the span of exchange contacts.

In southern Asia, evidence well dated to this period is still limited. An example from the foothills of the central Ganges Valley is the rockshelter of Laharia Dih. Layer 3 was occupied from about 22,500 BP (ca. 19,000 bp) over an area of only .015 ha. Geological evidence indicates a variable semiarid climate, perhaps with acacia parkland. The occupants used a later Upper Paleolithic industry (*16*), with tools made from either flints or quartzites from unspecified sources (Figure 6.10). One possible disc core also appears to have been used as a source of microblades (Figure 6.10f). Some blanks made large blades (Figure 6.10a), but most blanks were small blades or bladelets. These blanks could be made into end scrapers (Figure 6.10b, c), scrapers (Figure 6.10d), notched tools (Figure 6.10m), burins (Figure 6.10g–i), or steeply backed (Figure 6.10j–l) or modified on the end to make points (Figure 6.10n–r). Unfortunately, there is no report of subsistence remains.

To the north, on the steppe-tundra, there was a proliferation of sites early in the LGM. The site of Mal'ta, studied by several expeditions during the twentieth century, is located on a terrace overlooking a smaller tributary of the Angara River, which drains Lake Baikal. At the time of occupation, however, this river may have formed a small lake in the tundra (*17*). At least 16 individual houses in two rows, with adjacent artifact and bone concentrations, have been mapped. Multiple dates indicate the site was occupied ca. 24,000 BP (20,400 bp) (*19*), before the LGM. The primary hunted animal was reindeer. The tool industries were based largely on blades and some bladelets struck from pyramidal and wedge-shaped cores. The raw material sources are not discussed. The blades and bladelets are notably variable and often irregular, and are often retouched to make end scrapers, pointed pieces, burins on truncations, notched blades, and finely retouched blades. Backed blades and bladelets, so common

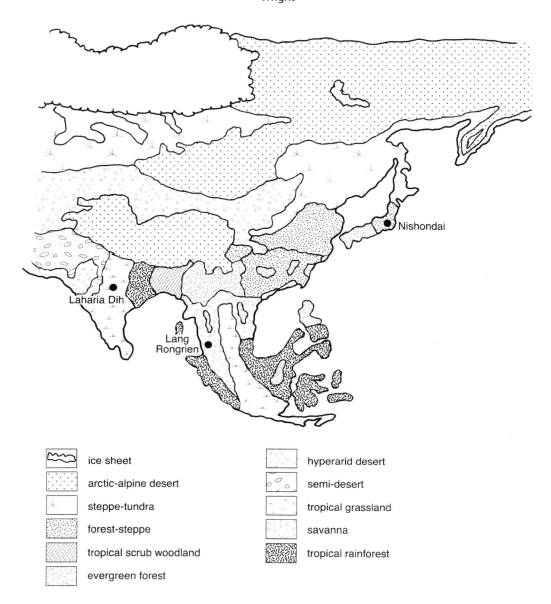

FIGURE 6.10. East Eurasian environments during the Last Glacial Maximum (adapted from Ray and Adams 2001).

to the west and south, appear to be absent. Flakes were used to make end scrapers of varying sizes. A striking feature of the Mal'ta assemblage is a range of mammoth ivory and antler items, including figurines representing women and animals, ornaments such as beads and pendants, and tools such as needles and awls. During the nadir of the LGM, between 22,500 and 21,000 BP, after the florescence represented by Mal'ta and many other sites, settlement became rare on the steppe-

tundra (20), and we must infer that the inhabitants died out or moved elsewhere.

In northeast Asia, there were some regions with rich networks of communities. Many sites on the Kanto Plain in southern Honshu have been well studied, though because of their acidic volcanic soils, they lack evidence other than stone artifacts. As an example, I take Nishinodai B, Layer IV (21), which dates to about 18,800 BP (ca. 16,300 bp) and is therefore after the nadir of

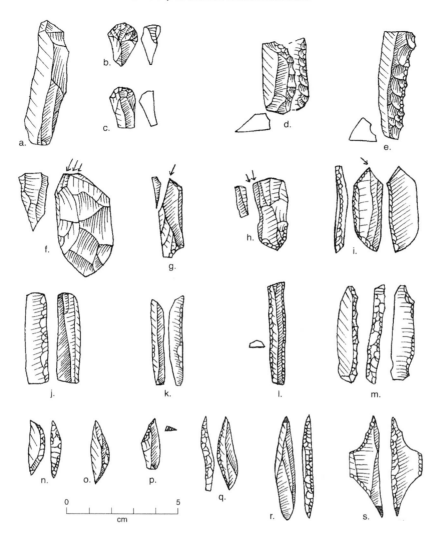

FIGURE 6.11. The industry from Laharia Dih, India (adapted from Jayaswal 1990: Fig. 12.6).

the LGM. It is a 2.4 ha campsite with some fire features; other sites have 6 m long huts. There is no surviving subsistence evidence on the sites, but a variety of deer and nuts would have been available in this cool, forested interior plain. The tools (Figure 6.12) are predominantly of local materials, but some are obsidian imported from as much as 200 km away. The stone tool industry is what Japanese archaeologists term a "Phase IIA" assemblage, with blanks made from flakes and some struck blades with a few rough microblade cores (Figure 6.12f) and microblades (Figure 6.12p). Among the retouched tools are end scrapers (Figure 6.12a, b), notched and retouched

pieces (Figure 6.12c–e) of flakes, and many small pointed pieces made mostly on distinctive "side-blow" flakes (Figure 6.12j–o). Backed blades and punched microblades occur for the first time about 14,000 bp, a relatively late occurrence in comparison with the rest of Eurasia. Grinding stones are also present. Like the Solutrean assemblages, the Japanese assemblages of the LGM are based on a different reduction sequence from those in most of Afri-Eurasia, but the end products, emphasizing small points, are similar.

Southeast Asia has long been thought to be an area where Middle Pleistocene traditions of pebble tools and expedient flake tools continued

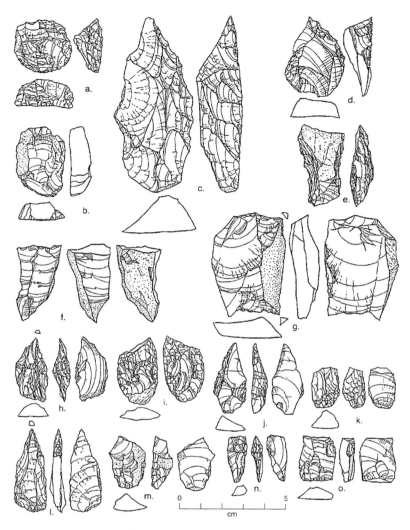

FIGURE 6.12. Stone tool assemblage from Nishinodai B, lower-middle Layer IV, southern Honshu, Japan (adapted from Akazawa, Oda, and Yamanaka 1980: Fig. 126).

into early Holocene times. Recent discoveries challenge this understanding. As an example, let us consider Lang Rongrien on the Kra Peninsula, Layers 8–10, dating from about 26,000 BP (ca. 23,000 bp) to 38,000 BP. Though well before the LGM, and thus provocative rather than definitive, this is the only well excavated Southeast Asian assemblage we have relevant to our problem. A large rockshelter, with a floor area of .045 ha (22), this site was in seasonally dry tropical forest (23) about 70 km from the sea. Several hearths were found in each layer, suggesting short-term use by a larger group with several nuclear families.

Hunting of a range of deer and small mammals and collecting of freshwater clams and turtles is attested (24). The Lang Rongrien sample from Layers 8–10 is small but provocative (Figure 6.13). A possible disc core (Figure 6.13a) and possible microblade core fragments (Figure 6.13b,c), a retouched flake fragment probably retouched as a scraper (Figure 6.13d), a flake with possible burin removal (Figure 6.13e), possible retouched blades (Figure 6.13f) and microblades (Figure 6.13g), and several flakes are reported. Raw materials include local sandstones, quartzites, and cherts, but so little work has been done in this area that

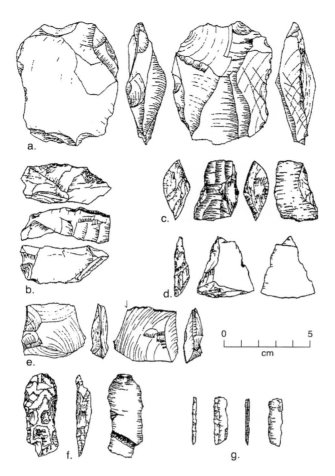

FIGURE 6.13. Stone tool assemblage from Lang Rongrien Rockshelter, southern Thailand (adapted from Anderson 1990).

sources are not well known, and it is difficult to assess the span of exchange networks. While flakes comprise a majority of the industry, the presence of prepared blade and microblade cores and tools in this area, not unlike those attested in every area of Africa and Eurasia discussed so far, would imply a broad industrial commonality. Larger samples and samples from sites actually dated to the LGM would clearly be of great interest.

Sahul

The great continent of Sahul—encompassing Tasmania, Australia, and New Guinea—formed when sea level was more than 70 m below its present level; it was never joined to Southeast Asia because of the deep oceanic

trenches of the western Indonesian archipelago, and its biota remained unique, as demonstrated long ago by Alfred Wallace. By 40,000 bp, people were established throughout the diverse environments of this continent, excepting hyperarid desert regions and high alpine areas. Although the earliest migrants may have crossed sea barriers on rafts, by 25,000 bp more sophisticated watercraft with sails must have been developed (25). During the LGM, the hyperarid central desert expanded, and areas easily exploitable by food collectors were limited to the coasts (Figure 6.13). Relict forest areas were limited in the south but substantial in New Guinea and northernmost Australia. The stone tool industries of southern and central Australia during the first 20,000 years of occupation were dominated by

71

large, single platform flake cores called "horse-shoe cores" and flakes; those of New Guinea had distinctive axes, thought to be tools for exploiting forest products. Northern Australian sites have all of these artifact categories. These tool industries appear to have continued in use until the end of the Pleistocene. To illustrate this, let us consider Nawamoyn Cave Layer III, in Arnhemland, dated to 22,500 BP (ca 19,000 bp) (26). This is a rock-shelter with about .01 ha of floor space. The stone tool industry used local quartz and quartzite pebbles, and includes horseshoe-shaped cores, other flake cores, and heavy scrapers on thick flakes. There is some mention of smaller flake tools, but little detailed illustration. There is no surviving subsistence evidence. Given what we know at the moment, it seems that the long-established people of Sahul continued their tool-making traditions and did not participate in the widespread technical developments documented throughout most of Africa and Eurasia.

Overview

This rapid consideration of a scattering of a few well reported archaeological sites and assemblages documents very similar industries throughout Africa and much of Eurasia around the time of the LGM. These industries used procedures that produced flakes and blades made on amorphous, disc, blade, and microblade cores, the larger preforms being used for various kinds of scrapers, burins, and other tools, and the smaller blades being steeply backed or retouched to produce small backed pieces and points. It has been suggested these were elements in projectiles with multiple, replaceable parts. If so, it is possible that new kinds of projectiles—coupled with other technological innovations in plant food processing, fishing, and food storage—could have given some populations an adaptive advantage in regions where populations were struggling with the harsh conditions of the full glacial maximum, which had forced the abandonment of regions and movement of populations. The fact that many groups had social contacts with areas more than 200 km away means that information about useful innovations and even social groups could move quickly across vast distances.

In contrast, in areas on the extremities of the vast Eurasian landmass these technological innovations were not adopted. To the far west, in the rich area around the Bay of Biscay, the distinctive Solutrean technology flourished, with an emphasis on flake industries and bifacially flaked projectile points (though blades made into scrapers and burins and backed bladelets also occurred). A similarly rich area in the far east, on the southern Japanese islands, had a distinctive stone technology of side-blow flakes often made into leaf-shaped points, with blades and bladelets becoming important only later. One can argue that these areas were sufficiently densely populated and ecologically distinctive that they could maintain their own cultural traditions. It is interesting that these rich refuge areas have in recent times been centers of language isolates difficult to relate to others—respectively, Basque and Ainu. This is not to claim that ancestors of Basque and Ainu were spoken at the time of the LGM, but only that these areas are known to nurture language isolates.

Another area that maintained local technologies was the diverse continent of Sahul, including New Guinea, Australia, and Tasmania. Although we lack evidence of regular communication, even with Southeast Asia, it is interesting that later in these areas there were local innovations of technologies, producing smaller tools and new kinds of projectiles.

In general, however, the broad cultural response to the LGM was a sphere in which similar technological solutions were widely communicated and in which groups could have moved and established their languages widely. With the return to less harsh conditions, populations could have recovered, and emergent local spheres of communication would have encouraged language differentiation.

Research Directions

This broad overview raises more questions than it answers, and several things might be done to improve and extend the analysis.

First, additional case material would be helpful. For many regions of the African and Eurasian landmass we still have little evidence of human responses to the LGM, and a number of these regions are particularly important for evaluating the implications of the preceding construction. For example, areas around the Black and Caspian seas and on the coasts of West Africa ought to have been rich refuge areas where larger populations could have flourished and maintained distinctive local technologies and styles as they did in Japan and around the Bay of Biscay. In contrast, in open, forested environments of northeastern China or the higher savanna-covered plateaus of eastern and northeastern Africa, there ought to have been more open community networks participating in the widespread struck blade and microblade technologies of the African and Eurasian heartlands.

Second, more rigorous analyses of the technologies are needed. The statements in this chapter are based on a visual assessment of classical typological reports and illustrations, which are no substitute for formal studies of the *chaîne opératoire*

of these industries. We need such studies not just for isolated sites, but for sequences of settlement systems before, during, and after the LGM. Thus far, such studies are common only in Japan and western Europe.

Third, as noted in the introduction, the language issues need to be discussed. If careful reconsideration of the lexico-statistics of the proto-languages indicates that widespread divergences occurred at some other time, then other archaeological evidence may be more relevant to language issues.

Fourth, the construct should be further evaluated with independent genetic and paleoanthropological evidence. I have intentionally avoided this biological evidence, but there are, in fact, some provocative studies that merit discussion.

Notes

1. D. Nettle, *Lingua* 108, 95–117 (1999).

2. S. Wichmann et al., Do Language Change Rates Depend on Population Size?(Internet resource, 2007).

3. K. Flannery, J. Marcus, *The Cloud People* (Academic, New York, 1983).

4. P. Kirch, *The Lapita Peoples* (Blackwell, Cambridge, 1997).

5. C. Gamble, O. Soffer, *The World at 18,000 BP*, vol. 2: *Low Latitudes* (Unwin Hyman, London, 1990).

6. O. Soffer, C. Gamble, *The World at 18,000 BP*, vol. 1: *High Latitudes* (Unwin Hyman, London, 1989).

7. N. Ray, J. Adams, *Internet Archaeology* 11 (2001).

8. R. Klein, *J. World Prehistory* 9(2), 167–198 (1995).

9. H. Deacon, *World Archaeology* 10, 241–257 (1979).

10. J. Deacon, in C. Gamble, O. Soffer, eds. *The World at 18,000 BP*, vol. 2: *Low Latitudes* (Unwin Hyman, London, 1990), pp. 171–183.

11. F. Wendorf, R. Schild, A. Close, *Loaves and Fishes,* (Pauls, New Delhi, 1980).

12. L. Straus and G. Clark, *La Riera Cave* (Arizona State University, Tempe, 1986).

13. L. Straus, *Evolutionary Anthropol.* 14, 145–158 (2005).

14. A. Montet-White, ed., *The Epigravettian Site of Grubgraben, Lower Austria* (Liège, Belique, 1990).

15. D. Nadel, *Ohalo II: A 23,000-year-old Fisher-Hunter-Gatherers Camp on the Shore of the Sea of Galilee.* University of Haifa Hecht Museum, Haifa, 2002).

16. D. Nadel, *Archaeology, Ethnology, and Anthropology of Eurasia* I/13 (2002).

17. V. Jayaswal in O. Soffer, C. Gamble, eds., *The World at 18,000 BP*, vol. 1: *High Latitudes* (Unwin Hyman, London, 1990), pp. 245–251, Fig. 12.6.

18. A. Derevianko, W. Powers, and D. Shimkin, eds., *The Paleolithic of Siberia* (Univ. of Illinois Press, Urbana, 1998), pp. 126–128, Figs. 101–109, 130–135.

19. L. Orlova, Radiocarbon Data Bank (2005).

20. T. Goebel, *Evolutionary Anthropol.* 8, 208–227 (1999).

21. T. Akazawa, S. Oda, I. Yamanaka, *The Japanese Paleolithic* (Rippu Shobo, Tokyo, 1980).

22. D. Anderson, *Lang Rongrien Rockshelter* (University Museum, Philadelphia, 1990).

23. J. White et al., *Quaternary International* 113, 114 (2003).

24. K. Mudar, D. Anderson, *Asian Perspectives* 46, 298–334 (2006).

25. G. Irwin, *The Prehistoric Exploration and Colonization of the Pacific* (Cambridge University Press, Cambridge, 1992).

26. Schrire, *The Alligator Rivers* (Australia National Univ., Canberra, 1982).

7

Why Are People Mortal?

World Mythology and the "Out-of-Africa" Scenario

Yuri E. Berezkin

The areal distribution of folklore and mythological motifs is a still unexplored source of data on early migrations and cultural contacts, but its use is possible in the context of culture as a set of elements subject to multiple replication.

The interpretation of culture as a system of acquired, borrowed patterns was elaborated after the mid-twentieth century by scholars whose prime aim was to study not the origin of these patterns but their meaning. Alfred Kroeber and Clyde Kluckhohn deduced that "Culture consists of patterns, explicit and implicit, of and for behavior acquired and transmitted by symbols" (1). Though "symbols" seems to be a key word of this definition, it is equally important that patterns of behavior are acquired, not invented. According to Clifford Geertz (2), patterns of culture function in a way fairly similar to the one in which DNA forms coded programs for the synthesis of proteins. Cultural patterns are "extrinsic sources of information" that provide blueprints, templates, or, more to the point, models for relations "among entities, processes or what-have-you in physical, organic, social, or psychological systems," but in each case such a pattern is reproduced from some earlier sample. The predominant trend in twentieth-century anthropology was to study cultural elements as "models for reality," as sets of symbols which are understood, recognized, and interpreted in a way peculiar to the bearers of a given culture. However, the study of elements of culture as "models of reality" that are copied unconsciously and selected only by the researcher is also possible.

Addressing traditional narratives, we can treat them either as entities that are meaningful for bearers of a particular culture and considered by them as expressing their unique cultural values, or as combinations of plots and images borrowed from earlier generations and neighboring groups, and which have mostly cross-cultural distribution. To a certain degree, the same can be said about any sphere of culture, but the place of narratives is special thanks to their weak dependence on the environmental and social factors.

Recent research demonstrates that the correlation between basic types of stone industries (Middle or Upper Paleolithic) and anatomical types of their creators (Neandertals and other "archaic" hominids and anatomically modern humans) is not unambiguous. The "Upper Paleolithic revolution" was but "a series of broadly coeval local transitions prompted by the need to intensify the resource procurement under conditions when escaping to free lands was no longer possible" (3). Unlike stone industries, the content of myths and tales does not directly influence people's lives and very often has almost nothing to do with the reality of the world in which people live. Narratives are reproduced not because they correspond to any reality, but either because they are considered sacred and are intentionally taught and learned and/or because they are "interesting"; that is, their learning does not need much effort and their further retelling provides psychological and social advantages.

The units of my research are not, however, narratives themselves but their motifs—the elements incorporated into the narratives whose existence is not necessarily recognized by the bearers of the tradition. The standard system for classifying motifs is that of Stith Thompson (*4*). For Thompson, "the main purpose of classification of traditional narratives, whether by type or motif," is "to furnish an exact style of reference, whether it be for analytical study or for the making of accurate inventories of large bodies of material." Accordingly, Thompson defined "motif" as "the smallest element in a tale having a power to persist in tradition" (*5*). This restriction ("the smallest") was necessary to make of the motifs the appropriate units for the formalized description of texts.

Although some of the motifs coincide with Thompson's (e.g., *Thunder-bird*, A284.2; *Land fished from the ocean*, A811.I; *Cosmic hunt*, F59.2), this correspondence is not systematic and is rarely complete. American anthropologists of the late nineteenth and early twentieth centuries also worked not with elementary motifs, but with those elements of the texts which were widespread across North American continent (*6–8*). The analytical units we speak about are sometimes similar to the tale types (*9*); however, unlike the latter, motifs do not have variants. For purposes of comparative analysis, motifs, be they elementary or complex, must be strictly defined. Elements of the texts that do not correspond precisely to the definition elaborated by the researcher are not included in the database. Distantly similar cases should be either ignored or linked to a precisely worded new motif to which all corresponding cases answer exactly. The practice of searching for the nearest similar motif in Thompson's index and supplying it with a plus (+) if no direct analogy is available (*10*) is unacceptable for the purposes of this research. If it is claimed that a given text contains a particular motif, it means that it contains all combinations of episodes or sets of images mentioned in the wording of this motif. Otherwise the inclusion of a particular case in a given series would depend on the subjective opinion of a researcher as about how near or distant a particular narrative is to the sample one.

The objectives of this project are connected not with describing particular texts but with selecting common elements in different traditions. Thompson's index contains more than 30,000 motifs. This number can be increased, but the series of themes addressed by traditional folklore is exhaustible, not infinite. The number of motifs relevant to the present purposes is much smaller (a few thousand at best). Potentially, however, it is infinite because I consider as motifs not only the elementary units but also any combinations and chains of such units shared by two or more traditions. The definitions of motifs are instrumental, and the list of motifs is subject to change and increases so long as the researcher processes more texts and finds previously unnoticed links. With only one text in hand, researchers are unable to select any motif. Instead, selection depends on the geographical scale and purpose of the research. My database has been created to facilitate the study of distant intercontinental folklore links that potentially preserve information on the early contacts between Africa, continental Eurasia, its Indo-Pacific borderlands, Oceania, Australia, and the Americas. Had this research been focused instead on North America or Australia, for example, the set of selected motifs would be different.

This work began in the late 1970s as a search for Andean and Amazonian parallels for mythological scenes on Moche ceramics (AD I–VII, North Peru). The processing of data on the mythology and folklore of Latin and North America, Siberia and the Far East, Central Asia and Eastern Europe, Southern Asia, Southeast Asia, Australia and Melanesia, Africa, Western Europe, and Polynesia have been major steps in the research. As of June 2006, the distribution of 1,281 motifs across 285 areas of the Old and New Worlds had been studied. The data on 55 such areas in Africa, Europe, the Near East, and Polynesia are still incomplete and in process of accumulation. However, I am basically familiar with the materials from corresponding regions, and the discovery of many new cases of the motifs discussed in this chapter does not seem plausible.

The data were selected from about 4,000 books and papers published in nine European languages (more than 35,000 texts). Two thousand or so tribal and local traditions are merged into areal clusters that are somewhat provisionally included in 60 or so large regions, including Eastern Brazil, Western Siberia, Caucasus–Asia Minor, Melanesia, and so on. Khasi and Tibeto-Burman groups of the northeast frontier of India and adjacent parts of Mianma and China form a separate region named Northeast India. The Coast–Plateau region of North America is the same as that defined by Bierhorst (11). All northern Athabaskan groups, together with the Inner Tlingit, form the Western Subarctic region.

The statistical processing of the folklore and mythology of Eurasia, America, Australia, and Oceania realized in 2003–2005 demonstrated the existence of two major interaction spheres: the Indo-Pacific and the Continental Eurasian (12–15). The factor analysis suggests that South and Central America, Australia, and Melanesia share many similar motifs that are very different from the motifs typical for Continental Eurasia. North America, Southeast Asia, and the Pacific Rim of East Asia share some sets of motifs with South America and Melanesia, and other sets with Eurasia. Some Siberian mythologies, though largely fitting Eurasian standards, also preserve significant elements of the Indo-Pacific mythological complex.

Since January 2006, abundant African, European, and Polynesian data have been added to the database. The statistical processing of these materials is currently being conducted. However, some particular cosmological and etiological motifs were studied before the statistical analysis, bringing together corresponding data from all over the world for the first time.

Death Motifs and Their Areal Distribution

Attempts to explain why humans are mortal can be found in almost every tradition. Some explanations are specific to particular regions or even particular ethnic groups, while others are too general and lack characteristic details. The worldwide processing of data on mythology has demonstrated, however, that there is a set of easily recognizable death motifs with extremely wide transcontinental, though not universal, territorial distribution.

- *Shed skin.* People are mortal because they cannot shed their skin. In many cases, people are contrasted to snakes, invertebrates, or trees that shed their skin or bark and rejuvenate.

- *Immortal moon.* Moon revives or rejuvenates every month, but people do not; those who live on the moon are immortal; the moon decides if people should die forever or regularly revive.

- *Strong and weak.* People are mortal because they have been likened to something subject to decay and easy destruction (e.g., soft wood, not stone).

- *Stone sinks, stick floats.* Humans are mortal because a stone thrown into the water sank, and they missed a chance to be like wood or other organic matter that floated.

- *Call of God.* Humans are mortal because they did not hear or answer the call of a being (or did not pronounce his name) who had promised them immortality, or they answered a call (pronounced the name) of a being who brought death.

- *Originator of death was the first sufferer.* A person insists that people should die forever. Somebody dear to him or her (usually his or her child) dies. This person consents for human beings to be revived after death, but the original decision cannot be changed.

- *Failed test.* People lose immortality because they do not dare to touch or drink something loathsome, poisonous, hot, or otherwise dangerous.

- *Vengeful cockroach.* A small animal asks God to make people mortal because they would be too numerous and step on it or deprive it of its food and habitat.

- *Personified death.* Death (Old Age, Disease) is a particular anthropomorphic person not identical with the Master of the Dead. Death comes and makes people die.

- *The muddled message.* A person is sent by God to bring instructions or certain objects but for some reason distorts, forgets, or replaces them. This has fatal consequences for humanity or for a certain class of beings.

- *Plants get the life medicine.* The life medicine is accidentally spilled not on humans but on plants.

In Africa, the biblical motif of prohibited fruit has numerous parallels that are probably independent there from the Old Testament (*16–19*). For many Eurasian traditions, however it is impossible to distinguish authentic cases of prohibited fruit from Christian and Muslim influences; therefore, this motif is excluded from the analysis.

Tribal groups (or localities) and regions where the death motifs in question have been recorded are listed below. Sources, being too numerous, are not provided. Readers who command Russian can get the abstracts and sources of texts online (*20*).

Shed Skin (Figure 7.1)

Bantu Africa (Ruanda, Fipa, Luya, Tabwa, Wemba, Bende, Gogo, Kongo, Luba, Chagga, Nyamwesi, Issansu, Bene Marungu, Zulu), **West Africa** (Ewe, Kone), **Australia** (Karadjari, unidentified group), **Sudan and non-Bantu East Africa** (Lur, Galla, Malagasi), **Near East** (Gilgamesh epics), **New Guinea** (Highland Arapesh, Lakalai, Marind Anim, Dugum Dani, Kiwai, Kukukuku, Kewa, Torres Strait Islands), **Melanesia** (Trobrian Islands, Dobu, Baining, Batom Islands, Admiralty Islands, San Cristobal, Florida, Banks Islands, Ambrim, Pentecost, Oba, Malekula, Eddystone Island, Kanaka), **Polynesia** (Hawaii, Tuamotu), **Northeast India** (Moklum, Wancho, unidentified group), **Southeast Asia** (Thai, Black Tai, Viet), **South Asia** (Dhanwar), **Malaysia/Indonesia** (Nias, Mentawei, Dusun, Toradja, To Mori, Loinang, Bangai Islands, Timor), **Philippines** (Atayal, Mangian), **China** (Meo), **Japan** (Miyako Islands, Ainu), **Coast-Plateau** (Klamath), **Northern Andes** (Embera, Kogi, Yupa), **Llanos** (Sicuani), **Southern Venezuela** (Sanema, Yanomami, Yanomam), **Guiana** (Warao, Dominica Caribs, Tamanak, Locono, Kariña, Kaliña, Aparai, Arikena), **Western and Northwestern Amazonia** (Secoya, Shuar, Karijona, Ufaina, Letuama,

FIGURE 7.1. Distribution of the "shed skin" motif.

77

Immortal Moon

Moon dies and revives, people are mortal

Those who live in the Moon are immortal

Moon pronounces a verdict if people
should revive or die forever

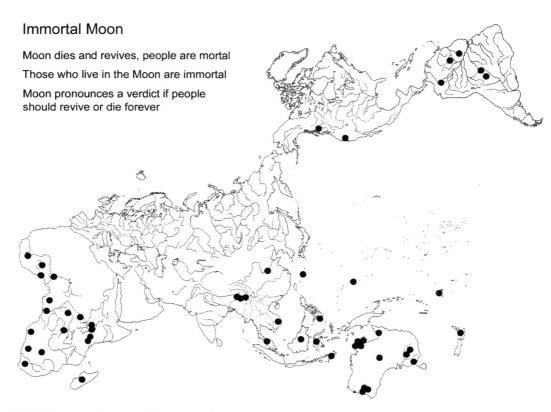

FIGURE 7.2. Distribution of the "immortal moon" motif.

Strong and Weak

People are mortal because they have
been likened to something subject to
decay and easy destruction (e.g. to
banana tree) and / or contrasted
with something hard and strong
(e.g. with stone)

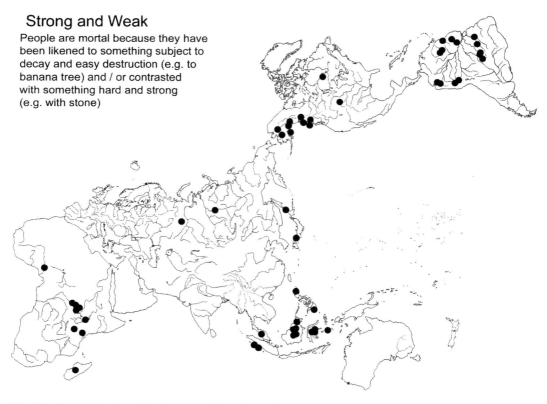

FIGURE 7.3. Distribution of the "strong and weak" motif.

Barasana, Tucano proper, Tucuna, Yagua), **Central Amazonia** (Maue, unidentified group, Teffé Lake), **Eastern Amazonia** (Shipaya, Juruna, Tenetehara, Urubu), **Central Andes** (Wanka), **Montaña** (Ashaninca, Amahuaca, Cashinahua, Harakmbet), **Southern Amazonia** (Kayabi, Nambikwara, Iránxe, Trumai, Kamaiura, Bakairi), **Eastern Brazil** (Caraja, Cayapo), **Chaco** (Ayoreo, Mataco, Nivakle).

The *shed skin* stories have an additional common element in Africa (Chagga, Gogo, Kongo, Luba, Lur), Indonesia (Toradja, Mori, Loilang), Melanesia (Lakalai, Dobu, Trobrian Islands, Admiralty Islands, Gazelle Peninsula, Solomon Islands, New Caledonia, New Hebrides) and South America (Yanomami, Secoya, Nambikwara). The process of rejuvenation is ruined and people become mortal because a person's relatives did not recognize him (or her) in his new state or disturbed him when he was shedding his skin.

The motif of snakes that become young every time they shed their skins was known in the Eastern Mediterranean in antiquity (by the Greeks, Phoenicians, and possibly others). However, the corresponding sources do not use this motif to explain the mortality of man. Only in Table 11 of the Akkadian Gilgamesh epics is the *shed skin* motif, though rather vaguely mentioned, linked to the motif of a failed attempt to make people revive after death (the snake steals from Gilgamesh the "flower of immortality" and, crawling back to its hole, it sheds its skin). In North America, the *shed skin* motif in its complete form is recorded only once, among the Klamath. The Baffin Land Inuit legend does not explain the etiology of death, but is about a particular woman who became young after shedding her skin.

Immortal Moon (Figure 7.2)

Koisan and Bantu Africa (Bushmen, Hottentot, Luba, Bemba, Poto, Yaka, Pare, Ambo, Vili, Kuta, Acholi, Chagga), **West Africa** (Mandingo, Fon, Hausa, Builsa), **Sudan and non-Bantu East Africa** (Bongo, Zande, Masai, Arusha, Nandi, Sanye, Malagasi), **Australia** (Djinang, Millingimbi, Wotjobaluk, Wuradjeri, Kulin, Yarra, Noongahburrah, Tiwi, Bibbulmum, Arunta, Wilman, Murngin, Yirrkalla, Maung), **Melanesia** (Fiji), **Micronesia** (Caroline Islands), **Polynesia**

(Maori), **Northeast India** (Aka, Kachin), **Southeast Asia** (Tjam), **Malaysia/Indonesia** (Semang, Kenya, Toradja, Timor), **China** (Ancient China), **Japan** (Miyako Islands), **Western Subarctic** (Carrier), **California** (Nisenan), **Guiana** (Hixkaryana), **Southern Venezuela** (Yanomami), **Southern Amazonia** (Iránxe), **Chaco** (Ayoreo).

Strong and Weak (Figure 7.3)

Bantu Africa (Issansu, Chagga), **West Africa** (Nupe), **Sudan and non-Bantu East Africa** (Acholi, Manja, Zande, Ngbetu, Efe, Malagasi), **Melanesia** (Jupta Valley, Urawa Valley), **Malaysia/Indonesia** (Semang, Mentawei, Nias, Ngadju, Bahau, Dusun, Toradja, Mori, Balantak, Wemale), **Philippines** (Tboli), **Siberia** (Mansi, Western Tungus), **East Asia** (Japanese, Ainu), **Eskimo** (Chugach), **Western Subarctic** (Ingalik, Koyukon, Upper Tanana, Athna, Tahltan), **Northwest Coast** (Tlingit, Tsimshian, Haida), **Eastern Subarctic** (Swampy Cree), **Plains** (Cheyenne), **Southern Venezuela** (Sanema, Yanomam), **Guiana** (Kaxúyana, Kariña, Trio), **Western Amazonia** (Shuar, Aguaruna), **Montaña** (Ashaninca, Machiguenga), **Southern Amazonia** (Kuikuru, Kamaiura, Bororo), **Eastern Brazil** (Caraja, Apinaye).

There is a particular modification of this motif in Circum-Pacific mythologies. A man must choose one of two women, one of them being associated with stone, another with a plant, or these two women are going to give birth. The plant-woman is preferred by the man or gives birth first, and because of this people are not immortal. Such stories are recorded in the North American Northwest Coast and adjacent area (Tsimshian, Tahltan), in Ancient Japan (Kojiki), among the Apayao of the Philippines, and in New Guinea (Urawa Valley).

Stone Sinks, Stick Floats (Figure 7.4)

Bantu Africa (Kwiri), **West Africa** (Fon, Ewe), **Sudan** (Dinka, Nuer), **Australia** (Noongahburrah), **Western Subarctic** (Tagish, Inner Tlingit, Tutchone, Kaska, Hare, Dogrib, Carrier), **Plains** (Blackfoot, Gros Ventre, Arapaho, Cheyenne, Comanchi, Kiowa-Apache), **Great Southwest** (Jicarilla, Western Apache, Chiricahua, Lipan), **Eastern Brazil** (Ramkokamekra, Botocudo).

Stone sinks, wood floats

People are mortal because stone thrown into the water or down slope sank, ran down. Usually one person throws a stone and another throws organic matter that floats. People, however, are like stone, not wood

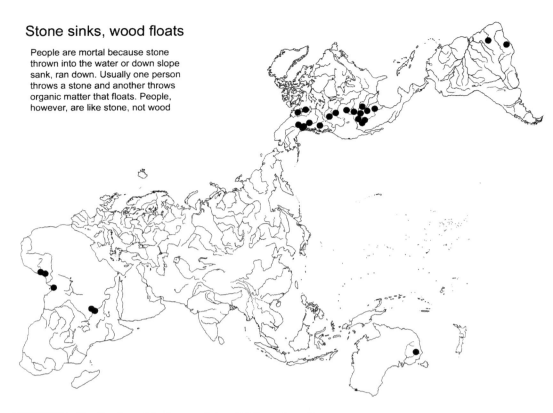

FIGURE 7.4. Distribution of the "stone sinks, stick floats" motif.

Call of God

People answer the call of a being who brings death or do not hear or answer the call of a being who promises immortality

FIGURE 7.5. Distribution of the "call of God" motif.

The Call of God (Figure 7.5)

Bantu Africa (Lunda, Pende, Ruanda, Kiwu Lake, Fipa, Bena Lulua, Ben Mbua, Chokwe, Bende), **West Africa** (Tiw), **Melanesia** (Baining), **Northeast India** (Aka), **Indonesia** (Dusun, Toradja), **North American Southeast** (Choctaw), **Northern Andes** (Yupa), **Llanos** (Sicuani), **Guiana** (Warao, Tamanak, Hixkaryana, Kariña, Locono, Trio), **Western and Northwestern Amazonia** (Secoya, Mai Huna, Karijona, Ufaina, Letuama, Tucuna, Tucano proper), **Central Amazonia** (Teffé Lake; unidentified group), **Eastern Amazonia** (Shipaya), **Montaña** (Amuesha, Ashaninca, Cashinahua, Shipibo), **Southern Amazonia** (Kuikuru, Kamaiura), **Eastern Brazil** (Caraja, Apinaye).

Originator of Death Was the First Sufferer (Figure 7.6)

North Africa (Marocco Berber, Kabyl), **Bantu Africa** (Ila, Lui, Mbala, Soto), **West Africa** (Fon), **Sudan and non-Bantu East Africa** (Masai, Arusha), **Coast–Plateau** (Thompson, Lillooet, Kutenai, Sanpoil, Quileute, Quinaulte, Alcea, Coos, Kalapuya, Takelma, Modoc), **Plains** (Blackfoot, Hidatsa, Kiowa), **North American Southeast** (Cherokee), **California** (Wiyot, Shasta, Wintu, Patwin, Pomo, Sinkyone, Coast Yuki, Yana, Achomawi, Sierra Miwok, Nisenan, Maidu, Tubatulabal), **Great Basin** (Northern Paiute, Paviotso, Western Shoshone, Gosiute, Ute), **Great Southwest** (Yavapai, Western Apache, Lipan), **Mato Grosso** (Caduveo).

Failed Test

Bantu Africa (Luia), **Taiwan** (Atayal), **Llanos** (Sicuani), **Guiana** (Arikena), **Western and Northwestern Amazonia** (Shuar, Barasana, Tucano proper, Tucuna, Yagua), **Central and Southern Amazonia** (Surui, Kayabi).

This motif is represented by the least number of cases and is widespread only in South America. However, the Amazonian stories are very similar to the only African one. Unlike the *shed skin* and *personified death* motifs, the *failed test* has not been noticed as a particular motif by specialists on African mythologies. It is possible that a more thorough search in the early sources will reveal additional African cases.

Vengeful Cockroach (Figure 7.7)

Bantu Africa (Embu, Gogo), **Europe** (Lithuanians), **Northeastern India** (Wancho), **Southeast Asia** (Banar), **Siberia** (Western Tungus), **NW Coast** (Haida), **Coast–Plateau** (Coos, Klamath), **North American Southeast** (Choctaw, Seminole, Cherokee), **Great Southwest/Northwestern Mexico** (Mohave, Papago, Seri, Tarahumara), **Mesoamerica** (Tepehua), **South Cone** (Tehuelche).

Personified Death (Figure 7.8)

Bantu Africa (Luba, Yaka, Mbundu, Rundi, Matumbi, Kerewe, Ganda, Banyoro), **West Africa** (Dan, Temne, Ashanti, Nzema, Ewe, Bamun, Munci, Jukun, Neio-Kru, Gagu, Lobi, Kraci, Hausa, unspecified groups in Liberia), **Sudan/non-Bantu East Africa** (Manju, Amhara), **Western, Central and Northern Europe, the Balcans** (practically everywhere including ancient Greece), **Near East** (Phoenicia, Ugarit, Sumer, modern and medieval Arabs), the **Caucasus/Asia Minor** (Abkhaz, Adygs, Avars, Georgians, Kurds), **Eastern Europe** (all Eastern Slavs, Chuvash, Mari, Udmurt), **Melanesia** (Banks Island), **South Asia** (Mahabharata, Dhanwar, Bugun), **Indo-China** (Sre), **Great Southwest** (Navajo), **Guiana** (Warao?), **Northwestern Amazonia** (Tucuna?), Eastern Amazonia (Shipaya?).

The Muddled Message (Figure 7.9)

Groups in which the *muddled message* motif is linked not to the etiology of death but to other themes are italicized:

Koisan and Bantu Africa (Bushmen, Hottentot, Suto, Chwana, Zulu, Cosa, Swasi, Ronga, Yaka, Kuta, Nyangi, Duala, Bube, Yaunde, Koko, Bulu, Ganda, Chuka, Embu, Emberre, Mwimbe, Kikuiyu, Kamba, Pare, Ngoni, Yao, Nyanja, Tonga, Ila, Safwa, Konde, Mkulwe, Bemba, Lamba, Ndau, Wenda, Fang), **West Africa** (Beng, Ibo, Ijo, Mende, Margi, Kilpa, Kone, Hausa, Dagomba, Builsa, Mende, not specified group in Liberia, Margi, Kraci, Ekoi, Wute), **Sudan and non-Bantu East Africa** (Bongo, Galla, Malagasi), **Melanesia** (Gazelle Peninsula), **Tibet–Northeastern India** ("*Tangut*," *Lepcha*, Apa Tani), **Southeast Asia** (*Tai*, Black Tai of Laos, Viets), **South Asia** (*Bondo, Saora, Parenga, Kond, Gond*), **Central Asia** (Tadjik), **Europe** (Lithuanians), **Southern**

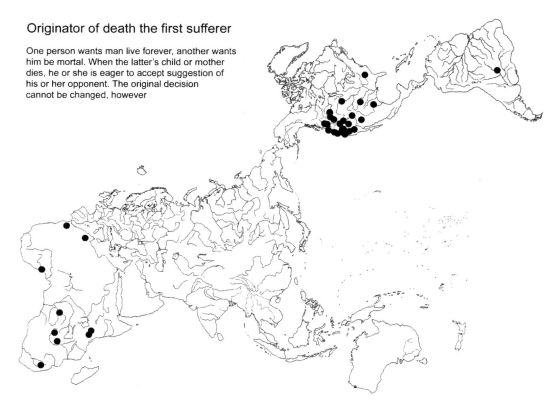

Originator of death the first sufferer

One person wants man live forever, another wants him be mortal. When the latter's child or mother dies, he or she is eager to accept suggestion of his or her opponent. The original decision cannot be changed, however

FIGURE 7.6. Distribution of "the originator of death was the first sufferer" motif.

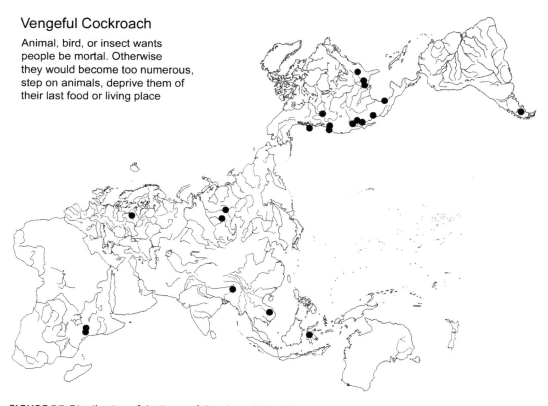

Vengeful Cockroach

Animal, bird, or insect wants people be mortal. Otherwise they would become too numerous, step on animals, deprive them of their last food or living place

FIGURE 7.7. Distribution of the "vengeful cockroach" motif.

Death as personification

Death (Old Age, Mortal Disease)
acts as a particular person (not
identical with the Master of the Dead
who rules in the land of the ghosts)

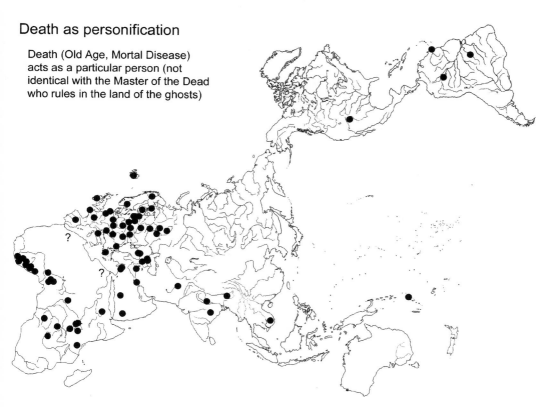

FIGURE 7.8. Distribution of the "personified death" motif.

The Muddled Message

Messenger distorts, forgets
or replaces instructions or
objects to be delivered.
This has fatal consequences
for a certain class of alive beings

● Origin of death   ◈ Other cases

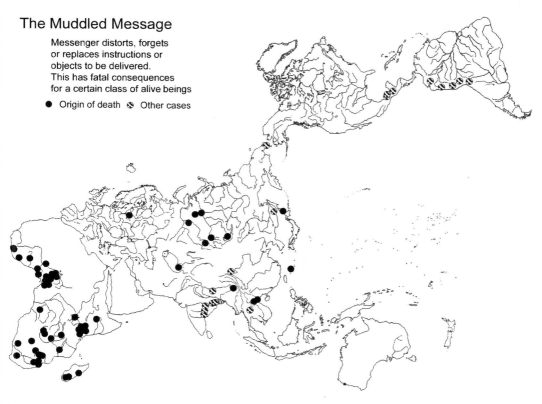

FIGURE 7.9. Distribution of "the muddled message" motif.

Plants get the Life-medicine

Life-medicine which must be applied
to humans falls on plants making
them evergreen, fruitful or capable
for regeneration from roots after the
upper parts have been destroyed

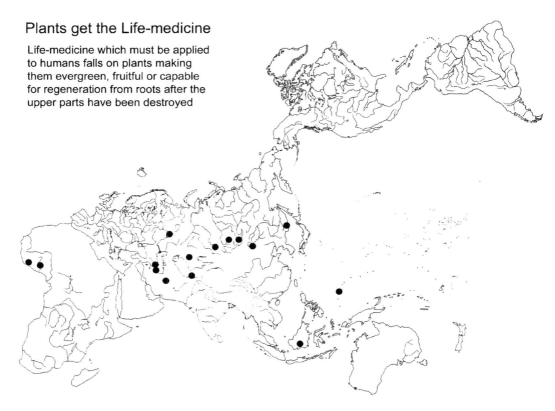

FIGURE 7.10. Distribution of "the plants get the life medicine" motif.

Siberia (Khakas, Altai, Buryat, Mongol), **Western Siberia** (Hanty, Northern Selkup, Ket), **Lower Amur** (*Oroch*), **Japan** (Miyako Islands, Ainu), **Arctic** (*Asiatic Eskimo*), **Mesoamerica** (*Veracruz Nahuatl, Sierra Popoluca, Chol*), **Western Amazonia** (*Napo*), **Central Andes** (*most of the Kechuan and Aimaran groups*).

Plants Get the Life Medicine (Figure 7.10)

West Africa (Kraci, not specified group in Liberia), **Micronesia** (Palau), **Indonesia** (Ngadju), the **Caucasus** (Talysh, Azerbaidjan), **Iran/Central Asia** (Persians, Tadjik), **Volga** (Tatars), **Turkestan** (Kazakhs), **Southern Siberia/Mongolia** (Altai, Tofa, Buryat, Mongols), **Lower Amur** (Udeghe).

There is a noticeable tendency in the areal distributions of the described motifs. The first seven are widely known across the Indo-Pacific part of the globe and in sub-Saharan Africa but almost completely absent in continental Eurasia. Three Siberian cases of the *strong and weak* motif, which are recorded among two groups of Mansi and

among Western Tungus, are the only exceptions. As mentioned above, mythology of the Western Siberian peoples and, to a lesser degree, of the Western Tungus demonstrates numerous parallels with the mythologies of the Lower Amur–Sakhalin and of the Kolyma–Chukotka–Kamchatka regions (*21–22*). The intrusion of Western Tungus into areas west of Baikal and Lena dates not before AD 1100–1200, and the influence of this substratum on their physical type and culture was very strong. Most or all assimilated groups were probably speaking Yenissei and Uralic languages (*23*). It is plausible that prior to the Yakut (*24*) and Tungus migrations—and before the introduction of the Central Eurasian cultural elements thanks to contacts with the stock-breeding people of the Steppe Belt—the folklore of all of Siberia, besides its southern rim, was nearer to the Indo-Pacific than to the Continental Eurasian type (*21–22, 25–27*).

The *vengeful cockroach* motif is represented in Africa by only two related cases. Its absence in Oceania and Australia and its sparse and unsystematic distribution in Eurasia (it is registered not only among the Western Tungus but also in Europe, at least among the Lithuanians) make its Old World history uncertain, but similar protagonists suggest historical links between at least the American cases. In most of them it is an insect (Tehuelche, Seri, Papago, Cherokee, Seminole, Choctaw, Coos, Klamath), but in others it is a toad or frog (Tarahumara, Cherokee), a lizard (Tepehua, Mohave), a wren (Haida), or a coyote (Kootenai). The idea of a corpse-eating animal that wants people to die (hyena in Africa, coyote among the Seri, raven among the Kootenai) is simple and probably could emerge independently.

The areal distribution of the *personified death* motif is much more systematic and significantly different from distribution of the first seven motifs. Being very popular in sub-Saharan Africa, it is only rarely found in the Indo-Pacific part of the globe. The idea behind this image is simple, and with unique isolated cases it would be difficult to exclude the possibility of their chance independent emergence. In all three South American narratives where personified death is mentioned, it is a vague image used in the *wrong call* myths (people welcome somebody who brings death and not the deity who brings eternal life). In several otherwise similar Guianan and Amazonian narratives, one who brings death is named just *stinking*, *dead wood*, and so on. There are no stories about personified death coming to take some man's life, so this South American image is very different from the African and Western Eurasian motif. In the Navajo myth, the hero decides for some reason not to kill Poverty, Old Age, Death, and Lice. There are no other American tales in which Death as a person is mentioned. Among the Arikara of the Great Plains, Death and Disease are dogs who bite people. At the same time, the *personified death* motif is known everywhere in Europe and Southwest Asia. Moreover, both in Africa and in Europe this motif is often used in a similar context (i.e., trickster stories). Their protagonists (from the ancient Greek Sisyphus to the heroes of Livonian, Russian, Georgian, Kurdish, or Chuvash tales recorded in the twentieth century) are successful in deceiving Death for some time but are ultimately overcome

by him or her, die, and thus introduce permanent death for all people. The Kazakh myth about Korkut, who managed to escape death for a long time, is of the same type though there is no anthropomorphic personification of death in Turkestan. It is reasonable to believe that the story about an old man and the death angel recorded in Pushtun folklore was brought to Afghanistan with Islam. In South and Southeast Asia, however, the motif in question can be early, and some additional cases will be possibly found here.

Discussion

What historical information might be extracted from the areal patterns of these motifs? The existence of corresponding motifs not only in tropical zones but in the Subarctic region of North America (and among not only agriculturists of the rain forests but also Australian, North American, and Patagonian hunters and gatherers, as well as their circulation in bands and tribes, in middle-range and also in some state-level societies) practically excludes their functional dependence on any ecological, social, or economic factors. A historical explanation (certain motifs were reproduced from generation to generation and spread to new territories together with their bearers) seems to be the most consistent. However, although the mythological data alone are good enough to supply us with facts for producing reasonably plausible hypotheses, they are not sufficient to make a choice among them. Considering the number of recorded cases, which is the greatest both in South America and in sub-Saharan Africa, both regions would be considered as having an equally good chance to be the original homeland of the corresponding populations. Or we could suggest that Southeast Asia was such a homeland from whence the death motif complex was brought to the New World, Australia, and Africa. Only genetic and, to a lesser degree, archaeological data on the spread of anatomical modern humans allow us to incorporate mythological data into a particular historic scenario.

About 60–50 kyr BP, *Homo sapiens* went out of Africa and began to move along the coasts of Indian Ocean (*28*). In the Persian Gulf region, or somewhere not far from it, the original population stream split into two major branches. One penetrated inner areas of Western Eurasia,

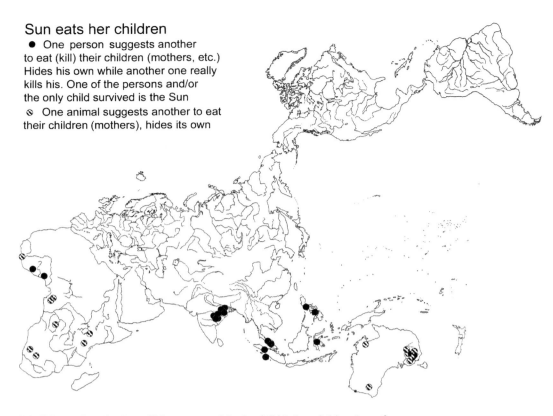

Sun eats her children

● One person suggests another to eat (kill) their children (mothers, etc.) Hides his own while another one really kills his. One of the persons and/or the only child survived is the Sun

⊘ One animal suggests another to eat their children (mothers), hides its own

FIGURE 7.11. Distribution of "the person tricked to kill his/her children" motif.

Sun caught in snare

Sun (rare: Moon) is caught (sometimes unintentionally) in snare and/or tied by a rope. Tales about the stolen sun that do not contain specific details on how it has been caught are not included

FIGURE 7.12. Distribution of "the sun caught in a snare" motif.

while another continued its movement to the east, reaching Sahul (Australia and New Guinea) probably before 45 kyr BP and certainly before 40 kyr BP. Some groups that split from this branch (in Southeast Asia?) began to move north along the Pacific Asian rim, reaching Japan at about 30–35 kyr BP and ultimately taking part in the peopling of the Americas 14 kyr BP. Taking these data into consideration, it appears that the death motifs in question initially emerged in Africa and then spread across the Indo-Pacific world.

It is probable that at the early stages of their dissemination all seven African-Indo-Pacific motifs were brought together, because in about one-third of corresponding texts two (much more rarely, three) motifs are linked. There are at least 14 such combined versions in sub-Saharan Africa, 2 in Australia and Melanesia, 5 in South and Southeast Asia and Micronesia, 2 in Japan, 7 in North America and 38 in South America. Not all relevant publications on African mythology have been considered, so the overall number of African and of South American cases is probably roughly similar. At the same time, the linkage between motifs is not strong enough to suggest that initially all of them were but episodes of the same tale. For example, *Shed skin* is never linked to *Stone sinks, wood floats* and *Originator of death*; similarly, *Call of God* is never combined with the *Muddled message*, and so on.

The greatest differences between areal distributions of particular motifs on this list are in the New World. The *shed skin* motif, so popular in South America, is rare in North America, whereas the distribution of the *originator of death* motif is exactly the opposite. I can explain this with the same "founder effect" that probably played its part during the initial differentiation between the Indo-Pacific and Continental Eurasian sets of motifs. With the extremely low demographic density at the early stages of the peopling of America, many chance factors could have led to the loss of cultural elements by different groups of people and the rapid increase of cultural differences between groups. This process could have begun during the peopling of Northeast Asia and Beringia.

Seven other motifs of probable African origin were also brought to the South Asian/Australian zone and in some cases also (much later)

penetrated into the New World. These are (1) *one animal pretends to kill its children (or mother) and tricks another to kill its own children* (Figure 7.11); (2) a related motif of *Moon tricks Sun to kill her children (mother)*; (3) *Sun caught in snare (29, 30)* (Figure 7.12); (4) *sky pushed up with a pestle to the present height by a person who had been grinding plant food* (Figure 7.13); (5) *Milky Way as a serpent* (Figure 7.14); (6) *rabbit or hare seen in the moon* (Figure 7.15); (7) *lost fishing hook* (a man borrows a hunting or fishing device and then loses it; when the owner claims it back, the man must retrieve it from the nonhuman world; Figure 7.16). Certainly there are others, but the overall number of such motifs—as well as the variability of African mythological, especially cosmological, plots themselves—is not large. It seems that after anatomically modern people established themselves in Southeast and East Asia, the complexity and diversity of their mythology increased tremendously. Dozens, if not hundreds, of these new (not known in Africa) motifs emerged and were shared in the recent past by peoples both to the east and west of the Pacific. The *vengeful cockroach* motif, if it is never found in Africa, could be one of such new Indo-Pacific motifs.

This complex can itself be divided into two parts, though the dividing line is not sharp. Some motifs are known not only in Asia, Oceania, and America, but also in Australia (Figure 7.17). Others are not registered in the latter region and probably have not crossed Wallace's line, at least not before Austronesian dispersal (Figure 7.18). I would provisionally connect the second group with the spread of the proto-Mongoloid populations.

The *personified death* motif could be just another member of original African death motif complex. However, it was further used and elaborated mainly by groups that took part in the peopling not of Indo-Pacific regions but of Western Eurasia.

The motif of the *muddled message* may have a more complicated history than other death motifs. In Africa, it is the most popular of all and is known in several versions (Figure 7.19). In many cases (Hottentot, Zulu, Soto, Swasi, Chwana, Ronga, Duala, Ngoni, Fang, Bemba, Yao, Nyanja, Tonga, Lui, Ndao, Kosa, Kwiri, Luia, Ganda, Bemba, Lamba, Ila, Wenda, Hausa, Margi,

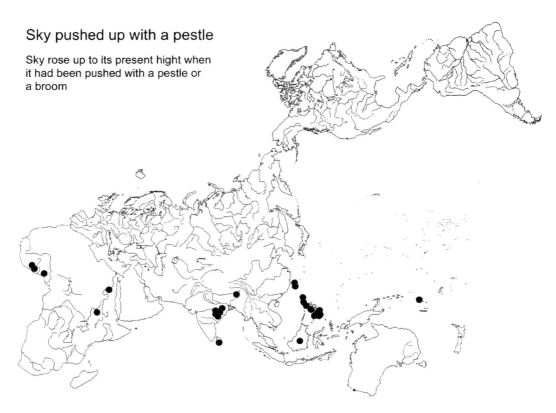

Sky pushed up with a pestle

Sky rose up to its present hight when it had been pushed with a pestle or a broom

FIGURE 7.13. Distribution of "the sky pushed up with a pestle" motif.

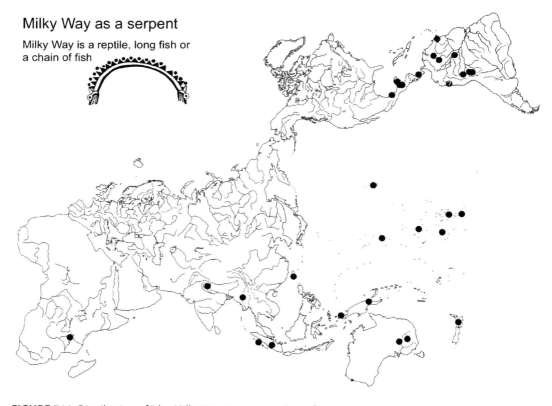

Milky Way as a serpent

Milky Way is a reptile, long fish or a chain of fish

FIGURE 7.14. Distribution of "the Milky Way as a serpent" motif.

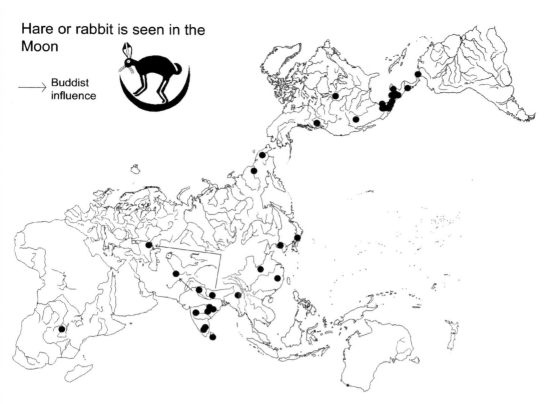

Hare or rabbit is seen in the Moon

→ Buddist influence

FIGURE 7.15. Distribution of the "rabbit or hare seen in the moon" motif.

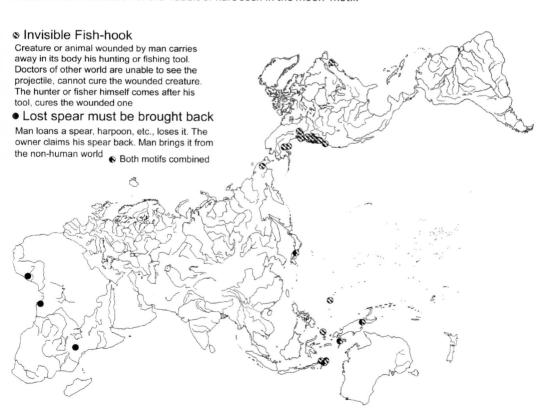

◔ **Invisible Fish-hook**

Creature or animal wounded by man carries away in its body his hunting or fishing tool. Doctors of other world are unable to see the projectile, cannot cure the wounded creature. The hunter or fisher himself comes after his tool, cures the wounded one

● **Lost spear must be brought back**

Man loans a spear, harpoon, etc., loses it. The owner claims his spear back. Man brings it from the non-human world ◕ Both motifs combined

FIGURE 7.16. Distribution of "the lost/invisible fishing hook" and "the lost spear that must be retrieved" motifs.

Chain of arrows

Every arrow or dart hits the back of the previous one and sticks to it forming a chain (ladder, bridge, pole, etc.)

FIGURE 7.17. Distribution of the "chain of arrows" motif.

The Dog Husband

It is described how a woman takes a dog for her marriage partner. Their children become ancestors of particular group of people

FIGURE 7.18. Distribution of "the dog-husband" motif.

Animals responsible for the introduction of death

- ◉ Dog
- ○ Sheep or goat
- ● Lizard and / or chameleon
- ◐ Hare

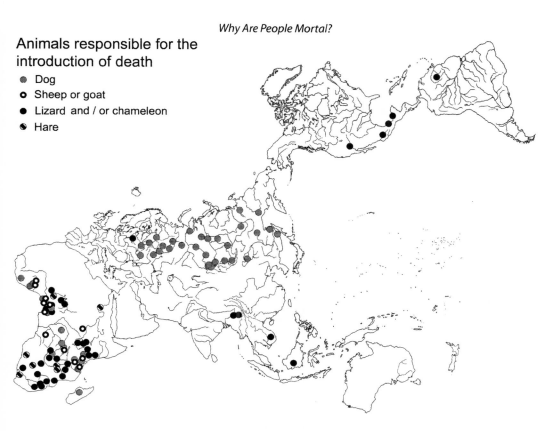

FIGURE 7.19. Distribution of the "animals responsible for introduction of death" motif.

Kilpa, Yaka, Wute, Acoli, Kikuyu, Kamba), the animal responsible for the introduction of permanent death is the chameleon, usually in company with the lizard. The chameleon also makes people mortal in the myths of Kachin (Northeastern India), Banar (Southeast Asia) and Ngadju (Indonesia). Because of ecological reasons, the chameleon could not have played any part in the more northern mythologies, but the lizard brings death both in Africa (Zulu, Soto, Swasi, Chwana, Duala, Lui, Fang, Ngoni, Yao, Nyanja, Tonga, Bemba, Lamba, Lower Zambezi, Ndau, Ronga, Kosa, Hausa, Margi, Kilpa, Sanye) and in Europe (Lithuanians), Northeastern India (Nagaland), and the Americas (Mohave, Tepehua, Veracruz Nahuatl, Makiritare). Though lizards do not live in the Arctic, the climate of the Pacific coast of the Beringian land bridge was possibly mild enough for small reptiles, so the historical links between the lizard in Asian and Amerindian myths are not completely excluded. Lizard, chameleon, and also hare (the protagonist of the *muddled message* stories among such African groups as the Bushmen,

Hottentot, Ila, Luba, Hausa and Nuba) could easily be Paleolithic in age. But in many other African stories the animals responsible for the introduction of permanent death are the dog (Luba, Bemba, Baule, Maka, Beng, Builsa, Kraci, Kone, Ibo, Nyangi, Kuta, Bongo, Kposso, Nandi, Safwa, Konde, Mkulwe) and the goat (Yaka, Kuta, Safwa, Konde, Mkulwe, Luba, Kraci, Dagomba, Ibo, Builsa, Ijo, Bongo). The domestication of dogs took place in Eurasia in the Terminal Paleolithic (*31–33*), and the domestic goat could not have been brought into Africa before the Pre-Pottery Neolithic B (PPNB) of the Levant (*34*). The goat, so far as I know, does not play any role in Eurasian death myths, but the dog does and is considered responsible for this misfortune in most traditions of Northern Eurasia from the Russians and Ukrainians to the Oroch and Negidals (*15, 34*). It seems plausible that the dog/goat versions of the *muddled message* appeared in Africa as a result of some later Eurasian influences, possibly related to the dispersal of the Afro-Asian languages.

The original chameleon/lizard version could

91

have been brought into both Continental Eurasia and the Indo-Pacific regions; however, the *muddled message* motif is not widely used to explain death outside of Africa, the most numerous cases being in Siberia. In all Amerindian and many Eurasian traditions the *muddled message* explains not the phenomenon of death but either the death of a particular person (in all Mesoamerican cases) or some habits of behavior of people and animals.

The *muddled message* motif is partly overlapped with the *plants get the life medicine*, another death motif that has been registered both in the Indo-Pacific and in Continental Eurasian regions and which could have originated in Africa or been brought there later from Eurasia. The latter possibility is preferable because the protagonists of one of the African versions (Kraci) are again the dog and the goat, and the protagonist of another is the cat, which is not a typical animal in etiological legends and possibly replaced the dog. The nature of Austronesian (Ngadju of Kalimantan) and Central Eurasian parallels concerning the *plants get the life medicine* motif is still unclear, not to say enigmatic. Many other motifs with similar cross-Eurasian distribution are found in Eastern European, Central Asian, and Siberian etiological tales that are usually considered to have been developed on the basis of Christian, Muslim, or Manichean traditions but which are absent in the Old Testament (35). In Northeast India and Southeast and East Asia some of these motifs seem to be well in place, and one version (finger- and toenails are remains of original hard skin that covered the entire human body) is also known to the Tsimshian of British Columbia.

Conclusions

The data presented above on the areal distribution of the mythological motifs fit well the "Out-of-Africa" scenario suggested by geneticists. The materials suggest two conclusions important for our understanding of the early history of humans. Anatomically modern people had some mythology (and consequently language adequate enough to retell myths) before they left their African homeland. The mortal nature of humans was among the earliest (if not the very first) themes treated in myths.

The Indo-Pacific borderlands of Eurasia and Sahul were reached by groups moving along the ocean coasts and preserving a significant part of their original culture. Later the elements of this culture, with some losses, were brought to Northern Asia and to the Americas. The fact of survival of African heritage in Indo-Pacific mythologies follows from the regional pattern of the distribution of motifs: the number of exclusive links between Africa and Eurasian borderlands (Figures 7.11, 7.13, 7.16) and between Eurasian borderlands and the Americas is much greater than between Africa and the Americas. The *originator of death* (Figure 7.6) is practically the only motif with exclusive African–American distribution.

Most of the African cases of the transcontinentally known death motifs are localized between 10° N and S from the equator. I have little data on the more northern mythologies of Songhai and the Saharan groups, but there is no doubt that Khoisan mythologies of the South Africa possess only two motifs of the list, the *muddled message* and *immortal moon*. The lack of the *shed skin* motif, which is the most popular and widespread death motifs in the world, is especially remarkable. Such a distribution suggests that the ancestors of the Khoisan were not in close contact with the ancestors of the future non-African populations.

Links between Africa and Western Eurasia also exist (the motif of *personified death* can be just one of them), but the situation is more complicated than in case of the African–Indo-Pacific links. Not only were the adjacent continents never in complete isolation from each other, but the "Neolithic revolution" in the Near East could have changed the picture and deleted many traces of earlier contacts. Demic growth and expansion during PPNB times resulted in the intrusion of peoples of Near Eastern origin into Europe, Central Asia (Jeitun Neolithic and possibly Caspian Mesolithic), Baluchistan (Merhgarh Neolithic), and Africa. Though consensus is lacking for particular areas concerning the relative number of newcomers in respect to the local inhabitants, these processes certainly influenced cultural development across all of Western Eurasia and Northern Africa. Which folklore motifs in particular could be followed back to the PPNB of the Levant and which had disseminated much earlier or later than 8–10 kyr BP is still impossible to say.

Although the Indo-Pacific set of motifs has been reconstructed with a reasonable degree of certainty, the Continental Eurasian set is more hypothetical. Although in the nineteenth and twentieth centuries (when most of our folklore materials were recorded) the distribution of motifs from the Atlantic to Mongolia and from Northern Europe to Northern Africa was relatively uniform (with many motifs also found in sub-Saharan Africa), such a uniformity was probably due more to continuous cultural interaction over many millennia, especially since the mid first millennia BCE, than a result of initial migration from Africa. The Continental Eurasian set of motifs is an extremely complex system of different influences and "inventions," and it is a challenge to unravel their succession.

Acknowledgments

At its different stages, my research has been supported by the Russian Foundation for Fundamental Research (Project No. 04-06-80238), special programs of the Presidium of Russian Academy of Sciences "Ethno-Cultural Interaction in Eurasia" and "Adaptation of Peoples and Cultures to Environmental Changes, Social and Technogenic transformations," the International Research and Exchange Board (IREX), Smithsonian Institution, James Soros Fund, Russian Fund of Humanities (Grant No. 97-00-00085), Dumbarton Oaks Libraries and Collections, and the St. Petersburg Scientific Center of Russian Academy of Sciences. It would take a page or more to name all the friends and colleagues in many countries who helped me in my work. I am deeply indebted to all of them.

Notes

1. A. Kroeber, C. Kluckhohn, *Culture: A Critical Review of Concepts of Definitions* (Peabody Museum, Cambridge, MA, 1952), p. 181.

2. C. Geertz, *The Interpretation of Cultures* (Basic Books, New York, 1973), pp. 92–94.

3. L. Vishnyatsky, *J. Israel Prehistoric Soc.* 35, 143–158 (2005).

4. S. Thompson, *Motif-Index of Folk Literature*, vols. 1–6 (Indiana Univ. Press, Bloomington, 1955).

5. S. Thompson, *The Folktale* (Dryden Press, New York, 1951), pp. 415, 427.

6. F. Boas, *Indian Myths and Legends from the North Pacific Coast of America* (Talonbooks, Vancouver, 2002), pp. 635–674.

7. A. Kroeber, *J. Am. Folklore* 21, 222–227 (1908).

8. J. Swanton, *Myths and Tales of the Southeastern Indians* (Smithsonian Institution, Washington, D.C., 1929), pp. 269–274.

9. A. Aarne, S. Thompson, *The Types of Folklore* (Suomalaisen Tiedeakatemia, Helsinki, 1964).

10. J. Wilbert, K. Simoneau, *Folk Literature of South America Indians, General Index* (UCLA Latin American Center Publications, Los Angeles, 1992).

11. J. Bierhorst, *The Mythology of North America* (Morrow, New York, 1985).

12. Y. Berezkin, *Archaeology, Ethnology and Anthropology of Eurasia* 14, 94–105 (2003).

13. Y. Berezkin, *Acta Americana* 12, 5–27 (2004).

14. Y. Berezkin, *Archaeology, Ethnology and Anthropology of Eurasia* 21, 146–151 (2005).

15. Y. Berezkin, *Forum for Anthropology and Culture* 2, 130–170 (2005).

16. H. Abrahamsson, *The Origin of Death: Studies in African Mythology* (Univ. of Uppsala, Uppsala, 1951), pp. 11–12, 39, 50–53, 94–96.

17. G. Parrinder, *African Mythology* (Hamlyn, London, 1967), p. 40.

18. R. Schott, *Paideuma* 35, 260 (1989).

19. J. Studstill, *Les Desseins d'Arc-en-ciel: Épopée chez les Luba du Zaïre* (Éditions du Centre Nacional de la Recherche Scientifique, Paris, 1984), pp. 125–128.

20. http://www.ruthenia.ru/folklore/berezkin

21. Y. Berezkin, in V. Vydrin et al., eds., *Ad hominem: To the Memory of Nikolai Girenko* (Museum of Anthropology and Ethnography, St. Petersburg, 2005), pp. 131–156.

22. Y. Berezkin, *Archaeology, Ethnology and Anthropology of Eurasia* 27, 112–122 (2006).

23. V. Tugolukov, *Tungusy (Eveny i Evenki) Srednei i Zapadnoi Sibiri* (Nauka, Moscow, 1985), pp. 272–273.

24. Intrusion of Turk-speaking people into the Middle Lena Basin began slightly before AD 1000. During AD 1200–1600 the local substratum was completely assimilated by the Yakut (36).

25. Y. Berezkin, *Archaeology, Ethnology and Anthropology of Eurasia* 22, 141–150 (2005).

26. Y. Berezkin, *Latin American Indian Literatures Journal* 21(2), 99–115 (2005).

27. Y. Berezkin, in A. Arkhipova, M. Gister, eds., *Stsenari Zhizni—Stsenari Narrativa* (Russian State Univ. of Humanities, Moscow, 2007).

28. Kyr BP: thousands of years before present. To estimate age using C^{14} dates, calibration has been considered (37).

29. K. Luomala, *Oceanic, American Indian, and African Myths of Snaring the Sun* (Bishop Museum, Honolulu, 1940).

30. K. Luomala, *Fabula* 6, 213–252 (1965).

31. M. Sablin, G. Khlopachev, *Curr. Anthropol.* 43(5), 795–799 (2002).

32. P. Savolainen et al., *Science* 298, 1610–1613 (2002).

33. E. Tchernov, *J. Anthropol. Sci.* 24, 65-95 (1997).

34. L. Horwitz, O. Lernau, *Paléorient* 29(1), 19–58 (2003).

35. Y. Berezkin, in Y. Berezkin, ed., *Kul'tura Aravii v Aziatskom Kontekste* (Museum of Anthropology and Ethnography, St. Petersburg, 2006), pp. 225–249.

36. A. Alekseev, in M. Turov, ed., *Narody i Kul'tury Sibiri* (Irkutski Mezhregional'ny Institut Obschestvennyh Nauk, Irkutsk, 2002), pp. 6–21.

37. P. Mellars, *Nature* 439, 931–935 (2006).

8

Neolithic Migrations in the Near East and the Aegean

Linguistic and Genetic Correlates

Roy King

The study of human migrations is a complex process which, at its best, integrates genetic, archaeological, and linguistic data. This chapter focuses on the phenomenon of migrations spanning from the Pre-Pottery Neolithic B (PPNB) period (ca. 8500 BCE) to the end of the Early Bronze Age (ca. 2000 BCE) within the geographic frame of the Arabian Peninsula, the Levant, Mesopotamia, central and eastern Anatolia, the Aegean Sea, and the Caucasus. We will also consider the connection between demographic events within this domain and the diversification of the Semitic and Northeast Caucasian languages, including the extinct languages of Hurrian and Uratian, proposed to be, through lexicographic and morphological relationships, akin to the Northeast Caucasian family (1). I will speculate on the poorly characterized substratal languages in the area, such as the Aegean substratum in Anatolia, Crete, and mainland Greece, and the so-called "Banana" and Proto-Tigridian substratal languages in northern Syria and Mesopotamia (2, 3). By limiting the temporal and geographic horizon under investigation, I have excluded from analysis those languages that dispersed earlier than the PPNB (e.g., Afro-Asiatic), and language families for which the attribution of their "homeland" to the region under study is widely disputed (e.g., Indo-European). Most of the genetic data used in this work are from studies on Y-chromosome markers and their associated short tandem repeats (STRs), employed both to localize and to date expansions and migrations. I will investigate in depth

one Y-chromosome haplogroup (Haplogroup J) whose origin is ascribed to the Taurus and Zagros mountain region circumscribing the fertile crescent of Mesopotamia and northern Syria (4). It is probable that any migration conveyed multiple Y lineages from different haplogroups; however, the use of one haplogroup to delineate the paths and temporal depth of a particular migration simplifies the analysis of migratory phenomena.

Prehistoric Archaeological Background

It is well known that agropastoralism—the domestication and cultivation of wheat and barley, and the taming and herding of goats, sheep, and cattle—first occurred in the Levant and the hilly flanks of the Taurus and Zagros mountains. An ovicaprid taming and herding economy may have had its origins in the Zagros (5), while einkorn wheat may have been first domesticated in southeast Anatolia (6).

These processes were somewhat gradual. After the Last Glacial Maximum (LGM) (ca. 21,000–16,000 BCE), the Levant, Anatolia, and Mesopotamia were sparsely occupied. In coastal Palestine, northern Lebanon, and northwest Syria, evidence of an Epipaleolithic culture, termed Kebaran, is found in the hilly piedmont areas of the Levant and can be dated to 15,000 to 20,000 BCE. Concurrent Epipaleolithic sites have been excavated in southwest Anatolia at Beldibi and Belbasi caves near Antalya and in the Zarzian horizon in the Zagros of northern Iraq and Iran (7).

Later, just prior to the Holocene, the Natufian

people in the mid-Euphrates region of the southern Levant and northern Syria began collecting wild grains and living in settled sites as early as 12,000 to 10,000 BCE. However, it was not until after 9000 BCE that the complete agropastoral package developed, spreading from northern Syria and southeastern Turkey to the southern Levant, Cyprus, and central Anatolia (7, 8). By 7500 BCE, the PPNB culture had diffused eastward to the upper Tigris. Cauvin has argued that the PPNB carried with it more than the economic innovations of cultivation and herding; he views the conceptual innovations of rectilinear architecture and the production of anthropomorphic figurines as part and parcel of the PPNB expansion (8). By the final PPNB (6500 BCE), archaeologists find nomadic sites particularly dense in the Sinai and the Trans-Jordan, as well as coastal occupation of the northern Levant (8). There may have been contact between the southern Levant and eastern Anatolia since by 9000 BCE the southern Levant began to obtain obsidian for the manufacture of lithics from sources near Lave Van in eastern Anatolia (8).

By 6000 BCE we also see the pervasive spread of agriculture to the southern Caucasus, northern Iraq and northwestern Iran with slightly different cultural refractions, suggesting an interaction between indigenous foragers and immigrant farmers in these areas (7, 8).

Farming economy diffused to the Aegean, first in Crete around 7000 BCE and then somewhat later to mainland Greece around 6500 BCE (9). The density of agropastoral sites during the Neolithic period is particularly high in Thessaly and central/western Macedonia, whereas the southern areas of Greece, such as the Peloponnesian Peninsula, only witnessed a major demographic expansion during the Early Bronze Age (9).

The appearance of herding/seminomadic agriculture in the southern and eastern Arabian Peninsula can be dated to as early as 5500 BCE, a cultural horizon associated with a specific lithic form, the Arabian Bifacial tradition (10). These stone tools resemble those of the Levant, with their elaborate notching. It is likely that during this period, a time prior to the severe desiccation of both central Arabia and the northeastern African Sahara (11), that groups migrated from the Levant throughout the Arabian Peninsula.

Although these two major migrations, the expansion of PPNB from southeast Anatolia and northern Syria and the expansion from the southern Levant into the Arabian Peninsula, may have yielded profound demographic changes in the region, later demographic movements may have contributed to the area's present gene pool. Eastern Anatolia and the Caucasus acquired agriculture relatively late (6000 BCE), but during the Late Chalcolithic era (3500 BCE) experienced a major cultural expansion termed the Kuro-Araxes horizon (12, 13). These communities, identified in the archaeological record through their production of Red-Black burnished pottery, are found across a broad expanse, from Georgia to Armenia, Azerbaijan, and eastern Anatolia. Slightly later (2600 BCE) the same pottery style is found as far south as the southern Levant, where it is termed Khirbet Kerak ware (12). The similarities in both pottery and architectural styles between Khirbet Kerak and Trans-Caucasian cultures suggest that there was some movement of people from the northeast Trans-Caucasian area to the southwest. This corridor of migration from northeast to southwest may also have been employed toward the end of the Early Bronze Age, a period for which we do have some historical documentation. By 2200 BCE, Hurrian personal names and toponyms are found throughout northern Syria and northern Iraq (14, 15). These names appear rather suddenly; prior to this period only Semitic names and names of unknown language affiliation are seen in the area's historical record (16). In addition, like the putative expansion from the southern Levant into the Arabian Peninsula during the Neolithic era, the epigraphic and archaeological data suggest that groups speaking Northwest Semitic languages moved from the southern Levant into northern Syria during the Late Bronze Age (17, 18).

Linguistic Considerations

Even though the location of the homeland of the Afro-Asiatic languages is under debate, most scholars would agree that the homeland of proto-Semitic is in the southern Levant and, as indicated by its lexical features, that it was associated with a Late Neolithic/Early Chalcolithic society (19). The earliest toponyms in present-day Israel are almost all Semitic in derivation, while those of the northern Levant are mostly non-Semitic of unknown linguistic affiliation, characterized by suffixal forms such as –uwa, -ija, -ik, -ka, -ashe (16). Likewise, it has been argued that the earliest onomastic data from northern Mesopotamia are pre-Akkadian and pre-Sumerian, with features such as syllabic duplication (e.g., divine names such as Kubaba, Zababa, Bunene, and Inana). This has led some to term this substratum the "Banana" language (3, 16).

Northward, Hurrian, the language found in tablets from northern Syria and northern Mesopotamia from 2200 BCE, and Uratian, the language of the Iron Age kingdom centered on Lake Van in eastern Anatolia, have been shown by both lexical and grammatical analysis to be affiliated with the Northeast Caucasian languages such as Lezgi and Chechen (1). These languages are ergative, agglutinative, predominantly suffixing, and verb final (1, 20). These typological and morphological features distinguish the Northeast Caucasian and Hurro-Urartian languages from Semitic, which aside from Akkadian and Ethiopic are verb initial, and from Proto-Indo-European, which is most probably an accusative rather than ergative language (21). As Diakanoff and Starostin (1) have shown, the Hurro-Uratian languages share many lexical isoglosses with the Northeastern Caucasian family. Furthermore, there are mutual borrowings between Northern Caucasian and Afro-Asiatic that must have occurred before the dispersion of the Afro-Asiatic languages (22). Lexical isoglosses for the words for goat ('ez [Hebrew], 'anz [Arabic], enzum [Akkadian] [23], aza [Kabardian], and awst [Chechen]) (24) demonstrate a likely sharing of lexemes across language families for the important cultural innovative process of domestication of caprids. Similarly, the word for wheat, grain, or barley (hnt [Egyptian], htt [Northwest Semitic], kut [Armenian], kade [Hurrian], gad [Lezghian], and chada [Lycian]) (19, 23, 25) follows the pattern of a pervasive *wanderwort* for cultivated grains in Afro-Asiatic, Northeast Caucasian and substratal languages to Indo-European in the regions under study.

The original languages of central and western Anatolia, Crete, and mainland Greece are also poorly characterized. Hattic, a language of central Anatolia that is prefixing and suffixing and shows affinities to the Northwest Caucasian family (20), is attested in the Late Bronze Age as a substratum to Hittite, an Indo-European language of Anatolia. Moreover, the Alishar Cappadocian cuneiform tablets, datable to the Assyrian colony period of the early second millennium BCE, contain non–Indo-European, non-Hattic, and non-Semitic person and place-names characterized by frequent reduplication and suffixes with the elements –t, -ass, or –na (52).

In the Aegean and Greece, it has been observed that pre-Greek toponyms often carry suffixal forms containing intervocalic sigmas (-ss- or -nth-/-nd-) (26, 27, 28). Place-names bearing these forms, such as Larissa, Knossos, Corinth, or Berekynthia, are found throughout the Aegean. Other lexical sets of items such as phytonyms (e.g., minthos, kypressos, coriander) also share similar suffixes. It is important to note that the Aegean substratal forms differ from those of northern Syria and Mesopotamia, suggesting that a variety of languages and/or language families were present early in the regions under consideration. The undeciphered languages of Crete— Linear A and Cretan Hieroglyphic—also differ morphologically from Greek and most likely differ from Anatolian languages in their apparent use of both prefixes and suffixes and their frequent reduplication of syllables (29); however, one prominent theory proposes that Linear A may be related to the Indo-European language Lycian (30, 31).

Genetic Correlates

As stated above, this chapter focuses on Y-chromosome studies that help to tease apart the archaeological and linguistic data and hypotheses. In the last decade several studies have been published using Y-chromosome data from modern populations covering the regions of interest. These include Turkey (32), Jordan (33), Oman and Egypt (34), Iraq (35), Iran (4, 36), the Aegean and the Middle East (37, 38, 39), and the Jewish, Kurdish, and Palestinian populations (40). This chapter also includes a report on a recent study from the laboratory on 88 diasporic Assyrian Christians who, though living in the United States, trace their geographic ancestry to northern Iraq, eastern Turkey, and northwestern Iran.

The dominant Y-chromosome haplogroup in the Middle East is J-M304. J bifurcates into two

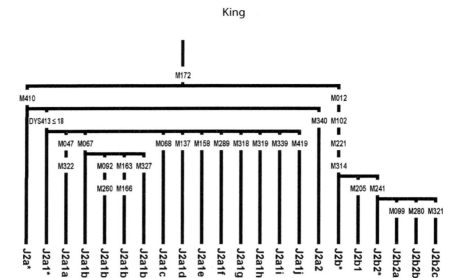

FIGURE 8.1. Genealogical tree of Y-chromosome J2 lineages. Figure is used with permission from Sengupta et al. 2006 (*44*).

clades: J1-M267 and J2-M172. As can been seen in Figure 8.1, J2-M172 in turn bifurcates into J2a-M410 and J2b-M12. Based on criteria such as STR variance, in which the source area of a particular haplogroup is more likely to be in a region of higher variance rather than lower variance, the source of J has been localized to the Zagros Mountains of Iran by Quintana-Murci and colleagues (*4*).

More recently, based on 9 STRs (excluding DYS388, which exhibits a jump transition on J1 lineages) on a J1 Y SNP background, J1 displays its highest variance in eastern Anatolia (.52) (*32*) and among Assyrians from Urmia in northwest Iran (.46). Dating the expansion times using the average square deviation (ASD) method (*41*) with an STR mutation rate of .0007 per generation (*42*) yields an expansion time for J1 lineages in eastern Anatolia of 17,000 BCE and in Urmia of 16,000 BCE. These dates are consistent with an expansion of J1 just after the LGM in the Taurus/Zagros area and the appearance of the Zarzian Epipaleolithic horizon at sites such as Shanidar Cave. It should be noted that all estimates of expansion times based on Y STR data have broad confidence intervals and are thus consistent with a large range of possible dates.

Likewise, J2, based on 10 STRs, has highest variance in the Mediterranean (.63), southeastern (.70) and eastern Anatolia (.63), and among

Assyrians from northwestern Iraq (.58) (*32*). Based on 6 STRs, J2 has a high variance of .52 for Palestinians living in coastal Israel near Kebaran Epipaleolithic sites (*40, 43*). This value is comparable to the 6 STR variance of J2 lineages from southeastern Anatolia. In addition, J2 has higher variance among Kurds of Anatolia than among populations from Iran and the Caucasus (*43*). The expansion times for these areas range from 19,000 BCE to 25,000 BCE, placing the J2 expansion during the LGM at presumed refugia areas in the middle Euphrates and southern Levant. J2 lineages were well located to participate in the expansion and subsequent migration of Neolithic farmers to southeastern Europe, Iran, and the Caucasus, and subsequently to India (*44*). Indeed, the data show that the presence of Neolithic ceramic figurines and painted pottery correlates best with the frequency distribution of J2 in Europe and the Middle East (*45*).

The two J2 sublineages, J2a-M410 and J2b-M12, have slightly different global distributions. J2b-M12 is rather localized to southeastern Anatolia, apart from major migrations to Greece and the Balkans to the west, and to Pakistan and India to the east (*37*). J2a-M410 is the major lineage that migrated to Crete, southern Greece, southern Italy, and even to Mediterranean Spain to the west and to Iran and the Caucasus to the east (*44*). A major sublineage of J2a, J2a1b-M67, is frequent in northwest Anatolia, eastern Crete, the Peloponnese, and southern Italy (*37, 38, 46*). We have postulated that J2a1b-M67 may have participated in Early Bronze Age expansions from western Anatolia into the Aegean and Crete. Of note, J2a1b-M67 frequencies correlate with the density of –nth- (*r* = .44, *n* = 36, *p* < .01, 2-tailed Spearman's) and –ss- (*r* = .35, *n* = 36, *p* < .05, 2-tailed Spearman's) place-names in Anatolia, the Aegean, the Balkans, and Italy. Although the remote parent lineage of J2ab1-M67 (J2a-M410) is of quite ancient northern Syrian/southeastern Anatolian origin and perforce must have been associated with many language families during its 20,000 year expansion, J2ab1-M67 is more recent in origin and expansion, and is clearly associated with the pre-Greek substratum in the Aegean.

As demonstrated, J1 may be of eastern Anatolian origin; it appears to bifurcate on the basis of a "jump" in a microsatellite repeat score for DYS388 to 13 repeats (*32, 37, 38*). Most J1 haplotypes have 15 or more repeats at the DYS388 site. However, in northeastern Anatolia, Azerbaijan (*38*), and among Assyrians, 13 repeats at DYS388 on a J1 background is not uncommon. In general, J1 is found at high frequencies in the Arabian Peninsula and the Levant, north Africa, and among the Semitic speakers of Ethiopia (*37*). A variance analysis of STRs on a J1 DYS388 long background suggests an expansion of J1 in the Levant at approximately 8000 BCE (*34*), coinciding with the presence of a PPNB horizon in the area. Perhaps individuals with a J1 background migrated from the Taurus/Zagros mountains with the domestication of sheep and goats, and adopted a proto-Semitic or Afro-Asiatic language in the Levant. Subsequently the J1 DYS388 long lineages may have migrated northward from the southern Levant into northern Syria, Cilicia, and Iraq with the expansion of the Eastern Semitic and Central Semitic languages (the Northwest Semitic and Arabic languages in the Arabian Peninsula and Mesopotamia).

Table 8.1 shows the calculated expansion times for various regions in the Arabian Peninsula and neighboring domains. Egypt and Oman have the oldest expansion times, dating to 7600 BCE, reflecting perhaps the Afro-Asiatic Egyptian languages and an Afro-Asiatic substratum in the southern Arabian Peninsula as postulated by

Militarev (*47*). It should be noted that Ethiopia also displays a comparable high STR variance of J1 long chromosomes (*37*). In the southern Levant, the Lebanese Muslim, Palestinian, and Damascus Syrian populations all expanded ca. 6000 BCE to 6600 BCE, near the onset of the Pottery Neolithic period in the region. Northward, in the coastal Mediterranean, are populations of the Maronite Christians of northern Lebanon who may derive from northern Syria, Mediterranean Turkey, southeastern Turkey, and Iraqi and Turkish Assyrians; the expansion times of these J1 lineages are later, 3500 BCE to 5000 BCE, and may correspond to the period of separation between East and West Semitic languages. Semino and colleagues (*37*) have noted that these J1 lineages among Arabs from the Arabian Peninsula and Morocco, and among both Ashkenazi and Sephardic Jewish populations, also have YCAIIa/b STR repeats of 22/22 with an estimated divergence time between 2300 BCE and 6700 BCE, broadly consistent with the expansion of the Central Semitic languages.

As mentioned, J1-short DYS388 lineages are found in eastern Anatolia and have an expansion time of 5700 +/- 3000 BCE among the Assyrian populations. This date matches that of the development of agriculture in eastern Anatolia and the Caucasus, and thus may furnish a useful marker tracing the subsequent migration of Trans-Caucasian and/or Hurrian populations southward. J1 DYS388 short chromosomes are found among Bedouins of the Negev (2/32), Palestinians in Galilee (1/54), northern Egyptians (1/147), Muslim Kurds (2/95), and Kurdish Jews (3/99) (*34, 40*). The J1 short chromosomes among the northern Egyptians, Negev Bedouins, and Palestinians have a variance on 6 STRs of .13, yielding an expansion time dating to 2700 BCE. This time is consistent with the presence of Trans-Caucasian ware in the southern Levant during the Early Bronze Age at sites such as Khirbet-Kerak. This distribution pattern and corresponding STR variance fit a model of subsequent migration from eastern Anatolia to northern Iraq (Kurds and Kurdish Jews) and the southern Levant (Bedouins and Galilean Palestinians).

The presence of J1-short DYS388 in Azerbaijan and eastern Anatolia and the high frequency of J1 lineages in northern East Caucasian populations

TABLE 8.1. Expansion Times for J1 (DYS388 > 13) Lineages

Population	n	10 STR Variance	Expansion Time
Assyrian-Iraq/Turk	4	.20	5100 BCE
Bedouin CEPH	18	.15	3400 BCE
Anatolia-Med/SE	6	.20	5100 BCE
Palestinian/Syrian	5	.22	5900 BCE
Egypt	30	.27	7600 BCE
Oman	30	.27	7600 BCE
		6 STR Variance	
Bedouin	18	.22	5500 BCE
Lebanese-North	4	.15	3400 BCE
Lebanese-South	12	.24	6600 BCE
Palestinian	54	.22	5900 BCE

Note: Expansion times were calculated using the ASD method (*41*) and the evolutionary STR mutation rate (*42*). For the 10 STR variances, the STRs are identical to those used in Cinnioglu et al. (*32*), while the 6 STRs are the same as those measured by Nebel et al. (*40*).

Sources: The Assyrian population is from R. King's unpublished ms.; the Bedouin population is from the CEPH collection; the Palestinian/Syrian samples are from CEPH and unpublished Syrian data; Oman and Egypt data are from Flores et al. (*34*); the 6 STR data on the Lebanese are from Capelli et al. (*39*); the data on Palestinians are from Nebel et al. (*40*).

(90 percent in Darginians, 67 percent in Avars, 58 percent in Lezgi, 58 percent in Rutulians, 32 percent in Chechens) (*48, 49*) support the proposition that the Hurrian-Uratian populations are related to those of the northeast Caucasus, both genetically and linguistically. These populations may have periodically migrated to northern Mesopotamia and Syria since the Late Chalcolithic/Early Bronze Age, conveying both personal names and toponyms to the region. In northern Syria, these groups may have encountered West Semitic–speaking populations characterized also by J1 Y chromosome lineages with a long DYS388 STR allele variety. Underlying both these migrations, there may have been a population dating to the LGM characterized by J2 Y lineages whose set of languages is unknown but may have included syllabic reduplication in their morphology.

Conclusion

The linguistic and Y-chromosome genetic maps of the Aegean, Anatolia, the Levant, and Mesopotamia portray an intricate and evolving picture.

Immediately after the LGM, southeast Anatolia, northern Syria, and coastal Palestine may have provided refugia to populations marked by J2 lineages of uncertain linguistic character. The LGM may be too remote temporally to reconstruct this linguistic superfamily. However, typological features such as ergativity may reflect ancient East Caucasian and Mesopotamian areality among a variety of language stocks (*50*).

In addition, if the undeciphered Linear A from Crete and Hattic from central Anatolia are related and can be linked to the Northwest Caucasian languages—with which they may share certain typological features like verbal prefixing, reduplication, and head-initial word order (*50*)—it is possible that the J2a lineages may carry a language group distantly related to the Caucasian family. It has recently been demonstrated that both the Y haplogroup frequency and J2a-M410 STR patterns of Crete and central Anatolia are quite similar (*52*). This common genetic association suggests that the underlying substratal languages, Linear A in Crete and Hattic/Cappadocian onomastics in central Anatolia (51), may also be connected either genetically or in an areal typological sense dating to the Neolithic period.

In the Zagros, the eastern Caucasus, and eastern Anatolia, J1 lineages expanded, perhaps contributing to the Zarzian horizon in the Zagros and involved in the obsidian trade from Lake Van. At the onset of the Holocene, a portion of this group may have migrated to the southern Levant, either ferrying a pastoral economy from the Zagros with them or adopting agropastoralism in Palestine/Sinai. This particular subset of J1 lineages carrying a YCAIIa,b pattern of 22/22 repeats spread the Semitic languages to the Arabian Peninsula from the southern Levant during a range expansion into more arid territory (53). Finally, the J1 lineages remaining in the eastern

Caucasus, northwestern Iran, and eastern Anatolia, marked in part by a short DYS388 repeat on a J1 background, were transported to northern Iraq, northern Syria, and ultimately to Palestine through the well-traversed corridor from eastern Anatolia to the Levant during the Early Bronze Age. The sudden appearance of Hurrian language, toponyms, and personal names in documented records may reflect the migrations.

It thus appears that both the linguistic and genetic patterns underlying the Levant, Anatolia, and Mesopotamia are complex, but that the Y-chromosome analysis of modern populations provides a means for testing hypotheses and can provide some insight into ancient patterns of migration.

Notes

1. I. M. Diakonoff, S. A. Starostin, *Hurro-Urartian as an East Caucasian Language* (Kitzinger, Munich, 1986).

2. G. Rubio, *J. Cuneiform Studies* 51, 1 (1999).

3. B. Landsberger, *Three Essays on the Sumerians*, M. Ellis, trans. (Undena Publications, Los Angeles, 1974).

4. L. Quintana-Murci et al., *Am. J. Hum. Genet.* 68, 537 (2001).

5. H. Fernandez et al., *PNAS* 103, 15375 (2006).

6. S. Colledge, J. Conolly, S. Shennan, *Current Anthropology* 45, S35 (2004).

7. J. Mellaart, *The Neolithic of the Near East* (Thames and Hudson, London, 1975).

8. J. Cauvin, *The Birth of the Gods and the Origins of Agriculture* (Cambridge University Press, Cambridge, 2000).

9. J-P. Demoule, C. Perles, *J. World Prehistory* 7, 355 (1993).

10. H. P. Uerpmann, M. Uerpmann, *Arabian Archaeology and Epigraphy* 7, 125 (1996).

11. R. Kuper, S. Kropelin, *Science* 313, 803 (2006).

12. J. Mellaart, *The Chalcolithic and Early Bronze Ages in the Near East and Anatolia* (Khayats, Beirut, 1966).

13. G. Palumbi, *Ancient Near Eastern Studies* 40, 80 (2003).

14. P. Steinkeller, in G. Buccellati, M. Kelly-Buccellati, eds., *Urkesh and the Hurrians* (Undena Publications, Malibu, CA, 1998), pp. 75–98.

15. M. Salvini, in G. Buccellati, M. Kelly-Buccellati, eds., *Urkesh and the Hurrians* (Undena Publications, Malibu, CA, 1998), pp. 99–116.

16. I. Gelb, *J. Cuneiform Studies* 15, 27 (1961).

17. P. Akkermans and G. Schwartz, *The Archaeology of Syria* (Cambridge University Press, Cambridge, 2003).

18. A. Mazar, *Archeology of the Land of the Bible* (Doubleday, New York, 1990).

19. I. Diakonoff, *J. Semitic Studies* 43(2), 209 (1998).

20. C. Justus, in C. Polome, W. Winter, eds., *Reconstructing Languages and Cultures* (Mouton de Gruyter, Berlin, 1992), pp. 443–467.

21. W. P. Lehmann, *Pre-Indo-European* (JIES Monograph 41, Washington, D.C., 2002).

22. A. Militarev, pers. comm.

23. J. Fox, *Semitic Noun Patterns* (Eisenbrauns, Winona Lake, IN, 2003).

24. S. L. Nikolayev, S. Starostin, *A North Caucasian Etymological Dictionary* (Asterick Press, Moscow, 1994).

25. J. Greppin, I. Diakonoff, *J. Am. Oriental Society* 111, 720 (1991).

26. J. Haley, *Am. J. Archaeology* 32, 141 (1928).

27. C. Blegen, *Am. J. Archaeology* 32, 146 (1928).

28. C. Renfrew, in R. Crossland, A. Birchall, eds., *Migrations in the Aegean* (Duckworth, London, 1973), pp. 263–276.

29. Y. Duhoux, *Journal of Indo-European Studies* 26, 1 (1998).

30. M. Finkelberg, *Classical World* 91, 3 (1997).

31. M. Finkelberg, in R. Drews, ed., *Greater Anatolia and the Indo-Hittite Language Family* (Institute for the Study of Man, Washington, D.C., 2001), pp. 81–105.

32. C. Cinnioglu et al., *Hum. Genet.* 114, 127 (2004).

33. C. Flores et al., *J. Hum. Genet.* 50, 435 (2005).

34. J. Luis et al., *Am. J. Hum. Genet.* 74, 532 (2004).

35. N. Al-Zahery et al., *Molecular Phylogenetics and Evolution* 28, 458 (2003).

36. M. Regueiro et al., *Hum. Hered.* 61, 132 (2006).

37. O. Semino et al., *Am. J. Hum. Genet.* 74, 1023 (2004).

38. F. Di Giacomo et al., *Hum. Genet.* 115, 357 (2004).

39. C. Capelli et al., *Ann. Hum. Genet.* 70, 207 (2006).

40. A. Nebel et al., *Am. J. Hum. Genet.* 69, 1095 (2001).

41. D. Goldstein et al., *Genetics* 139, 463 (1995).

42. L. Zhivotovsky et al., *Am. J. Hum. Genet.* 74, 50 (2004).

43. I. Nasidze et al., *Ann. Hum. Genet.* 69, 1 (2005).

44. S. Sengupta et al., *Am. J. Hum. Genet.* 78, 202 (2006).

45. R. King, P. Underhill, *Antiquity* 76, 707 (2002).

46. R. King, unpublished data; A. Novelletto, pers. comm.

47. A. Militarev, *J. Ancient History* 2, 113 (1995).

48. I. Nasidze et al., *Ann. Hum. Genet.* 68, 205 (2004).

49. T. Kivisild, pers. comm.

50. J. Nichols, in V. Yanko-Hombachet al., eds., *The Black Sea Flood Question* (Springer, Berlin, 2007), pp. 775–796.

51. I. Gelb, *Inscriptions from Alishar and Vicinity* (Univ. of Chicago Press, 1935).

52. R. King et al., *Ann. Hum. Genet.* 72, 205 (2008).

53. J. Chiaroni, R. King, P. Underhill, *Antiquity*, 82, 281 (2008).

9

Migratory Mechanism

Rus' and the Magyars in the Ninth Century

Vladimir Petrukhin

The emergence of Rus' (the Russians) and the Magyar migration were the main events in the history of eastern Europe in the ninth century. The famous treatise by Byzantine emperor Constantine Porphyrogenitus, "De administrando imperio" (DAI, ca. 950) and other, including Byzantine, sources (1–4) demonstrate the fact that despite the seeming suddenness and chaotic character of the "barbarian" migrations, the historical situation in eastern and southeastern Europe in the tenth century depended on certain general tendencies. The so-called barbarians longed for plunder or other profits within Byzantium, while the empire, in accordance with the old concept *divide et impera,* tried to take advantage of the contradictions between the barbarians:

> While the vasilevs [emperor] of the *Romaioi* [Greeks/Byzantines] maintains peace with the *Pachinakites* [Pechenegs: the steppe nomads of the Northern Black Sea region], neither the Rhos [the Greek name of Rus'] or the Turks [Magyars] dare attack the state of the *Romaioi* in the law of war or demand from them tremendous and excessive sums of money or things in exchange of peace fearing that when they attack the *Romaioi*, the vasilevs would use the strength of this people against them. (5)

Long ago scholars noted that the first appearance of the Magyars before the Danube Bulgarian boundaries and the first appearance of the Rus' ("the people Rhos") in Constantinople were linked events. The Danube Bulgarians called for Magyar help to hold the Byzantine captives who rushed home in 836 or 837. This fact does not evidence directly the hostility of the Magyars against Byzantium (or the hostility of Khazaria, the Magyars' sovereign), though it may mark their independent status in western regions north of the Black Sea (6–9). Probably, the Magyars were those "savage tribes" who blocked the way to the ambassadors of the "people Rhos" (Old Russian Rus') who appeared "as seekers after friendship" in Constantinople in 838 and had to search for a roundabout way back over the sea to "their people of Swedes" (according to the Frankish chronicle b [10]) via the Frankish empire (by the Rhine)(10–11). Consequently, in this period the Magyars could settle in the mysterious country Levedia to the west of the Don (Figure 9.1) and even penetrate into Etelköz, the country between the Dnieper and the Carpathians. It seems reasonable to suggest (as do many other authors) that the embassy of the people Rhos moved to Constantinople by the Dnieper via Kiev (the Khazarian boundary main road; the Don was the axial road of the Khazarian Khaganate). "The nomadic empire" controlled the south of eastern Europe as well as Volga, Don, and middle Dnieper River communications (the Khazars built Sarkel and other fortresses on the Don), and the Don could not be controlled by the Magyars (12–14).

The geopolitical context of the events that took place two decades later attracted less attention, though the Frankish emperor Louis the Pious, who received the embassy of the Rhos in

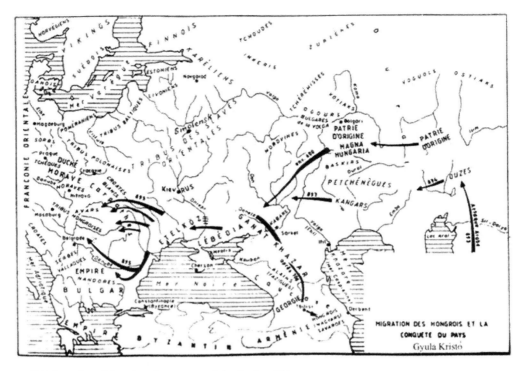

FIGURE 9.1. Possible migration routes of the Rus' and Magyars.

839, had warned his Byzantine partner Emperor Theophilos that those people more probably were spies rather than seekers of friendship (*10, 15–17*). In June 860, 200 ships of the "people Rhos" suddenly appeared in front of Constantinople's walls and, as Patriarch Photios evidences, threatened the city "with death by the sword." We do not know whether the Rhos possessed the data of a certain "intelligence service" and were aware of the absence of Emperor Michael III, but the fact is that such a raid would not have been possible without serious preparations. The major point here must have been the river routes; according to the Russian Primary Chronicle (*21*), Russian ships launched their first attack from Kiev on Constantinople by the Dnieper. In the tenth century the major obstacle on this route were the Dnieper rapids, a detailed description of which is contained in the above-mentioned treatise by Constantine Porphyrogenitus. To avoid the rapids, the Rhos boatmen had to haul their craft overland, providing the "savage tribes" (the Pechenegs) an opportunity to attack.

The Primary Chronicle's records, especially the dates, do not correspond to the information of a Byzantine source (unknown in Russia) on the raid of 860 (*18*) and therefore are often considered unreliable (*19, 20*). Meanwhile, the early chronicle dates have an obviously conventional character: from the report of a Greek chronograph it was known that the Rhos launched the first attack on Constantinople under the reign of Michael III, but the Russian chronicler did not possess the exact information and dated the attack by the end of Michael's reign (*21*). Using this date as a starting point, the chronicler calculated (subtracting four years) the date when Russian princes and Rus' retinue (of Scandinavian, "Varangian" kin) had been called from over the Baltic (Varangian) Sea in Novgorod (*21*), and the retinue men under Askold and Dyr had established their control over Kiev and obtained permission to launch a raid on Constantinople (*21*).

A more complicated problem is the lack of archaeological data: in eastern Europe the Scandinavian antiquities of the period of the embassy of 838 are known only in Volkhov Basin; in the towns of Ladoga and Gorodishche (Old Town) of Novgorod their appearance can be dated from 860, but in Kiev and even to the north on the

Dnieper route, in Gnëzdovo near Smolensk, the Scandinavian complexes can be reliably dated only from the tenth century. However, the early Kievan city layers have approximately the same dating: moreover, the earliest urban layers from the last quarter of the ninth century in the Podol region reveal close parallels to the planning of Swedish (Baltic) Viking-age towns (*22*). It is important that this purely archaeological problem of chronology should not be directly linked with the historical problems. Similarly, a few ninth-century Hungarian monuments can be marked out in eastern Europe on both banks of the lower Dnieper (*23*). For a long time this situation had a good explanation: the Magyars had adopted the "Khazarian" Saltovo-Mayaki culture, and it was not without reason that Constantine Porphyrogenitus, as well as the eastern authors, called them the Turks (*24*). But the final decades of the twentieth century were marked by the finds of many Ugrian elements in equipment and burial rituals of the Saltovo-Mayaki culture monuments in the forest-steppe zone, including such major centers as a white stone fortress near Sukhaja Gomel'sha (*25*) and Verkhnij Saltov in the (Severskij) Donets Basin (*26*).

In the ninth century the Magyars, like the Rus', were extremely active and demonstrated their independence. A new "splash" of their activity happened in 862: according to Annali Bertiniani, in 862 the Magyars (Ungri) invaded central Europe for the first time, having devastated the East Frankish kingdom (*27*). The annals do not comment on the invasion (more attention was traditionally given to the invasions of the Northmen, or Vikings) though for a long time scholars have thought that the Magyar raid was connected not only with the strifes in Khazaria, but also with the military pressure of the forming Varangian–Russian state upon the Magyars (*28, 29*). Nevertheless, the Magyar invasion influenced the balance of forces in central Europe and in the Balkans. Great Moravia, the earliest Slavic state on the Danube (in alliance with Byzantium), was clashing with Louis II ("the German"), king of the East Franks (840–876), allied with Bulgaria (*27*).

Concerning the situation in eastern Europe, Constantine Porphyrogenitus (DAI, Chap. 38) wrote about the three-year period when the Mag-

yars (Turks) lived under direct domination of the Khazars in the country of Levedia, named after their *voivoda* (military chief). After that the Pechenegs defeated by the Khazars occupied the territory of the Magyars, with one group moving to Persia (Caucasus?) and the other to the west, to Etelköz. The Khazarian khagan called Levedia from Etelköz and offered him the chance to become the archon of the Magyars. Levedia rejected the proposition, and the Magyars elected Arpad as their ruler. These data obviously demonstrate the beginning of Magyar autonomy. Further evidence of this autonomy is found in a work by an early tenth-century Arabian geographer, Ibn Rusta, whose information about the Magyars collecting tribute from the Slavs goes back to sources of the 870s. It is important that the Primary Chronicle named the only tribute collectors from the Slavs: the Khazars. Obviously, the migration to Etelköz was connected with the formation of the Hungarian ethnic identity, and Ibn Rusta was the first to mention their self-name, the Magyars (*30–32*).

Constantine's information about the Magyars (DAI, Chap. 38) reveals the situation characteristic of relations between the Slavs and the nomads. Their relations should not be reduced to a simple domination and tribute-paying: the Magyars had adopted important Slavic terms designating a military chief and law. Levedia was called their first *voivoda* (βοεβόδα), and Arpad was elected archon; according to a Khazarian custom, *zakana* (ζάκανα), the Magyars raised him on a shield. It is significant that the Pechenegs swore oaths to the Greeks according to their *zakan*. So the Slavic *zakon* became a term of international law; judging from the treaties between the Rus' and the Greeks, in the tenth century Russian law (*zakon russkij*) was recognized in Constantinople (*33*). Based on the data concerning Slavic-Hungarian relations, one can suggest that the transformation of Slavic culture in the left-bank Dnieper region—that is, the formation of the so-called Romny culture of the Slavic tribe of the Severians—was connected with the new Magyar domination, though judging from the Russian chronicle, the Slavic tribute was, as before, passed to the Khazars, obviously through their Hungarian vassals (*34*). The Romny culture area in the left-bank middle Dnieper lacks numerous Saltovo (Khazarian) antiquities (35); the Magyars could have isolated the Dnieper Slavs from Khazaria.

The archaeological aspects of the problem should also be taken into account. Hungarian material culture was formed in the tenth century with their conquest of homeland. The same is true of the antiquities of the original Rus', the Scandinavian antiquities of the ninth century in eastern Europe. They are not numerous in the north (in Ladoga, Novgorod [in Gorodishche], and in the Upper Volga) and are practically absent in the middle Dnieper, but spread in the first half of the tenth century, the epoch of formation of the Old Russian state with its center in Kiev.

An anonymous Arab author whose report used Ibn Rusta as a source describes the country of the Magyars as lying between the countries of the Pechenegs and the tribe of Eskel (a fraction of the Volga Bulgars). The Magyars collected tribute from the neighboring Slavs (*Saqaliba*), captured prisoners, and sold them as slaves to the Greeks from ar-Rum (Byzantium) in their port Kerch in Crimea (K.r.kh). The Magyars used to roam between two rivers in the country of the Saqaliba, Itil (flowing to the Khazars) and Duba (or Ruta): beyond one of these rivers lives a people, the Nandar, who belong to ar-Rum; over their land is a high mountain, and beyond it a Christian people, M.rwat, lives (31, 32, 36). Generations of scholars have tried to understand this text (32, 37–40). The main question deals with the rivers between which the Hungarian roaming territories lay. Long ago the river Duba was identified with the Danube, over which the real people known as Nandor lived (such was the Hungarian name for the Bulgars, the term going back to an old Turkic ethnonym, Onoghundur) (41, 42); the Danube Bulgarians settled within the empire of the Romaioi and so were affiliated to ar-Rum. The mountain over which the M.rwat lived appears to be the Carpathians; in fact, over the Carpathians lived the Slavs—the Moravians (from Great Moravia). More difficult is the problem of Itil: the Turkic term *itil* means "a river." Most scholars identify the Itil not with the Volga but with the Dnieper: the Magyars moved beyond the Dnieper to the country Atelkouzou (Etelköz) (the Hungarian term for "a country between two rivers").

No less difficult is the question of dating the events described. It is significant that both the anonymous author and Ibn Rusta do not mention the Rus' in the country of the Slavs. According to the Arab geographer, the people ar-Rus lived on a mysterious island, from where they sailed to the Slavs to collect tribute; they enslaved the Slavs like the Magyars. The Primary Chronicle reports the date when the Rus' appeared in the country of the Dnieper Slavs for the first time: Askold and Dir's retinue settled in Kiev after calling in the Varangian princes to Novgorod (see above); as we know, it happened before 860, the year when the Rus' launched their attack on Constantinople. By that time the Magyars had settled in Etelköz.

The Primary Chronicle reveals the geopolitical situation in eastern Europe: the chronicler reports (under the year 859) the tribute laid on the Novgorodian tribes Slovene, Krivichi, and Merja by the Varangians from over the sea, and the tribute collected by the Khazars from the Slavic tribes of Polianians (in Kiev), Severians, and Vjatichi. This report corresponds to the above-mentioned data of Ibn Rusta about the domination of the people ar-Rus over the Slavs in the north: they sailed to the Slavs from the "island of ar-Rus" (31, 43)—that is, from over the sea—and not from eastern Europe, and in the south, according to the Arab author, the tribute from the Slavs was collected by the Magyars and not by the Khazars proper: they were formal Khazarian vassals.

Meanwhile, the Slovene and other northern tribes had driven the Varangian violators away over the sea and had called back Russian (Varangian) princes to Novgorod; in 860 their retinue men launched the attack on Constantinople. Obviously, at that time Kiev and the Dnieper route, including the rapids (in the tenth century the Rus' feared them because of the Pechenegs' threat), were free. The Rus' gained a foothold in Polianian Kiev in 860, at the time of the Magyar-Pecheneg conflict (44), but the left-bank Dnieper still remained under the nominal domination of Khazaria (and the former Khazarian allies, the Magyars). The Rus' appropriated the Khazarian tribute later, under Oleg the Prophetic (880s, according to the chronicle dating).

The invasions of the Northmen (Magyars), as well as the raid of the Rus' on Constantinople, resulted in the mid-ninth century in an extraordinary upsurge in missionary activity both in the west and east, including Ansgar's mission to the Swedes from Hamburg, Constantine the Philosopher's mission to Khazaria and Great Moravia from Byzantium, and the rivalry of the eastern and western churches in the course of Bulgaria's baptism. Finally, Byzantine patriarch Photios reported that the barbarian "people Rhos" who had attacked Constantinople wished to be baptized and asked for a bishop in Byzantium. All of these facts were obviously connected not only with the ideas about Gog and Magog from eschatological prophecies of the Bible, the "prince Rhos" from the Septuagint, and other signs of the coming end of the world, the concepts characteristic of Christian Europe since the Migration period (*45, 48*). No less significant was the desire to "tame" the barbarian peoples and to draw them into the sphere of influence of the rival churches and great powers. The barbarians were capable of using these aspirations to further their own interests: Bulgarian prince Boris, who adopted Byzantine emperor Michael's baptismal name, had secured the independence of the Bulgarian church from Byzantium and thus positioned himself as not being a Byzantine subject (*3*). The ninth-century Magyars remained out of the sphere of this missionary activity; the spreading of the world religions among the nomads met certain difficulties, but after the Conquest of Homeland in the tenth century the Magyars were converted to Christianity, and the heritage of the Christian Great Moravia contributed a great deal to this event. The Hungarian Christian vocabulary contains Slavic adoptions, and there is a significant stratum of indirect adoptions from the Turkic forms of Slavic origin, in particular the terms for the Franks (*olasz*) and for a king (*király*). Besides that, the Magyars adopted from the Slavs the hydronyms of their conquered land (including the name of the Danube [Duna]) (*49–51*).

The consequences of "Photios' Baptism" of Rus' are practically unappreciable. G. Bakalov has suggested that the fragility of this event was conditioned by the fact that the Bulgarians of the 860s were unable to read and write the Slavic language and did not participate in the conversion of Rus' (cf. *3, 5*). It should also be noted that by the 860s the Varangian Rus' could hardly master the Slavic language. Nevertheless, the author of the Primary Chronicle was aware of the importance of Slavic writing for the Rus', and a special chronicle construction bears witness to this fact.

The Primary Chronicle reports the Magyar moving by Kiev (in 898) in order to link it with the Magyar invasion in Moravia and the Balkans, and the story about the beginning of the Slavic written language, which was brought to Moravia in the 860s by Saint Constantine and Methodios. The chronicler needed this anachronism for the assertion that "the Slovenian language and the Russian language are the same" (*52, 53*). The chronicle also tells that earlier, in 882, Rjurik's successor prince, Oleg, with his retinue of Rus' and Slovene which had moved from Novgorod and captured Smolensk on the upper Dnieper before the capture of Kiev, came to a stop lower on the Dnieper at the Ugorskoje site; it was named so (according to the record under 989) after the Magyars/Ugrians (Old Russian *Ugry*) had stood there (*54*). As noted above, the chronicle dates are of conventional character, but the whole geopolitical situation was described properly. It is significant that in 881 the Magyars, with a Khazarian fraction (the Kabars) who had freed themselves from the khagan's power, launched a new raid to the west in central Europe (on Vienna) acting as the allies of Moravia and the enemies of the Franks (*27, 55*). In Kiev, Oleg, in the guise of a trader sailing to the Greeks (the first mention of the route from the Varangians to the Greeks), lured Askold and Dir for a bargain, but then killed them as usurpers and proclaimed Kiev the capital ("the mother of Russian towns"). At that moment, Oleg's Varangians and Slovenes brought the names "Rus'" and "Russian land" to the middle Dnieper region. Then (under 883) the chronicler tells how the prince violated the right-bank Drevljane and collected tribute from them. He then appropriated tribute from the left-bank Severiane (884) and Radimichi (885) proclaiming hostility towards the Khazarians (*56*). Oleg could have easily appropriated the Khazarian tribute from the left-bank Dnieper Slavs thanks to the crisis in Khazaria after the Magyars had left Levedia occupied by the Pechenegs (the latter finally cut off the Dnieper Slavs from Khazaria) and moved to the west, to Etelköz and farther.

Now, we turn back to the epoch of Hungarian

Conquest of Homeland and the significance of this event for Rus'. The new collision had a traditional ninth-century form of conflict provoked by Byzantium in 894 (the conflict was described in the Chronicle by Simeon Logothete [57, 58] and by Constantine Porphyrogenitus in DAI, Chap. 40). The Greeks gave the Magyars gifts to make them attack the Bulgarians, who were at war with Byzantium. The Magyars managed to defeat the Bulgarian tsar Simeon and make headway to his capital, Preslav. After the Magyars had returned to Etelköz, Simeon in 895 concluded peace with the Greeks and a military alliance with the Pechenegs. When the Magyars launched a military campaign (Constantine Porphyrogenitus does not report its aim), the Bulgarians and Pechenegs devastated their country. It should be noted that at the same time in 894 the Magyars, as the Moravians' allies, again attacked the Franks (the Bulgarians' allies) and the Slavs in Pannonia (future Hungary) (59). The Magyars returned to their devastated country but soon had to leave it under pressure from the Pechenegs. They moved through the Carpathians to the Danube, occupied Transylvania, ravaged Great Moravia (taking advantage of the intense struggle there) and in 896–906 settled in this region (27, 59, 60). Constantine Porphyrogenitus noted that "the rest of the population" of Moravia "dispersed fleeing to the neighbouring peoples—Bulgarians, Turks [the term he used for the Magyars proper], Croats and others" (61).

It is not clear whether the Rus' participated directly in the events connected with the Magyar-Bulgarian war and how the Pechenegs' threat was estimated (the Pechenegs had already penetrated the limits of the Russian land in the forest-steppe zone). Nevertheless, to a certain degree the Rus' evidently appeared as the successor of Great Moravia; according to the archaeological data, Rus' was among "the other peoples" where the Moravians fled. Moravian antiquities have been found in two major areas, the middle and upper Dnieper, and even in Ladoga (62). It is significant that in Gnëzdovo, the main retinue settlement controlling the passage from the Volkhov (Novgorodian) water system to the Dnieper system Moravian things were found, and the Moravian ceramic tradition of manufacturing clay vessels of high quality had been maintained. Kiev and Gnëzdovo, on the route from the Varangians

to the Greeks, appeared attractive to the Moravians as well as the Varangians (63). The reason is quite obvious: here before Oleg, who was saved from the Magyars, lay the way from the Varangians to the Greeks. Oleg took advantage of this way, having gathered all the forces available with the aim of an attack on Constantinople (according to the chronicle dating, in 907); in 907 he concluded an unprecedented trade treaty with Byzantium. The Russian prince once more took advantage of the profitable geopolitical situation: according to the chronicle, under prince Igor in 915 "the Pechenegs for the first time came to the Russian land and concluded peace with Igor and came to the Danube"(64). In the northern Black Sea region, the Pechenegs replaced the Magyars, and became a new factor to be taken into account during the campaigns against the Greeks. On the Danube, the Greeks exploited the Pechenegs to fight against the Bulgarians, and the Russians evidently concluded peace with the Pechenegs in the interests of their trade relations with Byzantium. In 944 Igor engaged the Pechenegs for his expedition against Byzantium: he aimed to demonstrate force, frighten the Greeks, and make them conclude a new trade treaty. Having achieved the conclusion of this treaty on the Danube, he sent the Pechenegs to wage war in Bulgaria. After several decades, Prince Svjatoslav, son of Igor, was called by the Greeks against the Bulgarians, and then Byzantium had to appeal to the Pechenegs in order to restrain the ambitions of the Russian prince, who considered the center of his country to be on the Danube.

The ninth-century migratory mechanism in eastern Europe was connected with the system of east-west movements of the "steppe nomads" and the north-south movements of the "river nomads"—that is, the Rus' (65). It is significant that both groups were included in the geopolitical system of the relations between the great powers of the early Middle Ages and in the system of tribute-collecting from the east European Slavs (as well as in the system of alliances with Great Moravia). The Magyars were prepared for the meeting with the Pannonian Slavs in their conquered homeland: the linguists reconstruct the situation of Slavic-Hungarian bilingualism (the Koine) in the Arpad epoch (under the dynasty of the first Hungarian rulers in the tenth to eleventh centuries) *(49)*. This factor favored the intensive intrusion of the Magyars (as earlier, of the Bulgars) in the context of international relations in central Europe and the Balkans, and the formation of "national" states there *(66)*. At the same time, as Róna-Tas *(67)* has noted, the Slavs did not participate in the Magyars' military expeditions, which is why "the Magyars, unlike the Bulgars and the Avars, did not become assimilated" (cf. *68, 69*).

Notes

1. Cf. G. Litavrin, A. Novosel'tsev, eds., *Constantine Porphyrogenitus: Ob upravlenii imperiej* (Nauka, Moscow, 1989).

2. G. Moravcsik, R. Jenkins, eds., Constantine VII Porphyrogenitus, *De administrando imperio* (Dumbarton Oaks, Washington, D.C., 1967).

3. G. Bakalov, in O. Pritsak, I. Sevcenko, M. Labunka, eds., *Proceedings of International Congress Commemorating the Millennium of Christianity in Rus'-Ukraine* (Ukranian Research Institute, Harvard Univ., Cambridge, MA, 1990), pp. 387–399.

4. J. Shepard, in L. Brubaker, ed., *Byzantium in the Ninth Century* (Aldershot, Hampshire, UK, 1998), pp. 167–180.

5. G. Gennadij, *Vyzantija, Bolgaria, Drevnjaja Rus'* (Aleteja, St. Petersburg, 2000).

6. Cf. A. Róna-Tas, *Hungarians and Europe in the Early Middle Ages* (CEU Press, Budapest, 1999), pp. 387–388.

7. G. Vernadsky, *Kievskaia Rus'* (Tver, Moscow, 1996), p. 310.

8. V. P. Shusharin, in A. Zimin, V. Pasuto, eds., *Mezdunarodnye svjazi Rossii do XVII v.* (Nauka, Moscow, 1961), p. 134.

9. C. Zukerman, *Materialy po Archeologii, Istorii i Etnographii Tavrii* (*MAIET*) 4, 663–688 (1998).

10. G. Waitz, ed., *Annales Bertiniani* (Impensis Bibliopolii Hahniani, Hannover, 1895), p. 839.

11. Cf. A. Novosel'tsev, *Khazarskoje Gosudarstvo i Jego Rol' v Istorii Vostochnoj Evropy i Kavkaza* (Moscow, Nauka, 1990), p. 206.

12. V. Flerov, *Rossijskaja Archeologija* 2, 56 (2001). They suppose that Sarkel could have been built on the left bank of the Don to control the Hungarians who were moving to Etelköz.

13. Cf. I. Dienes, *The Hungarians Cross the Carpathians* (Corvina, Budapest, 1972), p. 9.

14. I. Zimonyi, in S. Csernus, K. Korompay, eds., *Les Hongrois et l'Europe: Conqête et Intégration* (Institut Hongroise de Paris, Paris, 1999), p. 41.

15. A. Nazarenko, in E. Mel'nikova, ed., *Drevnjaja Rus' v Svete Zarubezhnyh Istochnikov* (Logos, Moscow, 1999), p. 288. Louis's suspiciousness was valid because the Rhos did not assume their tribal name, though *sveoni* were well known to the emperor of the Franks. It could mean that the Rhos borrowed not the tribal name, but their "marching" east European name of the "rowers" and were going not to Sweden but farther, to eastern Europe.

16. E. Mel'nikova, V. Petruchin, *Tor.* 23, 203 (1990–1991).

17. Cf. the hypothetical reconstruction of the route by J. Shepard, *Early Medieval Europe* 4, 41–60 (1995).

18. P. Shreiner, *Vyzantijskij Vremennik* 52, 151 (1991).

19. Cf. the discussion by C. Zukerman, *Slavjanovedenije* 4, 55 (2001).

20. V. Petrukhin, *Slavjanovedenije* 4, 78 (2001).

21. D. Likhachev, M. Sverdlov, eds., *Povest' Vremennykh Let* (Nauka, St. Petersburg, 1996), p. 13.

22. M. Sahaidak, *Ruthenica* 4, 159 (2005).

23. A. Suprunenko, I. Kulatova, V. Prijmak, *Finno-ugrica* 1(3), 24 (1999).

24. Cf. I. Fodor, in V. Petrukhin, A. Fedorchuk, eds., *Khazary: Vtoroj Mezhdunarodnij Kolloqvium* (Institut Slavjanovedenija, Moscow, 2002), pp. 98–101.

25. V. Mikheev, *Sovetskaja Archeologija* 2, 165 (1982).

26. V. Aksjenov, in V. Petrukhin, V. Moskovich, eds., *Khazary*, Jews and Slavs 16 (Gesharim, Moscow, 2005), pp. 222–223. A single, though characteristic, element of a female dress—horse-like pendants— marks the connections of the burial monuments of the Donets Basin in eighth–ninth centuries with the Kama region on the one hand, and with the Taman' Peninsula on the other. If this element really is characteristic of east European Hungarian dress, one can reasonably suggest that the Magyars had reached not only Donets, but also the Bosporos.

27. C. Bowlus, *Franks, Moravians and Magyars* (Univ. of Pennsylvania Press, Philadelphia, 1995), pp. 236–237.

28. I. Boba, *Nomads, Northmen and Slavs* (Mouton, The Hague, 1967), pp. 95–97.

29. Correlation between the invasions of the Normans and the Hungarians (as well as the Muslims) as enemies of Christianity is characteristic for the later western European annals; see E. Czücs, *Hungarorossica* 9, 239 (2002).

30. V. Shusharin, *Rannij Etap Etnicheskoj Istorii Vengrov* (Rosspen, Moscow, 1997), pp. 111–113.

31. Cf. T. Lewicki, *Źródła Arabskie do Dziejów Słowiańszyzny* T. 2, cz. 2 (Widawnictwo Polskiej Akademii Nauk, Warsaw, 1977), pp. 32–35, 107.

32. B. N. Zakhoder, *Kaspijskij Svod Svedenij o Vostochnoj Evrope* (Glavnaja Redaktsija Vostochnoj Literatury, Moscow, 1967), vol. 2, p. 48.

33. G. G. Litvarin, A. P. Novosel'tsev, eds., *Constantine Porphyrogenitus: Ob upravlenii imperiej*, p. 290, comment 5 (Nauka, Moscow, 1989).

34. P. Tolochko, *Kochevyje Narody Stepej i Kievskaja Rus'* (Aleteja, St. Petersburg, 2003), p. 26.

35. A. Grigorjev, *Severskaja Semlja v VIII—Nachale XI Veka po Archeologicheskim Dannym* (Grif i K, Tula, 2000), p. 180.

36. T. Lewicki, *Slavia Antiqua* 14 (1967).

37. More exactly, one should speak about the code of texts, ascending to the *anonymous author* of the ninth century. See T. Lewicki, in L. Cherepnin, ed., *Vostochnaja Evropa v Drevnosty i Srednevekobje* (Nauka, Moscow, 1978), pp. 56–60.

38. V. Shusharin, *Rannij Etap Etnicheskoj Istorii Vengrov* (Rosspen, Moscow, 1997), p. 106.

39. G. Kristó, *Hungarian History in the 9th Century* (Szegedi Középkorász Mühely, Szeged, 1996), pp. 169–170.

40. D. Mishin, *Saqaliba: Slavjane v Islamskom Mire* (IV RAN-Kraft+, Moscow, 2002), pp. 54–60.

41. The Ravenna anonymous author (between the seventh and eighth centuries) mentions the country Onoghoria to the north from the Maeotis—the Sea of Azov (A. Podosinov, *Vostochnaja Evropa v Rimskoj Kartograficheskoj Traditsii* [Indrik, Moscow, 2002], pp. 192, 251–252).

42. V. Shusharin thought that the first contacts between the Bulgars-Onoghurs and the Magyars-Ugrians took place there, and since then the Magyars had called the Bulgars "the Nandor," while the Slavs had named the Magyars after their country, Onoghoria, and from this term an *ethnicon,* the Ugrians, developed in Proto-Slavic language (cf. *6, 26*).

43. Cf. A. Novosel'tsev, in A. P. Novosel'tsev et al., *Drevnerusskoje Gocudarstvo i Jego Mezhdunarodnoje Znachenije* (Nauka, Moscow, 1965), p. 397.

44. J. Marquart, *Osteuropäische und Ostasiatische Streifzüge* (Dieterich'sche Verlagsbuchhandlung, T. Weicher, Leipzig, 1903), pp. 33–35.

45. G. Litavrin, *Vyzantija, Bolgaria, Drevnjaja Rus'* (Aleteja, St. Petersburg, 2000), pp. 50–52.

46. Concerning eschatological expectations and identification of the Hungarians with Gog and Magog, see M. Bloch, *La Société Féodale* (Editions Albin Michel, Paris, 1986), p. 62.

47. E. Czücs, *Hungaro-Rossica* 9, 233 (2002).

48. L. Chekin, in V. Pashuto, ed., *Vostochnaja Evropa v Drevnosty i Srednevekobje* (Institut Rossiijskoij Istorii, Moscow, 1998), pp. 125–128.

49. E. Helimsky, *Comparativistica, Uralistica* (Jazyki Slavjanskoj Kul'tury, Moscow, 2000), p. 433.

50. A. V. Kuznetsova, in B. Florja, ed., *Christianstvo v Stranah Vostochnoj, Jugo-Vostochnoj i Central'noj Evropy* (Moscow, Jazyki Slavjanskoj Kul'tury, 2002), pp. 340–343.

51. L. Benkő, in S. Csernus, K. Korompay, eds., *Les Hongroise et l'Europe: Conqête et Intégration* (Institut Hongrois de Paris, Paris, 1997) pp. 121–136.

52. D. Likhachov, M. Serdov, eds., *Povest' Vremennykh Let (PVL)* (Nauk, Moscow, Akademi, 1950), p. 16.

53. V. Petrukhin, *Nachalo Etnokul'turnoj Istorii Rusi IX–XI Vekov* (Rusich, Smolensk, 1995), p. 80.

54. S. Franklin and J. Shepard noted a special role of the Hungarians in the emergence of Rus: the Ugorskoje (Hungarian) site near Kiev, mentioned in *PVL*, is interpreted as "the place where Hungarians in the khagan employ were encamped for a while" (S. Franklin, J. Shepard, *The Emergence of Rus* [Longman, London, 1996], p. 96).

55. A. Róna-Tas, *Hungarians and Europe in Early Middle Age* (CEU Press, Budapest, 1999), p. 331.

56. PVL, pp. 14–15.

57. Concerning chronology and geopolitical context of the conflict, see J. Howard-Johnston, *Materialy po Archeologii, Istorii i Etnographii Tavrii (MAIET)* 7, 342–356 (2000).

58. Chronology and localization of the military actions are under discussion in extensive literature. A. Turilov has recently found the mention of fortress M'dra Dr'storskaja in the Slavic "Story of inok Christodul": it is possible to conform the data of Constantine Porphyrogenitus that Bulgarian tsar Semion, defeated by the Hungarians, took cover in the fortress of Mundraga (slav. *M'dra*), to the data of Simeon Logothete, that the tsar found cover in Dorostol (cf. *M'dra Dr'storskaja*) (A. Turilov, in B. Florja, G. Litavrin, eds., *Slavjane i ich Sosedi*, [Nauka, Moscow, 2001], pp. 47–52). The certain parallels of the events of the first conflict between Byzantium, the Bulgarians, and Hungarians (in the 830s) and the events of the war of the 980s should be marked: particularly, the fate of the Byzantine prisoners should be decided.

59. Cf. P. Ratkoš, in *Velikaja Moravia: Je Istoricheskoje i Kul'turnoje Znachenije* (Moscow, Nauka, 1985), pp. 93–94.

60. R. Marsina, in A. Avenarius, G. Litavrin, eds., *Rannefeodal'nyje Gosudarstva i Narodnosti* (Nauka, Moscow, 1991), pp. 109–110.

61. G. G. Litvarin, A. P. Novosel'tsev, eds., *Constantine Porphyrogenitus: Ob upravlenii imperiej,* chaps. 40, 41, and comments. The Russian chronicler was also interested in these events (after his source—Continuation of the Byzantine George the Monk's Chronicle), though he told about them under the year 902 (*PVL*, p. 16), when the Hungarians had occupied their homeland.

62. W. Duczko, in M. Dulinicz, ed., *Słowianie i ich Sąsiedzi we Wczesnym Średniowieczu* (Wydawnictwo Universytetu Marii Curie, Lublin, 2003), pp. 127–132.

63. V. Petrukhin, in V. Murasheva, ed., *Archeologicheskij Sbornik: Gnëzdovo: 125-let Issledovanija Pamjatnika* (Gosudarstvennij Istoricheskij Muzej, Moscow, 2001), pp. 116–120.

64. *PVL*, p. 21.

65. B. Najmushin, in T. Stepanov, ed., *B'lgary i Khazary Prez Rannoto Srednevekovije* (Tangara, Sofia, 2003), p. 142.

66. I. Dienes, *The Hungarians Cross the Carpathians* (Corvina, Budapest, 1972), pp. 10–11.

67. A. Róna-Tas, *Hungarians and Europe in the Early Middle Ages* (CEU Press, Budapest, 1999), pp. 381–382.

68. It is significant that according to the eastern sources the Hungarians mobilized 20,000 horsemen for the invasion of their homeland: it was a typical nomadic tradition of mobilizing the attacking forces (two *tumens;* cf. 39).

69. I. Zimonyi, in *Hungaro-Rossica II* (Institut Vostokovedenija Akedemija Nauk Rosija, Moscow, 2005), pp. 32–51.

10

Migrations to the Americas

Merritt Ruhlen

The origins of the indigenous peoples of the New World have been of interest, and a topic of controversy, for centuries, and as early as 1789 Thomas Jefferson suggested that language could play a crucial role in the debate: "I endeavor to collect all the vocabularies I can, of American Indians, as of those of Asia, persuaded, that if they ever had a common parentage, it will appear in their languages." Clearly Jefferson's putative Asian homeland for Native Americans was based on the striking morphological similarities between Asians and American Indians. This chapter demonstrates that in the past two decades Jefferson's goal has finally been realized. In 1956, in a lecture at an international congress in Philadelphia, Joseph Greenberg announced that in his view the indigenous languages of the Americas belonged to just three families—Eskimo-Aleut, Na-Dene, and Amerind—but the evidence for this tripartite classification was not published until 1987 (1). The geographical distribution of these three families is shown in Figure 10.1.

Even if Greenberg's classification is correct—and there is certainly no shortage of critics—it would not necessarily mean that each family constituted a separate migration to the Americas: a single migration could have split into three families after reaching the New World. On the other hand, if each of these three families does represent a separate migration, it would be necessary to demonstrate that each is more closely related to a distinct set of Old World languages than they are to each other. As we shall see, this does appear to be the case.

In the mid-1980s Greenberg, Christy Turner, and Stephen Zegura presented evidence—linguistic, dental, and genetic—that New World populations fell into the three groups that Greenberg had identified thirty years earlier, and they suggested that each was indeed the result of a separate migration from Asia (2). I will summarize the linguistic evidence for these three migrations in reverse chronological order.

Eskimo-Aleut and Eurasiatic

The genetic affinity of Eskimo and Aleut was formulated by Rasmus Rask in 1819, and its validity as a linguistic family has not been questioned since. It was also Rask who first identified an Asian relative of Eskimo-Aleut, the Uralic family, when he noticed that both families shared a dual suffix -k and a plural suffix -t. During the nineteenth century the Uralic family was connected by different linguists with both the Altaic (Turkic, Mongolian, Tungus) and Indo-European families, indicating that Eskimo-Aleut was most closely related to a set of language families in Eurasia that in the twentieth century came to be called Nostratic or Eurasiatic. For Greenberg the Eurasiatic family included Indo-European, Uralic, Yukaghir, Altaic, Korean, Japanese, Ainu, Gilyak, Chukchi-Kamchatkan, and Eskimo-Aleut, as shown in Figure 10.2.

Greenberg provided abundant evidence connecting Eskimo-Aleut with these other Eurasian families in his final two volumes (3, 4), and Michael Fortescue has presented substantial additional evidence connecting Eskimo-Aleut with

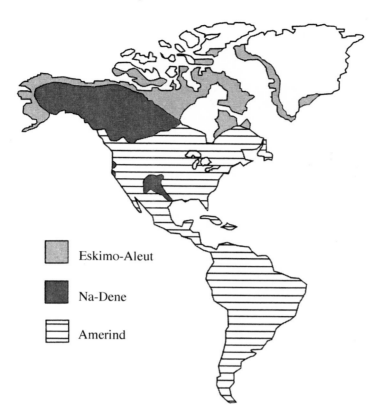

FIGURE 10.1. Language families in the Americas.

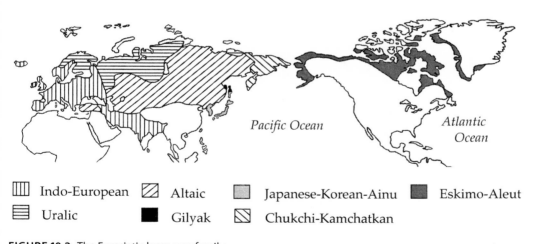

FIGURE 10.2. The Eurasiatic language family.

Uralic, Yukaghir, and Chukchi-Kamchatkan, though he did not consider the other branches of Eurasiatic (5). In addition to the dual -*k* and plural -*t* suffixes first noted by Rask, the Eurasiatic family is also defined by a first-person pronoun based on *m*- and a second-person pronoun based on *t*-, a pattern that had been noted by numerous scholars in the early twentieth century (6) and which is widely attested throughout northern Eurasia but extremely rare elsewhere in the

TABLE 10.1. Eurasiatic Cognates

	I, me, my	Thou, thy	Who?	What?	Two, dual	Plural	Fish, whale	Feather, hair
Indo-European	*mē-	*tu	*kʷi-	*ma			*kʷal-	
Uralic-Yukaghir	*-m	*te	*ke	*mi	*-k	*-t	*kala	*tulka
Turkic	men		*kim	*mi-	iki	-t		tülüg
Mongolian	mini	*ti	ken	*ma	ikire	*-t	kalimu	
Tungus	mini	-ti	*xa-	*ma		-te	*kali	
Korean	-ma		-ka	mai			kolai	th^l^k
(Old) Japanese				mī			kudira	
Ainu				mak	ki	-ti		trax
Gilyak		ti	-ka		-gi	-t	q'ol	
Chukchi-Kamchatkan	-m	-t	k'e	mi-	-k	-ti	klxin	ičelčlx
Eskimo-Aleut	-ma	-t	*kina	*mi	-k	-t	*iqałuy	tˢuluk

Note: Forms preceded by * are reconstructions. Chukchi-Kamchatkan *ičelčlx* is a phonetically eroded form of an original reduplication of something like Eskimo *tˢuluktˢuluk*.

world (7, 8). First- and second-person pronouns are among the most stable elements in human languages and often go much further back in time than other grammatical and lexical elements. Table 10.1 gives a small sample from the numerous grammatical and lexical parallels that connect Eskimo-Aleut with the other branches of the Eurasiatic family. The totality of this evidence leaves little doubt that Eskimo-Aleut represents a separate migration to the New World as the easternmost extension of the Eurasiatic family. It should be noted that Eskimo-Aleut has almost never been compared with other American families; virtually all proposed comparisons have been with Eurasian languages.

Linguists have estimated the age of Eskimo-Aleut at 4,000 BP. It would appear that the homeland of the Eskimo-Aleut family was in southwestern Alaska, where the two branches of the family meet. From this homeland the Aleut expanded westward through the Aleutian Islands, while the Eskimo expanded first northward to the Arctic Ocean and then eastward as far as Greenland.

Na-Dene and Dene-Caucasian

The Na-Dene family, which was identified by Edward Sapir in 1915, consists of four branches—Haida, Tlingit, Eyak, and Athabaskan—the first three of which are single languages spoken along the west coast of Alaska and Canada. Athabaskan, however, is a widespread, but homogeneous, family that occupies much of Alaska and western Canada, with outliers on the Pacific coast of Oregon and northern California and in the American Southwest (Navajo and Apache), as shown in Figure 10.3. Haida is the most divergent language, followed by Tlingit, whereas Eyak is closely related to Athabaskan, though not a member.

In the late twentieth century several scholars claimed that Haida was not in fact a member of Na-Dene, but was rather a language isolate with no known relatives (9, 10). However, Heinz-Jürgen Pinnow resolutely defended the inclusion of Haida in Na-Dene (11), as did Greenberg (1) and I (12). John Enrico, the world's expert on Haida, recently reconsidered the position of Haida and concluded that it is indeed a member of Na-Dene, exactly as Sapir had determined, and he supplied additional

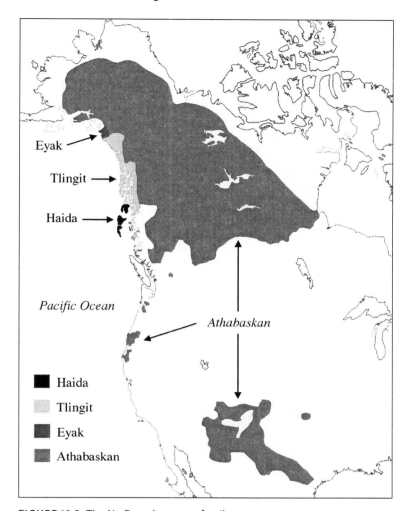

FIGURE 10.3. The Na-Dene language family.

evidence to support what had already been adduced by Sapir, Pinnow, and others (*13*).

Not only did Sapir discover the Na-Dene family, he was also the first to identify an Asian relative of Na-Dene—the Tibetan language, and implicitly the entire Sino-Tibetan family—thus identifying a second migration from Asia to the Americas. Sapir, however, never published any evidence for this putative Sino-Dene family, nor did he ever mention the hypothesis in print. The reason for this was no doubt that he had been severely criticized by Truman Michelson, the leading Algonquinist of the day, when he published an article connecting Algonquian with Wiyot and Yurok, two languages on the northern California coast, in a family called Algic. (Today Algic is

universally accepted.) Soon after Michelson's criticism of Algic, Sapir was attacked by Pliny Goddard for his Na-Dene proposal. Clearly Sapir saw that the time was not right for more exploratory taxonomic proposals, and he essentially ceased all such work around 1920. We know about Sapir's Sino-Dene hypothesis from letters he wrote to Alfred Kroeber (*14*), and from his unpublished "Comparative Sino-Tibetan and Na-Dene Dictionary," available from the American Philosophical Society. John Bengtson has examined this dictionary and published an article based on it that gives a number of Sapir's comparisons in support of the Sino-Dene hypothesis, as well as later comparisons by others (*15*).

Sapir was the leading Americanist of the first

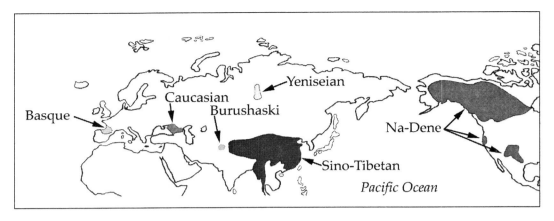

FIGURE 10.4. The six branches of the Dene-Caucasian language family.

TABLE 10.2. Dene-Caucasian Cognates

Family	Who?	What?	Dry	Sun, day(light)	Bone	Hungry	Name
Basque	no-r	se-r	agor	egun	-khoč	gose	isen
Caucasian	*na	*sa	*-ɢ^wVr-	*-ɢinV	*kŏc'a	*gaši	
Burushaski	ana	be-s¿-n	qaqər	goon			sen-as
Sino-Tibetan	*naai	*su	*qař	*kwaaŋ	*kūt	khusśĭ	*seŋ
Yeniseian	*ʔan-	*sV-	*qVr	*gəʔn			
Na-Dene		sa	*-ɢaŋ	kuuŋ	s-kut^s	*gas	sen

half of the twentieth century, and it was his classification of North American Indian languages, first published in the *Encyclopaedia Britannica* in 1929, that became the standard, so he clearly knew North American languages very well. Against this background he felt that Na-Dene stood out from the rest: "Nadene...is really quite alone in America.... The contrast between it and Eskimo, Wakashan, and Algonkin is tremendous." In 1920 he described Na-Dene as "a 'tremendous intrusive wedge,' driven from Asia into the older distribution of languages in North America." That same year he wrote to Kroeber: "Do not think me an ass if I am seriously entertaining the idea of an old Indo-Chinese offshoot into N. W. America."

During the twentieth century Sapir's putative Sino-Dene family was extended in various directions. First, Alfredo Trombetti argued in 1923 for a family consisting of Sino-Tibetan, Caucasian, and Basque (*16*). In 1982 Sergei Starostin proposed a Sino-Caucasian family that included Sino-Tibetan, Caucasian, and Yeniseian (*17*), and two years later Starostin's colleague, Sergei Nikolaev, offered evidence connecting Caucasian and Na-Dene (*18*). Finally, in the 1990s, Burushaski was added to the family by Bengtson (*19*). This enlarged version of Sapir's Sino-Dene family is today called Dene-Caucasian. The distribution of its six branches is shown in Figure 10.4.

A sample of proposed Dene-Caucasian cognates, taken from the literature cited above, is given in Table 10.2.

In 1998 I compared Yeniseian with Na-Dene—a comparison that had not previously been made by anyone—and found substantial additional evidence for the Dene-Caucasian family, as one would expect (*20*). In fact, some of this additional evidence is shared exclusively by Na-Dene and

TABLE 10.3. Yeniseian–Na-Dene Cognates

	Yeniseian	Na-Dene
Birch bark	qiʔy	*qʔəy
Stone, rock	tiʔś	tʔiːs (H)
Bow, arrow	qiʔt	*qʔaːʔ
Squirrel	*saʔqa	-tsʔaːkw (H)
Trough, dish	śiʔk	sʔixʔ (T)
River, ocean	*ses	siːskw (H)
Boat	*qä(ʔ)p	*-qeː-
Foot	*kiʔś	*-keːʔ
Head	*tsīʔG-	*-tsiʔ
Elbow, knee	*gid	*-god
Skin	*säːs	*-sətsʔ
Nit, louse	*yok	*yaʔ
Child	*gəʔt	gyiːtʔ (H)
Hunger, hungry	qəːt	qʔut (H)
Snow on ground	*tiːχ	tʔiːχʔ (T)
Falling snow	*beʔč	wehs (E)

Note: In the Yeniseian column, Proto-Yeniseian reconstructions are preceded by an asterisk; forms without an asterisk are taken from Ket. In the Na-Dene column, forms preceded by an asterisk are Proto-Athabaskan reconstructions; forms without an asterisk are taken from Haida (H), Tlingit (T), or Eyak (E).

Yeniseian, suggesting that Yeniseian may have been the branch of Dene-Caucasian from which Na-Dene emerged, though this is by means certain. Table 10.3 gives some of these Yeniseian–Na-Dene comparisons.

The resemblance between the Yeniseian and Na-Dene words for "birch bark" is particularly striking in that the words are virtually identical in sound and meaning, and yet "birch bark" is hardly part of the basic vocabulary, such as pronouns and body parts, which are often maintained for long periods of time. The reason this word has been retained for so long is that birch bark played a central role in the daily life of the Yeniseian people. Nearly all household items, including dishes and even the teepee, were made of birch bark, as well as the birch-bark boat. In addition, birch bark's impermeability to water means

it is effectively always dry, a very useful quality in a cold and wet environment.

There is, however, an interesting difference between Yeniseian *qiʔy* and Na-Dene *qʔəy*. The Na-Dene word begins with a glottalized consonant, *qʔ*, but in Yeniseian this glottalized consonant has broken up into its two components, and the second part has switched positions with the following vowel, *qiʔ*. This process, known as metathesis in linguistics, explains how Old English *waps* became modern English *wasp*. Usually metathesis affects single words, such as wasp, but as the words for "birch bark," "stone," "bow/arrow," "trough/dish," and "squirrel" in Table 10.3 show, in this case glottalized consonants in Na-Dene, *CʔV*, regularly correspond in Yeniseian to *CVʔ*, where *C* represents any consonant and *V*, any vowel. There is thus a regular sound correspondence

117

between Na-Dene and Yeniseian, and most linguists consider such correspondences the ultimate proof of genetic affinity. Whether Na-Dene and Yeniseian form a single taxon by themselves, and thus reveal the immediate origin of the Na-Dene, is not certain, but that Na-Dene is related to a different set of Eurasian languages than Eskimo-Aleut seems clear.

The homeland of the Na-Dene family is not known, but I would suggest that it may well have been on the Queen Charlotte Islands, where Haida, its most divergent language, is spoken. From here, part of the Haida population, at an unknown point in time, moved to the mainland and became the Tlingit. The time of separation between the Haida and the Tlingit must have been quite long, as the marked differences between these two languages attest, before the Tlingit expanded north along the coast, eventually giving rise to the Eyak and Athabaskan in southern Alaska. It was here that a major transition—the Athabaskan expansion—took place, when a coastal maritime people left their boats behind and colonized most of Alaska and western Canada. Some Athabaskans did, in fact, continue down the coast in boats, as the groups in Oregon and northern California attest. At a much later date, around 800 years ago, Athabaskans from western Canada moved to the American Southwest and became the Navajo and Apache.

The fact that Yeniseian and Na-Dene appear to share the same words for "river, ocean" and "boat" (Table 10.3) supports a maritime origin of the family, as would the Athabaskan groups on the coast of Oregon and California. The age of the Na-Dene family has been variously estimated at 7,000–9,000 BP, and the earliest archaeological evidence of human presence on the Queen Charlotte Islands is 7,000 BP, but could have been earlier.

Amerind

Greenberg's classification of New World languages into just three families provoked a firestorm of controversy that still rages today. This controversy did not involve Eskimo-Aleut or Na-Dene, both of which had long been accepted, as we have seen. The controversy focused solely on Greenberg's contention that all the other indigenous languages of the Americas belonged to a single family, Amerind. This proposal could hardly have contrasted more with the Americanist consensus that there were close to 200 independent families in the Americas, among which there was no evidence of any genetic connections (10, 21). The reason there were no connections among all of these families is quite simple. Languages change so rapidly that after 6,000 years all traces of earlier relationships would have been erased by the shifting sands of time, and it was clear that the first appearance of humans in the New World went back at least 13,500 years, and some would claim even earlier.

This temporal limit of the comparative method had become the mantra of twentieth-century historical linguists, even though there is no trace of it in the nineteenth century, and it is clearly false. I will give just two examples. In the reconstruction of Proto-Indo-European, which existed at least 6,000 years ago, the reconstructed word for "nephew" is *nepo:t. In modern Rumanian the word for "nephew" is nepot; in 6,000 years the only change has been that the long o: in Proto-Indo-European has become a short o in Rumanian, which lacks long vowels. Austronesian is a family of almost 1,000 languages spoken on islands from Madagascar to Easter Island. Proto-Austronesian is thought to have been spoken on Taiwan some 6,000 years ago. Following is a list of Proto-Austronesian reconstructions followed by the modern forms in the Rukai language, also spoken on Taiwan: *dusa "two" > dosa, *sepat "four" > sepate, *'enem "six" > eneme, *maca "eye" > maca, *calinga "ear" > calinga, *awang "canoe" > avange, *kucuh "head louse" > koco (22). As is obvious, the impression is not that everything has changed beyond recognition, but rather that almost nothing has changed at all. So much for the mythical 6,000 year limit on comparative linguistics.

The Amerind family was first discerned by Trombetti in 1905 in his book arguing for the monogenesis of all the world's languages. In this book he devoted an entire appendix to "The pronouns I and you in the principal American languages," in which he pointed out a specific American pronominal pattern, ni "I" and mi "you": "As can be seen, from the most northern regions of the Americas the pronouns NI 'I and MI 'thou' reach all the way to the southern tip of the New

World, to Tierra del Fuego. Although this sketch is far from complete, due to the insufficient materials at our disposal, it is certainly sufficient to give an idea of the broad distribution of these most ancient and essential elements" (6).

A decade later Sapir noticed the same pronominal pattern in the Americas, though there is no indication he was aware of Trombetti's appendix: "Getting down to brass tacks, how in the Hell are you going to explain general American *n*- 'I' except genetically? It's disturbing, I know, but (more) non-committal conservatism is only dodging, after all, isn't it? Great simplifications are in store for us" (23). This specifically American pronoun pattern was also emphasized in the work of Morris Swadesh, Sapir's student, as well as by Greenberg. In a survey of pronoun systems in the world's language families I showed that the *n/m* pattern is indeed essentially an American phenomenon; in fact, it is an Amerind phenomenon since this pattern is not found in either Eskimo-Aleut or Na-Dene (7).

How, then, did Greenberg's critics explain the presence of the *n/m* pronoun pattern throughout Amerind languages on two continents and virtually nowhere else in the world? According to Lyle Campbell, it simply wasn't true: "The *n/m* ['I/you'] pattern is not nearly as common in the Americas as Greenberg claimed...[and] his supposed *m/t* ['I/you'] pattern for his Eurasiatic languages is also found abundantly in the Americas (despite his and Ruhlen's assertions to the contrary)" (24). Elsewhere he claimed that "several Amerind groups exhibit pronoun forms (*m/t* ['I/you']) that Greenberg attributes to Europe and Northern Asia" and "the *n* 'first person'/*m* 'second person' is by no means unique to, diagnostic of, or ubiquitous in American Indian languages" (25). Johanna Nichols expressed similar views in 1992 (26). And then, in 1997, Campbell and Nichols had a debate in *Language* over which of them was the first to have noticed that the *n/m* pronominal pattern was found almost exclusively in the Amerind languages of North and South America, exactly as Trombetti had shown almost a century earlier, though Trombetti was not mentioned (27, 28).

But Nichols still denied that this pronoun pattern could have a genetic explanation since it must go back well beyond the 6,000-year limit of comparative linguistics, and therefore these two pronouns could not be genetic traits. Their distribution in the Americas must be explained, according to Nichols, by a mysterious unknown force, not simple evolution from a common original source. I will leave it to the historians of science to sort this all out. In any event, a world atlas of language structures, published in 2005, contained maps of the distribution of the Eurasiatic *m/t* pronoun pattern and the Amerind *n/m* pattern (8). Both maps confirm exactly what Trombetti had claimed in 1905.

A lexical item in Greenberg's book also provides evidence for the validity of Amerind that is even greater than the *n/m* pronoun pattern, though this was not apparent from the forms that Greenberg cited for this Amerind root. This root has the form *tVna* (where *V* indicates a vowel whose exact quality is unclear). The general meaning he gave was "girl," but other meanings included "child, son" and "daughter." Greenberg cited 16 variants of this root from 16 different languages, all in North America. When I later investigated this root, I found that it was vastly more widespread than Greenberg had realized; it is as widespread in South America as it is in North America (29). Greenberg apparently never looked for this root in his South American notebooks because otherwise he would surely have noticed it. In investigating this root, I first went through all 23 of Greenberg's Amerind notebooks, and then I consulted the literature in the Stanford library on Native American languages, thereby increasing the number of putative cognates from 16 to somewhere between 800 and 900, coming from all 13 branches of Amerind.

Furthermore, an analysis of all of these forms showed why the vowel in this root could seemingly be anything. The vowel, it turns out, is correlated with the gender of the child, at least at the beginning in Proto-Amerind, according to the pattern *i/u/a* "masculine/feminine/neutral." Greenberg had in fact noted the gender pattern *i/u* "masculine/feminine" in two South American branches of Amerind, but he had overlooked the third grade of this pattern, *a* "neutral," and he did not notice that this pattern was also found in North America. This specifically Amerind gender pattern—which I have not found elsewhere in the world—intersected with the *tVna* root to

TABLE 10.4. Variants of Three Proto-Amerind Roots

Proto-Amerind roots	*T'ANA "child, sibling"	*T'INA "son, brother"	*T'UNA "daughter, sister"
Almosan	t'an'a "child" (Nootka)	tˢin "young man" (Yurok)	tune "niece" (Coeur d'Alene)
Keresiouan	tane "brother" (Yuchi)	-ʔtsin "male, boy" (Mohawk)	tˢone "daughter, son" (Yuchi)
Penutian	t'ána-t "grandchild" (Totonac)	pnē-t'in "my elder brother"	tūne- "daughter" (Cent. Sierra Miwo)
Hokan	t'an-pam "child" (Coahuilteco)	t'inī-si "child, son, daughter" (Yana)	a-t'on "younger sister" (Salinan)
Central Amerind	*tana "daughter, son" (Uto-Aztecan)	ʔdíínó "brother" (Cuicatec)	-t'ŭt'ina "older sister" (Taos)
Chibchan	tuk-tan "child, boy" (Miskito)	sin "brother" (Changuena)	tuntu-rusko "younger sister" (Lenca)
Paezan	dani- "mother's sister" (Warrau)	tzhœng "son" (Millcayac)	tˢuh-ki "sister" (Cayapa)
Andean	tayna "first-born child" (Aymara)	den "brother" (Tehuelche)	thaun "sister" (Tehuelche)
Macro-Tucanoan	tani-mai "younger sister" (Masaca)	ten "son" (Tiquie)	ton "daughter" (Tiquie)
Equatorial	taʔin "child" (Urubu-Kaapor)	tin-gwa "son, boy" (Mocochi)	a-tune-sas "girl" (Morotoko)
Macro-Carib	tane "my son" (Pavishana)	dēnu "male child" (Yagua)	-tona "sister" (Nonuya)
Macro-Panoan	tawin "grandchild" (Lengua)	u-tse-kwa "grandchild" (Tacana)	-tóna "younger sister" (Tacana)
Macro-Ge	tog-tan "girl" (Tibagi)	čina "older brother" (Guato)	a-ton-kä "younger sister" (Piokobyé)

form a morphologically complex root that is the basis of much of the Amerind kinship terminology: Proto-Amerind *t'ina "son, brother," *t'una "daughter, sister," *t'ana "child, sibling." (The * indicates a hypothetical earlier form, while the apostrophe following the t indicates that the t was originally a glottalized consonant, as it still is in some languages.) Examples of this root are given in Table 10.4. For Greenberg's critics almost all these forms come from languages for which there is supposedly no evidence of genetic affinity.

No modern Amerind language preserves all three grades of this root intact, but some do retain two (e.g., Tiquie ten "son," ton "daughter";

Iranshe atina "male relative," atuna "female relative"), and many more retain only one. As is well known, gender systems often spread to numerals (cf. Russian odin "one masc.," odna "one fem.," odno "one neut."). The Amerind gender pattern has also spread to numerals, where the entire pattern is found in the South American language Tucano: nik-e "one masc.," nik-o "one fem.," nik-a "one neut.," which are reflexes of the Proto-Amerind word for "one" (30).

During the 13,000 years that the Amerind languages have been evolving, there have of course been both semantic and phonetic changes that have altered the original forms along predictable typological paths. With regard to semantic evolution, a common typological development is for the neutral form *t'ana* to become specialized as either masculine (e.g., Yuchi *tane* "brother") or feminine (e.g., Proto-Algonquian **ta:na* "daughter"). Sapir recognized this semantic development in Algonquian in 1923: "Proto-Algonquian **-tan-* must be presumed to have originally meant 'child' . . . and to have become specialized in its significance either to 'son' (Wiyot) or 'daughter' (Algonkin proper), while in Yurok its close relative *-ta-t⁵* ["child"] preserved a more primary genetic significance" (31). A common phonetic shift is for the masculine form *tin* to become *t⁵in* (e.g., Yurok *t⁵in* "young man"), with such changed forms further evolving in many cases to *sin* (e.g., Changuena *sin* "brother"). The reason for this common typological path is that the vowel *i* often causes this development, while the vowels *u* and *a* do not.

In addition, this morphologically complex root often occurs with specifically Amerind prefixes, such as the first-person pronoun (e.g., Proto-Algonquian **ne-ta:na* "my daughter"), or with Amerind suffixes such as **-kwa* "-in-law" (e.g., Proto-Algonquian **ne-ta:n-kwa* "my sister-in-law" and Iowa *ta-gwa* "son-in-law").

In sum, this complex root—with three variants determined by gender—is found on two continents in the same set of languages that have the *n/m* pronoun pattern. Both are exclusively shared innovations of the Amerind family, not found elsewhere in the world. The reason is quite simple. Both are founder effects deriving from the language of the first people who reached North America some 13,000 years ago. If we could find a dictionary of the Proto-Amerind language they spoke, I believe it would be relatively easy to find all of the following words in that dictionary, given their broad distribution in the Amerind languages of North and South America, as reflected in the current version of Greenberg's *Amerind Etymological Dictionary* (32): *ama* "earth," *aqʷa* "water," *iye* "wood," *ki ~ ka* "we two inclusive," *-ki ~ -ka* "reciprocal," *koko* "uncle," *k'apa* "cover, close," *k'api* "hand," *k'at⁵i* "fish," *k'uti* "small," *k'ʷači* "sew," *maliq'a* "swallow," *man/mak/mar* "hand, give, measure," *men* "wish," *mi* "you," *mikʷ* "person," *mo* "that," *mumu* "bee," *na* "I," *nana* "mother," *nekwe* "one," *new* "see," *nik* "talk,

tongue," *nuk'* "throat," *pale* "two," *patˡ* "broad, flat, wide," *pit⁵i* "skin," *po* "brother," *poq'u* "bow, arrow," *pos* "swell," *q'uča* "elbow," *qʷet⁵'* "left hand," *qʷal* "roast, cook," *sem* "one," *sokol* "hawk, eagle," *tala* "shoulder," *tik* "finger, one," *tuku* "owl," *tump* "fill (up)," *tup* "spit, saliva," *t'an* "cut," *t'ina/t'ana/t'una* "son, child, daughter," *t'umak* "get dark," *t⁵a* "bone," *t⁵aq* "go out," *t⁵ak* "rope," *t⁵'ik* "bird," *t⁵'ik'ʷa* "wash," *t⁵'iχ* "scratch," *t⁵uqʷ* "suck," *ču* "sit," *uqʷa* "drink," *uwi* "snake," *wa* "go," *win* "wife," *wok* "bark (dog)," *ya* "go," *ya* "that," *yaq* "speak," *ʔa-* "elder," *ʔako* "spider," *ʔaw* "fox," *ʔi* "he/she," *ʔo* "rock." Of course, no such dictionary exists, since writing would not be invented for another 8,000 years.

How can it be that a unique pronoun pattern is found throughout the Amerind family, as well as the complex *t'ina/t'ana/t'una* root, and yet Americanists maintain that there is no evidence of genetic affinity among any of the almost 200 language families in the Americas? There are four possible explanations for these patterns: (1) common origin, (2) borrowing, (3) accidental resemblance, and (4) sound symbolism. Only common origin can explain these two patterns. First- and second-person pronouns are almost never borrowed, and words in general could not have been borrowed over entire continents—much less two—until very recently. The Amerind *n/m* pronoun pattern can hardly be due to accidental resemblance, which should happen randomly around the world. If they are all found essentially in North and South America, they cannot be accidents. And that the distribution of the accidental *t'ina/t'ana/t'una* forms coincides with the distribution of the accidental *n/m* pronouns would truly be a remarkable coincidence.

What is behind the current vitriolic debate over Amerind, a taxon Greenberg and I consider among the most obvious in the world? The answer, I believe, is a complete misunderstanding during the twentieth century of what the comparative method really is. In linguistics, as worked out in the nineteenth century, the comparative method consists of two stages, taxonomy and historical linguistics. Taxonomy, or classification, identifies language families by comparing basic vocabulary, which is exactly how Jones identified Indo-European in 1786. Historical linguistics investigates families that have thus been identified and attempts to (1) identify the sound correspondences connecting the family's languages, (2) reconstruct the words in the original proto-language, (3) locate the homeland of the family, (4) identify the time that the proto-language existed, and so on. It should be obvious that the second stage must follow the first; after all, it is impossible to investigate a language family until one has been found. Historically, too, the first stage had to precede the second. Jones identified the Indo-European family in 1786 by pointing out that the similarities in the verbal paradigms of five languages could only be explained by assuming that all five paradigms must "have sprung from some common source, which, perhaps, no longer exists." The second stage in the comparative method did not begin seriously until the 1870s, when the regularity of sound change was fully recognized by the Neogrammarians, and its import for reconstruction was fully appreciated.

Greenberg made a strategic error in calling taxonomy first "mass comparison" and later "multilateral comparison," when what he was really doing was just taxonomy. Partially because of this error, the Indo-Europeanists came to believe that Greenberg had created a new approach to historical linguistics that was a substitute for historical reconstruction, when in fact he did nothing of the sort. As Greenberg opined more than once, "[W]hen I do historical linguistics I do it like anyone else." But what the twentieth-century Indo-Europeanists, and the Americanists who followed them, did not do was any taxonomy. Neither group made any taxonomic progress during the twentieth century; in fact, they actually regressed by breaking up valid families such as Altaic, which had been accepted since the nineteenth century.

The currently fashionable view is that Trombetti, Sapir, Greenberg, Illich-Svytich, and Dolgopolsky are renegades who have deviated from the splendid foundation laid out by the nineteenth-century Indo-Europeanists, while contemporary historical linguists are defending the faith. The reality is the exact opposite. Rather, it is Trombetti et al. who have followed religiously the nineteenth-century Indo-Europeanists, none of whom ever imagined that the reconstruction of Indo-European with regular sound correspondences had anything to do with "proving" Indo-

European, whose validity was doubted by no one. It was only in the twentieth century, and only in linguistics, that reconstruction came to be viewed as necessary to prove any taxon.

A final taxonomic point that seems not to be well understood by contemporary historical linguists is that more ancient nodes in a phylogenetic tree are not necessarily less clear than more recent ones. In fact, it is often just the opposite, as illustrated in Figure 10.5.

Let us assume that there is a population on Island A. At some point, part of that population moves to Island B. Later, part of that population moves to Island C, and finally part of that population moves to Island D. Let us further assume that there is no further contact between these populations. The correct phylogenetic tree would then be 10.5a, and many historical linguists believe that F_3 will be more obvious, and better supported, than F_2, and F_2 more obvious than F_1. Whether this is true or not depends on the amount of time between the separation of the populations. Let us assume that some people on Island A moved to B on Monday, then part of that population to C on Tuesday, and part of that population to D on Wednesday, and then 500 years pass. Under these circumstances the phylogenetic tree, based on linguistic evidence, would be as in 10.5b since there would not have been any time for innovations to develop that would distinguish F_2 and F_3. The language on each island would have been identical at the start, and each would have then gone its own way, in a process similar to genetic drift.

If, however, the time of the separations was 500 years, not one day, then both F_2 and F_3 would be well defined by innovations that had accumulated during the 500 years. In both scenarios, however, F_1 will be well defined by those words that have been preserved on Islands A, B, C, and D. Thus, whether the intermediate nodes can be identified or not depends on the rate of migration. With a rapid migration it is only the highest level node that will be clear, with the intermediate nodes often being unclear or even invisible. As we will see in the next section, archaeological evidence indicates that the initial peopling of the Americas was a very rapid migration that filled two empty continents with people in 1,000 years. Under these circumstances, it is the highest-level node—Proto-Amerind—that will be the most

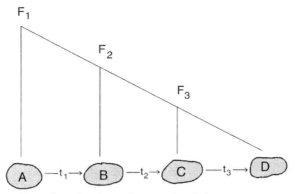

5a. when the time of separation is large

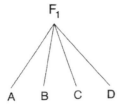

5b. when the time of separation is small

FIGURE 10.5. Time of separation and phylogenetic structure. Whether the correct phylogenetic tree can be ascertained on the basis of the linguistic evidence depends on the speed of the migration. If the speed of migration is slow, there will be time for innovations to develop, giving the correct tree (*a*). If, however, the speed of innovation is fast, there will be no time for innovations to develop, giving the incorrect tree (*b*).

obvious, as the *n/m* pronoun pattern and the *t'ina/ t'ana/t'una* root clearly show. Critics of Greenberg who claim that one cannot just jump to the top of a phylogentic tree without first working out every intermediate node obviously do not understand the fundamental principles of taxonomy.

Given its broad geographical distribution, covering most of North America and all of South America, and a degree of internal diversity far greater than that of either Eskimo-Aleut or Na-Dene, it seems obvious that Amerind represents the first migration to the New World by humans. If this is so, which were Amerind's closest relatives in the Old World? I have presented evidence that Amerind's closest relative in the Old World is the Eurasiatic family; Eskimo-Aleut is a member of Eurasiatic, whereas Amerind is a sister to Eurasiatic as a whole, with which it shares dozens of roots (33). Greenberg also considered Eurasiatic to be Amerind's closest relative, and the

two together to form a valid taxon (4). One piece of evidence given by Greenberg to connect these two families is a root *ma-* "hand," which appears in both families with the same three extensions: *-n*, *-k*, and *-r*. It appears that originally the extension modified the meaning according to the following pattern: *ma-n* "hand," *ma-k* "give," *ma-r* "measure of a hand, span," though the correlation between the extension and the meaning is imperfect. This is not surprising since English "hand" has all three meanings, showing the ease with which one meaning can change to another. The root *ma* itself is much more widespread than these two families, but the three extensions are only shared by Eurasiatic and Amerind.

If Amerind and Eurasiatic are more closely related to one another than to other families, there is one anomaly to be explained. As we have seen, both Amerind and Eurasiatic are defined by unique pronominal systems—Amerind *n/m* "I/

you" and Eurasiatic *m/t*—but at the same time the first- and second-person pronouns are the most stable items in language, being replaced very rarely. How then could *both* of these pronouns be replaced at essentially the same time? My hypothesis is that many of the world's languages have two kinds of "we"; "we inclusive" includes the person spoken to, while "we-exclusive" excludes the person spoken to (*34*). Eurasiatic, and even the larger Nostratic family, has this distinction, and "we-exclusive" is based on *n*, while "we-inclusive" is based on *m*. Amerind is known as being weak in the plural category. Furthermore, a well-known typological path for these two pronouns, if plurality is lost, is that "we-exclusive" can only become first-person singular "I," while "we-inclusive" (= you-me) can become either first-person "I" or second-person "you." If the plural category was lost in Proto-Amerind pronouns, "we-exclusive" *na* would have become "I" and "we-inclusive" *mi* would have become "you."

Archaeology

I have no intention of summarizing the archaeological and genetic evidence for the peopling of the New World, but I would like to make a few comments that bear on the linguistic evidence outlined in the preceding sections. First of all, linguistics is notoriously poor at providing dates for the origin of language families, as the current controversy over the age of Indo-European clearly shows. As mentioned above, linguists have estimated the age of Na-Dene as 7,000–9,000 BP and Eskimo-Aleut as 4,000 BP, but these are really just guesses. There is, of course, no estimate for Amerind since Americanists consider Amerind a conglomeration of 200 independent families, the origin of which is far beyond the supposed 6,000-year limit of comparative linguistics. However, if one accepts Amerind as a valid taxon—the evidence for which I have sketched above—then it is possible to date this family on the basis of archaeological evidence. In general, the archaeological record indicates that North and South America were both uninhabited by humans until around 13,500 BP, and yet there is abundant evidence of humans throughout North and South America a thousand years later. It was also 13,500 years ago that the ice-free corridor opened up between the two glaciers that had covered Canada for the

previous 10,000 years, preventing humans from walking from Alaska to the rest of the New World. Only a coastal route with boats would have been possible before 13,500 BP. What appears to have happened is that a small group of hunter-gatherers followed the game upon which they lived through the ice-free corridor, arriving at the end of the corridor in the area that is now the Canada–Montana border, which would almost by definition have been the Amerind homeland 13,500 years ago. It should be noted, however, that there is so far no archaeological evidence that people first entered the New World by this route.

This small population then split into many different groups that spread throughout North and South America in only a thousand years. At this same time some 35 genera of large mammals disappeared, almost certainly hunted to extinction by the first humans in the New World. There is also linguistic evidence for a rapid migration through North and South America—namely, the *t'ina/t'ana/t'una* root. Had the migration through North America been slow, this complex root would have broken up, and the original pattern would have been lost. The fact that this root is as well attested in South America as in North America indicates that this complex root made it to South America intact, and only later did the root start to break up into smaller parts, as it has in all extant Amerind languages. It has been suggested that the Amerind population derives from the Nenana Complex, which appeared in Alaska between 14,000 and 13,000 years ago, almost exactly when the ice-free corridor opened up. A different culture, the Denali Complex, appeared in Alaska a thousand years later, and this culture could be associated with the Na-Dene language family (*35*). Other archaeological evidence also supports a late, rather than early, entry into the Americas. It is now believed that dogs were first domesticated in east Asia around 15,000 years ago (*36*). Since the first Americans brought domesticated dogs with them, they could not have left Asia before 15,000 BP or they would have had no dogs. It thus appears that the first entry into North America took place not long after the domestication of dogs. For unknown reasons, all of these Asian dogs brought to America have gone extinct, replaced by European dogs that arrived much later.

Genetics

As mentioned earlier, Greenberg, Turner, and Zegura (2) argued more than twenty years ago that on the basis of linguistic, dental, and genetic evidence, New World populations fell into the same three groups: Eskimo-Aleut, Na-Dene, and Amerind. In 1988 Luca Cavalli-Sforza and colleagues also argued that, based on classical genetic markers, American populations fell into these three classes (37). However, subsequent work on mtDNA and the Y chromosome over the past two decades has not confirmed this early conclusion (38), and Zegura himself no longer subscribes to the tripartite classification, as he explains in this volume. For both mtDNA and the Y chromosome, different geneticists have supported one, two, and three migrations, but future work may well clarify the current impasse.

Although genetics has been able to provide estimated dates for certain events in human prehistory, Cavalli-Sforza's estimate of the time of the first migration to the Americas was 35,000–15,000 BP (39), which includes virtually all possible dates. Recently, however, Mark Seielstad et al. have found a mutation on the Y chromosome (M242) that lies between two mutations that are known to have occurred in Asia (M45, M74) and a mutation that arose in the Americas (M3) (40). They have dated the M242 mutation to the range 15,000–18,000 BP and have argued that this date provides a fairly certain upper bound on the time of the first entry into the Americas. This date corresponds well with the archaeological dates discussed above, supporting a first migration to the Americas at around the time that the ice-free corridor opened in Canada.

Conclusions

Linguistic evidence leaves little doubt that there were three pre-Columbian migrations from Asia to the New World. Combining this evidence with the evidence from archaeology and genetics suggests that the first migration took place around 13,500 BP, when the Bering land bridge was rapidly disappearing and an ice-free corridor was forming between the Laurentide and Cordilleran glaciers, opening a path from Alaska to Montana for the first time in 10,000 years. These Paleo-Indian people, with the Nenana culture, were almost certainly few in number, as are all hunter-gatherer societies. Their language, Proto-Amerind, would eventually give rise to almost all the languages of North and South America. Linguistic, archaeological, and genetic evidence all indicate a rapid dispersal of this population throughout North and South America in 1,000 years.

The second migration to the Americas brought the Na-Dene. If these people can be associated with the Denali culture, they arrived in Alaska 1,000 years after the Amerind people, around 12,500 BP. Though they arrived only one millennium later, their arrival had two important consequences. First, the Amerind people had already occupied the eastern part of Alaska where the ice-free corridor would soon open. Second, in only 1,000 years Beringia had disappeared, so the Na-Dene people would have had to have come to America by boat. If the Na-Dene and Denali culture represent the same people, then the Na-Dene homeland would have been in western Alaska. The linguistic evidence, however, tells a different, though not necessarily contradictory, story. As noted above, Na-Dene consists of two branches, Haida and all the rest, and Haida is in fact so different from all the rest that some linguists thought it was not even a member of Na-Dene at all. Since Haida, the most divergent Na-Dene language, is found (mostly) on the Queen Charlotte Islands, it seems likely that this was the Na-Dene homeland from a linguistic perspective. But the linguistic and archaeological scenarios are not necessarily contradictory. The Na-Dene could have arrived in Alaska before moving south, but there is no linguistic evidence for this.

The third, and final, migration brought the Eskimo-Aleut to the New World. The time has been estimated at 4,000 BP, and the homeland would have been in southwestern Alaska. From this homeland the Aleut expanded westward through the Aleutian Islands, while the Eskimo expanded northward to the Arctic Ocean and then eastward, eventually reaching Greenland.

Notes

1. J. Greenberg, *Language in the Americas* (Stanford Univ. Press, Stanford, 1987).

2. J. Greenberg, C. Turner, S. Zegura, *Curr. Anthropol.* 27, 477 (1986).

3. J. Greenberg, *Indo-European and Its Closest Relatives,* vol. 1 (Stanford Univ. Press, Stanford, 2000).

4. J. Greenberg, *Indo-European and Its Closest Relatives*, vol. 2 (Stanford Univ. Press, Stanford, 2002).

5. M. Fortescue, *Language Relations across the Bering Strait* (Cassell, London, 1998).

6. A. Trombetti, *L'Unità d'Origine del Linguaggio* (Beltrami, Bologna, 1905).

7. M. Ruhlen, *On the Origin of Languages* (Stanford Univ. Press, Stanford, 1994), pp. 252–260.

8. J. Nichols, D. Peterson, in M. Haspelmath et al., eds., *The World Atlas of Language Structures* (Oxford Univ. Press, Oxford, 2005), pp. 546–553.

9. R. Levine, *Int. J. Am. Linguist.* 45, 157 (1979).

10. L. Campbell, *American Indian Languages* (Oxford Univ. Press, Oxford, 1997).

11. H. Pinnow, *Die Na-Dene-Sprachen im Lichte der Greenberg-Klassifikation* (Völkerkundlichen Arbeitsgemeinschaft, Nortorf, 1990).

12. M. Ruhlen, *On the Origin of Languages* (Stanford Univ. Press, Stanford, 1994), pp. 93–110.

13. J. Enrico, *Anthropol. Linguist.* 46, 229 (2004).

14. V. Golla, ed., *The Sapir-Kroeber Correspondence* (Department of Linguistics, Univ. of California, Berkeley, 1984).

15. J. Bengtson, *Anthropol. Sci.* 102, 207 (1994).

16. A. Trombetti, *Elementi di Glottologia* (Zanichelli, Bologna, 1923).

17. S. Starostin, in V. Shevoroshkin, ed., *Dene-Sino-Caucasian Languages* (Brockmeyer, Bochum, 1991), pp. 12–41.

18. S. Nikolaev, in V. Shevoroshkin, ed., *Dene-Sino-Caucasian Languages* (Brockmeyer, Bochum, 1991), pp. 42–66.

19. J. Bengtson, in V. Shevoroshkin, ed., *Nostratic, Dene-Caucasian, Austric and Amerind* (Brockmeyer, Bochum, 1992), pp. 342–352.

20. M. Ruhlen, *Proc. Natl. Acad. Sci. USA* 95, 13994 (1998).

21. J. Nichols, in N. Jablonski, ed., *The First Americans,* (California Academy of Sciences, San Francisco, 2002), pp. 273–293.

22. P. Bellwood, *Sci. Am.* 265(1) (July), 88 (1991).

23. R. Darnell, J. Sherzer, *Int. J. Am. Linguist* 37, 27 (1971).

24. L. Campbell, *Mother Tongue* 23, 47 (1994).

25. L. Campbell, in M. Langdon, ed., *Survey of California and Other Indian Languages* (Department of Lingustics, Univ. of California, Berkeley, 1994), pp. 3, 9.

26. J. Nichols, *Linguistic Diversity in Space and Time* (Univ. of Chicago Press, Chicago, 1992).

27. J. Nichols, D. Peterson, *Language* 72, 336 (1996).

28. L. Campbell, *Language* 73, 339 (1997).

29. M. Ruhlen, *On the Origin of Languages* (Stanford Univ. Press, Stanford, 1994), pp. 183–206.

30. M. Ruhlen, *Anthropol. Sci.* 103, 209 (1995).

31. E. Sapir, *J. Société Am. Paris* 15, 41 (1923).

32. J. Greenberg, M. Ruhlen, *An Amerind Etymological Dictionary* (2007, available at http://www.merrittruhlen.com).

33. M. Ruhlen, *On the Origin of Languages* (Stanford Univ. Press, Stanford, 1994), pp. 207–241.

34. M. Ruhlen, in M. Chen, O. Tzeng, eds., *In Honor of William S-Y. Wang* (Pyramid Press, Taipei, 1995), pp. 405–407.

35. R. Klein, *The Human Career,* 2nd ed. (Univ. of Chicago Press, Chicago, 1999).

36. N. Wade, *Before the Dawn* (Penguin, New York, 2006).

37. L. Cavalli-Sforza et al., *Proc. Natl. Acad. Sci. USA* 85, 6002 (1988).

38. M. Jobling, M. Hurles, C. Tyler-Smith, *Human Evolutionary Genetics* (Garland Science, New York, 2004).

39. L. Cavalli-Sforza, *Genes, Peoples, and Languages* (North Point Press, New York, 2000), p. 94.

40. M. Seielstad, E. Minch, L. Cavalli-Sforza, *Am. J. Hum. Genet.* 73, 700 (2003).

11

The Peopling of the Americas as Viewed from the Y Chromosome

Stephen L. Zegura, Tatiana M. Karafet, and Michael F. Hammer

The early peopling of the Americas is a topic that has engendered tremendous interest among both scientists and the public in general. There is no widespread professional agreement, either within or among academic disciplines, about the answers to fundamental questions such as the timing of the initial entry, the number of early migrations, the route(s) taken, the proximate homeland(s) of the source populations(s), the number of early migrants, the subsistence strategies and ecological impact of the early colonists, the breadth of their technological capabilities, or what language(s) were spoken. Scientific opinions about these topics are legion, coming from fields as disparate as archaeology, skeletal biology, genetics, human biology, linguistics, sociocultural anthropology, paleoclimatology, biogeography, ecology, evolutionary biology, and the geosciences.

The task of forging a synthesis from the enormous amount of diverse data available today is vastly more daunting than that faced by Greenberg, Turner, and Zegura in 1986 when they collaborated to publish a widely cited and highly controversial position paper on the early peopling of the Americas that stressed the apparent congruence of the then-extant data from linguistics, dental anthropology, and traditional biparental nuclear genetic systems within a framework provided by the archaeological record (1). Their paper presented a "three-wave" hypothesis based on their claim that all Native American populations could be allocated to three distinct linguistically defined groups that were associated with

different tool traditions and that had origins in three chronologically separate migrations from different geographic areas of Asia (1). Although the model rose to paradigmatic status in textbooks and continues to find occasional adherents, its chief value has turned out to be heuristic. Literally hundreds of scholars have explored the issues it raised, and the vast majority of their studies have disagreed with one or more of the model's conclusions. More than twenty years later, researchers are faced with the inconvenient fact that different data sets often tell quite contradictory stories. For instance, within the field of genetics the maternally transmitted mitochondrial DNA (mtDNA), the paternally transmitted Y chromosome, and the biparentally transmitted nuclear genetic systems have led to contrasting inferences about the number and timing of early migration(s) to the Americas. Geneticists are actively engaged in trying to figure out why this is so, and some progress has recently been made in unifying the male- and female-based perspectives. This chapter concentrates on data derived from the male-specific region (MSR) of the Y chromosome, which used to be called the non-recombining region of the Y chromosome (NRY) until extensive intra-Y chromosomal recombination was discovered in 2003 (2). Thus, our scenario is both male-based and male-biased; however, appropriate data from other genetic systems and from nongenetic sources will be incorporated to "flesh out" one plausible model for the early peopling of the Americas. It should be kept firmly in mind that there are many other plausible models. Unfortunately, the genetic data necessary to test alternate hypotheses in a rigorous statistical framework do not yet exist.

The Beringian Connection

There is a general, though not universal, consensus that people first came to the Americas from Asia across the interior and/or along the southern coast of Beringia or its smaller remnant, the Bering land bridge (3). Beringia was a landmass continental in scope, extending from the Lena River in Siberia (135° E) to the MacKenzie River in western Canada (135° W) and for at least 1,000 km north of 50° N latitude. Beringia existed from approximately 25,000 years ago until its gradual breakup as temperatures warmed significantly between 15,000 and 13,000 years ago. Until rather recently, it was thought that people had not penetrated the northern reaches of Siberia before 20,000 years ago (3). For many, this meant that the Americas could not have been colonized until after the Last Glacial Maximum (LGM). The exact dating of the LGM varies according to the type of data used; however, the vast majority of dates place this extended period of cold temperatures at some time between 17,000 and 24,500 years ago (4–5).

An extremely important point to understand at this juncture is the difference between uncalibrated radiocarbon dates and calibrated (or calendar) dates. Because the atmospheric $^{14}C/^{12}C$ ratio (the starting point of the radiocarbon clock) varies over time, these fluctuations must be compensated for by applying a calibration curve to adjust time in radiocarbon years to actual calendar years (6). The calibration curve has recently been extended to cover the past 50,000 years, which corresponds to the current limit of ^{14}C dating resolution (7). In many books and articles the date of the LGM is simply given as 18,000–20,000 BP (years before the present). This is often an uncalibrated date referring to radiocarbon years (i.e., ^{14}C years BP), where the "present" is usually defined as 1950. The corresponding calibrated calendar year date would be close to 21,000–24,000 years ago (i.e., calendar years BP where the "present" corresponds to some recent datable event) (7). This difference between radiocarbon years and actual calendar years is important when com-

paring dates derived from archaeological studies with those derived from genetic studies. Another fact to keep in mind is that the standard deviations/errors and confidence limits associated with archaeologically derived dates are much smaller than those associated with the origin of a mutation or the dating of a population branching event in genetics. Thus, comparing dates from one publication to another requires considerable caution. Are the dates in calibrated calendar years or not? How confident can one be in a date reported as a point estimate? Are the standard deviations/errors or confidence limits given, and if so, how large are they?

Some Key Dates and Sites from Archaeology

The earliest (uncalibrated) radiocarbon-dated Upper Paleolithic industries in central Asia occur in the Altai Mountains (50° N) at 43,300 ± 1,600 years BP (8) (Figure 11.1). By ~40,000 calendar years ago people had also advanced northward as far as the Usa River at the Arctic Circle (66° N) just west of the Ural Mountains, and therefore just west of Siberia (9). Then, unexpectedly, in 2004 a potentially paradigm-shifting discovery was published by a team of Russian archaeologists and geologists (10). They described a rich human habitation site in the Yana River valley 500 km above the Arctic Circle at 70°43'N, about 100 km south of where the Yana River empties into the Laptev Sea. The most shocking revelation associated with this north Siberian assemblage of Gravettian-like stone and bone tools was the series of tightly spaced radiocarbon dates with relatively small standard deviations (i.e., all ± 750 years or less), proving that people were just east of the Verkhoyansk Mountains near the western edge of what was soon to become Beringia by approximately 30,000 calendar years ago. Thus, people were at (or close to) the Beringian gateway to the Americas well before the LGM, thereby making a pre-LGM entry a real possibility. But did it actually happen? It is just as possible that the Yana River population retreated to the south in Siberia or perished, leaving no descendants, when the LGM took hold and northern Siberia became uninhabitable. What we do know is that the earliest widely accepted archaeological site in the Americas dated at 14,700 calendar years

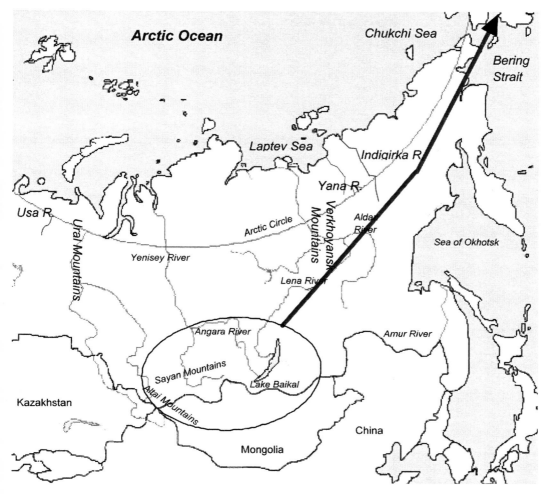

FIGURE. 11.1. North and central Asian geographical features and postulated ancestral source of Native American Y chromosomes (circled area).

ago is at Monte Verde, Chile, a full 13,500 km south of the southern margin of Beringia. The proposed earlier 30,000+ year-old occupation level at Monte Verde is not, however, thought to be an authentic human habitation site by most archaeologists who specialize in the early peopling of the Americas (*11*). Still, the 14,700-year date of Monte Verde means that colonists probably came via a coastal route because the interior ice-free corridor was impassable for at least another millennium. Thus, it seems most probable that the initial entry into the Americas took place sometime between 15,000 and 30,000 calendar years ago, but whether it was pre-LGM, post-LGM, or during the LGM is not known with any certainty. For instance, disparate dates based

on genetic data that occur in the literature actually support each of these three temporal periods, with biparental nuclear loci often favoring a pre-LGM date, mitochondrial DNA generally yielding pre-LGM or LGM dates, and Y-chromosome data indicating a post-LGM date as most probable (*12*).

The Y Chromosome: Nomenclature, Framework from Linguistics, and Data Synthesis

In 2002 the Y Chromosome Consortium (YCC) published a cladistically based standardized nomenclature system for a consensus Y-chromosome evolutionary tree derived from single-nucleotide polymorphism (SNP) and insertion-deletion (indel) markers (*13, 14*). The resulting 18 major clades/lineages are referred to as "haplo-groups" and are designated by capital letters (A–R). The term "haplotype" refers to all sublineages of the haplogroups defined by variation at short tandem repeat (STR) or "microsatellite" loci on the MSR of the Y chromosome. The haplogroups represent monophyletic entities defined by the presence of a derived allele that corresponds to a mutational change relative to the ancestral state of a trait found in a great ape outgroup. In this chapter we use the "short-hand" mutation-based haplogroup nomenclature system in which the capital letter is followed by a dash and then by the terminal mutation defining a given lineage. Thus, Q-M3 is the name of the most frequently occurring haplogroup in Native American populations (12).

The first Y-chromosome data from Native American populations were published in 1994 (15), almost a decade after the first human Y-chromosome polymorphisms were discovered. The first article to include data for what is now known as the Native American–specific Haplogroup Q-M3 appeared in 1996 (16). The number of STR and SNP markers surveyed in Native American populations increased tremendously after 1998, with a concomitant increase in the number of males assayed since 1997. In North America, geographic coverage has been very uneven, with populations from the Southwest and Arctic better represented than those in other culture/geographic areas. Note that most populations in Mexico are included within the North American Southwest culture area here, although many South American investigators group them with Central America (17). Within Central America, Panama is well represented. Brazil, Colombia, and Argentina are the best-represented countries in South America in terms of number of populations studied for Y-chromosome markers. Unfortunately, most studies concentrating on North America include few data from South America, and the reverse case is even more circumscribed in terms of geographic coverage, with North American data frequently not included in studies primarily designed to address microevolutionary relationships/processes within South America. More than 50 articles have now been published on Native American Y-chromosome polymorphisms; however, only a few attempts have been made to

synthesize data from North, Central, and South America (12, 17, 18). An even more inclusive synthesis is presented below.

Many of the articles dealing with the paternal population history and/or structure of Native Americans use a linguistic framework to group data as well as to test relationships among language, paternal genetic diversity, and geography. Greenberg's (1, 19) three major Native American language families (i.e., Eskimo-Aleut, spoken by Arctic populations distributed from Alaska to Greenland; Na-Dene, spoken primarily by Athabaskan populations in Alaska and northwest Canada, and by their southern relatives, the Apache and Navajo, in the Southwest; and Amerind, spoken by the vast majority of populations throughout the Americas) represent the most frequently employed classification. Occasionally, finer linguistic subdivisions reflecting subgroups of Greenberg's Amerind family have been used, as have alternative classifications (20), especially by those who reject the existence of Amerind as a valid linguistic unit. We follow Greenberg's (19) three-family classification system when addressing language-related issues.

Table 11.1 represents haplogroup frequency data on 1,756 Native American Y chromosomes. Haplogroups Q and C are thought to represent Native American founder haplogroups, while the majority of Haplogroup R chromosomes probably derive from admixture with Europeans (12, 23, 24). The category labeled "other" represents an amalgamation of eight additional haplogroups found in Native Americans. It should be noted that not all of the studies surveyed here typed the same battery of markers. Thus, in some cases further typing with additional more-derived markers would probably result in the placement of some of the "other" Y chromosomes into Haplogroups Q and R. The remaining "other" entries are almost entirely due to Eurasian and African admixture. The Haplogroup Q category includes the Native American–specific mutations Q-M3 and Q-M19, as well as the ancestral Haplogroup Q-P36 and its phylogenetic equivalents, Q-MEH2 and Q-M242. The Haplogroup C category includes the Native American–specific mutation C-P39 and ancestral markers C-M217 and C-RPS4Y$_{711}$. The Haplogroup R category is composed of numerous markers in different

TABLE 11.1. Native American Y-chromosome Haplogroup Frequencies and Percentages

	Language family	Number of populations	Sample size	Haplogroups			
				Q	C	R	Other
North America	Amerind	10	299	177 (59.2%)	12 (04.0%)	42 (14.0%)	68 (22.8%)
	Na-Dene	4	280	195 (69.6%)	24 (08.6%)	8 (02.9%)	53 (18.9%)
	Eskimo-Aleut	2	144	85 (59.0%)	2 (01.4%)	26 (18.1%)	31 (21.5%)
	Total for North America	16	723	457 (63.2%)	38 (05.3%)	76 (10.5%)	152 (21.0%)
Central America	Amerind	8	194	168 (86.6%)	0 (00.0%)	12 (06.2%)	14 (07.2%)
South America	Amerind	52	839	693 (82.6%)	2 (00.2%)	12 (01.4%)	132 (15.8%)
	Total for Amerind	70	1,332	1,038 (77.9%)	14 (01.1%)	66 (05.0%)	214 (16.0%)
	Total for North, Central, and South America	76	1,756	1,318 (75.0%)	40 (02.3%)	100 (05.7%)	298 (17.0%)

Sources: Language families from Greenberg 1987 (*19*). Other data compiled from Zegura et al. 2004 (*12*); Underhill et al. 1996 (*16*); Bortolini et al. 2003 (*18*); Bianchi et al. 1998 (*21*); Lell et al. 2002 (*22*); Bosch et al. 2003 (*23*); Karafet et al. 1999 (*24*); Karafet et al. 2006 (*25*).

studies, including R-M207, R-M173, R-M17, R-SRY$_{2627}$, R-SRY$_{10831.2}$, and R-P25. Admixture estimates from non–Native American sources have ranged from 17 percent (*12*) to 58 percent (*23*) for the Y chromosome. Based on the data in Table 11.1, an upper bound of 22.7 percent for a crude admixture estimate can be calculated simply by summing the R and "other" category relative frequencies; however, this is most likely a slight overestimate due to the less complete marker typing evidenced in some of the earlier studies.

As can be seen in Table 11.1, Haplotype Q predominates throughout the Americas, ranging from 59 percent of the Y chromosomes in the Eskimo-Aleut language family represented by Greenlandic and Alaskan Inuit populations, to 86.6 percent in Central America. Of the 1,756 Native American Y chromosomes assayed from 76 populations, 75 percent belong to Haplogroup Q. In general, South America exhibits a much higher frequency of Haplogroup Q (82.6 percent) than

does North America (63.2 percent). Also, the number of monomorphic populations (100 percent Haplogroup Q) was much higher in Central and South America than in North America (date not shown), indicating that a genetic bottleneck probably occurred in Central America and that genetic drift has been an especially important evolutionary force during the population history of both regions. In terms of language families, Amerind speakers have the highest frequency of Haplogroup Q (77.9 percent). Haplogroup C reaches its highest frequency among the Na-Dene speakers (8.6 percent), while the high prevalence of Haplogroup R among the Eskimo-Aleut speakers (18.1) is principally due to extensive male European gene flow into Greenlandic Inuit demes (*23*).

Contrasting global geographic distributions exist for Haplogroups Q and C (*24*). The ancestor of the Native American Q-M3 marker, known variously as Q-P36, Q-M242, and Q-MEH2 in different studies, is distributed primarily along an east-west axis, with its highest frequencies in populations near the Yenisey River in Siberia (see Figure 11.1). In the Americas, its frequency decreases from north to south, while the frequency of Q-M3 increases from north to south. With the exception of a few Q-M3 chromosomes identified in three Siberian populations and on one Polynesian island, thought to be due to admixture stemming from back-migration to Siberia and to the Peruvian slave trade, Haplogroup Q-M3 is confined to the Americas (25). This relatively circumscribed geographic distribution of Q-M3 chromosomes suggests that the M3 mutation arose very early in the process of entry into the Americas, perhaps while the ancestors of Native Americans still occupied Beringia. The genetic dating of this mutation is discussed further below.

Haplogroup C is distributed along a north-south axis from Australia all the way up the eastern side of Asia to northern Siberia, as well as to south-central Siberia (this latter region is denoted by a circle in Figure 11.1). Once in the Americas, Haplogroup C acquired a very patchy distribution. It has been found in only eight Native American populations, including four Na-Dene groups, two North American Amerind groups, one South American Amerind group, and the Greenlandic Inuit (18, 23, 24).

Discussion

Y-chromosome data have led to inferences about the geographic source region of the Native American population system, the number of migrations from Asia/Beringia, the dates of possible entry into the Americas, the genetic processes associated with colonization of the Americas, and the paternal population structure of Native Americans.

Candidate Asian Homelands

The circled area in Figure 11.1 represents our best candidate for a possible source region for Native American Y chromosomes. Evidence for this claim involves both haplogroup distribution data and a median-joining microsatellite network analysis of STR haplotype data (12). Three Siberian populations (the Kets, Selkups, and Altaians) possess both Haplogroups Q and C with the following frequencies: in 48 Kets (Q = 94 percent;

C = 6 percent), 131 Selkups (Q = 66 percent; C = 2 percent), and 98 southern Altaians (Q = 17 percent; C = 22 percent). Moreover, although the Kets and Selkups currently inhabit part of western Siberia and the Yenisey River valley, their ancient homelands are thought to lie on the slopes of the Sayan and Altai mountains (12). Thus, all three of these Siberian populations can claim roots within the circled area in Figure 11.1. The STR data proved to be of critical import for narrowing down the presumptive Asian source region to the geographic area included within this circle. Not only was Haplogroup Q-P36 found in these three populations, but the ancestral nodes leading to both Haplogroup Q-M3 and Haplogroup C-P39, the two Native American–specific founding lineages, were present in southern Altaian individuals (12). In fact, the ancestral node leading from Q-P36 to the Q-M3 mutation was present in three Altaians, one Ket, and one Selkup. The ancestral node leading from C-M217 to the C-P39 mutation was present in two Altaians and was only one STR mutational step away from a haplotype found in 11 Altaians (12). Thus, one of the three paternal founding lineages (Q-P36) and the direct predecessors of the other two founding lineages (Q-M3 and C-P39) were all found in the current southern Altai population system. It is quite possible that Haplogroups Q and C represent a major and minor component, respectively, of the Y-chromosome pool in a single polymorphic founding population with strong inter- and intragenerational genetic drift both on the way to, and subsequently in, the Americas, leading to today's patchy distribution of Haplogroup C and the overwhelming predominance of Haplogroup Q (especially in Central and South America).

A word of caution is appropriate at this point. Because extinction of chromosome lineages can occur both with and without population extinction, paternal lineages present in today's populations do not present a complete picture of the genetic variation in ancestral populations, either in the Americas or in Asia. For instance, Asian source populations may have suffered extinction, undergone fusion, or relocated quite a distance since the ancestors of Native Americans moved to Beringia. Additional Y-chromosome founding lineages may have disappeared, and future sampling may reveal more founding lineages or clarify the admixture status of possible rare founding haplogroups such as C-M217, found in two Wayuu individuals from Colombia, and a single N-M178 chromosome found in a Navajo. Our main intent was to locate those Asian populations that are genetically the closest paternal relatives of Native Americans, and who may have shared a common source with today's Native American population system. However, we may never be able to prove conclusively that modern Native Americans actually came from the circumscribed geographic region in Figure 11.1 (*12*). In any case, we consider it more than coincidental that a recent review paper on the peopling of the Americas from the perspective of molecular anthropology (*26*) presented an analysis based on mtDNA data that included a geographic circle locating the possible source populations for the five founding mtDNA haplogroups (A, B, C, D, and X) in the Americas that almost exactly replicates the circle in Figure 11.1 that we first published in 1999 (*24*). Of the five models graphically portrayed in Schurr's article (*26*), the model championing a south-central Asian source was one of the two best-supported by current mtDNA data.

The Number of Migrations

In his 2005 review of the history of physical anthropological (including genetic) studies on the peopling of the Americas, Turner (*27*) presents a synthetic table on the estimated number of early New World migrations that contains 45 entries. The only data sets that supported a single migration come from the two haploid genetic systems (with the exception of one red blood cell–based study). Autosomal-based systems generally supported two-, three-, or four-wave models, as did morphologically based data sets. The majority of early Y-chromosome studies concluded that a single founding wave was responsible for the early peopling of the Americas, with subsequent population differentiation within the Americas. Then, in 1999, we proposed a two-migration model (*24*) that was subsequently supported by additional Y-chromosome studies (*18, 22*) from other laboratories. By 2004 (*12*) we were right back where we started in 1997 (*28*). Our 2004 article employed a larger sample size, more microsatellite (STR) loci, and a much larger number of single-nucleotide polymorphism (SNP) markers than

our two previous studies. Unfortunately for our expectations, we no longer had any convincing statistical support for our two-migration model. Our SNP distribution data, our STR median networks, and our mutational ages and population branching dates (see below) all can more easily be accommodated by a single migration than by two or more separate dispersals from Asia to the Americas. Another recent review (*29*) of the population genetics and history of Native Americans concludes that both mtDNA and Y-chromosome data point to a single migration to the Americas carrying all haploid-founding lineages simultaneously as the most parsimonious and preferable explanation. These sentiments echo the position of Laughlin in a commentary accompanying the Greenberg, Turner, and Zegura (*1*) three-wave position paper, when he wrote with his characteristically clear and witty style: "The differences between American populations are not large enough to postulate more than one migration.... A single small migration some 16,000 years ago appears most parsimonious. Researchers who flirt with trinities should be reminded that Eskimos have walked on water for 10,000 years. They wait for it to freeze, and when on thin ice they avoid creating unnecessary waves" (*30*).

Chronological Framework from Genetics

A panoply of genetic dating techniques—including genetic distance/time ratios, mutational ages, mismatch distribution expansion dates, coalescence ages, and population divergence dates—have been used on STR, SNP, and traditional gene frequency data to date the colonization of the Americas. For instance, Cavalli-Sforza et al. (*31*) used autosomal gene frequencies and genetic distances as a basis for their estimate of 32,000 years ago for the divergence of the Native American population system from its Asian forbears. Most mtDNA-based dates have favored a pre-20,000 BP entry, with the exception of Haplogroup B, which may have arrived later (*26*). A more recent attempt to date the initial entry using a mismatch distribution analysis of mtDNA distinguished between the initial expansion of the mtDNA haplogroups in Siberia/Eurasia 25,000–18,000 calendar years BP and their actual expansion in the Americas 18,000–12,000 years ago (*32*). These authors concluded that the initial migration of both males and females most probably occurred 15,000–20,000 years ago, at least 1,500 years before the emergence of Clovis lithic sites in North America. Two 2004 review articles propose very similar dates based on both kinds of haploid data: 14,000–20,000 years ago (26) and about 17,000 years ago (29).

Early dating attempts employing Y-chromosome data lacked precision, with dates ranging from 2,100 years ago to approximately 30,000 years ago for the origin of the Q-M3 mutation (16). Larger data sets with increased numbers of subjects and markers, as well as more sophisticated dating techniques, have greatly narrowed the range of possible entry dates. For instance, four recent mutational age estimates for the ancestral Haplogroup Q marker Q-P36 (and its phylogenetic equivalent, Q-M242) are 17,700 ± 4,820 years (14), ~18,000 years (33), and 15,416 ± 4,722 years in Mongolians versus 13,611 ± 2,916 years in Amerinds (18). As expected, estimates for population divergence dates have been slightly younger on average, since polymorphism (produced by a new mutation) generally precedes polytypy (population branching) in human microevolution (34). All 14 of the STR-based SNP lineage divergence dates in Zegura et al. 2004 (12) range from 10,100 to 17,200 years, with standard errors ranging from ± 3,200 to ± 6,000 years. Also, the 11 Q-lineage–based dates were not temporally distinct from the three C-lineage dates. These divergence dates are all compatible with a post-20,000 BP entry, as are additional initial settlement date estimates from microsatellite diversity (14,000 years ago) (18), differing microsatellite mutation rates and male generation times (15,000–18,000 years ago) (33), and even linguistics (13,000–14,000 BP) (35), skeletal biology (< 14,000 BP) (12), and archaeology (14,700 calendar years BP at Monte Verde) (36). It should also be remembered that genetic data provide maximum age estimates for peopling of the Americas, whereas archaeology and skeletal biology only provide minimum estimates because the "real" earliest site in the Americas has probably not been found yet, especially if it is now underwater. In sum, paternal genetic data agree with a variety of other genetic and nongenetic data sets, and point to the conclusion that a relatively late entry (< 20,000 years ago) is most likely. We also speculate that the initial colonization of the Americas took place soon after the LGM and definitely pre-Clovis (with well-dated Clovis sites spanning 13,305–12,895 calendar years BP) (32). Our estimate of some 15,000–17,000 years BP for the initial colonization date is in general agreement with Laughlin's prediction of ~16,000 years made over 20 years ago with far fewer data than we have at our disposal today.

Colonization Routes and Models

Our Y-chromosome data are most parsimoniously explained by a single-source, single-wave model; however, many other types of data are better explained by multiple source regions and multiple migrations, or by a single migration with one or more re-expansions from a common source population in Asia and/or on Beringia (27, 37). Unfortunately, genetic predictions from a re-expansion model would likely be very difficult to distinguish from those of a single-wave coastal model in which back-and-forth migration took place all the way back from the leading edge deme to the source population(s) (38).

One possible scenario derived from a synthesis of well-accepted archaeological sites/data involves an initial coastal migration allowing people to occupy Monte Verde by 14,700 years ago followed by separate maritime migratory pulses using the coast, continental shelf, and nearby islands accompanied by a land-based re-expansion from Beringia once the ice-free corridor opened between the Laurentide and Cordilleran glaciers ~13,500 years ago. This subsequent dispersal may have involved extensive use of riverine environments, and the land-based population movements may have led to the widespread North American distribution of Clovis points between 12,895 and 13,350 calendar years ago. Using a budding deme model on Y-chromosome data, we concluded that it would take ~2,000 years to traverse a major portion of the length of Americas (i.e., ~14,500 km) (data not shown). This same result was arrived at using data from archaeology, geomorphology, and demography (39), with a coastal leapfrog model as the preferred scenario. Here, colonists from the population located behind the terminal group would occupy the next empty territory, thereby permitting rapid dispersal (38). In sum, it appears that the Americas were populated rather quickly, much as Martin (40) originally envisioned; however, his land-based megafauna extinction or "blitzkrieg" scenario probably needs to be augmented by a coastal component characterized by the use of boats and marine resources, perhaps following a leapfrog colonization mode, and with extensive gene flow between settlements. Moreover, there is a general consensus from nongenetic data that members of the Eskimo-Aleut language group represent a separate, later migration to the Americas than the rest of the Native American population system (*27*).

Caveats

Both the MSR of the Y chromosome and the mtDNA molecule behave evolutionarily like a single locus and are therefore subject to false and/or misleading inferences when reconstructing population history. Their trees are gene trees, not population trees, and they are assumed to be evolving neutrally (i.e., such that the structure of variation within and among populations is attributable to mutation and genetic drift rather than to selective processes). However, suggestive evidence for natural selection is accumulating both for the maleness-determining SRY gene (*41*) and for mtDNA Haplogroups A, C, D, G, and H in colder climatic regimes (*42*). Also, the general lack of recombination in these two haploid systems makes them especially vulnerable to selective sweeps, whereby selection somewhere in the system can lead to rapid unidirectional frequency change of other markers due to genetic hitchhiking (*34*). Other complicating factors that might cause misleading deductions about population history and/or structure from sole reliance on haploid systems include their smaller effective population sizes (N_e) relative to other genomic regions (i.e., Ne Y chromosome = N_e mtDNA = ¼ N_e autosome or ⅓ N_e X chromosome), contrasting postmarital residence patterns, warfare, kin-structured migration, lineage extinction, ancient gene flow, polygamy, large male reproductive variances, high levels of genetic drift (i.e., both intergenerational and via founder effects), repeated cycles of population fissions and fusions, and unrecognized selective sweeps (*34*). Thus, we must be extremely cautious about how we interpret patterns of variation at one (or two) loci with respect to the peopling of an entire continent. More accurate genetic reconstructions of

population processes will only emerge from the addition of data from multiple loci coupled with better geographic sampling of ethnohistorically/linguistically defined populations. We also need better haploid data, including more marker systems, more samples, and more analytically sophisticated dating techniques that will increase both the precision and the accuracy of the estimated dates. Indeed, the remarkably successful international Genographic Project cosponsored by the National Geographic Society, IBM, and the Watt Family Foundation will use a large (and increasing daily) global haploid database to address specific questions such as: "When did people first reach the New World, and what routes did they follow from Asia?" (*43, 44*).

Moreover, we must be prepared for the possibility that different genomic components will still lead to contrasting inferences because of different modes of inheritance, different recombination rates, different mutation rates, different demographic properties, and different responses to the four forces of evolution. For instance, traditional autosomal genetic systems have consistently led to the conclusion that there were multiple waves of migration to the Americas (*1, 27, 31*). The same is true for archaeological, skeletal, linguistic, and many other nongenetic data sets (*27, 45*). Thus, it is highly likely that there were numerous "early" dispersals to the Americas that are presently "invisible" from the vantage point of paternal genetics given the current data. Y-chromosome founding lineages may have gone extinct, and/or more extensive sampling may reveal heretofore unrecognized founding lineages. Furthermore, although all present-day genes definitely had an ancestor that is potentially recoverable by genetic analysis, there is absolutely no assurance that any particular early American skeleton or archaeological tradition can be directly connected to people alive today. Unfortunately, the western Pacific Continental Shelf may also be "hiding" much of the anthropological evidence for the early peopling of the Americas. It may well be that the vastly different natures of the data sets that have been used to decipher the early history of the peopling of the Americas will forever preclude a definitive consilience of induction of the kind attempted by Greenberg, Turner, and Zegura (*1*).

Notes

1. J. Greenberg, C. Turner, S. Zegura, *Curr. Anthropol.* 27, 477 (1986).
2. H. Skaletsky et al., *Nature* 423, 825 (2003).
3. F. West, ed., *American Beginnings* (Univ. Chicago Press, 1996).
4. L. Robinson et al., *Science* 310, 1469 (2005).
5. J. Schaefer et al., *Science* 312, 1510 (2006).
6. E. Bard, F. Rostek, G. Ménot-Combes, *Science* 303, 178 (2004).
7. K. Hugen et al., *Science* 303, 202 (2004).
8. Y. Kuzmin, L. Orlova, *J. World Prehist.* 12, 1 (1998).
9. P. Pavlov, J. Svendsen, S. Indrelid, *Nature* 413, 64 (2001).
10. V. Pitulko et al., *Science* 303, 52 (2004).
11. D. Meltzer, *Devel. Quat. Sci.* 1, 539 (2003).
12. S. Zegura et al., *Mol. Biol. Evol.* 21, 164 (2004).
13. YCC (The Y Chromosome Consortium), *Genome Res.* 12, 339 (2002).
14. M. Hammer, S. Zegura, *Annu. Rev. Anthropol.* 31, 303 (2002).
15. A. Torroni et al., *Am J. Hum. Genet.* 54, 303 (1994).
16. P. Underhill et al., *Proc. Natl. Acad. Sci. USA* 93, 196 (1996).
17. F. Salzano, *Annals Brazil. Acad. Sci.* 74, 223 (2002).
18. M.-C. Bortolini et al., *Am. J. Hum. Genet.* 73, 524 (2003).
19. J. Greenberg, *Language in the Americas* (Stanford Univ. Press, Stanford, 1987).
20. L. Campbell, *American Indian Languages* (Oxford Univ. Press, New York, 1997).
21. N. Bianchi et al., *Am. J. Hum. Genet.* 63, 1862 (1998).
22. J. Lell et al., *Am. J. Hum. Genet.* 70, 192 (2002).
23. E. Bosch et al., *Hum. Genet.* 112, 353 (2003).
24. T. Karafet et al., *Am J. Hum. Genet.* 64, 817 (1999).
25. T. Karafet, S. Zegura, M. Hammer, in D. Ubelaker, ed., *Handbook of North American Indians*, vol. 3: *Environment, Origins and Population* (Smithsonian Institution, Washington, D.C., 2006), pp. 831–839.
26. T. Schurr, *Ann. Rev. Anthropol.* 33, 551 (2004).
27. C. Turner, *Alaska J. Anthropol.* 3, 157 (2005).
28. T. Karafet et al., *Am. J. Phys. Anthropol.* 102, 302 (1997).
29. C. Mulligan et al., *Ann. Rev. Genomics Hum. Genet.* 5, 295 (2004).
30. W. Laughlin, *Curr. Anthropol.* 27, 490 (1986).
31. L. Cavalli-Sforza, P. Menozzi, A. Piazza, *The History and Geography of Human Genes* (Princeton Univ. Press, Princeton, 1994).
32. T. Schurr, S. Sherry, *Am. J. Hum. Biol.* 16, 420 (2004).
33. M. Seielstad et al., *Am. J. Hum. Genet.* 73, 700 (2003).
34. M. Jobling, M. Hurles, C. Tyler-Smith, *Human Evolutionary Genetics* (Garland Science, New York, 2004).
35. D. Nettle, *Proc. Natl. Acad. Sci. USA.* 96, 3325 (1999).
36. D. Meltzer, *Science* 276, 754 (1997).
37. P. Forster et al., *Am. J. Hum. Genet.* 59, 935 (1996).
38. D. Anthony, *Am. Anthropol.* 92, 895 (1990).
39. D. Anderson, J. Gillam, *Am. Antiquity* 65, 43 (2000).
40. P. Martin, *Science* 79, 969 (1973).
41. P. Sabeti et al., *Science* 312, 1614 (2006).
42. N. Wade, *Before the Dawn* (Penguin Press, New York, 2006).
43. J. Shreeve, *Natl. Geographic* 209, 60 (2006).
44. J. Shreeve, *Natl. Geographic* 209, 70 (2006).
45. M. Crawford, *The Origins of Native Americans* (Cambridge Univ. Press, Cambridge, 1998).

12

Y-Chromosome Japanese Roots

Tatiana M. Karafet, Stephen L. Zegura, and Michael F. Hammer

The island country of Japan lies off the eastern coast of continental Asia. Its four main islands—Kyushu, Shikoku, Honshu, and Hokkaido—describe a long, narrow arc from southwest to northeast (Figure 12.1). Japan's location has deeply affected its history and culture. Though it is now an island country, it was for much or most of the Pleistocene attached to the Asian continent. The most feasible land corridors connected Japan with the Korean Peninsula, Siberia, and Sakhalin. Human dispersals might have entered what are now the islands of Japan over dry land during long intervals of the Pleistocene epoch (1). Though the final swamping of land connections to the continent are not yet locally dated with precision, the faunal evidence and dating of worldwide sea-level fluctuations suggest that rising water would have finally made Japan fully insular between about 18,000 and 12,000 years ago (2).

Before the discovery of the Iwajuki site, most archaeologists believed that the Japanese islands were colonized at the beginning of the Early Neolithic (i.e., the Jomon period), arguing that the region was inhospitable during the Pleistocene due to active volcanism (3). The discovery of Paleolithic sites leads to questions about when the earliest colonization of Japan occurred, and where the first people came from. These questions are general and relevant for many populations around the globe. Although Japan is among the few ideal places to study migrations, these questions are particularly difficult to answer for Japanese history. This might sound surprising since

Japan is an island country and was geographically and culturally isolated from Western influences for millennia. Nevertheless, as Jared Diamond wrote in 1998: "The answers are difficult to come by, but not impossible.... Unearthing the origin of the Japanese is a much harder task than you might guess" (4).

Brief Historical, Linguistic, and Genetic Background

Japanese prehistory is commonly divided into four periods: the Japanese Paleolithic, Jomon, Yayoi, and Kofun (5). The beginning of the Japanese Paleolithic is controversial, with some archaeologists arguing for ages as early as 50,000 or 40,000 years ago or more, and others arguing that anything older than 35,000 years ago is invalid, either because it is not of human origin or it was not dated correctly. Several sites have yielded radiocarbon dates back to 33,000–31,000 BP, with the earliest being the Ishimoto site on Kyushu Island (3, 6). The Paleolithic in Japan ended around 12,000 BP, leading to the Jomon period. Jomon ("cord-pattern") culture developed out of the Late Paleolithic tradition of Japan, becoming recognizable archaeologically as a new cultural society with the introduction of pottery into the Japanese islands from the south, via Kyushu. Between about 12,500 and 10,000 years ago, Jomon pottery came into use throughout the three southern islands, and was established in Hokkaido by at least 8500 BP. The Jomon hunter-gatherer society (ca. 12,000 BP–400 BCE) was a very successful

137

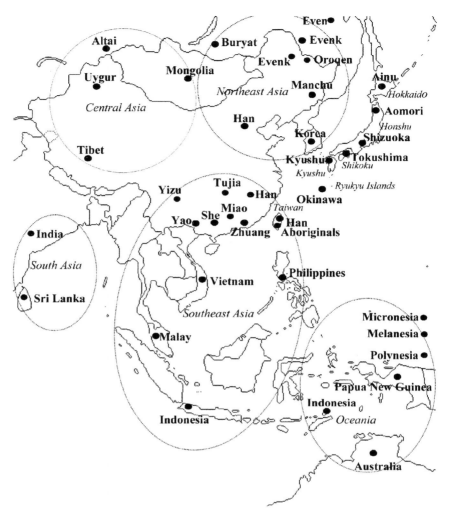

FIGURE 12.1. Map showing the approximate geographic positions of 39 populations sampled in this study.

culture, with the highest population densities ever estimated for hunter-gatherers (4). Jomon tradition dominated the Japanese islands for over 10,000 years with minor changes through time, thus demonstrating remarkable stability and continuity (7). However, Japan was not completely isolated (2). Pottery, obsidian, and fishhooks testify to some Jomon trade with the Russian Far East, Korea, and Okinawa (4, 8). Nevertheless, this limited trade with the outside world most probably had little influence on Jomon society.

A second important event in Japanese history happened around 400 BCE. Entering from the Korean Peninsula around 2,300 years ago, the Yayoi migration brought wet rice agriculture, weaving, and metalworking to Japan (9). The new period was named Yayoi after a district of Tokyo where a specific type of pottery was first found. The Yayoi migration initiated a series of radical changes starting in southwest Japan and moving towards the northeast, which led to the formation of the historic Japanese culture. The Yayoi period (ca. 400 BCE–AD 275/300) was characterized by an agrarian society that witnessed the initial development of Japanese social complexity and stratification. The later Kofun (ca. AD 275/300-650) was a period of early state formation in Japan.

The origin of the Japanese language is one of the most disputed questions in linguistics (4). More than half a dozen theories have connected

Japanese with different languages from Asia and Oceania (*10*). Most scholars believe that Japanese is an Altaic language, which makes a certain amount of sense considering that the Yayoi people seem to have migrated from Korea (*4, 10, 11*). Japanese was derived from a language spoken in northern Asia that would split off into several languages. According to Starostin's school, Proto-Altaic split into three branches—Turko-Mongolian, Tungus-Manchu, and Korean-Japanese—around the sixth millennium BCE (*11*). The Japanese language originated around the fifth century AD and was in part influenced by the Pacific Island (Austronesian) languages that surrounded the islands of Japan and thus formed an Austronesian substratum in Japanese (*12, 13*).

The modern inhabitants of Japan include the Ainu, the aboriginal population of Hokkaido Island; the Ryukyuans, who live in the southern islands; and the "mainland" Japanese, the inhabitants of Honshu, Shikoku, and Kyushu Islands. The Ainu and Ryukyuans are considered remnant populations descended from the Paleolithic-Neolithic (Jomon) people (*14–18*).

It is generally accepted that the modern Japanese are descendants of two populations: the Jomon and the Yayoi. The main controversy centers on the question of the relative genetic contribution of the Jomon and Yayoi people to contemporary mainland Japanese. Another question concerns the origins of the Japanese Paleolithic and Yayoi people. Unfortunately, only central and southern Ryukyu have produced well-preserved Paleolithic human fossils. Unquestionable Paleolithic human remains from mainland Japan are scarce (only three sites), and all are fragmentary (*3*). The Minatogawa remains from Okinawa have been extensively compared with other *Homo sapiens sapiens* fossils from Asia. Craniofacial and dental data from the remains of Japanese Paleolithic people led to the proposal of a southeast Asian and/or Pacific origin of early migrants to Japan (*18–20*).

Genetic surveys based on classical markers suggested a north Asian origin for the Upper Paleolithic people in Japan (*21–24*); however, Y-chromosomal and mtDNA studies showed closer connections for the Japanese with Koreans and Tibetans (*25–31*).

The Y chromosome, with its general lack of recombination, has been proven to be an excellent tool for reconstructing the history of human migrations (*32, 33*). This haploid system also provides opportunities to trace paternal ancestry and to uncover founding Y-chromosome lineages. In terms of markers, single nucleotide polymorphisms (SNPs) have helped to elucidate these founding lineages and to understand the pattern of migrations. The addition of fast-evolving short tandem repeats (STRs or "microsatellites") on the Y chromosome can lead to estimates of the ages of the SNPs, as well as facilitate the estimation of population divergence and supply time limits for historical events.

This genetic survey aims to (1) characterize patterns of Y-chromosome variation in Japan, (2) investigate the origins of Paleolithic/Jomon and Yayoi male lineages before they arrived in Japan, and (3) address questions concerning the relative genetic contribution of the Jomon and Yayoi people to the modern Japanese population system.

A Y-Chromosome Signature for the Peopling of Japan

Samples, Markers, Methods

We examined 259 males from six Japanese groups, representing Okinawa (Ryukyuans), Aomori, Shizuoka, Tokushima, Kyushu, and Hokkaido (the Ainu). We also included a total of 2,248 males from 33 non-Japanese populations (Figure 12.1). These populations are subdivided into regional groups: northeast Asia, southeast Asia, central Asia, south Asia, and Oceania (see circled areas in Figure 12.1). Many of the samples analyzed here were included in our previous studies (*25, 26, 34–37*). All sampling protocols were approved by the Human Subjects Committee at the University of Arizona.

We have followed the terminological conventions recommended by the Y Chromosome Consortium (YCC) (*38*) for naming NRY lineages. Capital letters A–R are used to identify the 18 major Y-chromosome clades or "haplogroups." Lineages not defined on the basis of a derived character state represent interior nodes of the tree and are potentially paraphyletic (*32*) and are called "paragroups." Paragroups are distinguished from haplogroups by an asterisk (*). For convenience, we generally refer to paragroups as haplogroups or lineages throughout the text. When no farther downstream markers in the YCC (38) tree were typed, we designated haplogroups by a capital letter corresponding to the major clade followed by a dash and the name of the most-derived typed marker (e.g., C-M8). As suggested by de Knijff (39), distinct Y-chromosome lineage identified by STRs are designated as "haplotypes."

A set of 81 Y-chromosome SNPs was used to trace the origins of the Paleolithic and Neolithic components of the Japanese paternal gene pool and to determine the relative contribution of Jomon and Yayoi Y-chromosome lineages to the modern Japanese population system (26). Ten STRs (DYS19, DYS388, DYS389I, DYS389II, DYS390, DYS391, DYS392, DYS393, DYS426, and DYS439) were used for the microsatellite analysis. Median-joining networks (40) were constructed using the NETWORK 4.0c program. Dating estimates of haplogroup age based on microsatellite diversity were obtained by two methods: BATWING (41) and YMRCA (42).

Geographic Distribution of NRY Haplogroups

Figure 12.2 shows the evolutionary relationships among the 44 haplogroups and their frequencies in Japan and in the six major geographic regions. Only 19 haplogroups were actually observed in the Japanese populations. Four lineages (C, D, N, and O) accounted for 98.8 percent of the Japanese chromosomes. Three samples from the I, Q, and R haplogroups are most probably due to recent admixture or unique historical events (34).

Six different M175-derived haplogroups within the O clade were observed in Japan. Altogether these haplogroups accounted for 51.7 percent of the Japanese Y chromosomes. Haplogroup O was found in all Japanese groups except the Ainu. Two major subclades of this haplogroup, O-P31 and O-M122 (Figure 12.2), are present at high frequencies in Japan. Approximately 20 percent of the Japanese samples belong to Haplogroup O-M122 and frequently carry additional derived markers: for example, O-M134 and O-LINE (Figure 12.2). Collectively these lineages are very common in eastern and southeastern Asia. Haplogroups

O-LINE and O-M134 probably originated in China, while haplogroup O-M122 is thought to have arisen in mainland southeast Asia. These lineages most likely migrated to northeast Asia, including Japan (43–45). Haplogroup O-P31 is present in Japan at a frequency of 31.8 percent and is split into two subclades, O-SRY$_{465}$ and O-M95 (Figure 12.2). Overall these haplogroups show a geographic distribution that is different from Haplogroups O-M122, O-M134, and O-LINE. O-SRY$_{465}$* and its derived haplogroup O-47z are almost entirely restricted to Korea and Japan. The high frequency of O-SRY$_{465}$ in Korea (33.3 percent), its high microsatellite diversity (0.31 versus 0.25 in Japan, data not shown), and notable microsatellite differentiation in Korea with several reticulations in the network (Figure 12.3a) suggest that the SRY$_{465}$ mutation might have originated in Korea. Haplogroup O-47z was found in all Japanese populations except the Ainu, with a higher frequency in mainland Japan (21.3–28.3 percent) than in Okinawa (11.1 percent). Outside of Japan this haplogroup was only marginally present in Korea and southeast Asia (34). A common Japanese haplotype accounts for 31 percent of the entire O-47z network (Figure 12.3b). Non-Japanese O-47z haplotypes from Korea and southeast Asia lie in the middle of the network and appear to be undifferentiated from Japanese haplotypes. On the basis of frequency data and the network analysis, we suggest that the 47z mutation might have arisen in Japan after the Yayoi migration and then later spread to Korea. Haplogroup O-M95, found at high or moderate frequencies in southeast Asia and in south Asian tribal populations but rarely in northeast Asia, occurred in 1.9 percent of the Japanese samples.

Lineage D, indisputably of Asian origin, is marked by the M174 mutation. Two subclades of D-M174 are present only in mainland Asia. The third sublineage, D-P37.1, is a remarkably long branch on the Y-haplogroup tree characterized by six mutations. Four of the resulting haplogroups (D-P37.1, D-M116.1, D-M125, and D-P42) were observed in 34.7 percent of the Japanese samples. Their frequencies varied greatly in Japan, from 75 percent in the Ainu to 25.7 percent in Tokushima. Outside of Japan these haplogroups were found only in three Korean males and one male from

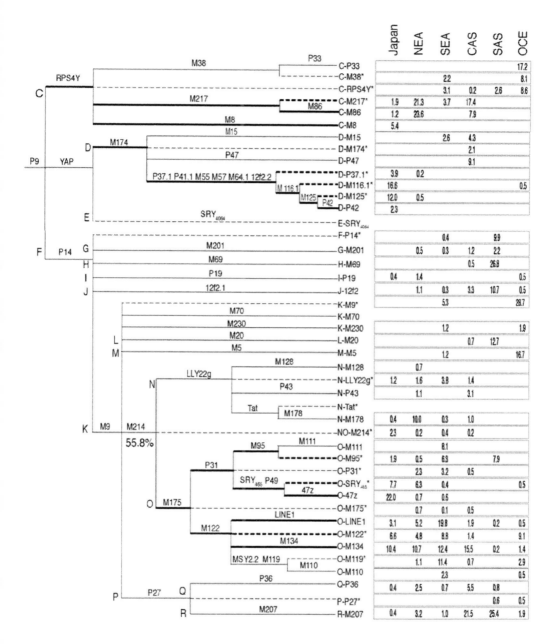

FIGURE 12.2. Maximum-parsimony tree of 44 Y-chromosome haplogroups along with their frequencies in Japan and five Asian regions (adapted from Hammer et al. 2006 [25]). Sample sizes for each region are Japan (259), northeast Asia (441), southeast Asia (683), central Asia (419), south Asia (496), and Oceania (209). Major clades (i.e., C–R) are labeled with large capital letters to the left of each clade. Mutation names are given along the branches. Dotted lines refer to internal nodes not defined by downstream markers (i.e., they represent paragroups). Haplogroup frequencies are shown on the far right.

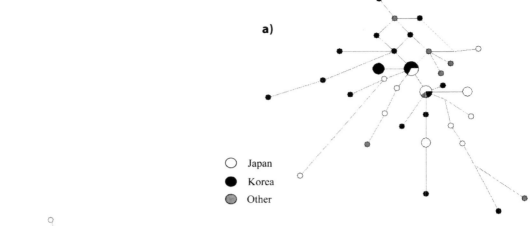

a)

○ Japan
● Korea
◉ Other

b)

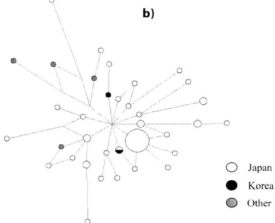

○ Japan
● Korea
◉ Other

FIGURE 12.3. Median-joining microsatellite networks for lineages: *a*, O-SRY$_{465}$*, *b*, O-47z, and *c*, C* (the position of the M8 mutation is denoted by cross-hatching) (adapted from Hammer et al. 2006 [26]). Microsatellite haplotypes are represented by circles with an area proportional to the number of individuals with that haplotype. Branch lengths are proportional to the number of one-repeat mutations separating the two haplotypes. Haplotypes are coded by geographic region (see key), with haplotype sharing indicated by pie chart divisions.

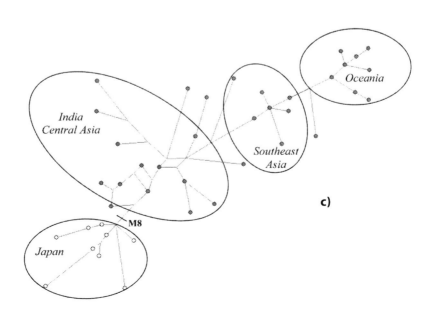

c)

Micronesia. The incidence of Japanese "specific" haplogroups in Korea and Micronesia can probably be explained by recent admixture. Microsatellite haplotypes of the Korean and Micronesian D haplogroups had one- or two-mutational step neighbors in the Japanese data set. This is not a surprising result since Korea was ruled by the Japanese from 1910 to 1945. Micronesia was under Japanese control for more than three decades, from 1914 until the end of the World War II.

Haplogroup C is the third most frequent major clade in Japan (8.5 percent)(Figure 12.2). Three subclades in haplogroup C demonstrate a high degree of geographic population structure. Haplogroup C-M217 is found at relatively high frequencies in northeast and central Asia. Interestingly, this haplogroup is observed in mainland Japan and in the Ainu, but not in Okinawa. The C-P39 lineage is restricted to Native Americans (46). C-M38 chromosomes are found in Oceania and east Indonesia (37). The M8 marker has drawn particular interest because C-M8 chromosomes are completely limited to the Japanese archipelago, albeit at low frequencies. Haplogroup C-M8 was present in 5.4 percent of our sample (14 men from mainland Japan and Okinawa), but was not observed in the Ainu. To investigate the origin of C-M8 chromosomes in Japan, a median-joining network of 41 different Y-STR haplotypes observed in 66 C-M8 and C* ancestral chromosomes is presented in Figure 12.3c. Clustering of haplotypes according to geographic regions is evident from the network, with a few exceptions. C* haplotypes exhibited three distinct clusters. Two clusters were characterized by simple connections of closely related haplotypes, with considerable haplotype sharing among populations within each geographic region. One of these clusters consists exclusively of Oceanian haplotypes. Another cluster contains haplotypes from southeast Asia. The third consists of C* chromosomes from India and central Asia. The Japanese C-M8 haplotypes are connected to an Indian–central Asian cluster.

Haplogroup N, the fourth most frequent haplogroup, was found only among mainland Japanese at a frequency of 1.5 percent (Figure 12.2). The Japanese are also characterized by the presence of NO* chromosomes, defined by marker M214. This haplogroup is found in Japan at a higher frequency than anywhere else, although it accounts for only 2.3 percent of the Japanese chromosomes. Deng et al. (47) found NO* chromosomes in Tibet and have suggested that the presence of this haplogroup could be a remnant of Tibetan ancestry (i.e., from the Di-Quiang population that occupied the upper Yellow River).

Ages of Haplogroups

To investigate whether Japanese founder Y lineages descended from different ancestral populations, we estimated haplogroup ages based on microsatellite diversity. Table 12.1 lists the time since the most recent common ancestor (TMRCA) for three Y-chromosome lineages. When a constant population size model was used in the BATWING program, there was good agreement between two methods for the age of the D-P37.1 lineage (20,180 and 19,350 years for BATWING and YMRCA methods, respectively). A notable discrepancy was observed between the estimates for the C-M8 and O-47z lineages in these two analyses. The YMRCA method gives a substantially younger age. Nonetheless, both dating methods produced a considerably younger coalescence time for O-47z compared with those for the C-M8 and D-P37.1 lineages. BATWING was also used to explore the influence of two alternative demographic models on the age of haplogroups (Table 12.1). Under the continuous growth model, the coalescence time for the D-P37.1, C-M8, and O-47z lineages is reduced (6,290 years, 9,710 years, and 3,810 years, respectively). The growth from a constant population size model reveals an age of the D-P37.1 lineage as old as 19,410 years, similar to a constant-size model, while C-M8 and O-47z yield intermediate ages (14,510 years and 8,690 years, respectively).

The Early Colonization of Japan: Paleolithic and Jomon Periods

Most scholars agree that there have been at least two major migrations to the Japanese archipelago. However, questions about the timing and particularly the source populations are still being debated by archeologists, geneticists, and linguists. An early wave brought the first people to Japan more than 30,000 years ago. One Japanese Paleolithic assemblage dates back to 34,000–31,000 BP, with the earliest Ishinomoto site on

TABLE 12.1. Estimates of Coalescence Time (and 95 percent Confidence Limits) for Y-chromosome Lineages Based on Variation at 10 STRs

| | | YMRCA | BATWING | | |
| | | | Constant-size population | Continuous population growth | Growth from constant-size population |
Lineage	n	TMRCA	TMRCA	TMRCA	TMRCA
C-M8	14	11,650 (8,460–18,690)[+]	20,010 (7,070–47,320)[+]	9,710 (3,470–22,860)	14,510 (6,140–30,410)
D-P37.1	88	19,350 (14,060–31,050)	20,180 (8,050–44,880)	6,290 (2,550–12,490)	19,410 (7,200–44,180)
O-47z	58	7,870 (5,720–12,630)	12,270 (4,680–27,630)	3,810 (1,640–7,960)	8,690 (3,840–17,640)

Note: TMRCA = time to the most recent common ancestor. All estimates are rounded to 10 years.

[+]YMRCA confidence limits are based on 95 percent CI of the mutation rate estimates, whereas BATWING age estimates are based on the median of the posterior distribution and the limits of the 95 percent even-tailed interval (see Hammer et al. 2006 [25]).

Kyushu island (3, 6). The early Upper Paleolithic portrayed similar trapezoid industries covering all Japanese islands. More than 10 years ago, Hammer and Horai (25) suggested that the YAP (Y Alu polymorphic) element existed in Japan before the Yayoi migration, and therefore the YAP element is a marker of Jomon male lineages. According to our present data, the Japanese have at least two lineages (C-M8 and D-P37.1) that most probably represent the descendants of Paleolithic founding haplogroups, only one of which (D-P37.1) represents a derived YAP marker. Both lineages suggest deep genealogical heritage. Their phylogenetic position and/or accumulated mutations (see Figure 12.2) might be explained by early dispersals of human populations into the Japanese archipelago and subsequent isolation from mainland Asia since these lineages are characterized by several mutations from predecessor haplogroups. Both lineages most likely arose in Japan. It is quite possible that they represent a major and a minor component of the Y chromosomes in a single polymorphic founding population. Our absolute dating estimates are based on two methods. Coalescence times ranged from 11,650 (8,460–18,690) years for the C-M8 lineage to 19,350 (14,060–31,050) years for the D-P37.1 lineage when we used the YMRCA method.

The ages obtained with BATWING depend on various assumptions. Constant population size is an unrealistic assumption for human populations. Pure exponential growth is also unlikely to provide a good model, since recent high growth rates would imply a vanishingly small population size a few thousand years ago. Koyama (48) estimated the number of Paleolithic inhabitants at 3,000 individuals. Taking into account marked population growth throughout the Jomon period, from 10,000 until about 4,500 BP, and exponential growth between 400 BCE and 600 AD during the Yayoi period (48), the model of exponential growth from a constant-size ancestral population might yield the most realistic dates. Under this model, the coalescent time of haplogroup C-M8 was estimated to be ~14,500 years, while the D-P37.1 lineage had a time back to the most recent ancestor of ~19,400 years (Table 12.1). That the same expansion is being detected can be inferred because of the large confidence intervals for these dates.

Our data support the hypothesis that the area between Tibet and the Altai Mountains in contemporary northwestern China is the primary candidate for the geographic source of the founding Japanese Y chromosomes (26). Although Tibetans and people from the Altai Mountains do not share the same D haplogroups with Japanese males, the ancestral paragroups that might have led to the Japanese D-P37.1 haplogroup were present in Tibetan and Altaian populations. Also, Japanese C-M8 haplotypes are connected to the Indian–central Asian cluster. Moreover, the presence of NO* chromosomes in Japan may signify remnant Tibetan ancestry (*47*). Historical records indicate that Tibetan populations were derived from ancient tribes of northwestern China which subsequently moved to the south and admixed with the southern natives during the last 2,600 years (*49–51*). Evidence exists that the Indian subcontinent played an essential role in the Late Pleistocene genetic differentiation of the Eurasian gene pools (*52*). A recent mtDNA study also posited close connections of Japanese haplotypes with Tibet (*30*).

The final Upper Paleolithic and incipient Jomon periods in Japan were distinguished by the appearance of a microblade tradition and the emergence of pottery at the end of this period, which covers the interval of approximately 14,000–12,000 years ago (*6*). The first appearance of the microblade industry in Hokkaido was comparatively earlier than in other parts of the Japanese islands. Located at the north end of the islands, Hokkaido was exposed to strong continental influence. From the preceramic to the recent Ainu period, the flow of various cultures both from the main islands of Japan and the Asian continent created some unique aspects of Hokkaido's culture. It seems possible that the Siberian microblade industry spread from Lake Baikal to the Amur region and from there to Japan. Traffic between these regions and Japan is also demonstrated by the finding of obsidian from Hokkaido Island in the Russian Far East. The radiocarbon age of the earliest site with obsidian on Sakhalin is $19,910 \pm 105$ BP (*8*). The most frequent Y lineages in these regions of Siberia belong to three major haplogroup divisions: C (C-M217* and C-M86), N (N-M178), and Q (Q-P36) (*53*). The age estimates of haplogroups C-M217 and Q ($11,900 \pm 10,100$ and $17,700 \pm 4,820$, respectively) (*31*) are consistent with the age of the Japanese Paleolithic. Given that these haplogroups are present in the Baikal and Amur regions, they were most likely brought to Japan through Hokkaido.

The Paleolithic in Japan ended around 12,000 years ago with the production of pottery ushering in the Jomon period. The use of pottery is often associated with early farming cultures. The Jomon culture was a remarkably successful adaptation to the biotic diversity in Japan. Throughout the approximately 10,000 years of its development, from around 10,000 BCE to around 400 BCE, local groups maintained a predominantly sedentary pattern of residence on the basis of a hunting-gathering-fishing-shellfishing economy (*7, 54*). The question of the origin of pottery is still unresolved. Since the mid-1960s, the Jomon culture had been considered to be the archaeological complex with the oldest pottery in the world (*55*). Later it was hypothesized that northern pottery emerged first within the Siberian microblade industry, spreading from Lake Baikal to the Amur region and from there to Japan (*56*). However, recent archaeological studies suggest multiple centers of pottery origin in east Asia. Based on dates and typology, three regions were proposed as independent centers of pottery origin: southern China, Japan, and the Russian Far East (*54, 57*).

The Yayoi Period

The Jomon period was succeeded by the Yayoi and Kofun periods, covering the millennium between 400 BCE and AD 650. This interval constitutes the formative period of traditional Japanese society. Presumably entering from or via the Korean Peninsula, the Yayoi culture brought wet-rice agriculture, metallurgy, weaving, and other cultural innovations to Japan (*20*). The Yayoi shift to wet-rice cultivation was of revolutionary significance, supporting rapid population growth. The density of Yayoi sites in southwestern Japan is many times greater than that known for Jomon sites in the same area, despite the fact that the Yayoi period was so much briefer than the Jomon.

Haplogroup O-SRY$_{465}$ fits criteria for a Yayoi founding lineage because it is widespread in both Japan and Korea. Moreover, this haplogroup is almost entirely restricted to Korea and Japan, with higher diversity in Korea. This is consistent with the hypothesis that this marker tracks a male lineage that originated in Korea and migrated to Japan. The O-47z lineage, the direct descendant of haplogroup O-SRY$_{465}$, was hypothesized to have entered Japan with the Yayoi migration from the Korean Peninsula (25, 26). Lin et al. (58) found O-47z chromosomes at low frequencies in two groups living in Taiwan. The ancestors of all men with the O-47z marker were traced to the province of Henan. Based on these data, the authors suggested that O-47z chromosomes might have originated in the Henan province near the Yellow River in China. However, in the present study and elsewhere (25, 26, 31, 45), this haplogroup has a high frequency only in Japan. Outside of Japan the geographic distribution of O-47z haplogroups is in remarkably good agreement with the territorial distribution and influence of the Japanese empire in 1940s (59). The coalescence time for the O-47z haplogroup is dependent on the demographic model employed. The model of pure exponential growth seems the most suitable for the age estimation of this lineage. During the Yayoi period the population increased rapidly as a result of a stable agricultural food supply, exceeding a million people by 650 AD (48). Population growth continued in Japan, and by the end of the Edo period (ca. 1868) the population reached a size of 3×10^7. Given the geographic distribution and the age of haplogroup O-47z (3,810 years, with a confidence limit of 1,640–7,960 years under a continuous population growth model), it is plausible that this lineage expanded in conjunction with the Yayoi culture (Table 12.1).

Other haplogroups might have been brought with the Yayoi expansion. Haplogroup O-M122, two derived haplogroups O-M134 and O-Line, and O-M95 are among the candidates for tracing the Yayoi migration. They probably originated in southeast Asia/south China and subsequently migrated into surrounding regions (43, 44), accompanying the proliferation of the Neolithic culture and rice cultivation. It seems likely that this expansion also brought O lineages first to Korea, and later to Japan with the Yayoi migration. The presence of O-M122-derived lineages in Japan may also be the result of direct relations with Chinese populations. It is well known that Japan maintained contacts with the successive dynasties of Korea and China as early as the Yayoi period (60). These contacts, political and cultural, intensified as the Japanese centralized state was established.

Dual Origin of the Modern Japanese

Three major hypotheses have been proposed to explain the origin of the mainland Japanese population and to account for the genetic differences among the Ainu, the Ryukyuans, and mainland Japanese (26). In the transformation or continuity model, the Jomon people are posited to be the ancestors of the mainland Japanese with no major genetic contribution from the Yayoi. The substitution or replacement model posits that the Yayoi people displaced the earlier Jomon populations, with only the Ainu and Ryukyuans representing the remnants of pre-Yayoi populations. According to the hybridization or admixture model, mainland Japanese are the result of admixture between the Jomon and Yayoi populations. These three models allow us to make tentative predictions, summarized in Table 12.2. In all three models, the Jomon people are considered the ancestors of both the Ainu and Ryukyuans, with high proportions of Paleolithic Y haplogroups in their gene pools. Under the transformation model, mainland Japanese are expected to have high frequencies of Jomon haplogroups, with small or negligible genetic input from the Yayoi migration. Under the replacement model, the Yayoi contribution is anticipated to be high in mainland Japan. Sokal and Thomson (61) examined the consequences for spatial variation of these three hypotheses and demonstrated that if the hybridization model is correct, there should be U-shaped (or inverted U-shaped) clines centered on Kyushu and southern Honshu. Ainu from Hokkaido and Ryukyuans from Okinawa are expected to be more similar to each other than either of them is to mainland Japanese populations. Under the transformation or replacement models no U-shaped clines are expected. Figure 12.4 shows Haplogroup O and Haplogroup D frequencies in six Japanese populations plotted against the approximate geographic distances from Kyushu Island. A U-shaped pattern for the D lineage is consistent with model predictions of a higher proportion of Paleolithic Y haplogroups among the Ainu and Ryukyuans. A similar, but opposite, trend was demonstrated for the O clade. There are higher frequencies of O haplogroups in the mainland Japanese than in Okinawa or Hokkaido. These results lend support to the hybridization model. We estimated

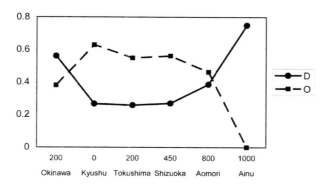

FIGURE 12.4. Haplogroup frequencies (Y–axis) for six Japanese samples plotted against their approximate geographic distances in kilometers from Kyushu (X-axis). Haplogroup D, solid line and circles; Haplogroup O, dashed line and squares.

TABLE 12.2. Predictions of Three Models for the Origin of Mainland Japanese

Model	Proportion of Jomon haplogroups		Proportion of Yayoi haplogroups		U-shaped distribution from the Yayoi entry
	Ainu, Ryukyuans	Mainland	Ainu, Ryukyuans	Mainland	
Transformation	Large	Large	Negligible	Negligible	Uncommon
Replacement	Large	Negligible	Negligible	Large	Uncommon
Hybridization	Larger	Smaller	Smaller	Larger	Common

the Jomon and Yayoi contribution to the modern Japanese gene pool based on the frequencies of these two clades (*26*). The Jomon contribution was found to be 40.3 percent, with the highest frequency in the Ainu (75 percent) and Ryukyuans (60 percent). The Yayoi Y chromosomes accounted for 51.9 percent of Japanese paternal lineages, with the highest contribution in Kyushu (62.3 percent), lower contributions in Okinawa (37.8 percent), and no evidence for Yayoi lineages in the Ainu (Figure 12.4).

Summary

Based on Y-chromosome data, we propose that Paleolithic people entered Japan about 12,000–20,000 years ago from the area between Tibet and the Altai Mountains in contemporary northwestern China. These people were isolated for thousands of years, although there is archaeological and genetic evidence of occasional traffic between Japan, Korea, and the Russian Far East. Later migration brought new people and Y-chromosome lineages to Japan via Korea. These lineages originated in southeast Asia and then expanded to Korea and Japan with the spread of wet-rice cultivation. Our data are in good agreement with the hypothesis that newly arrived Y chromosomes dispersed via a process of demic diffusion during the Yayoi period (*61*). Even though Japanese populations increased by a factor of 70 during the Yayoi period (*4*), our data indicate that almost 40 percent of the contemporary Japanese paternal gene pool can be traced back to Paleolithic/Jomon ancestors.

Notes

1. A. Melvin, T. Higuchi, *Prehistory of Japan* (Academic Press, New York, 1982).

2. Y. Kotani, *Arctic Anthropology* 5, 133 (1969).

3. H. Takamiya, O. Hiromi, *Radiocarbon* 44, 495 (2002).

4. J. Diamond, *Discover* 19, 86 (1998).

5. K. Mizoguchi, *An Archaeological History of Japan, 30,000 B.C. to A.D. 700* (Univ. of Pennsylvania Press, Philadelphia, 2002).

6. A. Ono et al., *Radiocarbon* 44, 477 (2002).

7. C. Aikens, T. Higuchi, *Prehistory of Japan* (Academic Press, London, 1982).

8. Y. Kuzmin, M. Glascock, H. Sato, *J. Archaeol. Sci.* 29, 741 (2002).

9. C. Chard, *Northeast Asia in Prehistory* (Univ. of Wisconsin Press, Madison, 1974).

10. R. Miller, *Languages and History* (White Orchid Press, Bangkok, 1996).

11. S. Starostin, A. Dybo, O. Mudrak, *Etymological Dictionary of the Altaic Languages, Part One [A–K]* (Brill, Leiden, 2003).

12. S. Murayama, *J. Jpn. Stud.* 2, 413 (1976).

13. P. Benedict, *Japanese/Austro-Tai* (Ann Arbor, MI, Karoma, 1990).

14. W. Howells, *Papers of the Peabody Museum of Archaeology and Ethnology, Harvard University* 57(1), 1 (1966).

15. K. Omoto, S. Misawa, in R. Kirk, A. Thorne, eds., *The Origins of the Australians* (Australian Institute of Aboriginal Studies, Canberra, 1976), pp. 365–376.

16. C. Turner, *Science* 193, 91 (1976).

17. N. Ossenberg, in T. Akazawa, C. Aikens, eds., *Prehistoric Hunter Gatherers in Japan* (University of Tokyo, 1986), Bulletin No. 27, pp. 199–215.

18. K. Hanihara, *Japan Review* 2, 1 (1991).

19. C. Turner, *Am. J. Phys. Anthropol.* 73, 305 (1987).

20. C. Brace, M. Brace, W. Leonard, *Am. J. Phys. Anthropol.* 78, 93 (1989).

21. H. Matsumoto, *Hum. Genet.* 80, 207 (1988).

22. M. Nei, in S. Brenner, K. Hanihara, eds., *The Original Past of Modern Humans as Viewed from DNA* (World Scientific, Singapore, 1995) pp. 71–91.

23. M. Bannai et al., *Am. J. Phys. Anthropol.* 101, 1 (1996).

24. K. Omoto, N. Saitou, *Am. J. Phys. Anthropol.* 102, 437 (1997).

25. M. Hammer, S. Horai, *Am. J. Hum. Genet.* 46, 115 (1995).

26. M. Hammer et al., *J. Hum. Genet.* 51, 41 (2006).

27. S. Horai et al., *Am. J. Hum. Genet.* 59, 579 (1996).

28. A. Tajima et al., *Hum. Genet.* 110, 80 (2002).

29. A. Tajima et al., *J. Hum. Genet.* 49, 187 (2004).

30. M. Tanaka et al., *Genome Research* 14, 1832 (2004).

31. T. Shinka et al., *J. Hum. Genet.* 44, 240 (1999).

32. M. Hammer, S. Zegura, *Ann. Rev. Anthropol.* 31, 303 (2002).

33. M. Jobling, C. Tyler-Smith, *Nat. Rev. Genet.* 4, 598 (2003).

34. M. Hammer et al., *Mol. Biol. Evol.* 18, 1189 (2001).

35. T. Karafet et al., *Am. J. Hum. Genet.* 69, 615 (2001).

36. A. Redd et al., *Curr. Biol.* 12, 673 (2002).

37. T. Karafet et al., *Hum. Biol.* 77, 93 (2005).

38. YCC, *Genome Res.* 12, 339 (2002).

39. P. de Knijff, *Am. J. Hum. Genet.* 67, 1055 (2000).

40. H. Bandelt, P. Forster, A. Rohl, *Mol. Biol. Evol.* 16, 37 (1999).

41. I. Wilson, D. Balding, *Genetics* 150, 499 (1998).

42. M. Stumpf, D. Goldstein, *Science* 291, 1738 (2001).

43. B. Su et al., *Hum. Genet.* 107, 582 (2000).

44. F. Santos et al., *Hum. Mol. Genet.* 9, 421 (2000).

45. H. Jin et al., *Hum. Genet.* 114, 27 (2003).

46. S. Zegura et al., *Mol. Biol. Evol.* 21, 164–175 (2004).

47. W. Deng et al., *J. Hum. Genet.* 49, 339 (2004).

48. S. Koyama, in K. Hanihara, ed., *Japanese as a Member of the Asian and Pacific Populations* (International Research Center for Japanese Studies, Kyoto, 1992), pp. 187–197.

49. D. Ruofu, V. Yip, *Ethnic Groups in China* (Science Press, Beijing, 1993).

50. L. Cavalli-Sforza, R. Scozzari, P. Underhill et al. *Am. J. Hum. Genet.* 70, 1197 (2002).

51. B. Wen et al., *Am. J. Hum. Genet.* 74, 856 (2004).

52. A. Basu et al., *Genome Res.* 13, 2277 (2003).

53. T. Karafet et al., *Hum. Biol.* 74, 761 (2002).

54. C. Keally et al., *Radiocarbon* 46, 345 (2004).

55. R. Morlan, *Arctic Anthropol.* 4, 180 (1967).

56. N. Naumann, *Japanese Prehistory* (Harrossowitz, Wiesbaden, 2000).

57. C. Keally, Y. Taniguchi, Y. Kuzmin, *Review of Archaeology* 24, 3 (2003).

58. S. J. Lin et al., *J. Hum. Gen.* 32, 299 (1994).

59. L. Menton et al., *The Rise of Modern Japan* (University of Hawai'i, Honolulu, 2003).

60. M. Kamei, in R. Pearson, ed., *Windows on the Japanese Past* (Center of Japanese Studies, Univ. of Michigan, Ann Arbor, 1986), pp. 405–414.

61. R. Sokal, B. Thomson, *Hum. Biol.* 70, 1 (1998).

13

Towards an Integrated Theory about the Indonesian Migrations to Madagascar

Alexander Adelaar

This chapter traces the Asian origins of the Malagasy people and their migrations to east Africa. It assesses the multidisciplinary evidence regarding these origins and migrations, discusses the way this evidence has been handled in previous research, and tries to combine it into an integrated theory. Aspects that are focused on include linguistic evidence (particularly the evidence of loanwords from Malay, Javanese, and South Sulawesi languages), possible migration routes from Asia to east Africa, possible migration dates, evidence from human genetics, and the establishment of the origins of Islam in east Madagascar as a possible way to determine sustained contacts with southeast Asia. Finally, this chapter presents some educated guesses on how Madagascar may have been populated.

The Linguistic Evidence

In a thesis defended more than fifty years ago, Otto Christian Dahl demonstrated that Malagasy is closely related to Maanyan, a language in southeast Borneo (1, 2). There are also some other languages in south Borneo with which Maanyan is directly related, including Dusun Witu, Paku, Samihim, and Lawangan, and together with Maanyan they form a genetic linguistic subgroup called Southeast Barito (3). Within the context of this subgroup, the genetic relationship between Malagasy and Maanyan is not unique: Malagasy is not directly related to Maanyan alone, but rather to the Southeast Barito subgroup as a whole, of which it is in fact a member for classificatory purposes (4).

In Austronesian historical linguistics, Dahl's thesis and the subsequent publications by him and Hudson solved an important mystery and put an end to various other, less well founded speculations about the origins of Malagasy. However, after half a century, it is still necessary to emphasise this genetic linguistic link. Although Dahl's theory has never officially been challenged since it was published in 1951, it has never quite obtained the recognition it deserved outside historical linguistics. There are several reasons for this.

From a historical linguistic perspective, there were problems with the way Dahl analyzed his data: some of the sound correspondences that he proposed were ambivalent, and a number of his etymologies were contrived. In hindsight, it is easy to see what was wrong with his phonological evidence. In his search for the closest next-of-kin of Malagasy, Dahl had overlooked the possibility that his lexical data in fact represented two Austronesian layers, one consisting of inherited vocabulary, and the other of loanwords from Austronesian languages outside the Southeast Barito group. As a result, many of his sound correspondences were ambivalent and lacked regularity. They were "blurred" because they yielded two correspondence sets instead of one: one for inherited (Southeast Barito) vocabulary, and one for loanwords from other Austronesian languages. Despite its shortcomings, historical linguists would soon come to accept Dahl's subgrouping claim, especially after Dyen's (5) endorsement of it on the basis of, among other things, lexicostatistical testing. In the meantime, more sources have become available for Southeast Barito languages, including Samihim comparative data (6), and linguistic studies of Maanyan (7), Lawangan (8), Paku (9) and other languages from the National Language Center (Pusat Bahasa) in Jakarta. My own research (10–13) has demonstrated that Malagasy has many loanwords from Malay, Javanese, and South Sulawesi languages. These new data and their analysis do not challenge Dahl's (2, 14) main claims; rather, they substantiate them more clearly than he himself had been able to do on the basis of the data available to him in 1951, and they add an important dimension to the history of Malagasy and its speakers. Identifying loanwords from Malay, Javanese, and South Sulawesi languages, and contrasting these with inherited Austronesian (Southeast Barito) vocabulary have made it possible to evaluate this vocabulary in its correct phonological perspective.

Another reason Dahl's theory failed to gain widespread acceptance is of a more typological linguistic nature. The morphosyntactic structure of Malagasy is in many ways more conservative than that of other Southeast Barito languages. It is more reminiscent of the structure of many of the languages of the Philippines, Sabah, North Sulawesi, and Taiwan, which are often considered to have remained typologically closer to Proto-Austronesian. This structural type is often referred to as the "Philippine-type structure" (15). In it, several parts of the sentence can become subject, such as actor, undergoer, recipient, location, or instrument, with an affix on the verb indicating which part of the sentence is the subject. On the other hand, Maanyan has evolved towards a West Indonesian (Malay-type) morphosyntactic structure. This structure basically allows only the actor and undergoer of the verb to become subject (in a way not unlike the active versus passive option in European languages).

The fact that Malagasy tends towards a Philippine-type structure, whereas Maanyan is more of a West Indonesian structural type, has aroused much suspicion among theoretical and typological linguists: how can languages that are supposedly so closely related be structurally so different? And is it not odd that Maanyan, which never left its traditional linguistic environment, has drifted so much further away from the morphosyntactic protostructure than Malagasy,

with its foreign influences and migratory history? As has become increasingly clear from recent typological comparisons, the morphosyntactic divergence between Malagasy and Maanyan must be a consequence of the longstanding and sustained influence of Malay on the languages of west Indonesia. Through the early migration of its speakers, Malagasy escaped this influence, while other Southeast Barito languages have been strongly affected by it because they are spoken in the vicinity of Banjarmasin, a Malay-speaking metropolis in south Borneo.

Malagasy and Maanyan are also very different in their phonologies, although here it is definitely Malagasy that appears to have undergone important innovations. These innovations also show similarities with phonological changes that have taken place in other (non-Southeast Barito) Austronesian languages, such as the development of vocalic endings, which is also observed in South Sulawesi and Polynesian languages. However, as Dahl (16) pointed out with his "Bantu substratum theory," the phonological developments of Malagasy can largely be explained through its common phonological history with Comorian, which, among others, show the same tendencies toward vocalic endings as Malagasy.

Finally, until recently, there was a lack of corroborating interdisciplinary evidence to support the alleged close genetic relationship between the Malagasy people and the speakers of Southeast Barito languages. If the linguistic connection was clear, there seemed to be little evidence outside linguistics to back it up.

Ethnological evidence is especially difficult to bring into alignment. This is due to several factors. One is, of course, the lack of ethnological research in both south Borneo and Madagascar. This is especially the case in the Southeast Barito area: although an appreciable amount of work has been done on the Maanyan people (cf. 17–19), we know little more than the names of some of the other groups. Another important factor is that ethnographic data do not lend themselves to genetically based historical comparison as readily as languages do. Similarities may be due to genetic relationship, contact, inherent systemic change, or chance, and it is imperative to distinguish between these causes in the search for the historical source of any phenomenon. In general,

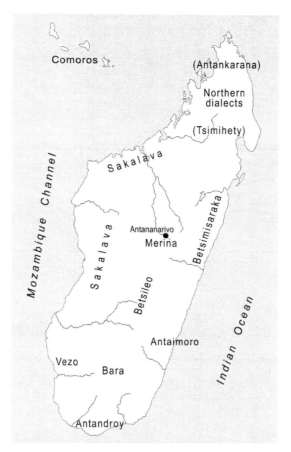

FIGURE 13.1. Dialects of Malagasy mentioned in the text.

such distinctions are more apparent in language than in ethnographic data. Finally, and very much as a result of the factors just mentioned, there do not seem to be salient cultural features that are shared exclusively among the Malagasy and Southeast Barito speakers. Obviously, both the Malagasy and the Southeast Barito speakers had undergone various cultural transformations after the Malagasy migration, including adaptation to external influences (from Malays and other Austronesian societies). In the case of the Malagasy, where the transformations must have been more dramatic, this also involved influence from Africa and the adaptation to a totally new environment.

In the past, there was also a lack of corroboration with human genetics and archaeology. Very recently, however, research in these domains has yielded promising new insights. In the case of ge-netics, these insights clearly bear out the linguistic evidence, and in the case of archaeology in east Africa and Madagascar, they are amenable to an integrated interpretation of the linguistic findings.

As a consequence of the initial lack of corroborating evidence for a Malagasy–Southeast Barito link outside linguistics, some authors resorted to looking for primary links with other ethnic groups, using evidence of cultural complexes (and their terminologies) that are not typically Southeast Barito. Apart from ignoring the linguistic evidence, they also failed to put their comparisons in a broader Austronesian context. There is little point in comparing, say, Malagasy rice cultivation techniques with Javanese ones (*20*), or Malagasy navigation skills with those of the Bugis and the Bajaus (*21*), without starting from a general ethnographic overview of these complexes in the wider Austronesian-speaking world. Such an approach tends to ignore the existence of cultural commonalities across the Austronesian world as well as cultural spread in certain areas within this world (e.g., the Indianized Malay and Indianized Javanese spheres of influence in large parts of Indonesia). It creates a tunnel vision with little predictive value for Malagasy culture history.

The historical relations between Madagascar and the rest of the Austronesian world can be studied effectively only from a general Austronesian perspective. In this respect, the Malgachisants are in a more disadvantaged position, as they start out from an individual case (Madagascar), which they have to test against a general variety. Apart from being experts in their own field, they will also need to be general Austronesianists and/or experts in Southeast Asian studies in order to make meaningful culture historical comparisons.

Borrowing from Malay

As indicated above, in order to properly understand the Austronesian element in Malagasy, a distinction must be drawn between features that are inherited and features that are borrowed from Austronesian languages not directly related to Malagasy. As far as I can see, these Austronesian languages are Malay, Javanese, Ngaju Dayak (2), and South Sulawesi languages. Among them, Malay takes a prominent position.

Loanwords can often be detected by the way their sounds correspond to those of the lending language. If a Malagasy word is related to a Malay word through inheritance from Proto-Austronesian, the way it phonologically agrees with the corresponding Malay word is usually different from the way a Malagasy word agrees with its Malay original form if it is borrowed from Malay. (As a rule, loanwords are more easily recognized than words related through common inheritance.) For instance, in borrowed vocabulary, Malagasy tends to have s and r where Malay also has s and r, as in Malagasy *suratră* (22) "writing" deriving from Malay *surat* "something written." On the other hand, in inherited vocabulary, Malagasy usually has no consonant at all where Malay has s and r—for instance, Malagasy *uni* "river" and Malay *suɲay* "id."; Malagasy *vau* "just

recently" and Malay *baru* "new." These and other correspondences between Malagasy and Malay concerning inherited and borrowed vocabulary are listed in Table 13.1.

Malay loanwords belong to many semantic domains but are most conspicuous in the domains of maritime life (including shipping, winds, and cardinal directions) and the human body. Some examples are presented in Appendix 13.1. Other loanwords do not appear to concentrate around such well-defined domains, although they do provide clear evidence of the great cultural influence the Malays must have had on Malagasy society (cf. *10, 13*).

Another way of demonstrating Malay influence in Malagasy is by contrasting word pairs, one member of which is inherited, and the other is borrowed from Malay. Examples are presented in Table 13.2.

Malay loanwords do not only give information about the cultural and technological impact of Malays on the Malagasy speech community. Sometimes they can also be stratified according to dialectal origin, or to the period in which they were borrowed.

Most Malay loanwords are borrowed from Sumatra (Srivijaya?) Malay. Some, however, bear the marks of a Bornean origin and are most probably borrowed from Banjar Malay. The main difference between the two dialects is that Sumatra Malay has a schwa (ə) in nonfinal syllables, whereas Banjar Malay has none and exhibits *a* instead. For instance, Sumatran Malay has the following words: *sǝmbah* "gesture of worship or honour"; *lǝmah* "weak"; *cecak* "k.o. lizard"; and *kǝmbar* "twins." Banjar Malay has the corresponding forms *sambah, lamah, cacak,* and *kambar* (with same meanings). These words were borrowed into Malagasy as *samba/samba* "expression of gratitude to God; *lama* "weak"; *tsatsaka* "k.o. lizard"; and (Sakalava) *hamba* "twins." In all these cases, the Malagasy form agrees with Banjar Malay in showing *a*, and not with Sumatran Malay, which has a corresponding ə (*10*). In contrast, Malagasy words that are borrowed from Sumatra Malay reflect the ə as *e*; for example, (Sumatra) Malay *rǝtak* "to burst" > Malagasy *retakă* "to collapse," and Malay *bǝsar* "big" > Malagasy *vesatră* "heavy."

Borrowing from Malay must have lasted for a considerable period. It persisted through two

TABLE 13.1. Sound Correspondences Between Proto-Austronesian Words, Inherited Malagasy Words, Borrowed Malagasy Words, and Malay Words

Proto-Austronesian	Malagasy (inherited)	Malagasy (borrowed)	Malay
*a	a	a	a
*-a, *-a(S,s,H,ʔ,R,l)	-i	-a, -i	a
*e	e	e; a	e (a in dialects)
*e (last syllable)	i	a	a
*i	i	i	i (e)
*u	u	u	u (o)
*-aw	u	u	-aw
*-iw, *-ey	-i	-i	-i
*-ay	-i	-i	-ay
*-uy	-u	-i	-i
*b	v,b	v,b	b
*-b	-kă, -tră	-kă, -tră	p
*c	-	ts (s)	c
*d, *j	r	tr, d	d
*-d, *-j	-tră	-tră	-t
*g	h	h, g	g, -k
*k	h,k; -kă	h,k; -kă	k
*l	l, -ø	l, -nă	l
*li	di	di	li
*m	m; -nă	m; -nă	m
*n, *N	n; -nă	n; -nă	n
*ŋ	n; -nă	n; -nă	ŋ
*ñ	n	n	ñ
*p	f, p	f, p	p
*-p	-kă, -tră	-kă, -tră	p
*q	ø	ø	h
*r	-	r; -tră, -nă	r
*R	ø	r; -tră, -nă	r
*s	ø (s)	s, -ø	s
*t	t; -tră	t; -tră	t
*ti	ts	tsi	ti

Proto-Austronesian	Malagasy (inherited)	Malagasy (borrowed)	Malay
*w	v	v	ø-, -w-
*y	ø (70)	z	y
*z	r	z	j
*ʔ, *S, *H	ø	ø	ø

Note: The following conventions are used in the table:

— A hyphen in isolation indicates that no Malagasy inherited words were found having a reflex of the Proto-Austronesian phoneme in question.

— A sound preceded by a hyphen (as in –i, -p) indicates that this sound occurs at the end of a word.

— A consonant between hyphens (as in –w-) indicates that it occurs between vowels.

— The symbol "ø" indicates that the corresponding Proto-Austronesian phoneme was lost.

— The symbol "ø-" indicates that the corresponding Proto-Austronesian phoneme was lost at the beginning of a word.

TABLE 13.2. Malagasy Word Pairs Contrasting Inherited and Borrowed Vocabulary

Proto-Austronesian	Malagasy (inherited)	Malay	Malagasy (borrowed)
*apuy "fire"	afu "id."	api	afi (Bara) "lightning"
*taneq "ground, soil"	tani "soil; country"	*tanah +-an	tanánă "town, village"
*ləmaq "weak"	lemi "id."	Banjar Malay lama "id."	lama "id."
*tulək "to push away; refuse"	tudikă "turn to look"	tolak "push away"	tulakă "turn on its hinges"
*tasik "sea"	taiky (dial.) "sea"	tasik "lake"	i/tasi (<i/tasihanaka)(23)
*tilik "observe"	tsidikă "peep in"	tilik "observe"	tilik/ambu "tower" (*ambu "above")

distinct stages of the phonological history of Malagasy, with loanwords adapting in different ways to each phonological stage. Dahl (16, 24) identified a common stage in Malagasy and Comorian phonological history. He attributed the effects of this common history on Malagasy phonology to a "Bantu substratum." I would rather call it a Bantu contact stage as I do not see much evidence for a substratum in present-day Malagasy (25). Dahl used this stage to distinguish between recent (Swahili) and not so recent (Comorian and other) Bantu loanwords. But it appears that the effects of the Bantu contact stage can also be distinguished in Malay loanwords. Most of these loanwords were also affected by it, but a few were not, to the effect that they remained more Malay in phonological shape (26). They must have entered Malagasy after its lexicon had already gone through the Bantu contact stage, which was probably towards the end of the first millennium BCE

(roughly the period between the migrations from southeast Asia to east Africa and the actual settlement of Madagascar itself). The phonological changes that took place in the Bantu contact stage had a considerable impact on the Malagasy sound system. They include:

*g, *k > h (with the proviso that word-final *k remained k)

*ŋg, *ŋk > k
  (*gh, *kh > k, a change that applies only to Bantu and Sanskrit loanwords)

*w > v

*p > f (word-final *p became -kă or -tră)

*nr > ndr

*d > tr

*-ey > -i, *-aw > -u

The tendency to develop z from *y (has not affected all dialects to same extent)

The tendency to develop vocalic endings (the extent and outcome of this tendency is different in various dialects)

Some of these changes, like *p > f and the development of vocalic endings (such as the addition of –ǎ in Merina Malagasy), outlived the Bantu contact stage and continued to affect later loanwords, but other changes, like *ŋk, *ŋg > k, did not. Examples of Malay loanwords that went through the Bantu contact stage, and those that did not, are presented in Appendix 13.1.

Borrowing from Javanese

Another lexical donor language, Javanese, is less important a source than Malay. Nevertheless, its legacy in Malagasy does include the honorific prefix *ra-*, which in Madagascar also occurs in many proper names: cf. Old Javanese *rānak* (< *ra-* + *anak*) "child," *rāma* "father" (< *ra-* + *ama* "father," modern Javanese *rāmā* "Roman Catholic priest"), *rahadyan* "Lord, Master" (modern Javanese *raden*, < *ra-* + *hadi* + *-an* < P(W)MP *qazi "ruler")(*27*), etc.; Malagasy *rafutsi* "term of address for old lady" (< *ra-* + *futsi* "white"); Comorian Malagasy *ravinantu* "child-in-law" (< *ra-* + *vinantu* < Proto-Austronesian *b-in-antu "child-in-law"); *Ranavalonă* (name of a series of Malagasy nineteenth-century queens), *Rantoandro, Rajaonarimanană, Razafintsalama* (Malagasy last names).

As a category, Javanese loans can be difficult to spot, and it is often not possible to establish with certainty that Javanese is indeed their source language.

Some loanwords in Malagasy can reasonably be assumed to be borrowed directly from Javanese because no cognate forms are found in any other language. This is the case with *tumutră* "close, imminent" (< Javane se *tumut* "to follow, accompany, participate"), *vulană* "word, speech" (< Javanese *wulang* "lesson, advice; admonition"), and *satrană* "fan palm; its leaves are used for making baskets and roofs" (< Javanese *saḍaŋ* "fan palm [*Livistonia rotundifolia Mart.*], the leaves of which are used for roofing").

Other loanwords occur in Javanese as well as in Malay but must ultimately be borrowed from Javanese because philological research and phonotactic probability clearly favor Javanese as an ultimate source. However, they were borrowed into Malay at a very early stage and have been totally adapted to the structure of this language. In such cases, these loanwords could also have been borrowed via Malay, especially since Malay is a major source for lexical borrowing, while Javanese is not. Words like these include *rutsakă* "fall downwards, slip on a slope" (in Tandroy Malagasy): "collapse." This word has a Malay corresponding form *rusak* (in Indonesia) or *rosak* (in Malaysia) meaning "spoiled, ruined," and a corresponding form in Javanese *rusak* "spoiled, ruined." These forms originally derive from an Old Javanese compound *rūg* "fall in, collapse, be smashed" + *sāk* "fallen apart, loosened, dispersed" (*28*). However, *rutsakă* could just as well have been borrowed via an older form of Malay, as *rusak/rosak* also became part of the core vocabulary of this language. Another such loanword is *fatutră* "to bind," which is borrowed from either Javanese or Malay *patut* "fitting, suitable." This word ultimately derives from Old Javanese *pa-tu:t* "id.," the root of which, *tu:t*, is a reflex of Proto-Austronesian *tuRut (Proto-Austronesian *R > Javanese ø) and corresponds regularly to Malay *turut* "to follow; to conform." However, *patut* has become so integrated in Malay that it could just as well be the direct source of *fatutră*. In both cases (*rutsakă* and *fatutră*), there is simply no way of telling which language was the direct lending source.

Other loanwords that are common to Malay and Javanese cannot be diagnosed as being borrowed from either one or the other because their development is unknown, and their shape in no way violates the phonotactic structure of either Malay or Javanese in any stage of their known history. Malagasy *lazu* "wilted, fading" is borrowed from either Malay or Javanese, which both have *layu* (same meaning); Malagasy *sala/sala* "doubtful, hesitating" could be from either Malay *salah* or Javanese *salah*, which both mean "wrong"; Malagasy *sudină* "flute" could be from either Malay *suling* or Javanese *suling* "flute," and so on.

In another, especially difficult category are the Sanskrit loanwords in Malagasy. These are known to have entered the language via Malay or Javanese. Considering that Malay loanwords in Malagasy outnumber by far loanwords from other Indonesian languages, it is likely that most Sanskrit loanwords in Malagasy were borrowed via Malay. But for reasons of documentation, this is impossible to demonstrate. Both Old Malay and Old Javanese had a large amount of Sanskrit loanwords. Since there are plenty of texts in Old Javanese (eighth to sixteenth century AD), but only very limited textual material for Old Malay (mainly seventh to tenth century AD), it is much easier to find a matching form for a Malagasy word of Sanskrit provenance in the rich Old Javanese literature than in the handful of Old Malay inscriptions. This creates the impression that Old Javanese was the "vehicular donor language" for these Sanskrit loanwords, but this is clearly too narrow an interpretation of what may have happened. We simply have better insight into what written Javanese must have looked like at the height of Indian intellectual influence in insular southeast Asia than we have for written Malay in the same period. Some reservation is therefore required in assessing the influence of Javanese on Malagasy. For instance, Malagasy *lapa* (*29*) "main residence; pavilion in the centre of a village where all public affairs and administration are done; court" reflects Javanese *pandåpå* "large open structure in front of Javanese house; open veranda, pavilion," which in turn is borrowed from Sanskrit *mandapa-* "open hall or temporary shed, pavilion"; Merina Malagasy *s-um-undrara* "having the breasts in a state of growth," and Tandroy Malagasy, Bara Malagasy *s-um-undrara* "adolescent girl" reflect Old Javanese *sundara* "beautiful" and Sanskrit *sundara-* "handsome" (*30*). Malay has no corresponding forms for these Sanskrit loanwords and their correspondences; however, it is still possible that these existed in the past, and that it was these now lost forms that were borrowed into Malagasy.

South Sulawesi Loanwords

A third important source for lexical borrowing into Malagasy was South Sulawesi, although it is not clear which South Sulawesi language or languages had an influence on the Southeast Barito lexicon (*31*). Certainly Buginese is a strong candidate to be one of the lending languages (*32*). However, although Buginese has been the most influential and cosmopolitan South Sulawesi language, it is not clear when it began to assume this role, and whether it had already done so before the

migrations took place. Furthermore, given that the Austronesian ancestors of the Malagasy left Borneo about halfway through the first millennium AD, it is not even clear whether at that time Buginese (or any other South Sulawesi language) already had become a separate linguistic entity. It is therefore safest to label the loanwords in question a generic South Sulawesi and not to specify their origin any further. The fact that there are South Sulawesi loanwords in Malagasy should not come as a surprise, given that several South Sulawesi communities have had a strong orientation towards the sea and have developed impressive navigational skills. The Buginese have traveled extensively and have had longstanding contacts with the coasts of Borneo, although historical sources do not provide evidence for any Buginese voyages and migrations prior to the seventeenth century (*33*). South Sulawesi history from before that period is simply unknown. However, what we do know from historical linguistic research is that the Tamanic communities (including the Embaloh or Maloh) living in the Upper Kapuas area in the northeastern part of west Kalimantan speak a number of related dialects that are very closely related to the South Sulawesi languages and in fact form a branch of the South Sulawesi language subgroup. Within this subgroup, Tamanic dialects appear to share most sound changes with Buginese. How and when the Tamanic communities ended up in central Borneo remains a mystery, and the argument for their relationship with South Sulawesi is still entirely linguistic. The Tamanic speakers themselves have no record of a homeland outside Borneo, although references to links with Macassarese or Buginese in scholarly literature have occasionally fed back into oral history (*34*). Be that as it may, the Tamanic case suggests that contacts between South Sulawesi and Borneo may be older and more complex than those documented in written records. If today there are some South Sulawesi loanwords in Malagasy, it probably means that there must already have been inter-insular contacts between South Sulawesi and Borneo long before the beginning of written history in that area. It could of course be argued, as various scholars have done, that at some stage in history the Buginese were in direct contact with Madagascar, but that would definitely be at a higher level of speculation, and an unnecessary one at that. Some of the more conspicuous South Sulawesi loanwords are presented in Appendix 13.2.

Borrowing from Other Austronesian Languages?

Various cases have been made for borrowing from other Indonesian languages, but apart from the occasional loanword from Ngaju Dayak, which is spoken in an area bordering that of the Southeast Barito languages (cf. 2), the evidence is weak and of little structural relevance. Beaujard (35) gives an inventory of possible loanwords from Austronesian and Indian languages into Malagasy. He does so in a recent article in which he argues that the contacts between Indonesia and Madagascar must have lasted for up to a millennium and must have left a considerable impact on Malagasy symbolic systems and political culture. He also proposes loanwords from Philippine languages, Dravidian languages, and Sulawesi languages other than those of South Sulawesi, but I do not find this part of his evidence convincing. In the first place, his Philippine and Sulawesi loanwords are collected from a large pool of alleged source languages. However, the more lending languages that are brought in from a certain area, the less persuasive the case for borrowing will be. In most contact situations involving the existence of many potential lending languages in a certain region, the receiving language will borrow systematically from one language only or, at best, from a restricted number of these languages. Furthermore, Beaujard's case for borrowing from Philippine and Sulawesi languages lacks a clear historical, cultural, or geographical context. In the context of Indonesian history, it is evident that many regional languages throughout insular southeast Asia have been strongly influenced by Malay or Javanese, or both. It is also documented that the Buginese and other South Sulawesi peoples played dominant roles in Indonesian maritime trade, and that the Buginese have had colonies in Borneo for many centuries. However, such context is lacking in the case of linguistic influence from other Sulawesi languages and languages from the Philippines. Finally, in some cases, more attention should have been paid to the regularity of sound correspondences, and some of the semantic connections are not quite in

agreement with the Austronesian cultural reality. Beaujard's (two) Dravidian loanwords are phonologically unjustified: *horakă* "rice field" cannot be derived from Tamil *kulam* "water reservoir"; *amberiky* "Vignata radiata (L.) Wilczek" may be derived from Malayalam *avarakka, amarakka* "id." but probably via Réunion French *ambérique* "id.," not directly from Malayalam. I also see no strong argument for borrowing from Bajau. One of the only two Sama Bajau loanwords proposed by Beaujard is a regular inherited reflex of Proto-Malayo-Polynesian: *òdi* "charm, remedy" is thought to originate from Sama Bangingi *uliʔ* "to look after," but it is more likely a regular inherited reflex of Proto-Malayo-Polynesian *uliq "go back; return something; restore, repair; repeat; motion to and fro" and must be inherited (36).

In summary, the evidence of loanwords allows us to draw some important conclusions. The main source of borrowing in early Malagasy was clearly Malay, and more particularly, Malay as it was spoken in Sumatra. Malay loanwords often relate to navigation and maritime life. They also reflect the high status that Malay must have had among early Malagasy speakers. Compared to Sumatran Malay, Banjarese Malay, Javanese, Sanskrit, and South Sulawesi languages were minor borrowing sources, although the loanwords they yielded give us some important information about the historical conditions in which the Asian ancestors of the Malagasy must have lived. Sanskrit loanwords must have entered Malagasy via Malay and Javanese, and South Sulawesi loanwords were probably already in the language of these Asian ancestors before they migrated to Africa. At any rate, Sanskrit loanwords in Malagasy do not suggest direct contacts between Madagascar and the Indian subcontinent, nor are South Sulawesi loanwords necessarily evidence of maritime contact between South Sulawesi and Madagascar. Apart from Malay, Javanese, South Sulawesi languages, and possibly some indigenous languages in Borneo, there is no convincing case for borrowing from other Austronesian languages in Malagasy. Some of these conclusions are discussed further below.

Migration Routes

An important question is whether the early migrants traveled to east Africa by navigating along the coasts of the Indian Ocean or by crossing it.

Many scholars tend to believe that the route must have been coastal (37–40). This is not surprising given the important trade routes from India to east Africa, and from India to southeast Asia. Furthermore, transoceanic crossings were apparently rare until very recently in navigational history, the Polynesian and Viking navigations being notable exceptions. However, one advocate for such crossings was Faublée (41), who used philological and oceanographic arguments to make his point. He drew attention to a Taimoro myth relating the arrival of Islam in Madagascar. In the story, Taimoro sailors return from Mecca to their country on the east coast of Madagascar while coming from the east. Mecca, however, lies north of Madagascar. According to Faublée, the name "Mecca" had to be a copyist's typo for an earlier "Malacca." He speculated that the myth refers to voyages back to southeast Asia, where the Taimoro would have learned about Islam. As a matter of fact, Malacca does lie to the east of Madagascar, but given the relatively recent foundation of Malacca in the early fifteenth century AD, this is not an obvious hypothesis (Islam had already been introduced to the Taimoro at that time). Faublée also argued that there is an Indian Ocean current that favors sailing from Sumatra to Madagascar. When Mount Krakatoa exploded at the end of the nineteenth century, pumice was washed ashore on Madagascar's east coast in a region where the Mananjary River opens into the sea. When Japanese aircraft bombed ships sailing between Java and Sumatra during World War II, pieces of wreckage ended up in this area, including a lifeboat with a survivor (41, p. 282).

Aside from the anecdotal nature of Faublée's evidence, transoceanic navigation may yet explain how Indonesian ships reached east Africa. For one thing, it would have saved these ships considerable travel time to make use of the ocean currents. Furthermore, Portuguese travelogues from the early sixteenth century mention "Javanese" (42) sailors in the Indian Ocean on their way to Madagascar. They also mention the availability of cloves on this island, a commodity which is demonstrably Moluccan in origin. Manguin (43), using Chinese and Portuguese sources, claims that southeast Asian cargo ships of up to 500 tonnes used to sail between southeast Asia and the Middle East between the third and sixteenth

centuries AD. These ships were originally built using lashed-lug and stitched-plank techniques, which were gradually replaced by techniques using planks and bulkheads fastened with doweling (and occasionally iron nailing). Manguin found that these techniques were also used on the Maldives, where they must have been introduced from southeast Asia. He was also able to trace an alternative navigation route between the eastern and western coasts of the Indian Ocean, which followed geographical latitudes instead of coasts, and which was used by southeast Asians. This route would connect the Sunda Strait to the Chagos Islands (with Diego Suarez) along the 6° south parallel, the Chagos Islands with the Maldives to the north, and the Maldives with Pulo We at the northern tip of Sumatra along the 6° north parallel (see Figure 13.2).

It would have taken Indonesian sailors less than 10 days to reach the Maldives along this route, which they used for slave trading (44). According to Manguin (43, p. 12): "We thus have proof, in the late 15th or 16th century, of shippers from insular South East Asia sailing along a route which is nowhere documented in Arabic, Chinese or Portuguese sea-pilots." Finally, the linguistic evidence is generally not in favor of early contacts between India and Madagascar. Indian loanwords in Malagasy are sometimes assumed to be borrowed directly from Indian languages, with which the early migrants were allegedly in contact during their voyages from Indonesia to east Africa (45). This assumption requires that the migrants also made use of coastal navigation. However, once it has become clear that almost all Indian loanwords were already in the language of the early migrants before they left Indonesia, this line of thinking becomes less compelling.

This does not mean that Austronesians never sailed via India, the Middle East, or other areas along the Indian Ocean on their way to east Africa (they obviously did). However, the evidence from maritime history and, indirectly, from historical linguistics shows that in their visits to east Africa they were not dependent on coastal navigation only. They also had the skills to make transoceanic crossings and may have preferred this mode of sailing at the time they migrated to east Africa.

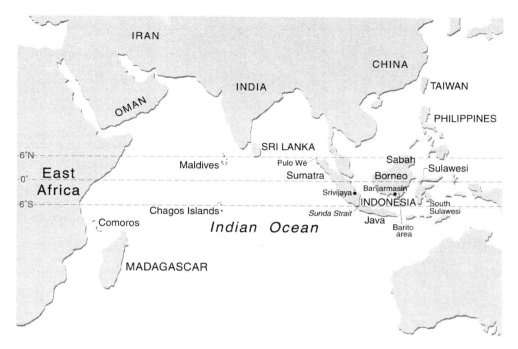

FIGURE 13.2. Indian Ocean navigation routes of the Malays in precolonial times.

Migration Dates

Dahl (2) used the presence (in his counting) of 30 Sanskrit loanwords in Malagasy as evidence that the migrations to east Africa must have taken place after the introduction of Indian influence in Indonesia. The oldest written evidence of Indian presence in this area is a Sanskrit inscription from around 400 AD found in Kutai, in southeast Borneo. Dahl therefore proposed the fifth century AD as the most likely migration period. In my 1989 article I interpret the Sanskrit influence in a different way (10). All but one of the Sanskrit loanwords in Malagasy have corresponding forms in Malay and/or Javanese. Moreover, many Sanskrit loanwords show the same phonological adaptations as their Malay and Javanese counterparts; I therefore conclude that the loanwords in question were actually borrowed via Malay or Javanese. Consequently, the migration date should not be correlated to the beginning of Indianization in the archipelago, but more specifically to the emergence of Sanskrit influence on Malay. This influence was the manifestation of an Indian Malay civilization, which was evidenced for the first time in the emergence of the maritime

polity of Srivijaya in the seventh century AD in south Sumatra (10, p. 32).

Dewar (46) points out that the dates proposed by Dahl (2) and Adelaar (10) should be reassessed in light of Ardika and Bellwood (47), who found that trade relations between India and insular southeast Asia go back much further in time, possibly as far as the second century BCE. While I appreciate the general importance of this finding, I do not think that it is immediately relevant to the Malagasy migration(s). The date in question is the oldest recorded date with regard to trade exchange with India. It is unlikely that such relations had an instant cultural impact on insular southeast Asia. The Indianized polities that developed in this area were of half a millennium later (cf. 48). On the other hand, evidence from seventh-century Old Malay inscriptions unequivocally shows that a thorough Indianization process was taking place in the (Malay) city of Srivijaya, reflected in, among other areas, political organization, religion, architecture, lexicon, the use of an Indian-based script, and the adaptation of writing itself. By the seventh century there had already been other Indianized polities in southeast

Asia, but Srivijaya was the first one clearly involving speakers of Malay. These inscriptions do not just provide a convenient "post quem" date for the first manifestation of Indian influence on Malay. They also date the emergence of a basically Malay society that (at least outwardly) embraced many aspects of Indian civilization.

The language of Srivijaya must have affected Malagasy, as the latter contains many Malay loanwords that reflect *e* for Malay penultimate *ə*. These loanwords can be opposed to Banjarese Malay loanwords in Malagasy that reflect the Malay penultimate schwa as *a*. Moreover, some of the Malay loanwords in Malagasy unmistakably stem from a southeast Sumatran environment, such as terms for cardinal directions and wind names, which could hardly have developed in Borneo, such as *varatraza* (< *barat daya) and *tsimilotru* or *tsimilautră* (< *timur *laut) (cf. *10*, pp. 9–11; *49*). One could add to this the occurrence of a few lines at the beginning of the Old Malay Telaga Batu and Kota Kapur inscriptions of 686, which seem to be a form of Maanyan (cf. *50, 51*), although attempts at their translation have not been entirely successful.

Correlating the immigration date with the beginning of Indian influence also involves another problem. It appears that several artifacts, food plants, and diseases had been transmitted between southeast Asia and Africa long before the migration dates proposed by Dahl and Adelaar. However, these events are not in contradiction and can be combined in a relative chronology, as discussed further below.

Genetic Research

Past research into the genetic origins of the Malagasy often yielded incomplete and conflicting results, which was partly due to the fact that only a subset of lineages present at any single locus could be identified. These results suggested that the Malagasy primarily descended from "Bantu-speaking Negroids" (*52*) or that they were genetically most closely linked to Javanese (*53*) or Polynesians (*54*).

In 2005 Hurles et al. issued a study involving "the detailed phylogenetic and geographic resolution of paternally inherited Y-chromosomal lineages and maternally inherited mitochondrial DNA lineages to apportion Malagasy lineages to ancestral populations." They claim that with their approach, "the contributions of different ancestral populations to the modern Malagasy gene pool can be estimated directly, and likely geographic origins can be pinpointed with precision" (*55*). The main findings of Hurles et al. are as follows:

1. The Malagasy are of mixed African–southeast Asian origin.
2. The Malagasy do not exhibit the same reduced genetic diversity as found in other recently colonized islands (as, for instance, in Pacific Island settlement). This supports direct, rather than multistep, migrations, or, alternatively, that successive waves of migration from Asia may have brought different sets of lineages to Madagascar.
3. Gene diversity for Asia-derived and Africa-derived maternal lineages in the Malagasy shows that Asian lineages are significantly more diverse. This would mean that migrations from Africa may have been more limited than those from Indonesia (p. 899).
4. The paternal and maternal estimates of the proportion of African ancestry in the Malagasy are statistically indistinguishable, which means that there is no evidence of ancient sex-based admixture (p. 899, col. 2).
5. There is a "mitochondrial Polynesian motif" among maternal Malagasy lineages (cf. *54*). However, direct migration from Polynesia can be discounted "since the predominant y-chromosomal haplogroups found in Polynesians (O3 and C) are not found at all among Malagasy paternal lineages."
6. Among 10 potential ancestral populations elsewhere in the Austronesian world, the Borneo populations (of Banjarmasin and Kota Kinabalu) had Y-chromosomal haplogroup distributions that were the most similar to those observed among the Malagasy.

The attraction of the study by Hurles et al. (*55*) is that it is the first genetic study of the Malagasy population that appears to be compatible with the linguistic evidence. It vindicates a more than 50-year-old argument entirely based on historical linguistics, which claims that the Asian origins of the Malagasy primarily have to be sought in south Borneo. The publication is therefore good news, although one wonders why the researchers selected the city of Banjarmasin as one of their testing areas instead of the Maanyan-speaking area itself, which is not far from Banjarmasin. Assuming that the approach of Hurles et al. (55) is generally sound and that it is a methodological improvement over previous research, it is a major step toward solving the problem of the origins of the Malagasy.

The research also leaves open the possibility that several southeast Asian groups migrated to Madagascar at different times. This correlates with the (socio)linguistic theory that the Asian ancestors of the Malagasy may have come from different parts of southeast Asia, provided that the first group of migrants included predominantly Southeast Barito speakers who became a nuclear group to whom all subsequent migrants would assimilate linguistically. Later migrants may have contributed to Malagasy regional and mainstream culture to such an extent that its distinct Southeast Barito features became less prominent or were lost. Linguistically, however, they would have had to adapt to the language of the nuclear group (12, 56). It also accommodates another theory proposing that links between southeast Asia and east Africa were primarily established by Malays, who were also the agents behind the migrations of Southeast Barito speakers to Madagascar (that is, Southeast Barito speakers as well as subsequent people who would adapt linguistically, if indeed the Southeast Barito speakers were only a nuclear group) (13, 56). The latter must have been used as subordinates (ship crew or slaves) in Malay-led voyages to east Africa. This theory supports the fact that neither the Southeast Barito Dayaks nor the Malagasy have ever developed the sort of seafaring skills required for the ambitious voyages that their ancestors made, while the Malays have. The Malays have a remarkable maritime past, were historically in contact with Sri Lanka and other places in the Indian Ocean, and held the cultural and political hegemony in insular southeast Asia for a long time. Their presence is evidenced by a very large number of cultural loanwords in Malagasy, and Malagasy terminology pertaining to the sea, winds, cardinal directions, and maritime skills is largely borrowed from Malay. Both the nuclear group theory and the theory proposing the Malays as the agents

behind the Malagasy migrations—which are compatible—presuppose that the migrants belonged to more than one ethnic group (57).

The conclusions of Hurles et al. (55) also lend support to Deschamps's (39) theory proposing that the early Austronesian migrants went to mainland Africa first before they populated Madagascar. Hurles et al. (55) point out that there is no indication of a sex-based admixture in the African ancestry of the Malagasy. This contradicts Dahl's observation that at an early stage in Malagasy society, migrants from Asia may have been predominantly males and that they married Bantu women. Many Bantu loanwords in Malagasy refer to names of edible plants and their fruits, as well as to terms related to food preparation, which are "words that have a special relation to women and their occupations" (16, p. 126). However, I am not convinced that these words are symptomatic of a gender bias in Bantu loanwords in general. Dahl's evidence consists of 14 correspondence sets, which are presented in Appendix 13.3. Words related to food preparation, such as cooking terms and names of dishes, are in most cultures gender-related, but this is not necessarily the case with terms for edible plants and their fruits, which make up a considerable part (six) of Dahl's loanwords. Another term, meaning "soot," does not typically belong to the female domain either. The remaining seven terms are interesting, but they have to be seen in the overall context of Bantu loanwords. Some other loanwords definitely belong to the male domain, which clearly undermines Dahl's claim. Many terms for animals are of Bantu origin, including the words for the main domestic animals, such as dog, goat, cow, sheep, donkey, chicken, and guinea fowl. Compare the animal correspondence sets presented in Appendix 13.3.

The large number of Bantu animal names in Appendix 13.3, especially the terms for large domestic animals, suggests a gender bias opposite in direction from the one claimed by Dahl. In Madagascar, as well as in Africa in general, the care of cattle is very much a male concern. It is clear, as Dahl (16) already pointed out, that the early Malagasy relied heavily on their Bantu neighbours to get acquainted with the local fauna and with cattle breeding, even when this involved animals also present in Borneo. Indonesian names for domestic animals seem to have been lost or to have become lexically unstable. An example of the latter is Malay *ləmbu* "cow, bull, ox," which was borrowed into Malagasy as *lambu* "wild pig" (*58*).

On balance, Dahl's inventory of Bantu loan-words includes domains that appear gender-related, but there are male as well as female domains, and Bantu loanwords in their totality are not biased towards any gender in particular.

The Advent of Islam

Islam was introduced at different times and in various places in Madagascar. The oldest evidence of Islam is the ruins of a thirteenth-century mosque in Mahilaka, an archaeological site representing one of the earliest towns on the island. Remains of many other more recent Islamicized towns with mosques are also found.

The Antalaotra (Antalaotse) on the west coast and the Antaimoro on the east coast are traditional Muslim Malagasy communities; other Muslim communities were converted in the nineteenth century (among the Antankarana in the northwest) or are ethnically Indians or Comorians (*59*).

The Antalaotra have had longstanding links with Muslim centers in the Comoros and on Africa's east coast. Many of them know Swahili (*59*). However, their origins and early history remain poorly known.

The Antaimoro, on the other hand, have a much more indigenized form of Islam, so much so that Gueunier (*59*) decided not to include them in his inventory of Muslim communities. The Antaimoro practice male circumcision, the ritual slaughter of animals, a taboo on pork meat, the use of the Arabic script, and various divination techniques (geomancy and astrology, including a zodiacal calendar). However, as Gueunier points out, ritual slaughter of animals, pork taboo, and circumcision are practices that already existed in some form before Islam. Moreover, slaughtering animals is traditionally a prerogative of Antaimoro aristocrats (one they already had before the advent of Islam), and pork is prohibited for the class of aristocrats only (other classes being characterized by different food taboos); divination is not part of orthodox Islam. Dahl (*51*) believed that this traditional and hybrid form of Islam was introduced

via Oman. This is understandable, given the relative proximity of this Arab sultanate and the leading political and religious role it played in east Africa in the past. However, the Antaimoro language and use of the Arabic script provide clues that suggest an Indonesian source and may be very important for dating postmigratory contacts with Indonesia. As I have demonstrated elsewhere (*10, 12*), the Antaimoro word *sumbili* "slaughtering in a ritual way" must be an adaptation of Malay *səmbəlih*, a word that now means "slaughtering" in general but historically had a sacral meaning specifically referring to slaughtering in a Muslim ritual way (*60*). It is the Malay transformation of the spoken Arabic term *bɛsmɛlɛːh*, which means "the utterance of *b'ismi'llāhi* as a requirement for the ritual slaughter of animals" and is in turn derived from the Classical Arabic formula *b'ismi'llāhi* "in the name of God." The Antaimoro version of the Arabic script, now called Sorabe, shows several adaptations that were also made in the Jawi (Malay) and Pégon (Javanese) adaptations of the Arabic script. More particularly, it uses the same graphic conventions for *p* and (velar nasal) *ŋ* as Jawi and Pégon do, and it uses the same graphic conventions for *d* and *t* as Pégon does for retroflex *d* and *t* (*61*). In contrast, Dahl traced Sorabe to Omani Arabic, but he did so on the false assumption that the Sorabe use of غ as a voiced velar stop *g* was copied from Omani Arabic (*12*, pp. 337–338).

A question that Dahl left unanswered is whether any particular branch of Islam can be recognized in the religion of the Antaimoro, which would help to find out the source of these adaptations. Indonesian Islam is basically Sunni, although it also shows (or showed in the past) some Shi'a tendencies. Oman, however, is remarkable for being neither Sunni nor Shi'a. It has always embraced its own, Ibadi, version of Islam. This is a moderate form of the Khariji doctrine rejecting a dynastic Caliphate and demanding that the role of Imam be given to the most pious Muslim in every community. It also maintains some formal distinctions, such as different postures during prayer. Taimoro Islam is essentially Sunni, with an admixture of Shi'a elements (*62*): does it exhibit these features? If so, then Dahl probably had a point; if not, the possibility that Islam was introduced to Madagascar from Indonesia is still on the table. The matter clearly deserves further attention.

First Contacts

The first contacts between Indonesia and east Africa and the migration of Southeast Barito speakers to Madagascar must have been two distinct historical events. Dahl (*2*) and I (*10*) have both proposed periods around the middle of the first millennium AD as possible (earliest) migration dates, primarily based on linguistic evidence. The difficulty with these dates is that they do not always tally with biological and material cultural evidence. Blench (*40*) discusses the cultural items, food plants, and diseases that were transmitted between southeast Asia and east Africa. He provides a conservative inventory, which basically consists of the following items:

- Food plants: the sweet banana (*Musa paradisiaca*), water yam (*Dioscora alata*), and taro (*Colocasia esculentum*)

- Boat types: outrigger boats, boats made of skins sewn together, and a type of large canoe found on Lake Victoria

- Diseases: elephantiasis

- Musical instruments: the stick-zither, the leaf-funnel clarinet, and the xylophone

Blench makes the point that some of these items can be shown to have been introduced in east Africa much earlier than the fifth or seventh century AD. This suggests that the first contacts between southeast Asia and east Africa must have happened perhaps as early as 2,200 years ago (*40*, p. 432). Blench's inventory deliberately leaves out some plants and diseases that are not unambiguously southeast Asian in origin and/or may have reached east Africa only indirectly from southeast Asia (for instance, along the "Sabaean Lane," the trade route connecting India with the Horn of Africa).

The point could be made that even this inventory is not waterproof, conservative as it is. While there is reasonable evidence to assume that the above food plants and at least outrigger boats were introduced from southeast Asia to Africa, things are less certain in the case of elephantiasis. For a long time, this disease was thought to have originated in southeast Asia, but this assumption is now open to doubt (*63*). With regard to the musical instruments, Blench makes a distinction between the stick-zither and the leaf-funnel clarinet,

which must have their origins in southeast Asia, and the xylophone. The latter is usually considered to have been borrowed from southeast Asia into Africa, but Blench makes a good case for transmission in the opposite direction. His arguments are that Africa has a wide typological variety of xylophones, including prototypical ones, whereas Asian xylophones basically represent one type of xylophone only; furthermore, xylophones are unknown among Malagasy speakers in Madagascar itself, Austronesia's westernmost outpost (*40*).

On a more positive note, there are also items that should be added to Blench's list. One such item is the *valiha* "zither", an instrument that is highly emblematic of Madagascar's traditional heritage. Beaujard (*35*, p. 145) traces its name back to Sanskrit *vādya(ka)*- "music," *vādiya*- "musical instrument." However, this name must have its archetypal counterpart in the *balikan* in Borneo. The latter is known as *balikan* among the Ambalo speakers (in Hulu Kapuas Regency in the northeastern part of west Kalimantan, Indonesia) and as *bəlikan* among the Iban (northwest Borneo) (*64*). The sound correspondences between *valiha* and *balikan* (*65*) are entirely regular, and the etymological link obviously supports the Borneo homeland hypothesis.

It is, however, not my intention here to try to fine-tune Blench's inventory. Allowing for the possibility that not all items in it may have been transmitted directly from southeast Asia to east Africa, there is little doubt that many of them did follow that road, implying that contacts between the two regions are much older than the fifth or seventh century AD.

These very old contacts are no reason to change our speculations on the time frame of the Austronesian migrations to Madagascar. Rather, they show that there were sustained contacts for at least half a millennium (and probably much longer), and that a drastic distinction should be made between the period in which the first contacts between Indonesians and east Africans took place, and the actual period that Southeast Barito speakers migrated to east Africa. These migrations took place much later, and most likely after the foundation of Srivijaya, which was in the seventh century AD at the latest. In other words, the first contacts may be more than two millennia old, but the actual migrations began around the seventh century AD.

Another point is that the migration to east Africa should not automatically be equated with the settlement of Madagascar itself. As proposed by Deschamps (39) and later authors, the Malagasy immigrants from Indonesia may first have spent time on the African mainland before they came to Madagascar. This "anteroom" scenario is less far-fetched than it seems. Madagascar is linguistically remarkably monolingual, and the effects of the common Bantu stage are witnessed in the phonologies of all present-day Malagasy dialects (66). Most Malagasy are to some extent of mixed African and Asian descent (55). Furthermore, recent archaeological excavations have shown that the island became systematically inhabited only after the eighth century AD, and there is no continuity between archaeological sites (ceramics, animal domestication) in the Austronesian world and those found in Madagascar, which are very similar to east African and Comorian sites (46, 67, 68). All these factors fit in rather nicely with the anteroom scenario and suggest that a mixed Austronesian-Bantu society had come into being before Madagascar became populated; one would not expect such a genetic and linguistic homogeneity if such a society had developed in Madagascar itself. But if the Asian ancestors of the Malagasy first arrived on the east African coast before they settled in Madagascar, the obvious questions concern why they made this detour, and why there are no longer any Malagasy on the African mainland. Also, is there any evidence left of mainland settlements? Of course, the usual explanation is that the Bantu migrations from central Africa into eastern and southern Africa, which began in the first millennium AD, must have swept away most evidence of earlier populations along the African coast. In the process, the ancestors of the present-day Malagasy population must have been pushed back into the Comoros and later on into Madagascar, which, it must be remembered, was basically uninhabited before the eighth century AD. (Or, rather than being pushed back, the Austronesians may at some point have occupied both sides of the Mozambique channel, whereby those living in Madagascar would eventually remain out of reach of the leveling Bantu influence on the African east coast

and the Comoros) (69). This explanation seems straightforward enough, but it needs further testing in order to lift it beyond the level of speculation. A supplementary explanation is that the perceived lack of evidence of an earlier Indonesian presence in east Africa may be due to a lack of research on the African mainland and to a possible reluctance among archaeologists and historians working on east Africa to interpret their data from this angle. These scholars understandably do not want to entertain undue speculations, but it is also hard to avoid the conclusion that Indonesians somehow must have had connections with mainland east Africa in the light of the genetic, linguistic, and archaeological research discussed above.

Conclusions

Malay loanwords in Malagasy clearly demonstrate the crucial role of the Malays in the contacts between southeast Asia and east Africa, and in bringing about the migration of the Indonesian ancestors of the Malagasy to the western shores of the Indian Ocean. Loanwords from other Austronesian languages in Malagasy had less of an impact.

The lexical evidence indirectly supports the theory that Indonesians were able to reach east Africa through direct ocean crossings. Sanskrit loanwords in Malagasy were borrowed via Malay (and possibly Javanese), and not directly from Indian languages. As a consequence, these loanwords were already in the language of the first migrants and do not testify to possible direct contacts (through coastal navigation or otherwise) between these migrants and the Indian subcontinent.

The combined evidence from archaeology, human genetics, and linguistics seems to support Deschamps's (39) theory that the early Austronesian migrants first stayed on the east African mainland before they settled in Madagascar.

The introduction of Islam to Madagascar by Indonesians is a possibility and needs further investigation.

The first contacts between southeast Asia and East Africa are possibly 2,200 years old. The migrations to east Africa and the settlement of Madagascar, however, are probably of the seventh and eighth centuries AD, respectively.

Appendix 13.1: Malay Loanwords

TABLE 13.3. Malay Marine Loanwords

Malagasy	Malay
a/varatră "north"	*barat* "west"
varatraza (Betsimisaraka) "south wind"	*barat daya* "southwest"
tsimilautru (Betsimisaraka) "north wind"	*timur laut* "northeast"
rivutră "wind"	(*angin*) *ribut* "storm wind"
rantu "1. go trading to far-out places or countries; 2. product of such trading"	*rantaw* "1. reach of a river; 2. go abroad for trading"
tanjună "cape, promontory"	*tanjung* "id."
fasikă, fasină "sand"	*pasir* "sand; beach"
truzună "whale"	*duyung* "sea cow"
lambuara "a species of fish"	*lembuara* "a giant fish (possibly a whale)" and Old Javanese *lembwara, lembora* "a very large fish (whale? porpoise?)"
harană "coral-reef, coral-rock"	*karang* "id."
hara "mother-of-pearl"	*karah* "tartar on teeth, stain; patchy in coloring (tortoise- shell)"
sambu "boat, vessel"	Old Malay *sāmvaw* "vessel"
tampikă (North) "outrigger"	Brunei Malay *sa-tampik* "on one side"
tuna "large nocturnal snake; enormous eel"	*tuna* name of a mud-snake or eel with yellowish body"
fanuhara (Sakalava) "turtle with a particular k.o. shell"	*penyu karah* "tortoise-shell turtle, *Ch. imbricata*"
vatuharanană, vatokaranană[1] "quartz"	*batu karang* "coral rock"
huala (North) "bay, inlet"; cf. also *Ankuala* (a region in northern Madagascar)	*kuala* "river mouth"
an-drefană "west"	*depan* "(in) front"
nusi "island"	Javanese (or Malay) *nusa* (with variant forms *nusya, nuswa* and *nungsa*)[2] "id."
sagari "a northeast wind"	*segara* "sea" < Sanskrit *sāgara-* "the ocean"
vidi (North) "k.o. small fish"	(*ikan*) *bilis* "anchovy, Macassar redfish; small fish, esp. *Stolephorus* spp."
hurita "octopus"	*gurita* "id."
vuntană (North) "k.o. fish"	(*ikan*) *buntal* "box-fish, globe-fish or sea-porcupine"
fanu "turtle"	*penyu* "id." (*fano* is probably from Banjarese Malay on account of its *a*)

Note: k.o. = kind of.

[1] The Malagasy forms must be derived from **+batu +karang** + **+**-an.

[2] The origin of this apparently non-Austronesian word is unknown.

Appendix 13.2: South Sulawesi Loanwords

Huta "a chew," Maanyan *kota* "eaten" corresponds with Proto–South Sulawesi **kota* "to chew" (Buginese *ota* "id."); it does not have corresponding forms in other Austronesian languages. The *–a* instead of expected *–i* in *huta* betrays that this word is borrowed.

Matua "the eldest" (used in conjunction with kinship terms) corresponds with Macassarese, Buginese, South Toraja *ma-tua* "old." The Malagasy default term for "old" is *antitra*. *Matua* is derived from Proto-Austronesian **tuqah* "old" but must ultimately be borrowed on account of its *–a* (compare this to another Malagasy term *ma-tui* "old, mature, serious, reasonable," which does exhibit the expected *–I* and must be inherited).

Sulu "a substitute": compare Macassarese, Buginese *pas-soloʔ*, Duri *soloʔ* "present(money, goods) given at celebrations," South Toraja *pas-suluʔ* "money borrowed on short term and without requiring interest" (< Proto–South Sulawesi **sulu(r)* "exchange, pay"). This set has no corresponding forms in other Austronesian languages. Malagasy *sulu* must be borrowed because it has maintained s- (elsewhere, Proto-Austronesian **s* > Malagasy ø).

Ta- This is a prefix forming an ethnic name or geographically definable group of people; for instance, *ta-lautra* denotes an ethnic group supposedly originating from across the Mozambique channel (cf. Malay *laut* "sea"); *ta-nusi* "island people (cf. Malagasy *nusi* "island"). It derives from Proto-Austronesian **taw* "human being, person." This etymon survived as a free form *taw and a prefix ta-, to- or tu- in South Sulawesi languages (cf. *To-raja* lit. "people from the inland," the name of an ethnic group). In East Barito languages, however, it was replaced by **hulun* (Malagasy *ulună*) as a default form for "human being." If Malagasy has a supplementary *ta-*, this could theoretically be an inherited reflex of Proto-Austronesian **taw*, but it is more likely to be a loan prefix from South Sulawesi languages.

Taneti "high and flat terrain, bare hill between two valleys; mainland, terra firma." This word has no Proto-Austronesian etymon, but it does have corresponding forms in South Sulawesi languages: Macassarese *tanete* "rolling (hills), hilly terrain"; Buginese *tanete* "elevated terrain, high country," South Toraja *tanete* "hill, low mountain."

Untsi "kind of banana" agrees with Macassarese *unti*, Buginese *utti* (< **unti*) "banana." All these forms ultimately derive from Proto-Austronesian **punti* "banana." However, the loss of **p-* is usual in Buginese, but not in Malagasy: it is therefore likely that Malagasy *untsi* is borrowed from South Sulawesi.

Vadi "spouse" corresponds with Macassarese *paʔbalibaliaŋ* "spouse," South Toraja *bali* "partner, associate, spouse, opponent," also South Toraja *si-bali-aŋ* "to get married." The latter three forms derive from Proto-Austronesian **baluy/*baliw*. This etymon must have meant (among other things) "to oppose, opposite part; friend, partner"; it has two reflexes in Malagasy, the aforementioned *vadi* "spouse" and *valu* "alteration." The Proto-Austronesian final diphthong **-uy* regularly becomes *–u* in Malagasy; I therefore assume that *vadi* is borrowed from a South Sulawesi language, and *valu* is inherited. Note also that the original Proto-Austronesian words for "spouse" were **sawa* "wife" and **bana* "husband."

Vuhu "the back of something" and *i-vuhu* "behind" correspond with Buginese, South Toraja *bokoʔ* "back (body-part)." These forms are reflexes of Proto–South Sulawesi **boko(tʔ)* "back," which replaced an earlier Proto-Austronesian **likud* "back" (the latter has many reflexes throughout the Austronesian language family).

TABLE 13.4. Body-part Terms Borrowed from Malay

Malagasy	Malay
*vuavits*i "calf of leg"	*buah betis* "id."
mulutră "upper lip"	*mulut* "mouth"; cf. Proto-Austronesian *vava
tsufină "outer ear"	*cuping* "lobe (e.g., of ear)"
tratra "chest"	*dada* "id."
tanană "hand"	*tangan* "id."; cf. Proto-Austronesian *lima
hihi "gums; (dialectally:) teeth"	*gigi* "teeth"; Proto-Austronesian *[n,l,ø]ipən
valahană "loins"	*bəlakang* "back; space behind"; cf. Proto-Austronesian *likud
haranka (dialectal) "chest," Bara Malagasy *haráka* "skeleton"	*kərangka* "skeleton"

TABLE 13.5. Body-part Terms Possibly Borrowed from Malay

Malagasy	Malay
vaukă (dialectal) "hair along the jawbones"	bauk
handrină "eyebrow"	*kəning* "forehead"
huhu "nail"	kuku
tumutră/tumitră "heel"	tumit
vua "fruit; kidneys"	buah ginjal
vutu "penis"	butuh
fifi "cheek"	pipi

TABLE 13.6. Malay Loanwords Affected by the Bantu Contact Stage

sakană	"anything put across, any obstacle or impediment" (Malay *sangkar* "diagonal, line across or athwart")
huntsană	"rinsing (of bottles)" (Malay *goñcaŋ* "shake")
harană	"coral-reef, coral-rock" (Malay *karaŋ* "id.")
vuruně	"bird" (Malay *buruŋ* "id.")
fara/fara	"bed-frame" (Malay *para-para* "[under-]frame")
sandratră	"elevated" (Malay *sandar* "reclining, resting on a support")
tranu	"house" (Malay *daŋaw* "id.")
trusa	"debt" (Malay *dosa* "sin" < Sanskrit *dośa* "id.")

TABLE 13.7. Malay Loanwords Not Affected by the Bantu Contact Stage

fiŋga	"plate" (Malay *piŋgan* "id.," possibly borrowed directly from Persian (cf. Persian *piŋgān* "cup")
sagari	"a northeast wind" (Malay, Javanese *səgara* "sea" < Sanskrit *sāgara-* "ocean")
kurintsană	"loud noise, as the sound of pieces of glass, gold or silver; small silver pieces used as ornament on hands and legs; jingle" (Malay *kərəñcaŋ* "to champ" "to clang; the crash of cymbals") (*11*)
budu	"infantile" (Malay *bodo(h)* "uneducated, stupid")
puki (Comorian dialects)	"(a curse)," *mi-puki* "swear, curse" (Malay *puki* "vagina," *puki mai* ("a grossly insulting expression") (*1*)
landaizană	"anvil" (Malay *landasan*, Minangkabau Malay *landehan* "id.")
tsingi	"mountain peak" (Malay *tiŋgi* "high")

Appendix 13.3. Correspondences between Bantu and Malagasy

These correspondences were proposed by Dahl (*14*). Malagasy forms are from the Merina dialect unless indicated otherwise.

mumba "sterile woman," Swahili *m-gumba* "id.";
< Proto-Bantu *gumba

Food Plants and Their Fruit

mangga-hazu "cassava" (< Bantu *mangga* "cassava" + Proto-Austronesian *kaSiw "wood; tree"; (various Bantu languages have *mangga* "cassava") (*72*)
ampembi, (Sakalava Malagasy) *ampemba* "millet";
< Proto–East Bantu *-pemba
akundru "banana," cf. Shingazije *ng-kudu* "id.";
Proto–Western Bantu *-kondo/koondro
vuan-tanggu "melon" (*vua* "fruit" < Proto-Austronesian *buaq "fruit" + Merina *-n-* (indicating possessive) + Proto-Bantu *-tangga "pumpkin, cucumber, melon"), cf. Swahili *tanggo* "pumpkin, watermelon"
vu-andzu "ground-nut" (< Proto-Austronesian *buaq "fruit" + Proto-Bantu *-jugu "ground-nut"), Swahili *n-džugu* "id."
tunggulu "onion," cf. Swahili *ki-tungguu* "id.";
Proto-Bantu *-tungguda

Preparation of Meals

hufa "to shake, sift, winnow," *akufa* "chaff";
*Proto-East Bantu *-kup- "to shake off"

ampumbu "husk, bran," cf. Swahili *pumba*, Mambwe *pumbu* "id."
sa-hafa "winnowing pan"; Proto-Bantu *-kapa "to spill moving to and fro"
(Sakalava Malagasy) *mutru* "fire," Swahili *m-oto*, Comorian *m-oro* "id."; < Proto-Bantu *-yoto
nunggu "earthen pot," cf. Swahili *nyunggu* "id.";
< Proto-Bantu *-yunggu "clay pot"
(*mu-*)*kuku* "crust in pot," cf. Swahili *u-koko* "id.";
Proto-Bantu *-koko
mulali, (Sakalava Malagasy) *mulale* "soot," cf. Swahili *m-lale* "id."

Domestic Animals

ambúa "dog," cf. Swahili, Comorian *mbwa*;
< Proto-Bantu *-bua
usi, (Sakalava Malagasy) *uze* "goat," cf. Swahili, Comorian *mbuzi*; < Proto-Bantu *-budi
umbi, (Sakalava Malagasy) *a-umbe*, (Vezo) *anumbe* "cattle," cf. Swahili *ngombe*, Shindzwani, Shimaore *ny-ombe*, Shingazije *mbe*; < Proto-Bantu *-gombe, *-ngombe
undri, (Sakalava Malagasy) *angundri* "sheep"; cf. Shimaore *gondzi*, northeast Bantu languages *ondi, gondi, gonzi*
akuhu "chicken," cf. Swahili *khuku*, Shimaore *kuhu*, Shingazije, Shindzwani *ng-kuhu* < Proto-Bantu *-kuku
ampundra "donkey," cf. Swahili *punda*, Shimaore *pundra*, Shingazije, Shindzwani *m-pundra*

akangga "guinea-fowl," cf. Swahili *khangga*, Shingazije *ng-kangga* < Proto-Bantu *-kangga

Other Animals

pili "large tree serpent," cf. Swahili *phili* "big, dangerous snake" < Proto-Bantu *pidi "puff-adder"

papanggu "vulture, *Milvus aegyptius*," cf. Swahili *phunggu* "k.o. vulture," Shimaore *papanggu* "carrion-eater" < Proto-Bantu *-punggu "k.o. eagle"

lulu butterfly, cf. Swahili *m-lulu* "insect; boogey man"

(Sakalava Malagasy) *ampaha* "wild cat," cf. Swahili

phaka, Shimaore *paha*, Shindzwani *m-paha*; < Proto-East Bantu *-paka "id."

kúnggună, (Sakalava) *kunggu* "bedbug," cf. Swahili *kungguni*; < Proto-Bantu *-kungguni

(Vezo Malagasy) *luvu, uluvu* "k.o. fish" < Proto-Bantu *-dûb "fish"

(Vezo Malagasy) *amban-tsui* "k.o. fish" < Proto-Bantu *cûi/cûî "fish"

mamba "big crocodile," (Vezo Malagasy) *ambamba* "k.o. fish," cf. Swahili *mamba* "scale of fish or reptile; crocodile; poisonous snake"; < Proto-Bantu *-bamba "k.o. poisonous snake," also "fish-scale"

Notes

1. Unless otherwise indicated, the lexical data in this chapter were taken from the sources listed below.

Arabic: H. Wehr, *A Dictionary of Modern Written Arabic* (*Arabic-English*), 4th ed. (Spoken Language Services, Inc., Ithaca, 1994).

Banjar Malay: A. Hapip, *Kamus Banjar-Indonesia* (Pusat Pembinaan dan Pengembangan Bahasa, Jakarta, 1977).

Bantu languages: O. Dahl, *Études Océan Indien* 9, 91–132 (1988).

Bara Malagasy: L. Elli, *Dizionario Bara-Italiano* (Ambozontany, Fianarantsona, 1988).

Betsimisaraka Malagasy: M. Dalmond, *Vocabulaire et grammaire pour les langues malgaches sakalave et betsimisaraka* (Imprimerie de Lahuppe, Saint Denis [Île Bourbon], 1842).

Brunei Malay: R. Wilkinson, *A Malay-English Dictionary* (Macmillan, London, 1959).

Buginese: B. Matthes, *Boegineesch—Hollandsch woordenboek* (Nijhoff, The Hague, 1874).

Comorian dialects: O. Dahl, *Études Océan Indien* 9, 91–132 (1988).

Comorian Malagasy: The two dialects spoken on Mayotte have converged considerably, although their origins are different. Kiantalaotsy is close to Malagasy as spoken in the Majunga region, and Kimaore is more akin to the dialect of Sambirano and Nosy Be (N. Gueunier, *Études Océan Indien* 7 [1986]).

Maanyan: O. Dahl, *Malgache et Maanyan*. Avhandlinger utgitt av Instituttet 3 (Egede Instituttet, Oslo, 1951).

Macassarese: A. Cense, *Makassaars—Nederlandsch Woordenboek* (Nijhoff, The Hague, 1979).

Malagasy: A. Abinal, V. Malzac, *Dictionnaire Malgache-Français* (Éditions Maritimes et d'Outre-Mer, Paris, 1963).

Malagasy "dialectal": J. Richardson, *A New Malagasy-English Dictionary* (London Missionary Society, Tananarivo, 1885).

Malay: R. Wilkinson, *A Malay-English Dictionary* (Macmillan, London, 1959).

Merina Malagasy: A. Abinal, V. Malzac, *Dictionnaire Malgache-Français* (Éditions Maritimes et d'Outre-Mer, Paris, 1963).

Northern Malagasy dialects (including Antankarana and Tsimihety): Velonandro, *Lexique des Dialectes du Nord de Madagaskar* (CEDRATOM, Tuléar, 1983).

Old Javanese: P. Zoetmulder, *Old Javanese-English Dictionary* (KITLV publication, Nijhoff, The Hague, 1982).

Old Malay: J. De Casparis, *Prasasti Indonesia II: Selected Inscriptions from the 7th to the 9th Century A.D.* (Masa Baru, Bandung, 1956).

Proto-Austronesian, Proto-Malayo-Polynesian: R. Blust, *Oceanic Linguistics* 19, 1–189 (1980); 22–23, 29–149 (1983–1984); 25, 1–123 (1986).

Proto–South Sulawesi: R. Mills, Proto-South-Sulawesi and Proto-Austronesian Phonology (Ph.D. diss., Univ. of Michigan, Ann Arbor, 1975).

Sakalava Malagasy: D. Thomas-Fattier, *Le Dialecte Sakalava du Nord-Ouest de Madagascar* (SELAF, Paris, 1982).

Sanskrit: J. Gonda, *Sanskrit in Indonesia* (International Academy of Indian Culture, New Delhi, 1973).

Shindzuani-, Shimaore-, Shingazije Comorian: O. Dahl, *Études Océan Indien* 9, 91–132 (1988).

South Toraja: H. Van der Veen, *Tae'* (*Zuid-Toradjasch)-Nederlandsch Woordenboek* (Nijhoff, The Hague, 1940).

Tandroy Malagasy: N. Rajaonarimanana, S. Fee, *Dictionnaire Malgache Dialectal–Français:*

Dialecte Tandroy (Langues & Mondes, L'Asia-thèque, Paris, 1996).

(Sumatran) Malay: see Malay.

Vezo Malagasy: O. Dahl, *Études Océan Indien* 9, 91–132 (1988).

2. O. Dahl, *Malgache et Maanyan* (Egede Institut-tet, Oslo, 1951).

3. A. Hudson, *The Barito Isolects of Borneo* (Cornell University Press, Ithaca, 1967), pp. 90–114.

4. Cf. also O. Dahl, *Acta Orientalia* 38, 77–134 (1977), which is an evaluation of Hudson's data and classification.

5. I. Dyen, *Language* 29, 577–590 (1953).

6. A. Adelaar, in B. Champion, ed., *L'Étranger Intime* (Océan Éditions, Saint-André, 1995).

7. K. Djantera, I. Abdurachman, W. Ranrung, *Struktur Bahasa Maanyan* (Departemen Pendidikan dan Kebudayaan, Jakarta, 1984).

8. Y. K. Andriastuti et al., *Morfologi dan Sintaks Bahasa Lawangan* (Departemen Pendidikan dan Kebudayaan Jakarta, 1992).

9. D. Mulyani Santoso et al., *Fonologi bahasa Paku* (Departemen Pendidikan dan Kebudayaan, Jakarta, 1989).

10. A. Adelaar, *Oceanic Linguistics* 28(1), 1–46 (1989).

11. A. Adelaar, *Bijdragen tot de Taal-, Land- en Volkenkunde* 150, 49–64 (1994).

12. A. Adelaar, *Bijdragen tot de Taal-, Land- en Volkenkunde* 151, 325–357 (1995).

13. A. Adelaar, in I. Hussain et al., eds., *Tamadun Melayu: Jilid Pertama* (Dewan Bahasa dan Pustaka, Kuala Lumpur, 1995), pp. 21–40.

14. O. Dahl, *Acta Orientalia* 38, 77–134 (1977).

15. L. Reid and H.-C. Liao (*Language and Linguistics* 5(2), 433–490 [2004]) reject this label as it assumes a greater structural uniformity among Philippine languages than is justified.

16. O. Dahl, *Études Océan Indien* 9, 91–132 (1988).

17. A. Hudson, in T. Harrison, ed., *Borneo Writing and Related Matters* (Special Monograph No. 1., Sarawak Museum Journal, 1963), pp. 341–415.

18. A. Hudson, *Padju Epat* (Holt, Rinehart and Winston, New York, 1972).

19. A. Hudson, J. Hudson, in Koentjaraningrat, ed., *Villages in Indonesia* (Cornell Univ. Press, Ithaca, 1967), pp. 90–114.

20. Y. Takaya, *Madagascar* (Kyoto Univ. Center for Southeast Asian Studies, Kyoto, 1988).

21. R. Dick-Read, *The Phantom Voyagers* (Thurlton, Winchester, 2005).

22. (Merina) Malagasy has added a whispered vowel *ă* to words that originally ended in a consonant.

23. The word *i/tasi* derives from an earlier *i/tasiha-nakă,* the name of a big lake (with back-formation:

< * i/tasih-anakă < *i + *tasik + *anak "small sea")(2, p. 316).

24. O. Dahl, *Norsk Tidsskrift for Sporgvidenskap* 16, 148–200 (1954).

25. Dahl believed in a Bantu substratum because he assumed that Madagascar originally had a Bantu population that abandoned its language for that of in-migrating Austronesians; I do not share this view. "Bantu contact stage" is not entirely accurate either, but I use it for want of a better term. Theoretically, one could also question the validity of the label "Bantu," as the phonological consequences of this stage are only typical of Comorian languages, and not of Bantu languages in general. Finally, "Comorian contact stage" may not be appropriate either as it is not possible to establish whether the changes are due to Comorian influence on Malagasy, to Malagasy influence on Comorian, or to an outside influence on both Comorian and Malagasy.

26. There are, of course, also other factors influencing the adaptation of loanwords to the phonology of the borrowing language, but these are not discussed here.

27. No relation to Arabic *qāḍī* "judge": reflexes of this etymon are well represented in languages in western Indonesia.

28. The resulting cluster in this compound is still witnessed in an altered form in Sundanese *rutsak;* see F. Eringa, *Soendaas-Nederlands Woordenboek* (Foris Publications, Dordrecht, 1984).

29. Note that initial *l* becomes *d* after a nasal; e.g., *an-dapa* "in court," etc.

30. J. Gonda, *Sanskrit in Indonesia* (International Academy of Indian Culture, New Delhi, 1973), p. 334.

31. Compare Waruno Mahdi, who also attributes the development of vocalic endings in Malagasy to South Sulawesi influence;see W. Mahdi, *Morphophonologische Besonderheiten und historische Phonologie des Malagasy* (Dietrich Reimer Verlag, Berlin-Hamburg, 1988), pp. 211–253. However, it is more likely that this development was due to contact with Bantu languages; see A. Adelaar, in H. Steinhauer, ed., *Papers in Austronesian Linguistics* No. 1 (Pacific Linguistics, Canberra, 1991), p. 27.

32. Incidentally, in the seventeenth century the Malagasy used to refer to themselves as "Buki," and this is still the term for Madagascar in Swahili; cf. P. Ottino, *Madagascar, les Comores et le Sudouest de l'Océan Indien* (Publications du Centre d'Anthropologie Culturelle en Sociale, Université de Madagascar, 1974), p. 42 fn. 18. Intriguingly similar as it is to the Malay exonym *bugis* (the present-day Buginese call themselves *Ugiʔ*), without further research it is impossible to determine the significance of this similarity, as there is a fair amount of homonymy in ethnic names.

33. Leonard Andaya, pers. comm.

34. In the same way, incidentally, as academic knowledge has provided a historical awareness "after the facts" among the Maanyan about their links with the Malagasy.

35. P. Beaujard, *Études Océan Indien* 35–36, 59–147 (2003).

36. Even if a borrowing hypothesis were justified, the semantic connection between "charm, remedy" and "to look after" is not obvious; moreover, there are countless reflexes of *uliq in other Austronesian languages that have a more straightforward semantic connection and would have been more obvious candidates as a lending form. Incidentally, a link between Malagasy and Bajau languages does seem to exist, but it is a genetic one. Robert Blust (2006) argues that the Samalan languages (to which Bajau belongs) are a branch of the wider Barito subgroup.

37. P. Ottino, *Madagascar, les Comores et le Sud-ouest de l'Océan Indien* (Publications du Centre d'Anthropologie Culturelle en Sociale, Université de Madagascar, 1974).

38. G. Murdock, *Africa: Its Peoples and Their Culture History* (McGraw-Hill, New York, 1959).

39. H. Deschamps, *Histoire de Madagascar* (Editions Berger-Levrault, Paris, 1960).

40. R. Blench, in J. Reade, ed., *The Indian Ocean in Antiquity* (Kegan Paul, London, 1996), pp. 417–438.

41. J. Faublée, *Revue Française d'histoire d'Outre-Mer* 57, 268–287 (1970).

42. Portuguese sources often use the term "Javanese" to refer to people from insular southeast Asia in general, in the same way British sources use the term "Malay" for this ethnic category.

43. P-Y. Manguin, *Pre-modern Southeast Asian Shipping* (1993).

44. The crossing took six or seven days according to the Portuguese author Pires of the Summa Oriental (see *43*).

45. Compare also P. Ottino, *Annuaire des Pays de l'Océan Indien 2,* 303–321 (1975). Ottino argues for the occurrence of Tamil loanwords in Malagasy terminology pertaining to rice cultivation (refuted by Adelaar [*49*]).

46. R. Dewar, *World Archaeology* 26(3), 301–318 (1995).

47. I. Ardika, P. Bellwood, *Antiquity* 65, 221–232 (1991).

48. B. Andaya, L. Andaya, *A History of Malaysia* (University of Hawai'i Press, Honolulu, 2001).

49. A. Adelaar, in J. Reade, ed., *The Indian Ocean in Antiquity* (Kegan Paul, London, 1996), pp. 487–500.

50. W. Aichele, *Oriens Extremus* 1, 107–122 (1954).

51. O. Dahl, *Migration from Kalimantan to Madagascar* (Norwegian Univ. Press, Oslo, 1991).

52. R. Hewitt et al., *Am. J. Hum. Genet.* 58, 1303–1308 (1996).

53. F. Migot et al., *Tissue Antigens* 46, 131–135 (1995).

54. H. Soodyall, T. Jenkins, M. Stoneking, *Nature Genet.* 10, 377–378 (1995).

55. M. Hurles et al., *Am. J. Hum. Genet.* 76, 894–901 (2005).

56. A. Adelaar, in H. Steinhauer, ed., *Papers in Austronesian Linguistics* No. 1 (Pacific Linguistics, Canberra, 1991), pp. 23–37. A similar theory was launched but later abandoned by Paul Ottino.

57. However, there is no serious evidence for the scenario developed by Dahl (*51*). In this scenario, some Ma'anyan had migrated to Bangka Island (where some of them would still live on in what has now become the Lom community). From there they would have been shipped to Madagascar by the Sekak, a maritime people also living on Bangka Island (see Adelaar [*10*] for a critical assessment).

58. P. Beaujard (*35*, p. 96) notes that *lambu* refers to "bovine" in certain names and proverbs in southeast Madagascar. This suggests that the semantic shift was not a total one, and the word kept its original meaning in certain set phrases. Beaujard, however, believes that the term, with its original meaning, was reintroduced by later waves of Austronesian migrants.

59. N. Gueunier, *Petit Journal du Musée de l'Homme, Exposition Madagasikara Tonga Soa* (25 June 1991).

60. This word, as well as Islam itself, probably reached the Antaimoro via the Zafiraminia, a Muslim ethnic group who settled in southeast Madagascar before the Antaimoro (P. Beaujard, pers. comm.).

61. In relation to this, it is noteworthy that Javanese speakers hear the alveolar *d* and *t* of various other languages (such as Malay, Dutch, and English) as a retroflex *ḍ* and *ṭ*. If Sorabe was introduced by Indonesian (and more in particular, Javanese) speakers, they may conceivably have taught Malagasy speakers to use retroflex letters for *d* and *t* because that is how they perceived Malagasy *d* and *t*.

62. P. Beaujard, pers. comm.

63. G. Nelson, in E. Cox, ed., *The Wellcome Trust Illustrated History of Tropical Diseases* (Wellcome Trust, London, 1996), pp. 294–303. Nelson notes that the swollen limbs of a statue of pharaoh Mentuhotep the Third (about 2000 BCE) strongly suggest that this king was affected by elephantiasis.

64. A. Richards, *An Iban-English Dictionary* (Clarendon, Oxford, 1981).

65. Valiha is a West Malagasy term. West Malagasy dialects lose original *-n and maintain *l before *i (if there were a Merina corresponding form, it would presumably have been *vadihană).

66. A point already made by Murdock (*38*), arguing against theories that the present-day ethnic variety in Madagascar is the result of migrations of several ethnic groups arriving on the island at different points in time.

67. R. Dewar, H. Wright, *J. World Prehistory* 7, 417–466 (1993).

68. H. Wright, J. Rakotorisoa, in S. Goodman, J. Bensted, eds., *Natural History of Madagascar* (University of Chicago Press, 2003), pp. 112–119.

69. A scenario proposed by Philippe Beaujard (pers. comm.). Note, however, that such a course of events still requires an initial period on the African mainland where a hybrid Asian-African community must have come into being before the settlement to Madagascar took place. Otherwise it would fail to account for the archaeological and human genetic data pointing to a mixed Asian-African population on Madagascar from the outset.

70. W. Mahdi, *Morphophonologische Besonderheiten und historische Phonologie des Malagasy*, Veröffentlichungen des Seminars für Indonesische und Südseesprachen der Universität Hamburg, Band 20 (Dietrich Reimer Verlag, Berlin-Hamburg, 1988), p. 150.

71. MLG often has final -*nǎ* for an -*r* in the original Malay form; cf. MLG *fantsunǎ* "waste-pipe" < ML *pañcur* "flowing along a conduit or pipe"; MLG *kambanǎ* "twins" < ML *kəmbar* id. (*8*, p. 22).

72. Cassava is originally a South American crop. It must have been introduced in Madagascar in colonial times, possibly by the Portuguese via Mozambique (Henry Wright, pers. comm.).

14

Problems and Prospects in the Study of Ancient Human Migrations

Peter N. Peregrine, Ilia Peiros, and Marcus Feldman

Migration is a basic process in human history. The study of ancient human migrations, while experiencing a period of neglect in the latter half of the twentieth century (1), is now of great interest to archaeologists, linguists, and geneticists. It seems to us, however, that there is a disjuncture between what many of the descriptions of ancient human migrations present and the results of the actual research upon which those descriptions are based. This is not to say the descriptions are inaccurate or misleading, but rather that they appear to be oversimplified.

We read in the general or popular literature of a migration out of Africa by two routes, one along the coast of southern Asia, the other into central Asia (2, 3). We do not read, at least not in the more popular literature, of back migration (4) or admixture of different migrating groups (5, 6) that complicated the process. Similarly, we read of the movement of agriculturalists into Europe from the Levant (7), but again not of the complications of back migration and admixture. Human migrations are often presented as recursive phenomena that lack complicating factors. Table 14.1, which summarizes the case studies presented in this volume, makes it clear that human migrations have varied tremendously, and the processes involved must have varied tremendously as well.

Looking at Table 14.1, we can see that there is great diversity even within the small group of migration cases presented in this book. Two major types of migrations are described—territorial expansion and peopling of new lands—but there is diversity even within these types. The distance across which migration takes place ranges from a few hundred to more than 10,000 km, and there is a similar, large range of variation in terms of the numbers of people and time frames involved. Migrants tend not to outnumber local residents, but rather to dominate them culturally and technologically, if not militarily. This makes some sense, as it would be difficult for us to recognize a case of migration if the migrants did not maintain and spread their culture or language. This insight raises a further point: the identified cases of migration probably represent only a small subset of all the migrations that have taken place in human history. It is likely that many migrations were unsuccessful, and that many successful ones probably resulted in the migrants adapting to local cultures and languages. Thus it is likely that migration is a more common process in human history than we may think.

A striking feature of the cases compared in Table 14.1 is the prevalence of admixture. Every case in which migrants encountered local populations resulted in at least some admixture. This is not to say that displacement or extermination has never occurred, but rather to suggest that admixture is a more common phenomenon, at least judging by these cases. And this makes sense. If most migrations are made by populations of about the same scale as those encountered, it would take a strongly dominant migrant culture to wholly displace or exterminate a resident population.

TABLE 14.1. Summary of Migration Case Studies Presented in this Volume

Cases	Type of migration	Distance	Size of migrating groups	Relative size
Out of Africa (Chapters 6 and 7)	Territorial expansion	Total of more than 10,000 km, though probably only 10 km or so at a time	Small, probably no more than 15–30 people in each group	Nonmodern groups were probably similar in size
Aegean (Chapter 8)	Territorial expansion	About 1,000 km	Small, probably individual families or small groups	Small compared to resident populations
Rus' and Magyar (Chapter 9)	Territorial expansion	About 2,000 km	Moderate, perhaps several hundred people in each group	Probably similar to local groups
The Americas (Chapters 10 and 11)	Peopling	More than 10,000 km, though probably a mixture of short- and long-distance movements by individual groups	Small, perhaps only 1,000 people total; individual groups probably no more than 15–30 people	Original inhabitants
Japan (Chapter 12)	Territorial expansion (though often seen as peopling)	Less than 1,000 km	Moderate, perhaps as many as several hundred at a time	Probably similar to local populations initially, but rapidly increasing over time
Madagascar (Chapter 13)	Peopling	At least 6,000 km across open ocean	Probably small— less than 100 people	Original inhabitants

Admixture is the more likely result. We suggest this is an area that requires much further research—but it is not the only one.

Important Questions

A basic question that remains unanswered is why groups migrate. Although numerous forces fostering migration have been proposed—the need for agricultural land or other resources, the desire or need for trade, population pressure, and the like—variation in these has not been well explained. The response to population pressure, for example, might include mechanisms for limiting population or intensifying resource production rather than migration. What factors promote migration over other possible options? One potential reason for migration that has not received enough focus, in our opinion, is the need for marriage partners. We know that most societies allow polygamy, and we also know that in many societies there are more men than available women. Men often resort to either wife-stealing or migration to obtain a spouse. We suggest that the movement of people as they seek or become spouses might

Duration of migration	Coercion or violence	Cultural dominance of migrants	Cultural persistence of migrants	Consequences
More than 10,000 years	Probably none	Complete	Complete	Drove nonmodern humans to extinction
About 3,000 years	Probably none	Apparently strong, as agriculture was adopted throughout the region, and languages also spread.	Strong, although local cultures persisted with agriculture.	Admixture of migrants with local populations
Several hundred years	Yes: military attacks and raids were common.	Strong, both culturally and linguistically	Complete	Admixture with and apparently some displacement of local populations
Several thousand years	None	Complete	Complete	Original inhabitants
Probably several hundred years	Unknown	Complete	Complete	Admixture with local populations
Less than 100 years	None	Complete, though borrowings from India and East Africa	Complete	Original inhabitants

be an important process fostering migration. One reason for suggesting the importance of marriage in migration is the fact that it is a key process in admixture, and, as noted earlier, a central lesson from the case studies presented here is that admixture is a common result of migration.

The prevalence of admixture raises the question of how languages migrate. As several of the case studies suggest, there are clear situations where languages have moved with people. On the other hand, there are also situations where language appears to have spread without large

numbers of people moving, as has been the case in many colonial settings (such as the spread of English in south Asia). There are also cases of people moving, but their language has not (as with the Irish migrations to the Americas in the 1840s). How and why does language move? Is it linked with technology? Is it linked to dominant cultures or peoples? These are questions that have been considered but clearly need further work.

What seems clear to us is that the study of human migrations is at a turning point in two ways. First, the field appears ready to shift from asking simple descriptive questions (who, what, when, and where) to more processual ones (how and why). In making this shift, the historical linguists, archaeologists, and geneticists who have been studying human migrations will need to engage the aid of sociolinguists, anthropologists, and demographers. This engagement will require an entirely new way of pursuing research, one we argue is best seen as multidisciplinary rather than interdisciplinary.

A Multidisciplinary Approach

This volume stems from a series of workshops held at the Santa Fe Institute. We believe these workshops have provided a foundation for the multidisciplinary approach that will be necessary to answer questions about the processes of human migrations. The workshops allowed scholars working in the disciplines of historical linguistics, genetics, and archaeology to share their insights and understandings of how human languages spread. The editors of this book realized that much of the discussion focused on the movement of peoples, and that migration is intimately linked to problems of interest to scholars in all these disciplines.

In the course of these workshops we realized that migration processes are so complex that no single scholar, nor single team of scholars, can reasonably be expected to examine them. Rather, scholars, or teams of scholars, will need to work on individual problems and then come together to try to grasp the larger processes at work. The Santa Fe Institute proved a particularly rich environment for these discussions, as many of its faculty had worked on similarly complex problems in physics, economics, and biology. With insight from these scholars, we realized that a multidisciplinary approach to the study of human migrations is possible—and necessary.

At the Santa Fe Institute we realized that archaeologists, linguists, and geneticists work within distinct frameworks, and each framework is both enabled and constrained in different ways. For example, the spread of technology as examined by the archaeologist may not be accompanied by a movement of genes. Alternatively, a conquest that results in the conquered being forced to adopt a new language might result in changes in genetic composition detectable in the present, while the

linguistic history might be masked. Reconciling observed patterns in different fields should give us multiple independent data sets for better understanding human history. This is the great benefit of a multidisciplinary approach.

A multidisciplinary approach begins with a group of scholars from distinct disciplines who share interest in a common problem. The group addresses the problem by, first, hypothesizing about the processes at work and then identifying individual questions that stem from these hypothesized processes. Scholars from the appropriate discipline take up these questions and attempt to answer them. Once answers are provided, the group returns to the hypotheses and evaluates them. This process continues until the group has agreed on a solution to the problem.

A multidisciplinary approach differs from an interdisciplinary one primarily in its scale: there are more people involved, and a longer time frame. But it also differs in that scholars are not expected to be experts in more than one discipline; rather, they are expected to provide specific expertise to the group as a whole. Synthesis comes not from scholars working in an interdisciplinary fashion, where an attempt is made to blend or merge disciplinary expertise, but from the group working in a multidisciplinary fashion, where disciplinary expertise remains separate, and each discipline provides a unique approach to the common problem.

But multidisciplinary research has many affiliated problems. A basic one is personnel. There is often little reward for this kind of work. Individual research that contributes to addressing a group problem may not be of interest or importance otherwise, and may not result in publications or support. This is particularly problematic for younger scholars who need to establish a track record for hiring, tenure, and promotion. There is also a problem in funding. Most funding agencies seek projects with simple, direct goals. Multidisciplinary research is designed for projects without such simple goals, and it is expensive: multiple researchers, each with their own assistants and labs, and numerous opportunities or mechanisms for group interaction must all be funded. Expensive projects that will produce complex and perhaps ambiguous results are not attractive to most funding agencies.

With these problems, why propose multi-disciplinary research? Because we believe it is necessary. Complex problems, such as ancient human migrations, necessarily require complex approaches. And the problem of ancient human migrations is important enough to justify the work needed to explore it.

The Importance of Further Research

Migration has been a basic process in producing the data for archaeology, genetics, and linguistics. The modern world has been shaped by migration and, as the cases in this book make clear, migration also shaped the ancient world. We are a species rooted in movement and admixture. We know that human genetic races as commonly understood do not exist, and we can see through the study of ancient human migrations why that is the case. Human groups have never been isolated or stagnant; rather, human groups have moved amoeba-like across the face of the earth—interacting, absorbing, repelling, intermixing, and being absorbed by other groups. This is a process we need to understand.

Today genetic information is available to anyone with a cotton swab and a hundred dollars (*8*). In a world where rural Englishmen use DNA markers to claim direct descent from Paleolithic Cheddar Man and Oprah from South African Zulus, there is a strong tendency for uninformed people to create a fictitious link between ethnicity, location, and genes (*9*). This is dangerous, for such a link between genes, ethnicity, and location has historically led to racism and genocide. Recognizing that the history of humankind is not one of genetic or geographical isolation, but rather one of movement and admixture, is essential for us to reinforce the fact that we are one species.

Notes

1. D. Anthony, *Am. Anthropol.* 92, 895–914 (1990).
2. N. Wade, *Before the Dawn* (Penguin, New York, 2006).
3. S. Wells, *The Journey of Man* (Princeton Univ. Press, Princeton, 2002).
4. F. Cruciani et al., *Am. J. Hum. Genet.* 70, 1197–1214 (2002).
5. N. Rosenberg et al., *Science* 298, 2381–2385 (2002).
6. L. Cavalli-Sforza, M. Feldman, *Nature Genet. Supp.* 33, 266–275 (2003).
7. A. Ammerman, L. Cavalli-Sforza, *The Neolithic Transition and the Genetics of Population in Europe* (Princeton Univ. Press, Princeton, 1984).
8. For example, through the National Geographic Foundation's Genographic Project, https://www3.nationalgeographic.com/genographic/participate.html
9. S. Lyall, *New York Times*, 24 March 1997, A4.

Bibliography

Aarne, A., and S. Thompson
1964   *The Types of the Folk-tale.* Helsinki: Suomalaisen Tiedeakatemia.

Abinal, A., and V. Malzac
1963   *Dictionnaire Malgache-Français.* Paris: Éditions Maritimes et d'Outre-Mer.

Abrahamsson, H.
1951   *The Origin of Death: Studies in African Mythology.* Uppsala: Theological Faculty of the University of Uppsala.

Adelaar, A.
1989   Malay Influence on Malagasy: Linguistic and Culture-Historical Inferences. *Oceanic Linguistics* 28(1):1–46.

1991   New Ideas on the Early History of Malagasy. In H. Steinhauer, ed., *Papers in Austronesian Linguistics* no. 1, pp. 23–37. Canberra: Pacific Linguistics.

1994   Malay and Javanese Loanwords in Malagasy, Tagalog and Siraya (Formosa). *Bijdragen tot de Taal-, Land- en Volkenkunde* 150(1):49–64.

1995   Asian Roots of the Malagasy: A Linguistic Perspective. *Bijdragen tot de Taal-, Land- en Volkenkunde* 151(3):325–357.

1995   Bentuk Pinjaman Bahasa Melayu dan Jawa di Malagasi. In Ismail Hussain, A. Aziz Deraman, and Abd. Rahman Al Ahmadi, eds., *Tamadun Melayu: Jilid Pertama,* pp. 21–40. Kuala Lumpur: Dewan Bahasa dan Pustaka.

1995   L'importance du Samihim (Bornéo du Sud) Pour l'Etymologie Malgache, in B. Champion, ed., *L'Étranger Intime: Mélanges Offerts à Paul Ottino, Madagascar, Tahiti, Insulinde, Monde Swahili, Comores, Réunio.* Saint-André: Océan Éditions.

1996   Malay Culture-History: Some Linguistic Evidence. In J. E. Reade, ed., *The Indian Ocean in Antiquity,* pp. 487–500. London: Kegan Paul.

2005   Austronesian Languages of Asia and Madagascar: A Historical Perspective. In A. Adelaar and N. Himmelmann, eds., *The Austronesian Languages of Asia and Madagascar,* pp. 1–42. London: Routledge.

Aichele, W.
1954   Sprachforschung und Geschichte im Indonesischen Raum. *Oriens Extremus* 1:107–122.

Aikens, C. M., and T. Higuchi
1982   *Prehistory of Japan.* London: Academic Press.

Akazawa, T., S. Oda, and I. Yamanaka
1980   *The Japanese Paleolithic.* Tokyo: Rippu Shobo.

Akkermans, P., and G. Schwartz
2003   *The Archaeology of Syria: From Complex Hunter-Gatherers to Early Urban Societies (ca. 16,000–300 BC).* Cambridge: Cambridge University Press.

Aksjenov, V.
2005   Kvoprosu o Cuschestvovanii Pamjatnikov Etnicheskih Khazar v Verhnem Techenii Severskogo Dontsa. In V. Petrukhin and V. Moskovich, eds., *Khazary* (Jews and Slavs 16), pp. 222–223. Moscow: Gesharim.

Alekseev, A. I.
2002   Proishozhdenie Naroda Sakha v Svete Novyh Arheologicheskih Dannyh. In *Narody i Kul'tury Sibiri,* M. Turov, ed., pp. 6–21. Irkutsk: Irkutski Mezhregional'ny Institut Obschestvennyh Nauk.

Al-Zahery, N., O. Semino, G. Benuzzi, C. Magri, G. Passarino, A. Torroni, and A. S. Santachiara-Benerecetti
2003   Y-chromosome and mtDNA Polymorphisms in Iraq: A Crossroad of the Early Human Dispersal and of Post-Neolithic Migrations. *Molecular Phylogenetics and Evolution* 28:458–472.

Ammerman, A. J., and L. L. Cavalli-Sforza
1971   Measuring the Rate of Spread of Early Farming in Europe. *Man* 6: 674–688.

1984   *The Neolithic Transition and the Genetics of Populations in Europe.* Princeton: Princeton University Press.

Andaya, B. W., and L. Y. Andaya
2001   *A History of Malaysia.* Honolulu: University of Hawai'i Press.

Anderson, D.
1990   *Lang Rongrien Rockshelter.* Philadelphia: University Museum.

Anderson, D., and J. C. Gillam
2000   Paleoindian Colonization of the Americas. *American Antiquity* 65: 43–66.

Anderson, M., and M. Ross
2002   Sudest. In J. Lynch, M. Ross, and T. Crowley, eds., *The Oceanic Languages*, pp. 322–346. London: Curzon Press.

Andriastuti, Y. K.
1992   *Morfologi dan Sintaksis Bahasa Lawangan.* Jakarta: Departemen Pendidikan dan Kebudayaan.

Anthony, D. W.
1990   Migration in Archaeology: The Baby and the Bathwater. *American Anthropologist* 92:895–914.

Ardika, I. W., and P. Bellwood
1991   Sembiran: The Beginnings of Indian Contact with Bali. *Antiquity* 65(247): 221–232.

Bakalov, G.
1990   Byzantium and Old Rus. In O. Pritsak and I. Sevcenko, eds., *Proceedings of International Congress Commemorating the millennium of Christianity of Rus'-Ukraine* (Harvard Ukranian Studies vols. 12–13), pp. 387–399. Cambridge: Ukrainian Research Institute.

Bandelt, H. J., P. Forster, and A. Rohl
1999   Median-joining Networks for Inferring Intraspecific Phylogenies. *Molecular Biology and Evolution* 16:37–48.

Bannai, M. Katsushi Tokunaga, Tadashi Imanishi, Shinji Harihara, Kiyoshi Fujisawa, Takeo Juji, Keiichi Omoto
1996   HLA Class II Alleles in Ainu Living in Hidaka District, Hokkaido, Northern Japan. *American Journal of Physical Anthropology* 101:1–9.

Bard, E., F. Rostek, G. Ménot-Combes
2004   A Better Radiocarbon Clock. *Science* 303:178–179.

Basu, A., N. Mukherjee, S. Roy, S. Sengupta, S. Banerjee, M. Chakraborty, B. Dey, M. Roy, B. Roy, N. P. Bhattacharyya, S. Roychoudhury, and P. P. Majumder
2003   Ethnic India: A Genomic View, With Special Reference to Peopling and Structure. *Genome Research* 13:2277–2290.

Beaujard, P.
2003 Les Arrivées Austronésiennes à Madagscar: Vagues ou Continuum? (Partie 1 + 2). *Études Océan Indien* 35–36:59–147.

Bellwood, P., and C. Renfrew, eds.
2003   *Examining the Language/Farming Dispersal Hypothesis.* Cambridge: McDonald Institute for Archaeological Research.

Bellwood, P.
1991   The Austronesian Dispersal and the Origins of Languages. *Scientific American* 265(1):88–93.

Benedict, P. K.
1990   *Japanese/Austro-Tai.* Ann Arbor: Karoma.

Bender, B., W. Goodenough, F. Jackson, J. Marck, K. Rehg, H-M. Sohn, S. Trussel, and J. Wang
2003   Proto-Micronesian Reconstructions. *Oceanic Linguistics* 42(1):2–110, 42(2):271–328.

Bengtson, J. D.
1991   Macro-Caucasian Phonology. In V. Shevoroshkin, ed., *Nostratic, Dene-Caucasian, Austric and Amerind.* Brockmeyer: Bochum.

1994   Edward Sapir and the "Sino-Dene" Hypothesis. *Anthropological Science* 102:207–230.

Benkő, L.
1997   La Situation Linguistique des Hongrois de la Conquête et ce qui en Résulte. In S. Csernus and K. Korompay, eds., *Les Hongroise et l'Europe: Conqête et Intégration*, pp. 121–136. Paris: Institut Hongrois de Paris.

Berezkin, Y. E.
2003   Southern Siberian–North American Links in Mythology. *Archaeology, Ethnology and Anthropology of Eurasia* 14:94–105.

2004   Southern Siberian–North American Links in Mythology. *Acta Americana* 12:5–27.

2005   The Black Dog at the River of Tears: Some Amerindian Representations of the Passage to the Land of the Dead and Their Eurasian Roots. *Forum for Anthropology and Culture* 2:130–170.

2005   Cosmic Hunt: Variations of a Siberian–North American Myth. *Archaeology, Ethnology and Anthropology of Eurasia* 21:141–150.

2005   Nekotorye Tendentsii v Global'nom Rasprostranenii Kompleksov Fol'klorno-Mifologicheskih Motivov. In V. Vydrin, ed., *Ad hominem: To the Memory of Niko-lai Girenko*, pp. 131–156. St. Petersburg: Museum of Anthropology and Ethnography.

2005   The Assessment of the Probable Age of Eurasian-American Mythological Links. *Archaeology, Ethnology and Anthropology of Eurasia* 1:146–151.

2005   Continental Eurasian and Pacific Links in American Mythologies and Their Possible Time-depth. *Latin American Indian Literatures Journal* 21(2):99–115.

2006   Do ili Posle Zaveta? "Oplevannoe tvore-nie" i Soputstvuyuschie Mifologicheskie Motify v Yevrazii. In Y. Berezkin, ed., *Kul'tura Aravii v Aziatskom Kontekste*, pp. 225–249. St. Petersburg: Museum of Anthropology and Ethnography.

2006   Alkor, Kotelok i Sobaka. In A. Arkhipova and M. Gister, eds., *Stsenari Zhizni–Stsenari Narrativa*. Moscow: Russian State University of Humanities.

2006   Fol'klorno-Mifologicheskie Paral-leli Mezhdu Zapadnoi Sibir'iu, Severo-Vostokom Azii i Priamur'iem–Primor'iem. *Archaeology, Ethnology and Anthropology of Eurasia* 27:112–122.

Bianchi, N. O., C. I. Catanesi, G. Bailliet, V. L. Martinez-Marignac, C. M. Bravi, L. B. Vidal-Rioja, R. J. Herrera, and J. S. López-Camelo

1998   Characterization of Ancestral and Derived Y-chromosome Haplotypes of New World Native Populations. *American Journal of Human Genetics* 63:1862–1871.

Bierhorst, J.

1985   *The Mythology of North America*. New York: Morrow.

Biggs, B.

1991   POLLEX (Comparative Polynesian Lexicon). Computer file.

Binford, L. R.

1990   Mobility, Housing, and Environment: A Comparative Study. *Journal of Anthropological Research* 46:119–152.

Blanton, R. E.

1993   *Houses and Households: A Comparative Study*. New York: Plenum.

Blegen, C.

1928   The Coming of the Greeks, Part II: The Geographical Distribution of Prehistoric Remains in Greece. *American Journal of Archaeology* 32:146–154.

Blench, R.

1996   The Ethnographic Evidence for Long-

Distance Contacts between Oceania and East Africa. In J. E. Reade, ed., *The Indian Ocean in Antiquity*, pp. 417–438. London: Kegan Paul.

Bloch, M.

1986   *La Société Féodale*. Paris: Editions Albin Michel.

Blust, R.

1970   Proto-Austronesian Addenda. *Oceanic Linguistics* 9:104–162.

1977   The Proto-Austronesian Pronouns and Austronesian Subgrouping. *Working Papers in Linguistics of the University of Hawai'i* 9(2):1–15.

1978   Eastern Malayo-Polynesian. In S. Wurm and L. Carrington, eds., *Second International Conference on Austronesian Linguistics: Proceedings* 1, pp. 181–234. Canberra: Pacific Linguistics.

1980   Austronesian Etymologies I. *Oceanic Linguistics* 19:1–189.

1983–1984   Austronesian Etymologies II. *Oceanic Linguistics* 22–23:29–149.

1986   Austronesian Etymologies III. *Oceanic Linguistics* 25:1–123.

1989   Austronesian Etymologies IV. *Oceanic Linguistics* 28:111–180.

1995   The Position of the Formosan Languages: Methods and Theory in Austronesian Comparative Linguistics. In J-K. Li, ed., *Austronesian Studies Relating to Taiwan*, pp. 585 –650. Symposium Series of the Institute of History and Philology, Academia Sinica 33. Taipei: Academia Sinica.

1999   Subgrouping, Circularity and Extinction: Some Issues in Austronesian Comparative Linguistics. In E. Zeitoun and P. Li, eds., *Selected Papers from the Eighth International Conference on Austronesian Linguistics*, pp. 31–94. Symposium Series of the Institute of Linguistics (Preparatory Office), Academia Sinica 1. Taipei: Academia Sinica.

2006   The Genetic Classification of Samalan Languages. Paper presented at the 10th International Conference of Austronesian Linguistics, Puerto Princesa (Palawan, Philippines), 17–20 January.

Boas, F.

2002   *Indian Myths and Legends from the North Pacific Coast of America*. Vancouver: Talonbooks.

Boba, I.

1967   *Nomads, Northmen and Slavs: Eastern*

Europe in the Ninth Century. The Hague: Mouton.

Bogucki, P., ed.
1993   *Case Studies in European Prehistory.* Boca Raton, FL: CRC.

Bortolini, M. C., F. M. Salzano, M. G. Thomas, S. Stuart, S. P. K. Nasanen, C. H. D. Bau, M. H. Hutz, Z. Layrisse, M. L. Petzl-Erler, L. T. Tsuneto, K. Hill, A. M. Hurtado, D. Castro-de-Guerra, M. M. Torres, H. Groot, R. Michalski, P. Nymadawa, G. Bedoya, N. Bradman, D. Labuda, and A. Ruiz-Linares
2003   Y-Chromosome Evidence for Differing Ancient Demographic Histories in the Americas. *American Journal of Human Genetics* 73:524–539.

Bosch, E., F. Calafell, Z. H. Rosser, S. Nørby, N. Lynnerup, M. E. Hurles, and M. A. Jobling
2003   High Level of Male-Biased Scandinavian Admixture in Greenlandic Inuit Shown by Y-chromosomal Analysis. *Human Genetics* 112:353–363.

Bowlus, R.
1995   *Franks, Moravians and Magyars.* Philadelphia: University of Pennsylvania Press.

Brace, C. L., M. L. Brace, and W. R. Leonard
1989   Reflections on the Face of Japan: A Multivariate Craniofacial and Odontometric Perspective. *American Journal of Physical Anthropology* 78:93–113.

Brown, B. M.
1987   Population Estimation from Floor Area: A Restudy of "Naroll's Constant." *Behavior Science Research* 21:1–49.

Burch, E., E. Jones, H. P. Loon, L. D. Kaplan
1999   The Ethnogenesis of the Kuuvaum Kaŋiaġmiut. *Ethnohistory* 46:291–327.

Burton, M., and D. White
1991   Regional Comparisons, Replications, and Historical Network Analysis. *Behavior Science Research* 25:55–78.

Campbell, L.
1994   Inside the American Indian Language Classification Debate. *Mother Tongue* 23:41–54.

1994   Problems with the Pronouns in Proposals of Remote Relationships among Native American Languages. In M. Langdon, ed., *Survey of California and Other Indian Languages*, pp. 1–20. Berkeley: Department of Lingustics, University of California, Berkeley.

1997   *American Indian Languages: The Historical Linguistics of Native America.* New York: Oxford University Press.

1997   Amerindian Personal Pronouns: A Second Opinion. *Language.* 73: 339–351.

Cann, R. L., M. Stoneking, and A. C. Wilson
1987   Mitochondrial DNA and Human Evolution. *Nature* 325:31–35.

Cann, Rebecca
2001   Genetic Clues to Dispersal in Human Populations: Retracing the Past from the Present. *Science* 291:1742–1748.

Capelli, C., N. Redhead, V. Romano, F. Calì, G. Lefranc, V. Delague, A. Megarbane, A. E. Felice, V. L. Pascali, P. I. Neophytou, Z. Poulli, A. Novelletto, P. Malaspina, L. Terrenato, A. Berebbi, M. Fellous, M. G. Thomas and D. B. Goldstein.
2006   Population Structure in the Mediterranean Basin: A Y Chromosome Perspective. *Annals of Human Genetics* 70:207.

Cauvin, J.
2000   *The Birth of the Gods and the Origins of Agriculture.* Cambridge: Cambridge University Press.

Cavalli-Sforza, L. L.
2001   *Genes, Peoples, and Languages.* New York: North Point Press.

Cavalli-Sforza, L. L., and W. F. Bodmer
1971   *The Genetics of Human Populations.* San Francisco: W. H. Freeman.

Cavalli-Sforza, L. L., and F. Cavalli-Sforza
1995   *The Great Human Diasporas.* New York: Addison-Wesley.

Cavalli-Sforza, L. L., and M. W. Feldman
1981   *Cultural Transmission and Evolution: A Quantitative Approach.* Princeton, NJ: Princeton University Press.

2003   The Application of Molecular Genetic Approaches to the Study of Human Evolution. *Nature Genetics* 33:266–275.

Cavalli-Sforza, L. L., P. Menozzi, and A. Piazza
1994   *The History and Geography of Human Genes.* Princeton, NJ: Princeton University Press.

Cavalli-Sforza, L. L., E. Minch, and J. L. Mountain
1992   Coevolution of Genes and Languages Revisited. *Proceedings of the National Academy of Science, USA* 89:5620–5624.

Cavalli-Sforza, L. L., A. Piazza, P. Menozzi, J. L. Mountain
1988   Reconstruction of Human Evolution: Bringing Together Genetic, Archaeological, and Linguistic Data. *Proceedings of the National Academy of Science, USA* 85:6002–6006.

Cavalli-Sforza, L. L., and W. S. Y. Wang
1986   Spatial Distance and Lexical Replacement. *Language* 62:38–55.

Cense, A. A.
1979   *Makassaars–Nederlandsch Woordenboek.*
        The Hague: Nijhoff.
Chard, C.
1974   *Northeast Asia in Prehistory.* Madison:
        University of Wisconsin Press.
Chekin, L.
1988   In V. Pashuto, ed., *Vostochnaja Evropa v
        Drevnosty i Srednevekobje,* pp. 125–128.
        Moscow: Institut Rossiijskoij Istorii.
Chen, J., R. Sokal, and M. Ruhlen
1995   Worldwide Analysis of Genetic and Lin-
        guistic Relationships of Human Popula-
        tions. *Human Biology* 67:595–612.
Chiaroni, J., R. King, and P. Underhill
2008   Correlation of Annual Precipitation with
        Human Y-chromosome Diversity and the
        Emergence of Neolithic Agricultural and
        Pastoral Economies in the Fertile Cres-
        cent. *Antiquity* 82:281–290.
Chick, G.
1998   Games in Culture Revisited: A Repli-
        cation and Extension of Roberts, Arth,
        and Bush (1959). *Cross-Cultural Research*
        32:185–206.
Cinnioglu, C., R. King, T. Kivisild, E. Kalfoğlu,
S. Atasoy, G. L. Cavalleri, A. S. Lillie, C. C. Roseman,
A. A. Lin, K. Prince, P. J. Oefner, P. Shen, O. Semino,
L. L. Cavalli-Sforza, and P. A. Underhill
2004   Excavating Y-chromosome Haplotype
        Strata in Anatolia. *Human Genetics*
        114:127–148.
Colledge, S., J. Conolly, and S. Shennan.
2004   Archaeobotanical Evidence for the Spread
        of Farming in the Eastern Mediterranean.
        Current Anthropology 45:S35–S58.
Cordaux, R., E. Deepa, H. Vishwanathan, and
M. Stoneking
2004   Genetic Evidence for the Demic Dif-
        fusion of Agriculture to India. *Science*
        304:1125.
Coyne, J. A., N. H. Barton, and M. Turelli
1997   A Critique of Sewall Wright's Shifting
        Balance Theory of Evolution. *Evolution*
        51:643–671.
Crawford, M. H.
1998   *The Origins of Native Americans: Evidence
        from Anthropological Genetics.* Cam-
        bridge: Cambridge University Press.
Cruciani, F., P. Santolamazza, P. Shen, V. Macaulay,
P. Moral, A. Olckers, D. Modiano, S. Holmes,
G. Destro-Bisol, V. Coia, D. C. Wallace, P. J. Oefner,
A. Torroni, L. L. Cavalli-Sforza, R. Scozzari, and
P. A. Underhill
2002   A Back Migration from Asia to Sub-
        Saharan Africa Is Supported by High-
        Resolution Analysis of Human Y-Chro-
        mosome Haplotypes. *American Journal of
        Human Genetics* 70:1197–1214.
Czücs, E.
2002   Ocherk Drevnej Istorii Vengrov. *Hungaro-
        Rossica* 9:231–271.
Dahl, O. C.
1951   *Malgache et Maanyan: Une Comparaison
        Linguistique.* Avhandlingerutgitt av Insti-
        tuttet 3. Oslo: Egede Instituttet.
1954   Le Substrat Banout en Malgache. *Norsk
        Tidsskrift for Sporfvidenskap* 16:148–200.
1977   La Subdivision de la Famille Barito et
        la Place du Malgache. *Acta Orientalia*
        38:77–134.
1988   Bantu Substratum in Malagasy. *Études
        Océan Indien* 9:91–132.
1991   *Migration from Kalimantan to Madagas-
        car.* Oslo: Norwegian University Press.
Dalmond, M.
1842   Vocabulaire et Grammaire pour les
        Langues Malgaches Sakalave et Betsi-
        misaraka. Saint Denis (Île Bourbon):
        Imprimerie de Lahuppe.
Darnell, R., and J. Sherzer
1971   Areal Linguistic Studies in North Amer-
        ica: A Historical Perspective. *Interna-
        tional Journal of American Linguistics*
        37:20–28.
Davis, W. D.
1971   Societal Complexity and the Nature of
        Primitive Man's Conception of the Super-
        natural. Ph.D. dissertation. University of
        North Carolina, Chapel Hill.
De Casparis, J. G.
1956   *Prasasti Indonesia II: Selected Inscriptions
        from the 7th to the 9th Century A.D.* Band-
        ung: Masa Baru.
Deacon, H. J.
1979   Excavations at Boomplaas Cave: A
        Sequence through the Upper Pleistocene
        and Holocene in South Africa. *World Ar-
        chaeology* 10:241–257.
Deacon, J.
1984   Changes in the Archaeological Record in
        South Africa at 18000 BP. In C. Gamble
        and O. Sofer, eds., *The World at 18,000 BP,*
        vol. 2: *Low Latitudes,* pp. 171–83. London:
        Unwin Hyman.
Demoule, J. P., and C. Perles
1993   The Greek Neolithic: A New Review.
        Journal of World Prehistory 7:355–416.
Dempwolff, O.
1934–1938 *Vergleichende Lautlehre des*

Austronesischen Wortschatzes. 1–3
Zeitschrift für Eingeborenen-Sprachen.
Berlin: Reimer.

Deng, W., B. Shi, X. He, Z. Zhang, J. Xu, B. Li, J. Yang,
L. Ling, C. Dai, B. Qiang, Y. Shen, and R. Chen

2004   Evolution and Migration History of the
Chinese Population Inferred from Chi-
nese Y-chromosome Evidence. *Journal of
Human Genetics* 49: 339–348.

Derevianko, A. P., W. R. Powers, and
D. B. Shimkin, eds.

1998   *The Paleolithic of Siberia: New Discoveries
and Interpretations.* Urbana: University of
Illinois Press.

Deschamps, H.

1960   *Histoire de Madagascar.* Paris: Editions
Berger-Levrault.

Dewar, R. E.

1995   Of Nets and Trees: Untangling the Retic-
ulate and Dendritic in Madagascar's Prehistory. *World Archaeology* 26(3):301–318.

Dewar, R. E., and H. T. Wright

1993   The Culture History of Madagascar. *Journal of World Prehistory* 7:417–466.

Di Giacomo, F., F. Luca, L. O. Popa, N. Akar,
N. Anagnou, J. Banyko, R. Brdicka, G. Barbujani,
F. Papola, G. Ciavarella, F. Cucci, L. Di Stasi, L. Gav-
rila, M. G. Kerimova, D. Kovatchev, A. I. Kozlov,
A. Loutradis, V. Mandarino, C. Mammi',
E. N. Michalodimitrakis, G. Paoli, K. I. Pappa,
G. Pedicini, L. Terrenato, S. Tofanelli, P. Malaspina,
and A. Novelletto

2004   Y-chromosomal Haplogroup J as a Signature of the Post-neolithic Colonization of
Europe. *Human Genetics* 115:357–371.

Diakonoff, I.

1998   The Earliest Semitic Society Linguistic Data. *Journal of Semitic Studies*
43(2):209–220.

Diakonoff, I. M., and S. A. Starostin

1986   *Hurro-Urartian as an East Caucasian
Language.* Munich: Kitzinger.

Diamond, Jared

1997   *Guns, Germs, and Steel.* New York:
Norton.

1998   Japanese Roots. *Discover* 19(6):86–95.

2000   Blitzkrieg Against the Moas. *Science*
287:2170–2171.

Diamond, J., and P. Bellwood

2003   Farmers and Their Languages: The First
Expansions. *Science* 300:597–603.

Dick-Read, R.

2005   *The Phantom Voyagers: Evidence of Indonesian Settlements in Africa in Ancient
Times.* Winchester: Thurlton Publishing.

Dienes, I.

1972   *The Hungarians Cross the Carpathians.*
Budapest: Corvina Press.

Divale, W. T.

1974   Migration, External Warfare, and
Matrilocal Residence. *Behavior Science
Research* 9:75–133.

1977   Living Floors and Marital Residence: A
Replication. *Behavior Science Research*
12:109–15.

Djantera, K., I. Abdurachman, and W. Ranrung

1984   *Struktur Bahasa Maanyan.* Jakarta:
Departemen Pendidikan dan
Kebudayaan.

Dobzhansky, T., and S. Wright

1941   Genetics of Natural Populations V: Relations Between Mutation Rate and Accumulation of Lethals in Populations of
Drosophila pseudoobscura. Genetics
26:23–51.

Duczko, W.

2003   The Ways Things Were Moving: Staraja
Ladoga–Birka–Staré Mesto–Gradešnica.
In M. Dulinicz, ed., *Słowianie i ich
Sąsiedzi we Wczesnym Średniowieczu,*
pp. 127–132. Lublin: Wydawnictwo Uni-
versytetu Marii Curie.

Duhoux, Y.

1998   Pre-Hellenic Language(s) of Crete. *Journal of Indo-European Studies* 26:1–41.

Dyen, I.

1953   Review of O.C. Dahl's Malgache et Maanyan. *Language* 29:577–590.

1963   The Position of the Malayo-Polynesian
Languages of Formosa. *Asian Perspectives*
7:261–271.

Ehret, C.

1998   *An African Classical Age.* Charlottesville:
University Press of Virginia.

Elena, S. F., V. S. Cooper, and R. E. Lenski

1996   Punctuated Evolution Caused by Selection of Rare Beneficial Mutations. *Science*
272:1802–1804.

Elli, L.

1988   *Dizionario Bara-Italiano.* Fianarantsona:
Ambozontany.

Ember, C. R.

1974   An Evaluation of Alternative Theories of
Matrilocal versus Patrilocal Residence.
Behavior Science Research 9:135–149.

1975   Residential Variation among Hunter-
Gatherers. *Behavior Science Research*
10:199–227.

Ember, C. R., and M. Ember

1972   The Conditions Favoring Multilocal

Residence. *Southwestern Journal of Anthropology* 28:382–400.

1992   Resource Unpredictability, Mistrust, and War: A Cross-Cultural Study. *Journal of Conflict Resolution* 36:242–262.

1992   Warfare, Aggression, and Resource Problems: Cross-Cultural Codes. *Behavior Science Research* 26:169–226.

2001   *Cross-Cultural Research Methods.* Walnut Creek, CA: AltaMira.

Ember, C. R., M. Ember and B. Pasternak

1974   On the Development of Unilineal Descent. *Journal of Anthropological Research* 30:69–94.

Ember, M.

1967   The Emergence of Neolocal Residence. *Transactions of the New York Academy of Sciences* 30:291–302.

1970   Taxonomy in Comparative Studies. In R. Naroll and R. Cohen, eds., *Handbook of Method in Cultural Anthropology*, pp. 697–706. Garden City, NY: Natural History Press.

1973   An Archaeological Indicator of Matrilocal versus Patrilocal Residence. *American Antiquity* 38:177–182.

1974   On the Origin and Extension of the Incest Taboo. *Behavior Science Research* 10:249–281.

Ember, M., and C. R. Ember

1971   The Conditions Favoring Matrilocal Residence versus Patrilocal Residence. *American Anthropologist* 73:571–594.

1995   Worldwide Cross-Cultural Studies and Their Relevance for Archaeology. *Journal of Archaeological Research* 3:87–111.

2000   Testing Theory and Why the "Units of Analysis" Problem Is Not a Problem. *Ethnology* 39:349–363.

Enrico, J.

2004   Toward Proto–Na-Dene. *Anthropological Linguistics* 46:229–302.

Eringa, F. S.

1984   *Soendaas-Nederlands Woordenboek.* Koninklijk Instituut voor Taal-, Land- en Volkenkunde. Dordrecht: Foris Publications.

Faublée, J.

1970   Les Manuscrits Arabico-Malgaches du Sud-Est. *Revue Française d'histoire d'Outre-Mer* 57:268–287.

Faurie, C., and M. Raymond

2004   Handedness Frequency Over More than Ten Thousand Years. *Biology Letters (Supplement to the Proceedings of the Royal Society B: Biological Sciences)* 271 (Supplement 3):S43–S45.

Fernandez, H., S. Hughes, J.-D. Vigne, D. Helmer, G. Hodgins, C. Miquel, G. Hänni, G. Luikart, and P. Taberlet

2006   Divergent mtDNA Lineages of Goats in an Early Neolithic Site, Far from the Initial Domestication Areas. *Proceedings of the National Academy of Science, USA* 103:15375–15379.

Finkelberg, M.

1997   Anatolian Languages and Indo-European Migrations to Greece. *Classical World* 91:3–21.

2001   The Language of Linear A: Greek, Semitic, or Anatolian? In R. Drews, ed., *Greater Anatolia and the Indo-Hittite Language Family*, pp. 81–105. Washington, D.C.: Institute for the Study of Man.

Fischer, J.

1961   Art Styles as Cultural Cognitive Maps. *American Anthropologist* 63:80–83.

Fisher, R. A.

1937   The Wave of Advance of Advantageous Genes. *Annals of Eugenics* 7:355–369.

Fix, A.

1999   *Migration and Colonization in Human Microevolution.* New York: Cambridge University Press.

Flannery, K. V., and J. Marcus

1983   *The Cloud People: The Divergent Evolution of the Zapotec and Mixtec Civilizations.* New York: Academic.

Flerov, V. S.

2001   "Semikarakory" — krepost'khazarskogo kaganata na Nizhnem Donu. *Rossijskaja archeologija* 2, 56.

Flores, C., N. Maca-Meyer, J. Larruga, V. Cabrera, N. Karadsheh, and A. Gonzalez

2005   Isolates in a Corridor of Migrations: A High-Resolution Analysis of Y-chromosome Variation in Jordan. *Journal of Human Genetics* 50:435.

Fodor, I.

2002   Vengry v Khazarii. In V. Petrukhin and A. Fedorchuk, eds., *Khazary: Vtoroj mezhdunarodnij colloqvium*, pp. 98–101. Moscow: Institut Slavjanovedenija.

Forster, P., R. Harding, A. Torroni, and H. J. Bandelt

1996   Origin and Evolution of Native American mtDNA Variation: A Reappraisal. *American Journal of Human Genetics* 59:935–945.

Fortescue, M.

1998   *Language Relations across the Bering Strait.* London: Cassell.

Fox, J.
2003   *Semitic Noun Patterns.* Winona Lake, IN: Eisenbrauns.

Franklin, S., and J. Shepard
1996   *The Emergence of Rus.* London: Longman

Frayer, D. W., and D. Martin
1997   *Troubled Times: Osteological and Archaeological Evidence of Violence.* Langhorne, PA: Gordon and Breach.

Gamble, C., and O. Soffer, eds.
1990   *The World at 18,000 BP,* vol. 2: *Low Latitudes.* London: Unwin Hyman.

Geertz, C.
1973   *The Interpretation of Cultures.* New York: Basic Books.

Gelb, I.
1935   *Inscriptions from Alishar and Vicinity.* Chicago: University of Chicago Press.
1961   The Early History of the West Semitic Peoples. *Journal of Cuneiform Studies* 15:27–47.

Gennadij, G.
2000   *Vyzantija, Bolgaria, Drevnjaja Rus'.* St. Petersburg: Aleteja.

Gibbons, A.
2001   The Peopling of the Pacific. *Science* 291:1735–1736.

Goebel, T.
1999   Pleistocene Human Colonization of Siberia and Peopling of the Americas: An Ecological Approach. *Evolutionary Anthropology* 8:208–227.

Goldstein, D., A. R. Linares, L. L. Cavalli-Sforza, and M. W. Feldman
1995   An Evaluation of Genetic Distances for Use With Microsatellite Loci. *Genetics* 139:463–471.

Golla, V., ed.
1984   *The Sapir-Kroeber Correspondence.* Berkeley: Department of Linguistics, University of California, Berkeley.

Gonda, J.
1973   *Sanskrit in Indonesia.* New Delhi: International Academy of Indian Culture.

Gordon, R. G., ed.
2005   *Ethnologue: Languages of the World.* 15th ed. Dallas: SIL International.

Greenberg, J. H.
1963   Some Universals of Grammar with Particular Reference to the Order of Meaningful Elements. In J. Greenberg, ed., *Universals of Grammar,* pp. 73–113. Cambridge: Massachusetts Institute of Technology Press.
1987   *Language in the Americas.* Stanford: Stanford University Press.
2000   *Indo-European and Its Closest Relatives,* vol. 1. Stanford, CA: Stanford University Press.
2002   *Indo-European and Its Closest Relatives,* vol. 2. Stanford, CA: Stanford University Press.

Greenberg, J. H., and M. Ruhlen
2006   *An Amerind Etymological Dictionary.* Available at http://merrittruhlen.com.

Greenberg, J. H., C. G. Turner, and S. L. Zegura
1986   The Settlement of the Americas: A Comparison of the Linguistic, Dental, and Genetic Evidence. *Current Anthropology* 27:477–497.

Greppin, J., and I. Diakonoff
1991   Some Effects of the Hurro-Urartian People and Their Languages upon the Earliest Armenians. *Journal of American Oriental Society* 111:720–730.

Grigorjev, A.
2000   *Severskaja Zemlja v VIII–Nachale XI Veka po Archeologicheskim Dannym.* Tula: Grif i K.

Gueunier, N. J.
1986   *Lexique du Dialecte Malgache de Mayotte (Comores).* Études Océan Indien 7 (numéro spécial). Paris: INALCO.
1991   Islam à Madagascar: Tradition Ancestrale et Conversions Récentes. In *Petit Journal du Musée de l'Homme, Exposition Madagasikara Tonga Soa.* Paris: Musée de l'Homme.

Haak, W. P. Forster, B. Bramanti, S. Matsumura, G. Brandt, M. Tänzer, R. Villems, C. Renfrew, D. Gronenborn, K. W. Alt, and J. Burger
2005   Ancient DNA from the First European Farmers in 7500-Year-Old Neolithic Sites. *Science* 310:1016–1018.

Haley, J.
1928   The Coming of the Greeks, Part I: The Geographical Distribution of Pre-Greek Place-Names. *American Journal of Archaeology* 32:141–145.

Hammer, M. F., and S. Horai
1995   Y Chromosomal DNA Variation and the Peopling of Japan. *American Journal of Human Genetics* 56:951–962.

Hammer, M. F., T. M. Karafet, H. Park, K. Omoto, S. Harihara, M. Stoneking, and S. Horai
2006   Dual Origins of the Japanese: Common Ground for Hunter-Gatherer and Farmer Y-chromosomes. *Journal of Human Genetics* 51:47–58.

Hammer, M. F., T. M. Karafet, A. J. Redd, H. Jarjanazi, S. Santachiara-Benerecetti, H. Soodyall, and S. L. Zegura
2001   Hierarchical Patterns of Global Human Y-chromosome Diversity. *Molecular Biology and Evolution* 18:1189–1203.

Hammer, M. F., and S. L. Zegura
2002   The Human Y Chromosome Haplogroup Tree: Nomenclature and Phylogeography of Its Major Divisions. *Annual Review of Anthropology* 31:303–321.

Hanihara, K.
1991   Dual Structure Model for the Population History of the Japanese. *Japan Review* 2:1–33.

Hapip, A.
1977   *Kamus Banjar-Indonesia.* Jakarta: Pusat Pembinaan dan Pengembangan Bahasa.

Harpending, H. C., S. Sherry, A. Rogers, and M. Stoneking
1993   The Genetic Structure of Ancient Human Populations. *Current Anthropology* 34:483–496.

Hart, J. P.
1999   Maize Agriculture Evolution in the Eastern Woodlands of North America: A Darwinian Perspective. *Journal of Archaeological Method and Theory* 6:137–180.

2001   Maize, Matrilocality, Migration, and Northern Iroquoian Evolution. *Journal of Archaeological Method and Theory* 8:151–182.

Hartl, D. L., and A. Clark
1997   *Principles of Population Genetics.* Sunderland, MA: Sinauer Press.

Helimsky, E.
2000   *Comparativistica, Uralistica.* Moscow: Jazyki Slavjanskoj Kul'tury.

Hewitt, R., A. Krause, A. Goldman, G. Campbell, and T. Jenkins
1996   B-globin Haplotype Analysis Suggests That a Major Source of Malagasy Ancestry Is Derived from Bantu-Speaking Negroids. *American Journal of Human Genetics* 58:1303–1308.

Hewlett, B. S., A. De Silvestri, C. R. Guglielmino
2002   Semes and Genes in Africa. *Current Anthropology* 43:313–321.

Hofmeister, B.
1961   *Erdkunde.* Bonn: University of Bonn.

Holman, E. W., C. Schulze, D. Stauffer, and S. Wichmann
2007   On the Relation between Structural Diversity and Geographical Distance among Languages: Observations and Computer Simulations. *Linguistic Typology* 11:395–423.

Horai, S., K. Murayama, K. Hayasaka, S. Matsubayashi, Y. Hattori, G. Fucharoen, S. Harihara, K. S. Park, K. Omoto, and I. H. Panet
1996   mtDNA Polymorphism in East Asian Populations, with Special Reference to the Peopling of Japan. *American Journal of Human Genetics* 59:579–590.

Horwitz, L. K., and O. Lernau
2003   Temporal and Spatial Variation in Neolithic Caprine Explotation Strategies: A Case of Fauna from the Site of Yuftah'el (Israel). *Paléorient.* 29(1):19–58.

Howard-Johnston, J.
2000   Byzantium, Bulgaria and the Peoples of Ukraine in the 890s. *Materialy po Archeologii, Istorii i Etnographii Tavrii (MAIET)* VII:342–356.

Howells, W. W.
1966   Jomon Population of Japan. *Papers of the Peabody Museum of Archaeology and Ethnology, Harvard University* 57(1):1–67.

Hudson, A. B.
1963   Death Ceremonies of the Padju Epat Ma'anyan Dayaks. In Thomas H. Harrison, ed., *Borneo Writing and Related Matters*, pp. 341–415. Special monograph no. 1. Sarawak Museum Journal.

1972   *Padju Epat: The Ma'anyan of Indonesian Borneo.* New York: Holt, Rinehart and Winston.

Hudson, A. B., and J. M. Hudson
1967   Telang: A Ma'anyan Village of Central Kalimantan. In Koentjaraningrat, ed., *Villages in Indonesia*, pp. 90–114. Ithaca, NY: Cornell University Press.

Hugen, K., S. Lehman, J. Southon, J. Overpeck, O. Marchal, C. Herring, and J. Turnbull
2004   14C Activity and Global Carbon Cycle Changes over the Past 50,000 Years. *Science* 303:202–207.

Hurles, M. E., B. C. Sykes, M. A. Jobling, and P. Forster
2005   The Dual Origin of the Malagasy in Island Southeast Asia and East Africa: Evidence from Maternal and Paternal Lineages. *American Journal of Human Genetics* 76:894–901.

Irwin, G.
1992   *The Prehistoric Exploration and Colonization of the Pacific.* Cambridge: Cambridge University Press.

Jayaswal, V.
1989   Hunter Gatherers of the Terminal

Pleistocene in Uttar Pradesh, India. In O.Soffer and C. Gamble, eds., *The World at 18,000 BP,* vol. 1: *High Latitudes,* pp. 237–254. London: Unwin Hyman.

Jin, H. J., K.-D. Kwak, M. F. Hammer, Y. Nakahori, T. Shinka, J.-W. Lee, F. Jin, X. Jia, C. Tyler-Smith, and W. Kim

2003   Y-chromosomal DNA Haplogroups and Their Implications for the Dual Origins of the Koreans. *Human Genetics* 114:27–35.

Jobling, M. A., M. E. Hurles, and C. Tyler-Smith

2004   *Human Evolutionary Genetics: Origins, Peoples and Disease.* New York: Garland Science.

Jobling, M. A., and C. Tyler-Smith

2004   The Human Y-chromosome: An Evolutionary Marker Comes of Age. *Nature Reviews: Genetics* 4:598–612.

Jorgenson, J.

1980   *Western Indians: Comparative Environments, Languages, and Cultures of 172 Western American Indian Tribes.* San Francisco: W. H. Freeman.

Justus, C.

1992   The Impact of Non-Indo-European Languages on Anatolian. In C. Polome and W. Winter, eds., *Reconstructing Languages and Cultures,* pp. 443–467. Berlin: Mouton de Gruyter.

Kamei, M.

1986   Cultural Contacts between Japan and China as Reflected by Tang Sansai. In R. J. Pearson, ed., *Windows on the Japanese Past: Studies in Archaeology and Prehistory,* pp. 405–414. Ann Arbor: Center of Japanese Studies, University of Michigan.

Kamp, K. A.

1998   Social Hierarchy and Burial Treatments: A Comparative Assessment. *Cross-Cultural Research* 32:79–115

Karafet, T. M., J. S. Lansing, A. J. Redd, J. C. Watkins, S. P. K. Surata, W. A. Arthawiguna, L. Mayer, M. Bamshad, L. B. Jorde, M. F. Hammer

2005   Balinese Y-Chromosome Perspective on the Peopling of Indonesia: Genetic Contributions from Pre-Neolithic Hunter-Gatherers, Austronesian Farmers, and Indian Traders. *Human Biology* 77:93–114.

Karafet, T. M., L. P. Osipova, M. A. Gubina, O. L. Posukh, S. L. Zegura, M. F. Hammer

2002   High Levels of Y-Chromosome Differentiation among Native Siberian Populations and the Genetic Signature of a Boreal Hunter-Gatherer Way of Life. *Human Biology* 74:761–789.

Karafet, T. M., L. Xu, R. Du, W. Wang, S. Feng, R. S. Wells, A. J. Redd, S. L. Zegura, and M. F. Hammer

2001   Paternal Population History of East Asia: Sources, Patterns, and Microevolutionary Processes. *American Journal of Human Genetics* 69:615–628.

Karafet, T. M., S. L. Zegura, and M. F. Hammer

2006   Y-Chromosomes. In D. Ubelaker, ed., *Handbook of North American Indians: Environment, Origins and Population,* pp. 831–839. Washington D.C.: Smithsonian Institution.

Karafet, T. M., S. L. Zegura, O. Posukh, L. Osipova, A. Bergen, J. Long, D. Goldman, W. Klitz, S. Harihara, P. de Knijff, V. Wiebe, R. C. Griffiths, A. R. Templeton, and M. F. Hammer

1999   Ancestral Asian Source(s) of New World Y-chromosome Founder Haplotypes. *American Journal of Human Genetics* 64:817–831.

Karafet, T. M., S. L. Zegura, J. Vuturo-Brady, O. Posukh, L. Osipova, V. Wiebe, F. Romero, J. C. Long, S. Harihara, F. Jin, B. Dashnyam, T. Gerelsaikhan, K. Omoto, M. F. Hammer

1997   Y chromosome Markers and Trans-Bering Strait Dispersals. *American Journal of Physical Anthropology* 102:302–314.

Kawi, D., A. Ismail, and W. Ranrung

1984   *Struktur Bahasa Maanyan.* Jakarta: Departemen Pendidikan dan Kebudayaan.

Keally, C. T., Y. Taniguchi, Y. V. Kuzmin

2003   Understanding the Beginnings of Pottery Technology in Japan and Neighboring East Asia. *Review of Archaeology* 24:3–9.

Keally, C. T., Y. Taniguchi, Y. V. Kuzmin, I. Y. Shewkomud

2004   Chronology of the Beginning of Pottery Manufacture in East Asia. *Radiocarbon* 46:345–362.

Kimura, M., and T. Maruyama

1971   Pattern of Neutral Polymorphism in a Geographically Structured Population. *Genetical Research* 18:125–131.

King, R., and P. Underhill

2002   Congruent Distribution of Neolithic Painted Pottery and Ceramic Figurines with Y-chromosome Lineages. *Antiquity* 76:707–714.

King, R., S. Ozcan, T. Carter, E. Kalfoğlu, S. Atasoy, C. Triantaphyllidis, A. Kouvatsi, A. Lin, C-E. Chow,

L. Zhivotovsky, M. Michalodimitrakis, and
P. Underhill
2008   Differential Y-Chromosome Anatolian Influences on the Greek and Cretan Neolithic. *Annals of Human Genetics*
72:205–214.

Kirch, P. V.
1997   *The Lapita Peoples: Ancestors of the Oceanic World.* Cambridge, MA: Blackwell.

Klein, Richard G.
1995   Anatomy, Behavior, and Modern Human
Origins. *Journal of World Prehistory*
9:167–198.
1999   *The Human Career.* 2nd ed. Chicago:
University of Chicago Press.

Knijff, P. de
2000   Messages through Bottlenecks: On the
Combined Use of Slow and Fast Evolv-
ing Polymorphic Markers on the Human
Y Chromosome. *American Journal of
Human Genetics* 67:1055–1061.

Kotani, Y.
1969   Upper Pleistocene and Holocene Environmental Conditions in Japan. *Arctic
Anthropology* 5:133–158.

Koyama, S.
1992   Prehistoric Japanese Populations: A
Subsistence-Demographic Approach. In
K. Hanihara, ed., *Japanese as a Member of
the Asian and Pacific Populations: International Symposium 4*, pp. 187–197. Kyoto:
International Center for Japanese Studies.

Kozlowski, J.
1990   North Central Europe c. 18,000 BP. In
C. Gamble and O. Sofer, eds., *The World
at 18,000 BP*, vol. 1: *High Latitudes*,
pp. 204–247. London: Unwin Hyman.

Kristó, G.
1996   *Hungarian History in the 9th Century.*
Szeged: Szegedi Középkorász Műhely.

Kroeber, A. L.
1908   Catch-Words in American Mythology.
Journal of American Folklore 21:222–227.

Kroeber, A. L., and C. Kluckhohn
1952   *Culture: A Critical Review of Concepts of
Definitions.* Cambridge, MA: Peabody
Museum.

Kuper, R., and S. Kropelin
2006   Climate-Controlled Holocene Occupation in the Sahara: Motor of Africa's Evolution. *Science* 313:803–807.

Kuzmin, Y. V., M. D. Glascock, and H. Sato
2002   Sources of Archaeological Obsidian on
Sakhalin Island (Russian Far East). *Journal of Archaeological Science* 29:741–749.

Kuzmin, Y. V., and L. A. Orlova
1998   Radiocarbon Chronology of the Siberian
Paleolithic. *Journal of World Prehistory*
12:1–53.

Kuznetsova, A. V.
2002   Christianstvo v Vengrii na Poroge
Vtorogo Tysjacheletija. In B. Florja, ed.,
*Christianstvo v Stranah Vostochnoj, Jugo-
Vostochnoj i Central'noj Evropy*, pp. 340–
343. Moscow: Jazyki Slavjanskoj Kul'tury.

Landsberger, B.
1974   *Three Essays on the Sumerians.* Los
Angeles: Undena Publications.

Larsen, C. S.
1997   *Bioarchaeology: Interpreting Behavior
from the Human Skeleton.* New York:
Cambridge University Press.

Laughlin, W. S.
1986   Comment. *Current Anthropology* 27:490.

Lee, E.
1969   A Theory of Migration. In J. A. Jackson,
ed., *Migration*, pp. 282–297. Cambridge:
Cambridge University Press.

Lehmann, W. P.
2002   *Pre-Indo-European.* Monograph 41.
Washington, D.C.: JIES.

Lell, J. T., R. I. Sukernik, Y. B. Starikovskaya,
B. Su, L. Jin, T. G. Schurr, P. A. Underhill, and
D. C. Wallace
2002   The Dual Origin and Siberian Affinities
of Native American Y Chromosomes.
American Journal of Human Genetics
70:192–206.

Levine, R. E.
1979   Haida and Na-Dene: A New Look at the
Evidence. *International Journal American
Linguistics* 45:157–170.

Lewicki, T.
1967   Uwagi o Niektórych
Wzcesnośredniowiecznych Węgierskich
Drogach Handlowych. *Slavia Antiqua* 14.
1977   Źródła Arabskie do Dziejów
Słowiańszyzny. T. 2. cz. 2. Warsaw:
Widawnictwo Polskiej Akademii Nauk.
1978   "Madjary" u Srednevekovyh Arabskyh i
Persidskyh Geografov. In L. Cherepnin,
ed., *Vostochnaja Evropa v Drevnosty i Srednevekobje*, pp. 56–60. Moscow: Nauka.

Lewontin, R. C.
1972   The Apportionment of Human Diversity.
Evolutionary Biology 6:381–398.

Li, P.
1988   A Comparative Study of Bunun Dialects.
*Bulletin of the Institute of History and Phi-
lology* 59(2):479–508.

Likhachev, D. S., and M. B. Sverdlov, eds.
1996   *Povest' Vremennykh Let* (PVL). St. Peters-
        burg: Nauka.
Lin, S. J., K. Tanaka, W. Leonard, T. Gerelsaikhan,
B. Dashnyam, S. Nyamkhishig, A. Hida, Y. Nakahori,
K. Omoto, M. H. Crawford, and Y. Nakagome
1994   A Y-associated Allele Is Shared Among
        a Few Ethnic Groups of Asia. *Journal of
        Human Genetics* 39:299–304.
Litvarin, G. G.
2000   *Vyzantija, Bolgaria, Drevnjaja Rus'.*
        St. Petersburg: Aleteja.
Litvarin, G. G., and A. P. Novosel'tsev, eds.
1989   *Constantine Porphyrogenitus: Ob uprav-
        lenii imperiej.* Moscow: Nauka.
Lubell, D.
1974   *The Fakhurian.* Cairo: Geological Survey
        of Egypt.
Luis, J., D. J. Rowold, M. Regueiro, B. Caeiro,
C. Cinnioğlu, C. Roseman, P. A. Underhill,
L. L. Cavalli-Sforza, and R. J. Herrera
2004   The Levant versus the Horn of Africa:
        Evidence for Bidirectional Corridors of
        Human Migrations. *American Journal of
        Human Genetics* 74:532–544.
Luomala, K.
1940   *Oceanic, American Indian, and African
        Myths of Snaring the Sun.* Honolulu:
        Berenice P. Bishop Museum.
1965   Motif A728: Sun Caught in Snare and
        Certain Related Motifs. *Fabula* 6:213–252.
Lyall, S.
1997   Tracing Your Family Tree to Cheddar
        Man's Mum. *New York Times*, March 24,
        p. A4.
Lynch, J.
2002   Marquesan. In J. Lynch, M. Ross, and
        T. Crowley, eds., *The Oceanic Languages*,
        pp. 865–876. London: Curzon Press.
Lynch, J., M. Ross and T. Crowley, eds.
2002   *The Oceanic Languages.* London: Curzon
        Press.
Mahdi, W.
1988   *Morphophonologische Besonderheiten
        und historische Phonologie des Malagasy.*
        Veröffentlichungen des Seminars für
        Indonesische und Südseesprachen der
        Universität Hamburg, Band 20. Berlin-
        Hamburg: Dietrich Reimer Verlag.
Malecot, G.
1948   *The Mathematics of Heredity.* Paris:
        Masson.
Malhi, R. S., B. A. Schultz, and D. G. Smith
2001   Distribution of Mitochondrial DNA Lin-
        eages Among Native American Tribes of

Northeastern North America. *Human
        Biology* 73:17–55.
Mallory, J. P.
1989   *In Search of the Indo-Europeans: Lan-
        guage, Archaeology and Myth.* New York:
        Thames and Hudson.
Mallory, J. P., and T. E. McNeill
1991   *The Archaeology of Ulster: From Coloniza-
        tion to Plantation.* Belfast: Institute of
        Irish Studies, Queen's University of
        Belfast.
Manguin, P-Y.
1993   Pre-modern Southeast Asian Shipping in
        the Indian Ocean: The Maldives Connec-
        tion. Paper presented at the Australian
        Association for Maritime History Con-
        ference, Fremantle, December. *Techniques
        and Culture* 35–36:21–47.
Marck, J.
2000   *Topics in Polynesian Language and
        Cultural History.* Canberra: Pacific
        Linguistics.
Marquart, J.
1903   *Osteuropäische und Ostasiatische
        Streifzüge.* Leipzig: Dieterich'sche
        Verlagsbuchhandlung, T. Weicher.
Marsina, R.
1991   Slavjane i Madjary v Kontse IX–X v.
        In A. Avenarius and G. Litavrin, eds.,
        *Rannefeodal'nyje Gosudarstva i Narod-
        nosti*, pp. 109–110. Moscow: Nauka.
Martin, P. S.
1973   The Discovery of America: The First
        Americans May Have Swept the Western
        Hemisphere and Decimated Its Fauna
        Within 1000 Years. *Science* 179:969–974.
Matsumoto, H.
1988   Characteristics of Mongoloid and Neigh-
        boring Populations Based on the Genetic
        Markers of Human Immunoglobulins.
        Human Genetics 80:207–218.
Matthes, B. F.
1874   *Boegineesch-Hollandsch Woordenboek.*
        The Hague: Nijhoff.
Mazar, A.
1990   *Archeology of the Land of the Bible.* New
        York: Doubleday.
McNett, C. W.
1967   The Inference of Socio-Cultural Traits
        in Archaeology: A Statistical Approach.
        Ph.D. dissertation, Tulane University,
        New Orleans.
1970   A Settlement Pattern Scale of Cultural
        Complexity. In R. Naroll and R. Cohen,
        eds., *Handbook of Method in Cultural*

Anthropology, pp. 872–886. Garden City, NY: Natural History Press.

McWhorter, J.
2003   *The Power of Babel.* New York: HarperCollins.

Mellaart, J.
1966   *The Chalcolithic and Early Bronze Ages in the Near East and Anatolia.* Beirut: Khayats.
1975   *The Neolithic of the Near East.* London: Thames and Hudson.

Mellars, P.
2006   A New Radiocarbon Revolution and the Dispersal of Modern Humans in Eurasia. *Nature* 439:931–935.

Mel'chuk, I.
1988   *Dependency Syntax.* New York: State University of New York Press.

Mel'nikova, E., and V. Petruchin
1990–1991 The Origin and Evolution of the Name Rus': The Scandinavians in Eastern-European Ethno-political Processes before the 11th Century. *Tor* 23:203–234.

Meltzer, D. J.
1997   Anthropology: Monte Verde and the Pleistocene Peopling of the Americas. *Science* 276:754–755.
2003   Peopling of North America. In A. R. Gilespie, S. C. Porter, and B. F. Atwater, eds., *The Quaternary Period in the United States* (Developments in Quaternary Science 1), pp. 539–549. Oxford: Elsevier.

Melvin, A. C., and T. Higuchi
1982   *Prehistory of Japan.* Academic Press: New York.

Menton, L. K., N. W. Lush, H. Tamura, and C. I. Gusukuma
2003   *The Rise of Modern Japan.* University of Hawai'i: Honolulu.

Migot, F., B. Perichon, P. M. Danze, L. Raharimalala, J. P. Lepers, P. Deloron, R. Krishnamoorthy
1995   HLA Class II Haplotype Studies Bring Molecular Evidence for Population Affinity between Madagascans and Javanese. *Tissue Antigens* 46:131–135.

Mikheev, V.
1982   Kon'kovyje Podvesky iz Mogil'nika Suhaja Gomol'sha. *Sovetskaja Archeologija* 2:165.

Militarev, A.
1995   Sumerians and Afrasians. *Journal of Ancient History* 2:113–127.

Militarev, A., L. Kogan, A. G. Belova
2000–2005 *Semitic Etymological Dictionary.* Münster: Ugarit-Verlag.

Miller, R. A.
1996   *Languages and History: Japanese, Korean and Altaic.* Bangkok: White Orchid Press.

Mills, R. F.
1975   *Proto-South-Sulawesi and Proto-Austronesian Phonology.* 2 vols. Ph.D. dissertation, University of Michigan. Ann Arbor: University Microfilms International, 1978.

Milner-Gulland, R.
1997   *The Russians.* Oxford: Blackwell.

Mishin, D.
2002   *Saqaliba: Slavjane v Islamskom Mire.* Moscow: IV RAN– Kraft+.

Mizoguchi, K.
2002   *An Archaeological History of Japan: 30,000 B.C. to A.D. 700.* Philadelphia: University of Pennsylvania Press.

Molnár, M.
2001   *A Concise History of Hungary.* Cambridge: Cambridge University Press.

Montet-White, A., ed.
1990   *The Epigravettian Site of Grubgraben, Lower Austria: The 1986 and 1987 Excavations.* Etudes et Recherche Archaeologique de l'Université de Liège no. 40. Liège: Belique.

Moore, C., and A. K. Romney
1994   Material Culture, Geographic Propinquity, and Linguistic Affiliation on the North Coast of New Guinea: A Reanalysis of Welsch, Terrell, and Nadolski. *American Anthropologist* 96:370–392.

Moore, J. H.
1987   *The Cheyenne Nation.* Lincoln: University of Nebraska Press.
1994   Putting Anthropology Back Together Again: The Ethnogenetic Critique of Cladistic Theory. *American Anthropologist* 96:925–948.
1996   *The Cheyenne.* Cambridge, MA: Blackwell.

Moravcsik, G., and R. J. H. Jenkins, eds.
1967   *Constantine VII Porphyrogenitus: De Administrando Imperio.* Washington, D.C.: Dumbarton Oaks.

Morlan, R. E.
1967   Chronometric Dating in Japan. *Arctic Anthropology* 4:180–211.

Mudar, K., and D. Anderson
2007   New Evidence for Southeast Asian Pleistocene Foraging Economies: Faunal Remains from the Early Levels of Lang Rongrien Rockshelter, Krabi, Thailand. *Asian Perspectives* 46:298–334.

Murdock, G. P.
1949   *Social Structure.* New York: Macmillan.

1959   *Africa: Its Peoples and Their Culture His-
          tory.* New York: McGraw-Hill.

Mulligan, C. G., K. Hunley, S. Cole, and J. C. Long

2004   Population Genetics, History, and Health
          Patterns in Native Americans. *Annual
          Review of Genomics and Human Genetics*
          5:295–315.

Mulyani Santoso, D., R. B. Santoso, A. L. Tobing,
C. Nisa, and W. H. Toendan

1989   *Fonologi Bahasa Paku.* Jakarta: Departe-
          men Pendidikan dan Kebudayaan.

Murayama, S.

1976   The Malayo-Polynesian Component in
          the Japanese Language. *Journal of Japa-
          nese Studies* 2:413–436.

Mussi, M.

1990   Continuity and Change in Italy at the
          Last Glacial Maximum. In C. Gamble
          and O. Sofer, eds., *The World at 18,000 BP,*
          vol. 1: *High Latitudes,* pp. 126–147. Lon-
          don: Unwin Hyman.

Nadel, D.

2002   *Ohalo II: A 23,000 Year Old Fisher-
          Hunter-Gatherers Camp on the Shore of
          the Sea of Galilee.* Haifa: University of
          Haifa, Hecht Museum.

2003   Ohalo II Brush Huts. *Archaeology, Eth-
          nology, and Anthropology of Eurasia* I/13.
          Available electronically at http://ohalo
          .haifa.ac.il/brush_huts_nadel.pdf.

Najmushin, B.

2003   Khazarskijat Kaganat i Iztochna Jevropa:
          Sbl's'tsy Mezhdu "Nomadite na na Stepta"
          i "Nomadite na Rekita." In T. Stepanov,
          ed., *B'lgary i Khazary Prez Rannoto
          Srednevekovije,* pp. 142–158. Sofia: Tangra.

Naroll, Raoul

1962   Floor Area and Settlement Population.
          American Antiquity 27:587–89.

Nasidze, I., E. Y. S. Ling, D. Quinque, I. Dupanloup,
R. Cordaux, S. Rychkov, O. Naumova, O. Zhukova,
N. Sarraf-Zadegan, G. A. Naderi, S. Asgary, S. Sardas,
D. D. Farhud, T. Sarkisian, C. Asadov, A. Kerimov,
and M. Stoneking

2004   Mitochondrial DNA and Y-Chromosome
          Variation in the Caucasus. *Annals of
          Human Genetics* 68:205–221.

Nasidze, I., D. Quinque, M. Ozturk, N. Bendukidze,
and M. Stoneking

2005   MtDNA and Y-chromosome Variation
          in Kurdish Groups. *Annals of Human
          Genetics* 69:401–412.

Naumann, N.

2000   *Japanese Prehistory: The Material and*

          Spiritual Culture of the Jomon Period.
          Harrossowitz: Wiesbaden.

Nazarenko, A. V.

1999   Zapadnoevropejskije Istochniki. In
          E. A. Mel'nikova, ed., *Drevnjaja Rus' v
          Svete Zarubezhnyh Istochnikov,* 288. Mos-
          cow: Logos.

Nebel, A., D. Filon, B. Brinkmann, P. P. Majumder,
M. Faerman, and A. Oppenheim

2001   The Y Chromosome Pool of Jews as Part
          of the Genetic Landscape of the Middle
          East. *American Journal of Human Genetics*
          69:1095–1112.

Nei, M.

1995   The Origins of Human Populations:
          Genetic, Linguistic and Archeological
          Data. In S. Brenner and K. Hanihara, eds.,
          *The Original Past of Modern Humans as
          Viewed from DNA,* pp. 71–91. Singapore:
          World Scientific.

Nelson, G.

1996   Lymphatic Filariasis. In E. G. Cox, ed.,
          *The Wellcome Trust Illustrated History of
          Tropical Diseases,* pp. 294–303. London:
          Wellcome Trust.

Nettle, D.

1999   Linguistic Diversity of the Americas Can
          Be Reconciled with a Recent Colonization.
          *Proceedings of the National Academy of
          Science, U.S.A.* 96:3325–3329.

1999   Using Social Impact Theory to Simulate
          Language Change. *Lingua* 108:95–117.

Nichols, J.

1992   *Linguistic Diversity in Space and Time.*
          Chicago: University of Chicago Press.

2002   Personal Pronouns. In N. G. Jablonski,
          ed., *The First Americans,* pp. 273–293. San
          Francisco: California Academy of Sciences.

2007   The First American Languages. In
          V. Yanko-Hombach, A. Gilbert, N. Panin,
          and P. Dolukhanov, eds., *The Black Sea
          Flood Question: Changes in Coastline,
          Climate, and Human Settlement,* pp. 775–
          796. Berlin: Springer.

Nichols, J., and D. A. Peterson

1996   *The Amerind Personal Pronouns. Lan-
          guage* 72:336–352.

2005   Sino-Caucasian Languages in America.
          In M. Haspelmath, M. S. Dryer, D. Gil,
          and B. Comrie, eds., *The World Atlas of
          Language Structures,* pp. 546–553. Oxford:
          Oxford University Press.

Nikolaev, S. L.

1991   Sino-Caucasian Languages in the

Americas. In V. Shevoroshkin, ed., *Dene-Sino-Caucasian Languages*, pp. 42–66. Brockmeyer: Bochum.

Nikolayev, S. L., and S. Starostin
1994   *A North Caucasian Etymological Dictionary*. Moscow: Asterick Press.

Noonan, James P., G. Coop, S. Kudaravalli, D. Smith, J. Krause, J. Alessi, F. Chen, D. Platt, S. Paabo, J. Prichard, and E. Rubin
2006   Sequencing and Analysis of Neanderthal Genomic DNA. *Science* 314:1113–1118.

Novosel'tsev, A. P.
1965   Vostochnyje Istochniki o Vostochnyh Slavjanah i Rusi. In A.P. Novosel'tsev et al., Drevnerusskoje Gocudarstvo i Jego Mezhdunarodnoje Znachenije, pp. 355–419. Moscow: Nauka.
1990   *Khazarskoje Gosudarstvo i Jego rol' v Istorii Vostochnoj Evropy i Kavkaza*. Moscow: Nauka.

Ochman, H., J. G. Lawrence, and E. A. Groisman
2000   Lateral Gene Transfer and the Nature of Bacterial Innovation. *Nature* 405:299–304.

Omoto, K., and S. Misawa
1976   The Genetic Relations of the Ainu. In R. L. Kirk and A. G. Thorne, eds., *The Origins of the Australians*, pp. 365–376. Canberra: Australian Institute of Aboriginal Studies.

Omoto, K., and N. Saitou
1997   Genetic Origins of the Japanese: A Partial Support for the Dual Structure Hypothesis. *American Journal of Physical Anthropology* 102:437–446.

Ono, A., H. Sato, T. Tsutsumi, and Y. Kudo
2002   Radiocarbon Dates and Archaeology of the Late Pliestocene in the Japanese Islands. *Radiocarbon* 44:477–494.

Oota, H., W. Settheetham-Ishida, D. Tiwawech, T. Ishida, and M. Stoneking
2001   Human mtDNA and Y-Chromosome Variation is Correlated with Matrilocal versus Patrilocal Residence. *Nature Genetics* 29:20–21.

Orlova, L. O.
2005   Radiocarbon Data Bank for Siberia and the Far East. http//:www.uiggm.nsc.ru/ uiggm/geology/ evol/lab924/orlova.
2006   *Pleistocene Megafauna and the Person in a Paleolith of Siberia: Chronology, Paleoenvironment and Interaction*. http//: www.uiggm.nsc.ru/uiggm/geology/evol/ lab924/orlova.

Ossenberg, N.
1986   Isolate Conservation and Hybridization in the Population History of Japan: The Evidence of Nonmetric Cranial Traits. In T. Akazawa and C. M. Aikens, eds., *Prehistoric Hunter Gatherers in Japan* 27:199–215. Tokyo: University of Tokyo.

Ottino, P.
1974   *Madagascar: Les Comores et le Sud-ouest de l'Océan Indien*. Publications du Centre d'Anthropologie Culturelle en Sociale. Université de Madagascar.
1977   L'Origine Dravidienne du Vocabulaire du Riz et Certains Termes de Riziculture à Madagascar. *Annuaire des Pays de l'Océan Indien* 2:303–321. Marseille: Presses Universitaires d'Aix.

Pagel, M., Q. D. Atkinson, and A Meade
2007   Frequency of Word-Use Predicts Rates of Lexical Evolution throughout Indo-European History. *Nature* 449:717–720.

Palumbi, G.
2003   Red-Black Pottery: Eastern Anatolian and Transcaucasian Relationships during the Mid-Fourth Millennium BC. *Ancient Near Eastern Studies* 40:80–134.

Parrinder, G.
1967   *African Mythology*. London: Hamlyn.

Pavlov, P., J. I. Svendsen, S. Indrelid
2001   Human Presence in the European Arctic Nearly 40,000 Years Ago. *Nature* 413: 64–66.

Peiros, I.
1998   *Comparative Linguistics in Southeast Asia*. Canberra: National University of Australia.

Peiros, I., and S. Starostin
1984   Sino-Tibetan and Austro-Tai. *Computational Analyses of Asian and African Languages* 22:123–127.
2005   Austric Etymologies. Computer database.
2005   Sino-Tibetan Classification. Manuscript.

Peregrine, P. N.
1993   An Archaeological Correlate of War. *North American Archaeologist* 14:139–151.
1996   The Birth of the Gods Revisited: A Partial Replication of Guy Swanson's (1960) Cross-Cultural Study of Religion. *Cross-Cultural Research* 30:84–112.
2001   Cross-Cultural Comparative Archaeology. *Annual Review of Anthropology* 31:1–18.
2004   Cross-Cultural Approaches in Archaeology: Comparative Ethnology, Comparative Archaeology, and Archaeoethnology.

Journal of Archaeological Research 12:281–309.

2007 Cultural Correlates of Ceramic Styles. *Cross-Cultural Research* 41(3):223–235.

Peregrine, P. N., and M. Ember, eds.

2001–2002 *Encyclopedia of Prehistory.* 9 vols. New York: Kluwer Academic/Plenum Publishers.

Petrukhin, V.

1995 *Nachalo Etnokul'turnoj Istorii Rusi IX–XI Vekov.* Smolensk: Rusich.

2001 Gnjezdovo Mezhdu Kijevom, Birkoj i Moravijej. In V. Murasheva, ed., *Archeologicheskij Sbornik: Gnëzdovo: 125–let Issledovanija Pamjatnika,* pp. 116–120. Moscow: Gosudarstvennij Istoricheskij Muzej.

2001 O "Ruskom kaganate," Nachal'nom Letopisanii, Poiskah i Nedorazumenijah v Sovremennoj Istoriografii. *Slavjanovedenije* 4:78–82.

Pinhasi, R., J. Fort, and A. Ammerman

2005 Tracing the Origin and Spread of Agriculture in Europe. *PloS Biology* 3:410.

Pinnow, H. J.

1990 *Die Na-Dene-Sprachen im Lichte der Greenberg-Klassifikation.* Nortorf: Völkerkundlichen Arbeitsgemeinschaft.

Pitulko, V. V., P. A. Nikolsky, E. Yu. Girya, A. E. Basilyan, V. E. Tumskoy, S. A. Koulakov, S. N. Astakhov, E. Yu. Pavlova, and M. A. Anisimov

2004 The Yana RHS Site: Humans in the Arctic Before the Last Glacial Maximum. *Science* 303:52–56.

Podosinov, A.

2002 *Vostochnaja Evropa v Rimskoj Kartograficheskoj Traditsii.* Moscow: Indrik.

Quintana-Murci, L., C. Krausz, T. Zerjal, S. H. Sayar, M. F. Hammer, S. Q. Mehdi, Q. Ayub, R. Qamar, A. Mohyuddin, U. Radhakrishna, M. A. Jobling, C. Tyler-Smith, and K. McElreavey

2001 Y-Chromosome Lineages Trace Diffusion of People and Languages in Southwestern Asia. *American Journal of Human Genetics* 68:537–542.

Rajaonarimanana, N., and S. Fee

1996 *Dictionnaire Malgache Dialectal–Français.* Dialecte Tandroy, Dictionnaires des Langues O', Langues de l'Océan Indien Occidental. Paris: Langues et Mondes, L'Asiathèque.

Ramachandran, S., O. Deshpande, C. C. Roseman, N. A. Rosenberg, M. W. Feldman, and L. L. Cavalli-Sforza

2005 Support from the Relationship of Genetic and Geographic Distance in Human Populations for a Serial Founder Effect Originating in Africa. *Proceedings of the National Academy of Science, USA.* 102:15942–15947.

Ratkoš, P.

1985 *Velikaja Moravia: Je Istoricheskoje i Kul'turnoje Znachenije.* Moscow: Nauka.

Ray, N., and J. M. Adams

2001 A GIS-based Vegetation Map of the World at the Last Glacial Maximum (25,000–15,000 BP). *Internet Archaeology* 11. http://intarch.ac.uk/journal/issue11/rayadams_index.html.

Redd, A. J., J. Roberts-Thomson, T. Karafet, M. Bamshad, L. B. Jorde, J. M. Naidu, B. Walsh, and M. F. Hammer

2002 Gene Flow from the Indian Subcontinent to Australia: Evidence from the Y Chromosome. *Current Biology* 12:673–677.

Reed, D. L.

2005 *Biomolecular Archaeology: Genetic Approaches to the Past.* Carbondale: Southern Illinois University Press.

Reed, D. L., V. S. Smith, S. L. Hammond, A. R. Rogers, and D. H. Clayton

2004 Genetic Analysis of Lice Supports Direct Contact between Modern and Archaic Humans. *PLoS Biology* 2(11): e340 DOI: 10.1371/journal.pbio.0020340.

Regueiro, M., A. M. Cadenas, T. Gayden, P. A. Underhill, R. J. Herrera

2006 Iran: Tricontinental Nexus for Y-Chromosome Driven Migration. *Human Heredity* 61:132–143.

Reid, L. A., and H-C Liao

2004 A Brief Syntactic Typology of Philippine Languages. *Language and Linguistics* (Taipei) 5(2):433–490.

Renfrew, C.

1973 Problems in the General Correlation of Archaeological and Linguistic Strata in Prehistoric Greece: The Model of Autochthonous. In R. Crossland and A. Birchall, eds., *Migrations in the Aegean,* pp. 263–276. London: Duckworth.

1987 *Archaeology and Language: The Puzzle of Indo-European Origins.* New York: Cambridge University Press.

Renfrew, C., and K. Boyle, eds.

2000 *Archaeogenetics: DNA and the Population Prehistory of Europe.* Cambridge: McDonald Institute for Archaeological Research.

Richards, A.
1981   *An Iban-English Dictionary.* Oxford: Clarendon Press.
Richardson, J.
1885   *A New Malagasy-English Dictionary.* Tananarivo: London Missionary Society.
Robbins, M. C.
1966   House Types and Settlement Patterns. *Minnesota Archaeologist* 28:2–26.
Roberts, J., M. J. Arth, and R. R. Bush
1959   Games in Culture. *American Anthropologist* 61:597–605.
Roberts, J., C. Moore, and A. K. Romney
1995   Predicting Similarity in Material Culture among New Guinea Villages from Propinquity and Language: A Log-Linear Approach. *Current Anthropology* 36: 769–788.
Robinson, L. F., F. Adkins, L. D. Keigwin, J. Southon, D. P. Fernandez, S-L Wang, and D. S. Scheirer
2005   Radiocarbon Variability in the Western North Atlantic During the Last Deglaciation. *Science* 310:1469–1473.
Róna-Tas, A.
1999   *Hungarians and Europe in the Early Middle Ages.* Budapest: CEU Press.
Rosenberg, N. A., L. M. Li, R. Ward, and J. K. Pritchard
2003   Informativeness of Genetic Markers for Inference of Ancestry. *American Journal of Human Genetics* 73:1402–1422.
Rosenberg, N. A., J. K. Pritchard, J. L. Weber, H. M. Cann, K. Kidd, L. A. Zhivotvosky, and M. W. Feldman
2002   Genetic Structure of Human Populations. *Science* 298:2381–2385.
Ross, M.
1988   *Proto-Oceanic and the Austronesian Languages of Western Melanesia.* Canberra: Pacific Linguistics.
2005   Pronouns as a Preliminary Diagnostic for Grouping Papuan Languages. In Andrew Pawley, Robert Attenborough, Jack Golson, and Robin Hide, eds., *Papuan Pasts: Cultural, Linguistic and Biological Histories of Papuan-speaking Peoples,* pp. 15–66. Canberra: Pacific Linguistics.
Ross, M., A. Pawley, and M. Osmond, eds.
2003   *The Lexicon of Proto-Oceanic: The Culture and Environment of Ancestral Oceanic Society.* Canberra: Pacific Linguistics.
Rouse, I.
1958   The Inference of Migrations from Anthropological Information. In R. H. Thompson, ed., *Migrations in New World*

Culture History, pp. 63–68. Social Science Bulletin. Tucson: University of Arizona.
1986   *Migrations in Prehistory: Inferring Population Movement from Cultural Remains.* New Haven: Yale University Press.
Rousset, F.
1997   Genetic Differentiation and Estimation of Gene Flow from F-Statistics under Isolation by Distance. *Genetics* 145:1219–1228.
1999   Genetic Differentiation within and between Two Habitats. *Genetics* 151:397–407.
Rubio, G.
1999   On the Alleged "Pre-Sumerian Substratum." *Journal of Cuneiform Studies* 51:1–16.
Ruhlen, M.
1994   *On the Origin of Languages.* Stanford, CA: Stanford University Press.
1994   *The Origin of Language: Tracing the Evolution of the Mother Tongue.* New York: John Wiley and Sons.
1995   Proto-Amerind Numerals. *Anthropological Science* 103:209–225.
1995   On the Origin of the Amerind Pronominal Pattern. In M. Y. Chen and O. J. L. Tzeng, eds., *In Honor of William S-Y. Wang,* pp. 405–407. Taipei: Pyramid Press.
1998   The Origin of the Na-Dene. *Proceedings of the National Academy of Science, USA* 95:13994–13996.
Ruofu, D., and V. F. Yip
1993   *Ethnic Groups in China.* Beijing: Science Press.
Sabeti, P. C., S. F. Schaffner, B. Fry, J. Lohmueller, P. Varilly, O. Shamovsky, A. Palma, T. S. Mikkelsen, D. Altshuler, and E. S. Lander
2006   Positive Natural Selection in the Human Lineage. *Science* 312:1614–1620.
Sablin, M. V., and G. A. Khlopachev
2002   The Earliest Ice Age Dogs: Evidence from Eliseevichi I. *Current Anthropology* 43(5): 795–799.
Sagart, L.
1995   Some Remarks on Ancestry of Chinese. *Journal of Chinese Studies* 8:195–223.
Sahaidak, M.
2005   Medieval Kiev from the Perspective of an Archaeological Study of the Podil District. *Ruthenica* IV:159.
Salvini, M.
1998   The Earliest Evidence of the Hurrians Before the Formation of the Reign of Mittani. In G. Buccellati and M. Kelly-Buccellati, eds., *Urkesh and*

the Hurrians: Studies in Honor of Lloyd Cotsen, pp. 99–116. Malibu, CA: Undena Publications.

Salzano, F. M.

2002   Molecular Variability in Amerindians: Widespread but Uneven Information. *Annals of Brazilian Academy of Science* 74:223–263.

Sanger, D.

1975   Culture Change as an Adaptive Process in the Maine-Maritimes Region. *Arctic Anthropology* 12:60–75.

Santos, F. R., A. Pandya, M. Kayser, R. J. Mitchell, A. Liu, L. Singh, G. Destro-Bisol, A. Novelletto, R. Qamar, S. Q. Mehdi, R. Adhikari, P. de Knijff, and C. Tyler-Smith

2000   A Polymorphic L1 Retroposon Insertion in the Centromere of the Human Y-chromosome. *Human Molecular Genetics* 9:421–430.

Sapir, E.

1921   *Language: An Introduction to the Study of Speech.* New York: Harcourt, Brace.

1923   The Algonkin Affinity of Yurok and Wiyot Kinship Terms. *Journal de la Société des Américanistes de Paris* 15:37–74.

Savolainen, P., Y. Zhang, J. Luo, J. Lundeberg, and T. Leitner

2002   Genetic Evidence for an East Asian Origin of Domestic Dogs. *Science* 298:1610–1613.

Schaefer, J. M., G. H. Denton, D. J. A. Barrell, S. Ivy-Ochs, P. W. Kubik, B. G. Andersen, F. M. Phillips, T. V. Lowell, and C. Schlüchter

2006   Near-Synchronous Interhemispheric Termination of the Last Glacial Maximum in Mid-Latitudes. *Science* 312:1510–1513.

Schott, R.

1989   Gott in Erzählungen der Bulsa (Nord-Ghana). *Paideuma* 35:260.

Schrire, C.

1982   *The Alligator Rivers: Prehistory and Ecology in Western Arnhem Land.* Canberra: Department of Prehistory, Australia National University.

Schurr, T. G.

2004   The Peopling of the New World: Perspectives from Molecular Anthropology. *Annual Review of Anthropology* 33:551–583.

Schurr, T. G., and S. T. Sherry

2004   Mitochondrial DNA and Y-Chromosome Diversity and the Peopling of the Americas: Evolutionary and Demographic Evidence. *American Journal of Human Biology* 16:420–439.

Seielstad, M. T., E. Minch, and L. L. Cavalli-Sforza

1998   Genetic Evidence for a Higher Female Migration Rate in Humans. *Nature Genetics* 20:278–280.

Seielstad, M. T., N. Yuldasheva, N. Singh, P. Underhill, P. Oefner, P. Shen, and R. S. Wells

2003   A Novel Y-Chromosome Variant Puts an Upper Limit on the Timing of First Entry into the Americas. *American Journal of Human Genetics* 73:700.

Semino, O., C. Magri, G. Benuzzi, A. A. Lin, N. Al-Zahery, V. Battaglia, L. Maccioni, C. Triantaphyllidis, P. Shen, P. J. Oefner, L. A. Zhivotovsky, R. King, A. Torroni, L. L. Cavalli-Sforza, P. A. Underhill, and A. Silvana Santachiara-Benerecetti

2004   Origin, Diffusion, and Differentiation of Y-Chromosome Haplogroups E and J: Inferences on the Neolithization of Europe and Later Migratory Events in the Mediterranean Area. *American Journal of Human Genetics* 74:1023–1034.

Sengupta, S., L. A. Zhivotovsky, R. King, S. Q. Mehdi, C. A. Edmonds, C. T. Chow, A. A. Lin, M. Mitra, S. K. Sil, A. Ramesh, M. V. Usha Rani, C. M. Thakur, L. L. Cavalli-Sforza, P. P. Majumder, and P. A. Underhill

2006   Polarity and Temporality of High-Resolution Y-Chromosome Distributions in India Identify Both Indigenous and Exogenous Expansions and Reveal Minor Genetic Influence of Central Asian Pastoralists. *American Journal of Human Genetics* 78:202–221.

Shepard, J.

1995   The Rhos Guests of Louis the Pious: Whence and Wherefore? *Early Medieval Europe* 4:41–60.

1998   Byzantine Relations with the Outside World in the Ninth Century: An Introduction. In L. Brubaker, ed., *Byzantium in the Ninth Century: Dead or Alive?* pp. 167–180. Hampshire, UK: Aldershot.

Shinka, T., K. Tomita, T. Toda, S. E. Kotliarova, J. Lee, Y. Kuroki, D. K. Jin, K. Tokunaga, H. Nakamura and Y. Nakahori

1999   Genetic Variations on the Y-chromosome in the Japanese Population and Implications for Modern Human Y-chromosome Lineage. *Journal of Human Genetics* 44:240–245.

Shreeve, J.

2006   The Greatest Journey. *National Geographic* 209 (March):60–70.

Shreiner, P.

1991   Miscellanea Byzantino-Rusica. *Vyzantijskij vremennik* 52:151.

Shusharin, V. P.

1961   Russko-vengerskije otnoshenija v Ix v. In A. Zimin and V. Pasuto, eds., *Mezdunarodnye svjazi Rossii do XVII v.*, p. 134. Moscow: Nauka.

1997   *Rannij Etap Etnicheskoj Istorii Vengrov.* Moscow, Rosspen.

Skaletsky, H., T. Kuroda-Kawaguchi, P. J. Minx, H. S. Cordum, L. Hillier, L. G. Brown, S. Repping, T. Pyntikova, J. Ali, T. Bieri, A. Chinwalla, A. Delehaunty, K. Delehaunty, H. Du, G. Fewell, L. Fulton, R. Fulton, T. Graves, S.-F. Hou, P. Latrielle, S. Leonard, E. Mardis, R. Maupin, J. McPherson, T. Miner, W. Nash, C. Nguyen, P. Ozersky, K. Pepin, S. Rock, T. Rohlfing, K. Scott, B. Schultz, C. Strong, A. Tin-Wollam, S.-P. Yang, R. H. Waterston, R. K. Wilson, S. Rozen and D. C. Page

2003   The Male-Specific Region of the Human Y-chromosome Is a Mosaic of Discrete Sequence Classes. *Nature* 423:825–837.

Slatkin, M.

1985   Rare Alleles as Indicators of Gene Flow. *Evolution* 39:53–65.

1991   Inbreeding Coefficients and Coalescence Times. *Genetical Research* 58:167–175.

1995   A Measure of Population Subdivision Based on Microsatellite Allele Frequencies. *Genetics* 139:457–462.

Snow, D. R.

1993   Using MapInfo to Map Archaeological Data. Paper presented at the Methods in the Mountains: Proceedings of Congrès International des Sciences Prèhistoriques et Protohistoriques Commission IV Meeting, Mount Victoria, Australia, August.

1995   Migration in Prehistory: The Northern Iroquoian Case. *American Antiquity* 60:59–79.

1996   More on Migration in Prehistory: Accommodating New Evidence in the Northern Iroquoian Case. *American Antiquity* 61:791–796.

2002   Individuals. In J. P. Hart and E. Terrell, eds., *Darwin and Archaeology: A Handbook of Key Concepts*, pp. 161–181. Westport: Bergin and Garvey.

Soffer, O., and C. Gamble, eds.

1989   *The World at 18,000 BP,* vol. 1: *High Latitudes.* London: Unwin Hyman.

Sokal, R. R., N. L. Oden, and C. Wilson

1991   Genetic Evidence for the Spread of Agriculture in Europe by Demic Diffusion. *Nature* 351:143–144.

Sokal, R. R., and B. A. Thomson

1998   Spatial Genetic Structure of Human Populations in Japan. *Human Biology* 70:1–22.

Soodyall, H., T. Jenkins, and M. Stoneking

1995   Polynesian mtDNA in the Malagasy. *Nature Genetics* 10:377–378.

Starostin, S. A.

1991   On the Hypothesis of a Genetic Connection between the Sino-Tibetan Languages in the Yeniseian and North Caucasian Languages. In V. Shevoroshkin, ed., *Dene-Sino-Caucasian Languages*, pp. 12–41. Bochum: Brockmeyer.

1995   Old Chinese Basic Vocabulary: A Historical Perspective. *Journal of Chinese Studies* 8:225–251.

Starostin, S., A. Dybo, and O. Mudrak

2003   *Etymological Dictionary of the Altaic Languages, Part One [A-K].* Leiden: Brill.

Steinkeller, P.

1998   The Historical Background of Urkesh and the Hurrian Beginnings in Northern Mesopotamia. In G. Buccellati and M. Kelly-Buccellati, eds., *Urkesh and the Hurrians: Studies in Honor of Lloyd Cotsen*, pp. 75–98. Malibu, CA: Undena Publications.

Straus, L. G.

2005   The Upper Paleolithic of Cantabrian Spain. *Evolutionary Anthropology* 14:145–158.

Straus, L. G., and G. A. Clark

1986   *La Riera Cave: Stone Age Hunter-Gatherer Adaptations in Northern Spain.* Anthropological Research Paper no. 36. Tempe: Arizona State University.

Studstill, J. D.

1984   *Les Desseins d'Arc-en-ciel: Épopée chez les Luba du Zaïre.* Paris: Éditions du Centre Nacional de la Recherche Scientifique.

Stumpf, M. P., and D. B. Goldstein

2001   Genealogical and Evolutionary Inference with the Human Y Chromosome. *Science* 291:1738–1742.

Su, B., C. Xiao, R. Deka, M. T. Seielstad, D. Kangwanpong, J. Xiao, D. Lu, P. Underhill, L. Cavalli-Sforza, R. Chakraborty, and L. Jin

2000   Y-chromosome Haplotypes Reveal Prehistorical Migrations to the Himalayas. *Human Genetics* 107:582.

Suprunenko, A., Kulatova, I., and V. Prijmak

1999   Vengerskoje Pogrebenije s Juga Poltavschiny. *Finno-ugrica* 1(3):24.

Swanson, Guy E.
1960   *The Birth of the Gods: The Origin of Prim-
        itive Beliefs.* Ann Arbor: University of
        Michigan Press.
Swanton, J. R.
1929   *Myths and Tales of the Southeastern
        Indians.* Washington D.C.: Smithsonian
        Institution, Bureau of American
        Ethnology.
Tajima, A., M. Hayami, K. Tokunaga, T. Juji,
M. Matsuo, S. Marzuki, K. Omoto and S. Horai
2004   Genetic Origins of the Ainu Inferred
        from Combined DNA Analyses of
        Maternal and Paternal Lineages. *Journal
        of Human Genetics* 49:187–193.
Tajima, A., I-H. Pan, G. Fucharoen, S. Fucharoen,
M. Matsuo, K. Tokunaga, T. Juji, M. Hayami,
K. Omoto, and S. Horai
2002   Three Major Lineages of Asian
        Y-chromosomes: Implications for the
        Peopling of East and Southeast Asia.
        Human Genetics 110:80–88.
Takamiya, H., and O. Hiromi
2002   Peopling of Western Japan, Focusing on
        Kyushu, Shikoku, and Ryukyu Archipel-
        ago. *Radiocarbon* 44:495–502.
Takaya, Yoshikazu, ed.
1988   *Madagascar.* Kyoto: Kyoto University
        Center for Southeast Asian Studies.
Tanaka, M., V. M. Cabrera, A. M. González, J. M. Lar-
ruga, T. Takeyasu, N. Fuku, L.-J. Guo, R. Hirose,
Y. Fujita, M. Kurata, K. Shinoda, K. Umetsu,
Y. Yamada, Y. Oshida, Y. Sato, N. Hattori, Y. Mizuno,
Y. Arai, N. Hirose, S. Ohta, O. Ogawa, Y. Tanaka,
R. Kawamori, M. Shamoto-Nagai, W. Maruyama,
H. Shimokata, R. Suzuki, and H. Shimodaira
2004   Mitochondrial Genome Variation in
        Eastern Asia and the Peopling of Japan.
        Genome Research 14:1832–1850.
Tchernov, E.
1997   Two New Dogs, and Other Natufian
        Dogs, from the Southern Levant. *Journal
        of Anthropological Science* 24:65–95.
Thomas-Fattier, D.
1982   *Le Dialecte Sakalava du Nord-Ouest de
        Madagascar.* Paris: SELAF.
Thomason, S., and T. Kaufman
1988   *Language Contact, Creolization, and
        Genetic Linguistics.* Berkeley: Univ. of
        California Press.
Thompson, E. A.
1996   *The Huns.* Oxford: Blackwell.
Thompson, S.
1951   *The Folktale.* New York: Dryden Press.

1955–1958   *Motif-index of Folk Literature.* Blooming-
            ton: Indiana University Press.
Thurgood, G.
1999   *From Ancient Chamic to Modern Dia-
        lects, 2000 Years of Language Contact and
        Change.* Honolulu: University of Hawaii
        Press.
Tolochko, P.
2003   *Kochevyje Narody Stepej i Kievskaja Rus'.*
        St. Petersburg: Aleteja.
Torroni, A., Y. S. Chen, O. Semino, A. S. Santachiara-
Beneceretti, C. R. Scott, M. T. Lott, M. Winter, and
D. C. Wallace
1994   mtDNA and Y-chromosome Polymor-
        phisms in Four Native American Popula-
        tions from Southern Mexico. *American
        Journal of Human Genetics* 54:303–318.
Trombetti, A.
1905   *L'Unità d'Origine del Linguaggio.* Bologna:
        Beltrami.
1923   *Elementi di Glottologia.* Bologna: Zani-
        chelli.
Tugolukov, V. A.
1985   *Tungusy (Eveny i Evenki) Srednei i Zapad-
        noi Sibiri.* Moscow: Nauka.
Turilov, A.
2001   "M'dra Pl'skovskaja" i "M'dra
        Dr'storskaja"—Dve Mundragi Pervoj
        Vengero-Bolgarskij Vojny. In B. Florja
        and G. Litavrin, eds., *Slavjane i ich
        Sosedi,* pp. 47–52. Moscow: Nauka.
Turner, C. G.
1976   Dental Evidence on the Origins of the
        Ainu and Japanese. *Science* 193:911–913.
1987   Late Pleistocene and Holocene Popula-
        tion History of East Asia Based on Dental
        Variation. *American Journal of Physical
        Anthropology* 73:305–321.
2005   A Synoptic History of Physical Anthro-
        pological Studies on the Peopling of
        Alaska and the Americas. *Alaska Journal
        of Anthropology* 3:157–170.
Uerpmann, H. P., and M. Uerpmann
1996   'Ubaid Pottery in the Eastern Gulf:
        New Evidence from Umm al-Qaiwain
        (U.A.E.). *Arabian Archaeology and Epig-
        raphy* 7:125–139.
Underhill, P. A., L. Jin, R. Zemans, P. J. Oefner,
L. L. Cavalli-Sforza
1996   A Pre-Columbian Y-chromosome-
        specific Transition and Its Implications
        for Human Evolutionary History. *Pro-
        ceedings of the National Academy of Sci-
        ences, USA,* 93:196–200.

Underhill, Peter, G. Passarino, A. A. Lin, P. Shen, M. M. Lahr, R.A. Foley, P. J. Oefner, and L. L. Cavalli-Sforza

2001 The Phylogeography of Y Chromosome Binary Haplotypes and the Origins of Modern Human Populations. *Annals of Human Genetics* 65:43–62.

Van der Veen, H.

1940 *Tae' (Zuid-Toradjasch)—Nederlandsch Woordenboek.* The Hague: Nijhoff.

Velonandro

1983 *Lexique des Dialectes du Nord de Madagaskar.* Tuléar: CEDRATOM.

Vernadsky, G.

1996 *Kievskaia Rus'.* Moscow: Tver.

Vishnyatsky, L. B.

2005 How Many Core Areas? The "Upper Paleolithic Revolution" in an East Eurasian Perspective. *Journal of the Israel Prehistoric Society* 35:143–158.

Wade, N.

2006 *Before the Dawn.* New York: Penguin.

Waitz, G., ed.

1895 *Annales Bertiniani.* Hannover: Impensis Bibliopolii Hahniani.

Wehr, H.

1994 *A Dictionary of Modern Written Arabic* (Arabic-English). Ithaca, NY: Spoken Language Services.

Wells, S.

2002 *The Journey of Man: A Genetic Odyssey.* New York: Random House.

Welsh, R., J. Terrell, and J. Nadolski

1992 Language and Culture on the North Coast of New Guinea. *American Anthropologist* 94:568–600.

Wen, B., X. Xie, S. Gao, H. Li, H. Shi, X. Song, T. Qian, C. Xiao, J. Jin, B. Su, D. Lu, R. Chakraborty, and L. Jin

2004 Analyses of Genetic Structure of Tibeto-Burman Populations Reveals Sex-Biased Admixture in Southern Tibeto-Burmans. *American Journal of Human Genetics* 74:856–865.

Wendorf, F., R. Schild, and A. E. Close.

1980 *Loaves and Fishes.* New Delhi: Pauls.

West, F. H., ed.

1996 *American Beginnings: The Prehistory and Paleoecology of Beringia.* Chicago: University of Chicago Press.

White, J., D. Penny, L. Kealhofer, and B. Maloney

2003 Vegetation Changes from the Late Pleistocene through the Holocene from Three Areas of Archaeological Significance in Thailand. *Quaternary International* 113:111–132.

Whiting, J. W. M., and B. Ayres

1968 Inferences from the Shape of Dwellings. In K. C. Chang, ed., *Settlement Archaeology,* pp. 117–133. Palo Alto, CA: National Press Books.

Wichmann, S., and A. Saunders

2007 How to Use Typological Databases in Historical Linguistic Research. *Diachronica* 24:373–404.

Wichmann, S., D. Stauffer, C. Schulze, and E. Holman

2007 Do Language Change Rates Depend on Population Size? http//: rxiv preprint physics/0607031, 2006 - arxiv.org

Wilbert, J., and K. Simoneau

1992 *Folk Literature of South America Indians: General Index.* UCLA Latin American Center Publication. Los Angeles: University of California.

Wilder, J. A., S. B. Kingan, Z. Mobasher, M. M. Pilkington, and M. F. Hammer

2004 Global Patterns of Human Mitochondrial DNA and Y-Chromosome Structure Are Not Influenced by Higher Migration Rates of Females versus Males. *Nature Genetics* 36:1122–1125.

Wilkinson, R. J.

1959 *A Malay–English Dictionary.* London: Macmillan.

Wilson, I. J., and D. J. Balding

1998 Genealogical Inference from Microsatellite Data. *Genetics* 150:499–510.

Winkelman, M.

1986 Magico-Religious Practitioner Types and Socioeconomic Conditions. *Behavior Science Research* 20:17–46.

Wood, W. R.

1971 *Biesterfeldt: A Post-Contact Coalescent Site on the Northeastern Plains.* Smithsonian Contributions to Anthropology 15. Washington, D.C.: Smithsonian Institution.

Wright, H. T., and J. A. Rakotorisoa

2003 The Rise of Malagasy Societies: New Developments in the Archaeology of Madagascar. In S. M. Goodman and Jonathan P. Bensted, eds., *The Natural History of Madagascar,* pp. 112–119. Chicago: University of Chicago Press.

Wright, S.

1921 Systems of Mating. *Genetics* 6:111–178.

1931 Evolution in Mendelian Populations. *Genetics* 16:97–159.

1943   Isolation by Distance. *Genetics* 28:114–138.
1951   The Genetical Structure of Populations. *Annals of Eugenics* 15:323–354.
1969   *Evolution and the Genetics of Populations, II: The Theory of Gene Frequencies.* Chicago: University of Chicago Press.

Wurm, S., and B. Wilson
1975   *English Finderlist of Reconstructions in Austronesian Languages (post-Brandstetter).* Canberra: Pacific Linguistics.

YCC
2002   The Y Chromosome Consortium. *Genome Research* 12:339.

Zakhoder, B. N.
1967   *Kaspijskij Svod Svedenij o Vostochnoj Evrope.* Moscow: Glavnaja Redaktsija Vostochnoj Literatury.

Zegura, S. L., T. M. Karafet, L. A. Zhivotovsky, M. F. Hammer
2004   High-Resolution SNPs and Microsatellite Haplotypes Point to a Single, Recent Entry of Native American Y Chromosomes into the Americas. *Molecular Biology and Evolution* 21:164–175.

Zhivotovsky, L., P. A. Underhill, C. Cinnioğlu, M. Kayser, B. Morar, T. Kivisild, R. Scozzari, F. Cruciani, G. Destro-Bisol, G. Spedini, G. K. Chambers, R. J. Herrera, K. K. Yong, D. Gresham, I. Tournev, M. W. Feldman, and L. Kalaydjieva
2004   The Effective Mutation Rate at Y Chromosome Short Tandem Repeats, with Application to Human Population-Divergence Time. *American Journal of Human Genetics* 74:50–61.

Zimonyi, I.
1999   Préhistoir Hongroise: Méthode de Recherche et Vue d'Ensemble. In S. Csernus and K. Korompay, eds., *Les Hongrois et l'Europe: Conqête et Intégration,* pp. 41–52. Paris: Institut Hongroise de Paris.
2005   Voennye Sily Vengrov Pri Obretenii Rodiny: Kolièestvo Voinov Srednevekovyh Koèevyh na- Rodov Evrazijskih Stepej. In *Hungaro-Rossica II*, pp. 32–51. Moscow: Institut Vostokovedenija Akedemija Nauk Rosija.

Zoetmulder, P. J.
1982   *Old Javanese–English Dictionary.* 2 parts. KITLV Publication. The Hague: Nijhoff.

Zukerman, C.
1998   Vengry v Strane Lebedii: Novaja Derzhava na Granitsah Vyzantii b Khazarii ok. 836–889. *Materialy po Archeologii, Istorii i Etnographii Tavrii (MAIET)* 4:663–688.
2001   Dva Etapa Formirovanija Drevnerusskogo Gosudarstva. *Slavjanovedenije* 4:55.

Index

absorption, and large-scale migrations, 11, 19
acculturation, and cultural diffusion, 12
adaptation, and concept of migration, 10
adaptive expansions, 11
Adelaar, Alexander, 4–5, 159, 160
Admiralties language family, 52
admixture: and case studies of migration, 173–74, 175; definition of in genetics, 21; and interpretations of Japanese prehistory, 146–47; and linguistic evolution, 29
Aegean, linguistic and genetic evidence for Neolithic migrations in, 95–101, 174–75
Africa: contacts between Indonesia and east Africa, 163; Paleolithic archaeology and Last Glacial Maximum in, 57–59, 60; mythology and folklore as evidence for "Out-of-Africa" hypothesis, 74–93, 174–75. See also Bantu
Afro-Asiatic language family, 97. See also Proto-Afriasiatic
agriculture: and agropastoralism in Neolithic Near East, 95–96; and contacts between Indonesia and east Africa, 163, 168; and Yayoi shift to wet-rice cultivation in Japan, 145
Ainu: and Eurasiatic language family, 112, 114; and interpretations of Japanese prehistory, 139, 140, 143, 146–47; and refuge areas during Last Glacial Maximum, 72
Aleut (Alaska), 125. See also Eskimo-Aleut language family
Algic language family, 115
Algonquian language, 115, 121
Altaic language, 33, 139
Altai Mountains (China), 144–45, 147
Americas: genetic studies and peopling of, 127–35, 174–75; linguistics and interpretation of migrations to, 112–25, 174–75
Amerind language family, 118–25, 130, 131
Amish (Pennsylvania), 18
Ammerman, A. J., 15, 27
Anatolia, and Neolithic migrations, 95, 96, 97, 98, 99, 100–101
animals: and Bantu loanwords in Malagasy language, 161–62, 168–69; domestication of, 91, 97, 124. See also horses
animals responsible for the introduction of death (folklore motif), 91
Annali Bertiniani, 105

Anthony, David, 14, 19
Apache language, 118
Arabian Bifacial tradition, 96
Arabian Peninsula, and Neolithic migrations, 96, 99, 101
Arabic languages, 99
archaeology: and agropastoralism in Near East, 95–96; comparative ethnology and indicators of behavior, 34–36; and evidence for migrations to North and South America, 124, 128–29; and evidence for warfare, 32; and linguistic reconstruction of Austronesian language family, 46–53; and multidisciplinary studies of migration, 7, 8; and sources of information about Pleistocene, 56–57
Ardika, I. W., 159
Arem language, 46
Arikaras (Great Plains), 13
Asia, and Paleolithic archaeology, 66–71. See also Afro-Asiatic language family; Eurasiatic language family; Middle East; Southeast Asia; *specific countries*
assemblage similarity, and association between material culture and language, 37–40
Assyrian language, 98, 99
Athabaskan language, 114, 118
Attila (Hun), 17
Australia, and Last Glacial Maximum, 71–72. See also Austronesian language family
Austric language macrofamily, 53
Austronesian (AN) language family, 46–53, 118, 139, 149, 152
Azerbaijan, and Neolithic migrations, 99

Bahnaric languages, 45
Bajau language, 157, 171n36
Bakalov, G., 107
"Banana" language, 97
Bantu: and languages of Madagascar, 150, 154, 161, 167, 168, 170n25; and migrations from central to eastern and southern Africa, 164, 168–69
"barbarian" migrations, in eastern and southeastern Europe, 103, 107
Basques: as case study of migration, 16–17; and Dene-Caucasian language family, 116; and refuge areas during Last Glacial Maximum, 72
Beaujard, Philippe, 157, 163, 171n58, 172n69
Bedouins, and genetic studies, 99

201